JUSTICE
NOT
VENGEANCE

SIMON WIESENTHAL
JUSTICE
NOT
VENGEANCE

Translated from the German by
Ewald Osers

Weidenfeld and Nicolson
London

First published in Great Britain in 1989 by
George Weidenfeld & Nicolson Limited
91 Clapham High Street, London SW4 7TA

ISBN 0 297 79683 6

Printed and bound in Great Britain by
Butler and Tanner Ltd, Frome and London

Contents

Preface

When you are writing a book at the age of eighty you assume that it will be your last. This makes you pedantic. I would have preferred to record the full details of every one of the many hundreds of cases on which I have worked since 1945, because to me every one of these cases was important. Thus, for instance, Josef Schwammberger, the commandant of the Przemyśl ghetto, will shortly be facing trial on charges of murdering thousands after I succeeded in tracking him down in Argentina. Yet his story, along with a hundred other stories, is not in this book – or it would have turned out three times as thick. I have been able to include only those cases which seemed to me typical for a variety of reasons – some because of the difficulties of the search, some because of the significance of the criminal or the crime, and others because of their importance to the present day.

It is only the most spectacular part of my activities that I am reporting here – but this doesn't mean that the less spectacular part is less important. I realize that the publisher of this book is inevitably concerned with stories – I am concerned with the killed and the killers.

Another problem about a book like this is that it creates the impression that I alone am responsible for all the successes and failures of the cases reported here. This is partly due to its presentation in the first person singular, and partly to the peculiarity of my work: security considerations compel me to sketch my colleagues as vaguely as possible. If I receive a strictly confidential piece of information from Paraguay it will be obvious to everybody that this is not the result of clairvoyance on my part, but that someone is working for me there, someone whom I would jeopardize by naming, or even by relating how he came by his information.

I should, nevertheless, like to seize the opportunity of this last book to express by gratitude to certain people who have supported my work. I realize that this is of no interest to the reader, but I feel my eighty years justify me in using a few pages here to tell these people that I am happy to count them among my friends.

In Austria they include, in particular, the late President of the Jewish Community, Dr Ivan Hacker, and his successor, Paul Grosz. In the Catholic camp the person closest to me was the late author and philosopher Fritz Heer: he contributed significantly to my knowledge of Jewish–Christian relations. I also had repeated opportunity to discuss these relations with Cardinal Dr Franz König, who, more than any other dignitary of the Catholic church, was ready to admit the guilt which the Church has heaped upon itself *vis-à-vis* the Jews over the centuries. Time and again, whenever anti-Semitism flared up in Austria, Cardinal König has found the right words against it.

When it came to the crunch, when Bruno Kreisky attacked me infamously, when the attempt was made, by means of an illegal parliamentary committee, to drive me out of the country, two journalists, above all, stood by my side: Peter Michael Lingens of *profil* and Alfred Payrleitner of *Kurier*, now working for Austrian radio. The Austrian Opposition also resisted, and that, at a time when Bruno Kreisky was venerated in Austria like God Almighty, was a deed of considerable civil courage, especially by its chairman, the Social Democrat Bruno Czermak.

In spite of such valuable friendships I sometimes felt rather lonely in Kreisky's Austria. At such moments it was good to know that, to compensate for it, I had, and still have, more friends in other countries than, with the best will in the world, I can enumerate.

In Israel, where my daughter lives, these include above all the President of Yad Vashem and Prosecutor-General in the Eichmann trial, Gideon Hauser, the scientific director of Yad Vashem, Dr Kiermisz, and the journalist Chaim Maas, whom I have known for forty years and who has translated my articles and my books into Hebrew.

I am happy to be able to list, next to my friends in Israel, those in West Germany. They are, in particular, Heinrich Guenthert and Adolf Kohlrautz, both of whom saved my life during the Third Reich, and to whom I am tied in equal measure by gratitude and admiration. But through my work, too, I have come to know many people in West Germany, whom I would describe as my friends today. They include, first and foremost, the Principal Public Prosecutor at the *Landgericht* Stuttgart, Rolf Sichting, and also a number of employees of the Central Office for the investigation of Nazi crimes in Ludwigsburg. Few if any of my more recent successes would have been possible without the helpful cooperation of Ludwigsburg, more particularly of Dr Rückerl and of Chief Public Prosecutor Streim.

Another friend and helper was the late publisher Axel Cäsar Springer, whose attitude to the Jews and to Israel was invariably regarded with respect even by his fiercest critics. I shall mention the helpful part played by Federal Chancellor Helmut Kohl at various points in this book.

In 1963 I joined the then newly founded Organization of Resistance Fighters and Deportees and was thus able to make the acquaintance of its president, the Belgian general Albert Guérisse [who died earlier this year]. The persons I have come to admire in that organization include, above all, its Secretary-General Hubert Hallin and the French Resistance heroine Madeleine Foucarde, Colonel Bjarke Schou of Denmark, Colonel Wolfgang Müller of West Germany, and the Preacher of Nôtre Dame de Paris, Père Riquet, who paid for his resistance by being my concentration camp companion in Mauthausen.

In 1965 I met Charles Ronsac, then director of the Opera Mundi literary agency in Paris. It was he who persuaded me to write the first book about my work, *The Murderers Among Us*. He has not only looked after my literary activity ever since, but our collaboration has grown into a cordial friendship, for which I should like to thank him in this, my last, book.

There have been countless people who supported our bureau financially. I am indebted to all of them, and with some their financial contributions have led to mutual friendship. Thus our first office in Linz was able to operate only because Dr Israel Silberschein transmitted a monthly sum to us to cover postal and telephone expenses. (Later I was able to use part of my restitution payments from West Germany for this purpose.)

After a brief intermediate phase, when the Association of Jewish Communities and the Vienna Jewish Community met the costs of our new office in Vienna, we received decisive assistance from Holland: Thom Roth, Simon Speijer and Hans Jacobs founded the Stiftung Wiesenthal Fonds (the Wiesenthal Foundation), which obtained from the government the concession that contributions made to it were tax-deductible. For twenty-five years now we have been receiving monthly financial assistance from Holland. Unfortunately the long-term president of the foundation, A. Stempel, died last year, so that he cannot read these lines. His successor is the well-known historian and former director of the Rijksinstitut voor Oorlogsdokumentatie, Professor Lou de Jong, with whom I have likewise been associated by many years of joint work. The same is true of the deputy director of the Rijksinstitut, Professor Ben Sijes, who was not only an advisor but also a personal friend of mine. He too, unfortunately, died a few years ago. The gap he has left cannot be filled by anyone.

My thanks, however, are due not only to individual friends in Holland, but to the Dutch people as a whole: in no other country, I believe, has there been so much interest in my work. This was largely due to Jules

Huf, who, as the Vienna correspondent of the Dutch media, time and again reported on cases I had been working on. In many of these cases Jules Huf himself conducted valuable research, and in every situation he has been a reliable friend. Not even the Waldheim affair, when many Dutchmen, including Huf, were unable to understand my attitude, has been able to cloud our relationship.

What the Stiftung Wiesenthal Fonds has been in Holland, the Jewish Documentation Center has been in the USA. This foundation, too, was authorized to collect contributions which were tax-deductible. The initiator and the soul of this institution was Hermann Katz, who also placed one of his firm's offices in New York at the Center's disposal.

Thanks to the flow of money from the JDC we were able to conduct a series of costly investigations overseas, investigations which would probably have been impossible otherwise. From New York also came those seven thousand dollars which I had to pay for information on the whereabouts of the commandant of Treblinka, Franz Stangl. Hermann Katz died in 1977, and his attorney and co-founder of the New York office, Martin Rosen, took over his function. As my family was exterminated by the Nazis and as I have scarcely any relations left, I once said to Martin how nice it would be if one could choose a new family for oneself – in which case I would choose him as a brother.

Thus we became brothers.

My first American friend was a soldier. His name was Jacob Katzmann, and I met him in 1945 immediately after my liberation from the Maut-hausen concentration camp, when he took it upon himself to look after the liberated Jewish inmates. This friendship between Jacob, my wife and myself has now endured for four decades and has also occasionally brought up together in our work: Jacob was Secretary-General of the Association of the Jewish Working Class Movement and subsequently a member of the World Zionist Executive. At present he is devoting himself to adult education in New York by transmitting his knowledge of the Holocaust to younger people.

Of the numerous other friends I have made in America over the years I should like to name just two: my attorneys Martin Mendelsson in Washington and Jerry Bender in Chicago, who give me whatever support they can in every respect.

In conclusion I should like to mention briefly the Holocaust Center in Los Angeles, which bears my name. I owe this honour to Rabbi Marvin Hier, Roland Arnal and the Belzberg brothers of the Yeshiva University. For over ten years the Simon Wiesenthal Center in California has been engaged in educational activities, supporting scholarly projects and, in particular, seeking to make contact with American youth. Among other things it produced the film *Genocide* which was awarded an Oscar in 1983 for best documentary.

In 1987 the Senate and House of Representatives of California voted a donation of five million dollars for the creation, within the framework of the Simon Wiesenthal Center, of a 'Museum of Tolerance'. I am well aware that it should really be called a 'Museum of Intolerance', for it shows mainly instances of persecution.

A portion of the exhibits, however, is devoted to the resistance which was alive even in those cruel times of persecution. And I simply happen to be an optimist, and believe that intolerance can dominate our lives only intermittently – ultimately tolerance will prevail.

Simon Wiesenthal
Vienna, September 1988

P.S. For their dedicated assistance while I was writing this book I should like to thank my secretaries Rosa-Maria Austraat and Maggie Glecer.

1

In Lieu of
a Self-Portrait

My publishers have urged me to write my 'memoirs'. I don't know if that is a correct description of this book, because what it contains about my private life is uninteresting: I am married, I have a daughter, I have grandchildren – they mean everything to me, but they are of no interest to the general public. Of interest alone is my life in relation to Nazism: I have survived the Holocaust and I have tried to preserve the memory of the dead.

At the age of eighty I am one of the last surviving witnesses. It is solely in this function, as a witness, that I write now.

I have left it to my friend of many decades, Peter Michael Lingens, to write about me; he has worked for some time in my office and I believe he knows me in a way few others do. What he has written seems to me – in as far as one can judge that oneself – essentially correct.

WHO IS SIMON WIESENTHAL
by Peter Michael Lingens

As the 'Eichmann hunter' he has become a magazine cliché in his lifetime: not a person but a name which arouses emotions in others. These emotions are entirely different in Austria and Germany from what they are, for instance, in France or in the USA. While in the free world Simon Wiesenthal is seen as one of the Just, most of his Austrian fellow-countrymen see him as a merciless avenger. Abroad one of the most highly esteemed Austrians – Wiesenthal has five honorary doctorates; he is also a Commander of the Order of the House of Orange, Commendatore della Repubblica Italiana, Chevalier of the French Légion d'Honneur, holder of the Grand Cross of Merit with Ribbon of the Federal Republic of Germany and of the Gold Medal of the Congress of the United States, to mention only the most important distinctions – in Austria itself he was an outcast for decades. A repressed (and hence violently denied) guilty conscience has endowed the old man in his tiny office on Vienna's Rudolfsplatz, and later in the Salztorgasse, with the demonic features of a merciless Nazi hunter. His frequently changing staff have been promoted to a 'network of agents'. The Documentation Center – for which he had to spend years begging money from wealthy American Jews – became his 'organization', conspiring with foreign powers and disposing of inexhaustible resources. Except when one of his numerous adversaries claims that he had absolutely nothing to do with the arrest of Eichmann, 'the Eichmann hunter' is credited with downright superhuman capabilities in capturing war criminals: a Jewish James Bond with a cabinet full of secret dossiers, who has access to the most hidden safes and who can strike mercilessly at any point on the globe. For the attributes of demons (whether gods or devils) are omnipresence, omniscience and omnipotence.

No one really wishes to know what Simon Wiesenthal is actually like: such knowledge might turn the avenging deity into a human being.

The man who chose Vienna as his new home was born in Buchach, a small town on the eastern fringe of the Austro-Hungarian monarchy (Sigmund Freud's family came from there too – Wiesenthal's mother-in-law was born a Freud). While most Jews grow up in a predominantly non-Jewish environment, or, conversely, in a ghetto, Jews represented the majority population in Buchach. There were 6000 Jews alongside only 2000 Poles and 1000 Ukrainians. This gave rise to a different kind of self-assurance: as a Jew one was not at the bottom of the pile (the Ukrainians were), but one was proud of one's Jewish origins.

In contrast to other Jews, for whom humiliation became second nature, a man like Wiesenthal found the physical sufferings under the Third Reich less painful than the humiliation.

To be a Jew could never, to him, mean not wanting to be one, as, for instance, it did to his great Austrian adversary Bruno Kreisky. Nor, on the other hand, has it ever meant regarding himself as a member of the chosen people: Wiesenthal is a Jew as a matter of course.

Like nearly all the Jewish families in Buchach, Wiesenthal's too was religious – with a touch of that strange eastern mysticism which was just then experiencing a renaissance there.

Galicia was the land of the miracle-working rabbis. The rabbi – not a priest but a sage – was the ultimate recourse for right and justice. As the Jews were almost invariably surrounded by stronger nations, they had to suppress conflicts among themselves as far as possible. Just as they maintained the strict sexual morality of their forefathers (which eventually caused Sigmund Freud to break out), so their concept of justice was hard and precise: time and again Simon Wiesenthal has told the story of how as a boy he was led past a house behind whose windows a man was sitting who had not spoken for years and who would eat only the most necessary food. The 'silent one', as he was called, had one day ended a quarrel with his wife by exclaiming: 'Wish you burnt!' That night his house was burned down – through no fault of his – and his wife perished in the flames. The man took his heavy conscience to the rabbi. The rabbi decided that he must never speak another word as long as he lived and that he must ceaselessly pray for forgiveness of his guilt.

This mystical concept of justice has remained with Wiesenthal to this day. He holds the conviction (which requires no further justification) that in each life there is a balance between crime and punishment, and he expresses this conviction in the oft-repeated phrase: 'Everything in this life has its price.'

Guilt cannot be forgiven but only paid for by expiation. Step by step.

Expiation in the sense demanded by Wiesenthal was made by Albert Speer, Hitler's Minister for Armaments: 'He didn't try to talk himself out of the charges, even though he could probably have done so more easily than any of the others accused at Nuremberg. He said: I enjoyed the advantage, so I won't dodge the disadvantage. And he got twenty years, although others, who had done a lot more, were given sentences no heavier. But Speer realized that this punishment matched his guilt.'

Wiesenthal has a very fine yardstick for both 'guilt' and 'expiation': he measures not the extent but the content.

To him, a man who had committed not one punishable offence but had merely written postcards bore a heavier burden of guilt than many murderers: that man, a railway official from Linz, was married to a postal employee. She was one-quarter Jewish, and although the marriage would have been protected under the law, he obtained a divorce from her.

From the moment of his divorce he wrote up to ten postcards a day to her, on which he abused her, pasted anti-Semitic slogans from the newspapers, or simply reviled her.

These were open cards, so that every colleague of the divorced woman was able to read them.

After the war Wiesenthal had a victim's card issued to her. In support of her application she had brought along only one piece of evidence: a crate, carried by two men, containing thousands of postcards.

'That was a Chinese torture,' Wiesenthal said. 'It should burn on the man's conscience, it should burn him every day.'

Contrary to the ideas which are current on the subject among the German and Austrian public, Wiesenthal painstakingly relates every action to the circumstances in which it was committed: a man who, as a member of an ad-hoc execution squad, shot dead ten Jews is less guilty in his eyes than one who, without any order or any pressure, broke a detainee's limbs by beating. And no blow by an SS man hurt Wiesenthal as much as the one dealt him by a Polish camp clerk a few days after the liberation of the Mauthausen concentration camp – 'because that was a continuation of anti-Semitism in the knowledge of what the Jews had suffered under Hitler'.

When the offender – forced by the Americans to apologize to Wiesenthal publicly – extended his hand to him in front of the assembled inmates, Wiesenthal stood motionless. 'I accept your apology, but I will not shake hands with you.'

Simon Wiesenthal – in this respect he matches the clichéd image the public has of him – does not forgive easily. Not so much in the intellectual sphere – there he is too clever and has too fine a concept of guilt never to cease blaming a person for his behaviour – but in the emotional sphere. He does not offer his forgiveness; he trades it against appropriate punishment.

Wiesenthal has repeatedly – he himself calls it his 'unredeemed past' – reflected on the problem of forgiveness. In his best book, *The Sunflower* (chosen in France as Book of the Year) he describes a wartime experience which raises this problem with tremendous self-critical precision: he was at the time assigned to work in an army hospital. Suddenly a nurse called him and took him to a terminal ward. The man on the verge of death was an SS man. He seized Wiesenthal's hand and began his confession. Gripped by fear of death, he told him about the most horrible crimes he had committed against Jews. When he had finished he begged the Jewish forced-labour worker to forgive him. Wiesenthal rose and walked out. Later he visited the mother of the dead man but did not tell the bereaved woman about her son's deeds.

There are other ways of dealing with that kind of situation: after the war a number of former concentration camp inmates were locked up by the Communists in Poland because they refused to be silent even under the new dictatorship. Some of them, including a woman, were sentenced to death. In 1946 she was waiting to be executed in the prison's death row.

One day she was taken to the shower room. The warders also brought in another woman – the most notorious and most brutal of the guards from Birkenau camp, the women's section of Auschwitz, the Austrian Maria

Mandl. She too had been sentenced to death. The two women stood naked under the showers and didn't look at each other.

Suddenly Mandl walked over and said just one sentence: 'Can you forgive me?'

The Polish woman, who was subsequently pardoned, described her reaction as follows: 'There we were, two naked women expecting to die. I realized that none of those whom Mandl had maltreated could hear me. So I said: Yes.'

Wiesenthal is aware of both options. And he is uncertain to this day whether the one he chose was the right one. So uncertain that in *The Sunflower* he initiated a survey, asking people whom he regarded as moral authorities to judge whether he had acted correctly. The discussion which followed, filling the pages of leading papers in France and elsewhere for weeks on end, failed to produced a conclusion. Wiesenthal himself now believes he found it in the letter of a Norwegian peasant woman: 'You should have told him to pray to his God that he may forgive him. And God will forgive.'

Wiesenthal today is not a regularly practising religious Jew. While many Jews of his generation have imperceptibly, in the process of assimilation, loosened their ties with the faith of their people, Wiesenthal preserved for himself the ethical principles of the Jewish faith, of which, as a Jew, he is proud. When he saw a rabbi loaning out his prayer book for half an hour to other inmates in return for a cup of soup, he swore never again to enter a synagogue. Friends changed his mind after the war by putting forward the only argument he was prepared to accept: 'Why do you only see those who took and not those who gave?' It was an argument against collective guilt.

Zionism, to whose worldwide conspiracy he is time and again linked, is to Wiesenthal more than a mere historical phenomenon: it is the Jews' hope of a homeland, which was realized with the foundation of the state of Israel, a hope which today 'probably calls for new forms'.

But unlike the former Austrian Chancellor Bruno Kreisky, who likewise is a non-religious, non-Zionist, assimilated Jew, Wiesenthal displays sympathy for the religiosity and the nationalism of his people as part of what he calls the real bond of Jewry: the common destiny, from the expulsion from Egypt through the pogroms of the Middle Ages to Auschwitz. 'To be a Jew means to be a remnant of persecution. The sum total of the remnants is the whole. Whereas prior to Auschwitz it may have been possible to sever oneself from the common fate of the Jews, after Auschwitz this is no longer conceivable.'

As an illustration of what he means Wiesenthal quotes a young American Jew who, brought up as an agnostic, deliberately tried after the war to recapture the faith of his forefathers: 'After what has happened to them I want to do everything to feel kinship with them.'

It is only against this background that the conflict with Bruno Kreisky, which Wiensenthal describes in detail in this book, can be understood. 'Kreisky' – Wiesenthal thus sums up his essential feelings in a single sentence – 'has severed himself from the Jewish community of destiny. And, in my eyes, anyone who does that is a deserter.'

Two Just Men

The special fate of the Galician Jews was characterized by Russia's brutal anti-Semitism: Buchach was full of people who had only just escaped with their lives from Russian pogroms. By contrast, the Austro-Hungarian monarchy – above all, the Emperor – was regarded, from a distance which lent enchantment to the view, as a patron and protector of the Jews. When the Cossacks burst into Buchach in 1915, during the First World War, Wiesenthal's mother with her two sons fled to where Jews could feel safe – to Vienna. For two years Simon Wiesenthal attended a primary school in Vienna's Bäuerlgasse. His father, a merchant, had been called up and was killed as an Austrian soldier on the Russian front.

In 1917 the Russians withdrew from Galicia and countless Jewish refugees – including the Wiesenthals – returned home. For a short period Galicia was proclaimed a 'West Ukrainian Republic', then it was occupied by the Poles. Until the Polish–Russian war.

The little town was overrun almost every week, either by one side or the other. The brutality of the Bolshevik troops was surpassed only by that of Petlyura's Ukrainian cavalry: the twelve-year-old Wiesenthal had his thigh cut to the bone by a drunken Ukrainian's sabre – an enormous scar remains to this day. And an important realization remains as well: bestiality is not the prerogative of any particular nation.

Though Wiesenthal's work has time and again focused the attention of the world public on Austrian or German war criminals, he has always refused to brand those two nations as the chosen people of evil. In Israel he caused a riot when, at a kibbutz of ghetto fighters, he declared that to him young Austrians or young Germans were no better and no worse than young Israelis.

Some of the animosity which Wiesenthal has encountered from the Viennese Jewish community is due to the fact that he has pursued Jews who sullied their hands under the Third Reich with the same relentlessness as SS men. 'There is only one yardstick for measuring guilt.' In 1961, when a certain Dr Friedrich Kaul from East Berlin, who attended the Eichmann trial as an observer, was engaged in loud propaganda against

West Germany, Wiesenthal at a tumultuous press conference denied him any right to open his mouth. 'Today we also know about Stalin's crimes. Whether we know all about them we don't know. But we do know that, just as with Hitler, he had thousands of henchmen who, as members of the secret police, extorted confessions, that there were secret tribunals which handed down sentences of long years of punishment without as much as having seen the accused. That there were inhuman camp commandants, who treated the inmates criminally. Until a Dr Kaul or some other representative of the eastern bloc countries can inform us that the thousands of henchmen from the ranks of the NKVD, the tribunals, and the camp command offices have similarly been sentenced, the representatives of the eastern bloc have forfeited the right to accuse Germans.'

In contrast to other resistance fighters who ceaselessly talk about Fascist anti-Semitism in order not to see Communist anti-Semitism, Wiesenthal has for some years now pilloried the new (and old) anti-Semitism in the Soviet Union.

The eastern bloc therefore unleashed a furious propaganda campaign against him. The Polish secret service manufactured a series of forgeries in which Wiesenthal was accused of being an agent of Zionism and of the CIA, and also of having been a collaborator with the Nazis. These documents found their way into Austria, where they were carefully translated by the Austrian state police and kept by the then Minister of the Interior Otto Rösch in a special safe. When in 1975 Wiesenthal pointed out that one of Bruno Kreisky's closest confidants, Friedrich Peter, had been a member of a murder squad during the National Socialist period, the Austrian Federal Chancellor assaulted him with the collected arguments of the Polish secret service: 'Herr Wiesenthal, I assert, had a different connection with the Gestapo from mine, demonstrably so. My connection with the Gestapo was unambiguous: I was their prisoner, their detainee, and I underwent interrogation. His connection – I believe I know this – was of a different nature.' Kreisky defamed the survivor of half a dozen concentration camps as a Gestapo informer.

In point of fact, Wiesenthal's survival during the Third Reich was a succession of miracles. Only a person who reminds himself of the pure luck which, time and again, let him escape certain death, can understand the inevitability with which he feels obliged to serve the dead. His *via dolorosa* began in June 1941 with Hitler's attack against the Soviet Union. Eight days later the last Russians left Lvov and the first German uniforms appeared: they were worn by Ukrainian auxiliary troops who celebrated their return by three days and three nights of continous pogroms. Six thousand Jews lost their lives.

In the afternoon of 6 July 1941 Simon Wiesenthal, who was hiding in a cellar, was arrested and, along with about a hundred lawyers, doctors and teachers, marched to the Brygidki prison. The Jews were ordered to stand up in several rows facing the wall and to fold their arms behind their necks. Beside each of them was an empty wooden box. A Ukrainian started the execution by shooting from the left end of the first row; two of his helpers flung the bodies into the boxes standing ready and dragged them away. This lasted throughout an afternoon.

Suddenly the church bells rang, and somebody called: 'Enough for now, vespers!'

The shooting stopped. Ten yards from Wiesenthal.

The next thing he remembers was a brilliant cone of light and behind it a Polish voice: 'But Mr Wiesenthal, what are you doing here?' Wiesenthal recognized a foreman he used to know, by the name of Bodnar. He was wearing civilian clothes with the armband of a Ukrainian police auxiliary. 'I've got to get you out of here tonight.'

Bodnar told the Ukrainians that among the captured Jews he had discovered a Soviet spy and that he was taking him to the district police commissar. In actual fact he took Wiesenthal back to his own flat, on the grounds that it was unlikely to be searched so soon again. This was the first time Wiesenthal survived.

Shortly afterwards – the German army proper had followed up in the meantime and proved considerably less trigger-happy – all Jews were made to give up their homes and move into the ghetto. From there Wiesenthal and his wife were taken to the nearby Janowska concentration camp. His mother stayed behind in the ghetto. Towards the middle of 1942 Wiesenthal and his wife were assigned to forced labour at the eastern railway repair shops.

To this day there is a man wandering about Austria, offering as sensational news evidence that Wiesenthal had 'worked for the Germans' and thus saved his own life. Wiesenthal described this in detail in his books: his wife was sent to work in a railway engine plant, where she polished brass fittings. He himself had to paint German eagles and swastikas on captured locomotives.

In May the Gestapo chief Reinhard Heydrich was assassinated in Prague. The retribution measure throughout the occupied territories resulted in mass deportations of Jews to the Polish extermination camps. In August the SS was loading elderly Jewish women into a goods truck at Lvov station. One of them was Simon Wiesenthal's mother, then sixty-three. She died at the extermination camp of Belzec. His wife's mother was shortly afterwards shot dead by a Ukrainian police auxiliary on the steps of her house.

Wiesenthal, able to move with relative freedom within the railway repair shop, tried to save his wife. He established contact with Polish resistance fighters and promised them plans of the railway station (which they wanted to blow up) if they helped his wife to escape and provided her with false papers. It was a deal.

Not until several months after the war did Wiesenthal find his wife again, under dramatic circumstances. Today he lives with her in a detached house on the edge of Vienna. In 1946 the couple's only child, their daughter Paulinka, was born: 'No one ever wanted a child as deliberately as we did.'

Today Paulinka is married. The photos of his three grandchildren – playing by the sea, on a sandy beach under Israel's sun – are always with Wiesenthal. 'If somebody then had told me that I'd live to see this, I would have thought him mad.'

While Cyla Wiesenthal managed to survive, as it were submerged, thanks to her blonde hair, Simon Wiesenthal, with his draughtsman's talent and training as an architect, was painting swastikas and slogans at the railway shop.

The 'collaboration' of which Bruno Kreisky accused him in all serious-ness did in fact exist – not, however, as Wiesenthal's collaboration with the Nazis, but the other way around: as the help of two Nazis for Wiesenthal.

The eastern railway repair shops came under the control of a German railway official called Heinrich Guenthert. Wiesenthal's immediate superior was likewise a German, Chief Inspector Adolf Kohlrautz. Both of them were Nazis. But the longer they were in Poland the more critical they became. Kohlrautz went so far as to murmur at one point, in Wiesenthal's hearing, that one day they would all be ashamed for what the SS were doing. Within their own sphere – in addition to the forced labour men they had fifty German railway officials under them – they saw to it strictly that the Jews were treated fairly. Not even in the Third Reich was there an official order that Jews must be beaten, spat on or left to starve.

However, on 20 April 1943, the miracle within the inferno came to an end: Wiesenthal and three other men were collected early in the morning, against the protestations of Guenthert and Kohlrautz, and taken to a concentration camp. The SS intended to celebrate the Führer's birthday with a sacrifice of Jews.

Those selected for execution by shooting, about twenty men, were made to stand by the so-called 'tube' – a two-metre-wide corridor between barbed wire fences. At the end of the tube was a sandpit. Into that they would fall, one after another.

For the second time in his life Wiesenthal was – almost like the doctor's, 'Next please' – waiting for his death. (He describes his fear of death in the second chapter of this book.)

The fact that he once more escaped death – the only one to do so –

weighs heavily on him as a sense of guilt to this day, though differently from the way Kreisky sees it. 'Why me, in particular?' is a question which Wiesenthal has been unable to shake off in over forty years. 'When hundreds of thousands were murdered, why was I allowed to live?' It runs counter to his mystical concept of justice: after all, he had not done anything that would justify his survival. This sense of guilt is a key to Wiesenthal's present activity: by bringing the murderers to justice he believes he is performing a deed which in retrospect justifies his survival then.

Wiesenthal's rescuers were Germans, and members of the Nazi party. On Guenthert's instructions Kohlrautz drove to the concentration camp and at the camp office demanded the return of his 'painter'. A big banner with a swastika on a white ground had to be urgently painted in time for the celebrations that afternoon. Wiesenthal was fetched out of the tube and taken back to the engine repair shop. The text of the banner he completed was: 'We thank our Führer'.

When Wiesenthal's daughter Paulinka was married in 1965, the 'Nazi hunter' invited Heinrich Guenthert to the wedding. To Simon Wiesenthal his rescue by two Nazi's was an experience which moulded him at least as much as his persecution by others: 'You are living proof that it was possible to survive the Third Reich with clean hands. You are proof that there is no such thing as collective guilt.'

The man who (though only in Austria) is regarded as the standard-bearer of the charge of 'collective guilt' has since the first day of his liberation fiercely opposed that thesis. There is scarcely a major article, scarcely a speech, by Wiesenthal in which he does not directly or indirectly reject it. When time and again religious Israelis argued that Germans and Austrians were stained for all time, Wiesenthal, normally chary of religious parables, quoted the Bible to them: the whole struggle of Abraham with God and the destruction of Sodom and Gomorrah, he said, was one great parable against collective guilt: a mere handful of just men would have sufficed to save the cities from destruction. He, Wiesenthal, knew at least two just men personally – and he knew of numerous others.

Shortly after the war – Wiesenthal was still working with the Americans – there was a rumour among Jews that an SS Untersturmführer by name of Beck was awaiting trial at the American internment camp at Dachau, although he had treated the inmates decently. Wiesenthal dropped everything and obtained affidavits by witnesses confirming Beck's decent behaviour. On the strength of this evidence he was discharged.

In 1943, when the SS started to deport the last surviving Jewish forced labourers from industrial plants, the Nazi Kohlrautz encouraged Simon Wiesenthal to escape. 'What more are you waiting for?' Without a word the German issued a pass to his sign-painter, authorizing him to buy painting materials in the town. As an escort he chose for him a feeble-minded Ukrainian police auxiliary who was unfamiliar with the neighbourhood. Wiesenthal entered the stationery shop by the front door and left it by the back door. He was saved.

A short while later, as Wiesenthal subsequently learned, Kohlrautz volunteered for front-line service because – with part of his heart still a Nazi – he believed he had to do his duty there. He was killed in action at the end of the war in Berlin.

Along with another Jew Wiesenthal made his way to the home of friends. Under the ground-floor floorboards of the old house was sand. They removed the boards, shovelled out the sand and created a hideaway. When strangers came near the house they lifted up the boards and lay down in the sand. Their friends pushed a heavy oak table over them. The safest place then was a grave.

One evening in April 1943 a German soldier was shot dead in the street. The alarm was raised: SS and Polish police officers in civilian clothes searched the nearby houses for hidden weapons. Instead they found Simon Wiesenthal. He was marched off for the third time to, as he believed, his certain execution.

While the memories of most victims of the Third Reich are marked by the passive endurance of a camp, Wiesenthal's memories are marked by the experience of escape, by the fear of being discovered at any moment, in any place. The continual listening for footsteps between heartbeats.

No matter how much Wiesenthal – credibly in so many respects – maintains that his work is not motivated by vengeance, his activity nevertheless puts his former tormentors in the same situation that he was in. The mere fact of his existence prevents them from finding respite anywhere in the world. One of them – Wiesenthal describes his case in this book – was unable to bear the tension any longer and committed suicide.

On 15 April 1943 Simon Wiesenthal could no longer bear the strain of constantly being on the run: while being taken to the Gestapo he cut his wrists with a razor blade he kept hidden in his clothes. The Gestapo nursed him back to health in prison, on special rations, in order to shoot him according to regulations.

By that time, however, the prevailing chaos was sufficient to save a man from death. Over Sapieha Street an aircraft was shot down; the explosion turned Gestapo headquarters into a smoke-filled pandemonium. Wiesenthal ran across the yard and joined a group of Jews lined up, evidently, for deportation. Along with them he was loaded on to a lorry and before long found himself back in the place he had escaped from earlier – the Janowska concentration camp.

The camp commandant, SS Hauptsturmführer Friedrich Warzog,

welcomed him with great cordiality as 'one of my regulars'. He introduced him to his colleagues as the 'prodigal son returned home'.

'No doubt you thought I'd have you shot along with the others,' he said to Wiesenthal. 'But in this place a man dies when I say so. Get off to your hut! No work for you, and you'll have double rations.'

It is well-nigh impossible for anyone not familiar with the conditions then to believe in such capricious twists of fate. Yet they are the stuff of the memories of nearly all the Jews who survived the extermination machinery of the Third Reich: in the midst of madness salvation, too, was a kind of madness. The absolute power which the SS had arrogated to itself over the lives of humans would now and again, after a thousand murders, manifest itself in someone, without any reason, being granted life.

One day, in the midst of millions of deaths, a commission arrived in Auschwitz from the Reich to verify the effect of corrective detention on a female inmate whose parents had requested it. The woman official from Berlin asked the young woman prisoner whether she had now come to realize that the Führer was doing things the right way. The woman said yes, and two hours later she was released. A Nazi historian might quote this as evidence that the duration of detention in Auschwitz was supervised by regular German authorities.

Wiesenthal's absurd salvation from death was followed a few days later by a clemency order. The reasons were entirely rational: the SS needed to have prisoners to guard. Lvov by then was under heavy artillery bombardment. SS men without specific duties were being sent to the front. Thus the thirty-four Jews who had survived along with Wiesenthal became a life insurance for two hundred SS men. Warzog, who no doubt had been considering what they had best say if taken prisoner by the Russians, invited the Jews to form 'a big family' with the SS men. They would try to reach the forests of Slovakia and await the end of the war there. While the German troops were engaged in their costly battles of retreat, Warzog's SS were guarding a handful of half-starved, severely weakened men and were anxious to find the quickest way back. Partly on foot and partly in vehicles taken from the fighting units, this strange party moved westwards.

At the beginning of 1945 the Red Army was close to Gross-Rosen. The internees had to march as far as Chemnitz, and from there they were taken by train to the Buchenwald concentration camp. On 3 February the flight backwards entered its last phase. Three thousand internees were loaded on to open lorries and transported to Mauthausen in Austria. Those who froze to death could not fall over because they were packed so tightly. When the convoy reached Mauthausen on 7 February, only 1200 of the 3000 men who had left Buchenwald were still alive. Simon Wiesenthal was one of them.

He weighed only about 110 pounds and lay in Hut B of the so-called death block, where those unfit for work were left to die. On the morning of 5 May 1945 he staggered outside – 'I don't know how I managed to get up and walk' – to meet the first American tank.

Former inmates took over command. One of them was the future Polish Cabinet Minister Kazimierz Rusinek. Wiesenthal needed to see him at his office to get a pass. The Pole, who was about to lock up, struck him across the face – just as some camp officials had frequently treated Jews. It hurt Wiesenthal more than all the blows received from SS men in three years: 'Now the war is over, and the Jews are still being beaten.'

In the second chapter of this book he relates how he sought out the American camp command to make a complaint. He stepped through a door which was marked with a piece of paper saying 'War Crimes'. Thus Simon Wiesenthal became a staff member of the 'Office of War Crimes'.

Hare into Huntsman

It was on one of the first few days he was serving in that office that the door opened and an SS man was brought in. Wiesenthal pressed his hands to his trouser seams and turned his head aside, as was proper for a subhuman. Only slowly, with the prisoner's ever-present readiness to retreat, did he turn his head in order to watch something his mind still failed to comprehend: the other man was shaking, a bundle of fear.

The image of the Teutonic superman who, equipped with power over life and death, commands fate rather than obeys it, was still so deeply ingrained in Wiesenthal that he found it difficult to recognize him in that bundle of fear: 'It was as if a hare was expected to grasp that the huntsman is afraid of it. It took me a long time to understand how much alike people are in certain situations. He had the same fear as one of us Jews would have when the SS found him in his hideout.'

This astonishing difference between the image of the SS men held by the inmates of the camps and the same SS men after their arrest, interrogation and trial in court led to a number of wrong verdicts: it was difficult even for the victims to realize that these were the men who had mown down helpless people with their machine guns.

The concept of the SS man with satanic eyes, a cynical smile, black jackboots and a menacing Alsatian dog was itself a cliché. It represented the extreme, not the average. Indeed, they were sometimes the less danger-ous ones: sadists who might have an orgy of beating, emptying their revolvers and stringing people up – and quite often then stopping. More dangerous – because it was they who kept the system going – were the seemingly average men. The ones who looked like everybody else. Whose emotional life seemed normal. The ones who sent Christmas greetings to their children from Auschwitz while sending the children of others to the gas chambers. Not enjoying it but because it was their job.

There was a guard in Auschwitz, a nice ordinary girl from the Black Forest, who described her work like this: 'I have to go on doing this for another six months. By then we'll have our little house furnished.' Each month she sent a few grains of gold, prised from the teeth of murdered Jews, to her family back home.

No one having to judge such a guard or such an SS man today would consider it possible even for a second that they had a part in killing people in the most bestial manner. But shortly after the war the evidence was more verifiable: when Simon Wiesenthal was searching one of those trembling SS men for papers he found a picture in his wallet: it showed a young man who had been strung up by his testicles.

This was the only time that Wiesenthal was tempted physically – without questioning, without establishing guilt – to hurl himself on a man. The American officers restrained him.

Wiesenthal's immediate superior was a Captain Taracusio, in civilian life a professor of international law in Cambridge, Massachusetts. He now had an opportunity to watch a form of prosecution of Nazi criminals that was not the rule everywhere: a differentiated approach from the outset, never primitive revenge or generalization. 'Only the law', Taracusio said, 'can be our answer to an age of lawlessness.'

Hardly anyone could have felt this more poignantly than Simon Wiesenthal. After this, his entire life had been a continous experience of what happens when laws designed to protect the individual against arbitrary persecution lose their power.

Wiesenthal did not seek revenge; he sought justice.

During those first few post-war years Wiesenthal was time and again visited by young Jewish commandos or former partisans who tried to win him over for secret retributory action: 'Give us the names, give us the addresses. And we'll do it ourselves.' But Wiesenthal spent hours making them see reason. To him the decisive victory over the ancient principle of 'an eye for an eye, a tooth for a tooth, was in the victim's readiness to transfer his need for retribution to society, to subject it to certain rules – the rules of establishing the truth by courts of law – and to respect their judgement absolutely.

'You will be asked: What difference is there between you and the Nazis? They killed people because they believed they were entitled to do so. And you too believe you have a right to do so.'

'But they killed millions of innocent people. We kill a hundred guilty ones.'

'I accept that there is a difference. But I am hoping for a society in which that difference is not enough.'

The intensity with which Wiesenthal presented his arguments converted even people whose longing for retribution would probably have been understood by everybody. In his book *The Murderers Among Us* he describes one such case: one of the murderers is alive because of Wiesenthal.

It happened in 1947, a week before Yom Kippur, the Day of Atonement. The pious Jews of the Admont camp wanted to observe their greatest holiday once again in the way they had been accustomed to: the men were to sacrifice a cockerel, the women were to sacrifice a hen. They decided to barter some tinned food and chocolate they had received from their British liberators for poultry. With this purpose two young Jews, Mair Blitz and Moses Kussowsky, went, with their inadequate command of German, to try their luck at illicit trading in the neighbourhood of Admont.

But the peasants were poor. Most avoided a deal by advising them to try elsewhere. And one of these pieces of advice stuck in the ears of the two young Jews: 'Why don't you try the man up there. He owns a big farm and has at least two thousand chickens. But he might kick you out. He hates Jews. Said to have been a big Nazi.'

The two men let Yom Kippur be Yom Kippur, about-turned and travelled to Linz, where Wiesenthal then had his office. 'We must catch Eichmann,' they told him.

'What makes you think he is Eichmann?' asked Wiesenthal.

'This fellow has two thousand chickens, he hates the Jews and he was a big Nazi. Why shouldn't he be Eichmann?' they asked in turn, with their own brand of logic.

In his book Wiesenthal poked fun at the strange belief that such assumptions are always correct in the hunt for a criminal. In actual fact it was not unlike his own mode of procedure: a kind of mystical certainty that he would find the people he was seeking. It was based on the equally mystical conviction that nothing in life is mere chance: to Wiesenthal it is a hint of destiny that he reads a certain file on a certain evening. To him it is even a hint of destiny when he fails in something. It is meant to keep him free for a more important task.

Looking for a man called Schultz in Frankfurt, Wiesenthal opens the telephone directory, finds a Schulz whose wife is called Heidrun, and is convinced: 'That's him.' And most of the time it is.

All good criminal investigators (and journalists) need this irrational mystical identification: they have to be convinced of a trail in order to follow it. The process of criminal investigation only rarely consists of the painstaking compilation of evidence, on the strength of which one bases one's suspicions. Almost invariably it runs in the opposite direction: one has a suspicion and painstakingly confronts it with the accumulating evidence. Soundness does not consist in rejecting intuition but in verifying it: not to utter a suspicion until, to the best of one's knowledge and belief, it is correct. Wiesenthal was capable of doing this to an almost incredible degree. In over forty years of searching for Nazi culprits there has only been one case when his 'client' was able in court to prove that he had made an error: the SS man Erich Rajakowitsch, who had accused Wiesenthal of four incorrect assertions, succeeded with one of them. (Wiesenthal's quotation from an Italian newspaper to the effect that Rajakowitsch had also operated as an Eastern bloc spy could not be proved.)

During the first few years of the war, admittedly, Wiesenthal's intuition was based on solid ground: whenever the police acted on suspicion there would be a high degree of probability that they actually held a guilty man. When Wiesenthal, just before Yom Kippur, travelled to Gaishorn – seven miles from the Admont camp – with his companions, he did not find Adolf Eichmann at the two-thousand-chicken farm, but he did find Franz Murer. As acting regional commissioner of Wilno, Murer bore a decisive responsibility for the extermination of approximately 80,000 Lithuanian Jews.

Among the witnesses' statements which Wiesenthal compiled over the months to prepare the case against Murer, there was that of a man called Jakob Brodi. One day the SS had formed up into two groups outside the gates of the Wilno ghetto. Assigned to one group were those fit for work; the other, consisting of those to be shot, included Brodi's seven-year-old son Daniel. While the two columns were still standing there, waiting, the little boy tried to sneak across to his father. One of the Germans spotted him and shot him dead. From a number of photographs Jakob Brodi identified Franz Murer as that man.

Murer is living on his farm in Admont to this day, unmolested.

At that time, however, things were different. Murer was arrested, handed over by the British to the Russians (in whose territory Wilno, or, as they called it, Vilnius, now lay), and sentenced to twenty-five years' imprisonment for the murder of 'Soviet citizens'. In 1955 the Soviet Union, in connection wih the Austrian State Treaty, undertook to repatriate all prisoners of war, including convicts such as Murer, though Austria agreed to try the latter in her own courts. Murer, repatriated, returned to his (still large) farm and became a respected member of the Austrian People's Party. He was chairman of the Regional Chamber of Agriculture, and was decorated in the presence of government ministers.

Wiesenthal went wild: he believed – a belief in other cases fully shared by the public – that it was intolerable for a murderer to be set free after a mere seven years. But the authorities – all political parties were then eagerly wooing former Nazis, found reasons for clemency: Russian prisons, they explained to Wiesenthal, were three times harder than Austrian ones, so Murer in fact had served twenty-one years. Even if an Austrian court had sentenced him to life imprisonment he would have been released after twenty years.

When Wiesenthal was reluctant to accept this surprising legal point of view, the official concerned became more officious: Murer was a free man; an action against him could be started only if new evidence were discovered.

It is the good fortune of those investigating Nazi crimes that such evidence is almost invariably discovered – not because, as is sometimes alleged, witnesses' statements are 'managed', but because men like Murer committed such countless atrocities that the difficulty lies in limiting the scope of evidence. Wiesenthal produced seventeen witnesses of personal murders committed by Murer.

There was no reaction from the Ministry of Justice. Not for several years, not even in response to countless domestic and foreign submissions.

Not until after the Eichmann trial did Wiesenthal take the step which brought the accusation that he was fouling his own nest: he appealed to the public. In 1963, nearly ten years after Murer's return from the Soviet Union, the judiciary graciously decided to schedule the case against him before a jury in Graz. One of the witnesses was Jakob Brodi.

It was the fourth day of the trial, and Brodi and Wiesenthal were sitting at the Hotel Sonne in Graz.

'I am told that Murer's two sons and his wife are sitting in the front row in court, poking fun at the witnesses,' Brodi said.

Wiesenthal nodded.

'They'll stop poking fun when I am in the witness box. I haven't come here to give evidence, I have come to act.' Slowly he unbuttoned his waistcoat and gripped the handle of an enormous knife concealed in his waistband. 'Murer killed my child before my eyes. And I'm now going to kill him before the eyes of his wife and his children.'

Wiesenthal remembered the affidavit he had read, and when he spoke he had to convince himself, too, for the first time in many years: 'We cannot achieve our ends by using their methods. If you try to kill Murer you're a murderer yourself.'

But Brodi did not understand. He was still filled with a thirst for revenge. He saw before him his son and he saw before him the man who had shot him, and he believed that there was only one justice for him: to kill Murer.

Wiesenthal thought of his own small daughter, and his words came out with effort: 'I too cried, Herr Brodi, when I read about your boy . . .'

Jakob Brodi put his knife on the table and cried.

The following day he gave his evidence in a toneless voice.

A few days later the jury produced their verdict: 'Not guilty.' Amidst cheers and masses of flowers Franz Murer left the courtroom.

The Supreme Court later (in 1963) reversed the acquittal. Since then Wiesenthal has been pressing, verbally and in writing, for a retrial to be scheduled. Meanwhile the Public Prosecutor's office has definitively closed the case.

A Bullet for Novak

This situation, straight out of the theatre of the absurd – Simon Wiesenthal guaranteeing the safety of a defendant in a Nazi trial – occurred for a second time in Vienna. The man whom Wiesenthal protected was Franz Novak. The 'stationmaster of death', as the press dubbed him, was responsible, at a time when the fighting forces were short of even the most primitive means of transport, for providing trains, week after week, to transport Jews across the Third Reich to Auschwitz. Vienna juries tried him three times: the first time they sentenced him to eight years, the second time they acquitted him, and the third time they sentenced him to nine years, of which, thanks to 'good behaviour', he only had to serve six.

Thereupon a fifty-five-year-old Jewish writer from England turned up at Simon Wiesenthal's office on the Rudolfsplatz. Single. Without relations: they had all been loaded on to Novak's trains for Auschwitz. The man was armed. 'Someone's got to do something. The Austrians can't simply release Novak after six years. The world needs reminding that this can't go on.'

But Simon Wiesenthal, the 'Nazi hunter', fought for the right of the Nazi criminal Franz Novak to stay alive, now that he had served his sentence. 'Revenge killings cannot and must not be a way of administering justice. We differ from the Nazis precisely in that we accept the judgements of courts of law, even if we consider them monstrous or unjust. If you are convinced that Novak is a murderer then you shouldn't become Novak's murderer.'

This fundamental attitude explains why Wiesenthal, to an almost bureaucratic degree, insists that every move of his must be in strict agreement with the law. Invariably his first, now almost automatic, action upon receiving new facts, a new testimony, or a tip-off, is to notify the appropriate department of the Ministry of Justice in Vienna and the Central Office for the investigation of Nazi crimes in Ludwigsburg, West Germany.

If one wished to be malicious, one might even claim that his real work consisted of passing on to the authorities those criminal investigations which the general public attributes to him.

A typical Wiesenthal correspondence runs something like this: 'Yad Vashem, the archive entrusted in Israel with the commemoration of the Holocaust, reports that it has transmitted to the Central Office for the investigation of Nazi crimes in Ludwigsburg a statement by a witness on executions by shooting in a Russian village; this statement also mentions Austrians.' Wiesenthal addresses a copy of the Yad Vashem letter to the Austrian Ministry of the Interior and suggests that a copy of the relevant file should be requested from Ludwigsburg; Ludwigsburg, in response to an inquiry by Wiesenthal, states that it has not so far received such a request from Austria; Wiesenthal sends a copy of the letter from Ludwigsburg to Yad Vashem and inquires from the Austrian authorities why no interest is being shown by them in the German proceedings. This so-called 'agent's activity' of Simon Wiesenthal is an unceasing, gigantic bureaucratic battle with reluctant officials, archives lacking the necessary authority or hostile departments demanding 'more details'.

The tracking down of Nazi criminals is, in point of fact, Wiesenthal's lesser merit; a more important function, for at least the past thirty years, has been the fact that his persistent writing of letters has prevented Austrian and German authorities from allowing the prosecution of Nazi criminals to be quietly shelved. Immediately after the war things were different. Wiesenthal then was something like an authority himself: by virtue of powers vested in him by the Allies he operated with a kind of police prerogative which even allowed him to make arrests himself or have them made by the military police. But even that early search for war criminals was soon swamped by other activities: issuing victim's cards and, above all, reuniting countless families dispersed throughout Europe by persecution.

As the first Allied soldiers, who had with their own eyes seen the camps in their original state, were relieved by new contingents, the new officials were less able to identify with the persecuted. The Americans were the victims of their totally mistaken ideas about the western part of the Third Reich: they expected savage barbarians and they found people who looked like Americans, worked like Americans, and whose bathtubs and flushing lavatories were evidence of civilization. Surely these could not be the people who wove the hair of murdered Jews into mats.

Simon Wiesenthal was more of a stranger to them than the countless German former officers who were increasingly offering their services to the CIC, the Counter-Intelligence Corps. The breach between the Americans who were looking to the future and Wiesenthal who had not yet finished with the past was bound to come. The occasion was one of those friendly conversations which 'well-meaning people who are not really anti-Semites' (as they usually describe themselves) have with Jews.

'You're such a smart guy,' Wiesenthal's new superior, a certain Mr

Essex who had succeeded Taracusio, commended his Jewish underling. 'People like you can make a great career back home. I can tell you one thing: traffic in the States is controlled by red and green lights, everything else is controlled by the Jews.'

Wiesenthal rose and left.

A few weeks later, at the beginning of 1947, he notified the department responsible for licensing organizations of the founding of a 'Jewish Documentation Center'.

The 'Network'

Then followed the only brief span of time when Simon Wiesenthal really had a 'network': some thirty young Jews from various camps who joined him in order to collect material against Nazi criminals. The costs were minimal: as former detainees all his staff were still living in their camps (waiting to emigrate) and were also fed there. The monthly postage and telephone costs, fifty US dollars, were met by a Jewish lawyer, Aron Silberschein, in Geneva. The organization was really already in place, as in each camp there was a man with a typewriter and paper, who asked the ex-prisoners to let him record their experiences. In this way a collection of places, events and names came into existence; this still forms the nucleus of the Wiesenthal archives.

While the official authorities did not know where to start in the prevailing chaos, Wiesenthal had his records copied and sent to all the authorities he thought should see them. There was nothing else at the time, and so the 'Jewish Documentation Center' became well known throughout Europe overnight.

The thirty helpers were soon to disperse: they were getting their emigration papers. But the reputation lived on: the knowledge that in Austria there was a man called Wiesenthal who was searching for Nazi criminals. And that one could write to him. And that there would be a reply. In that sense a worldwide network continues to exist, far greater than the one his adversaries accuse him of: all victims and opponents of the Nazi regime, wherever they may live – from Israel to South America, from Poland to Turkey – are potential colleagues of Simon Wiesenthal; all they need do is write to him. The address on their letters, frequently, is not much more than 'Wiesenthal, Austria'.

Wiesenthal's most important primary activity consists of the evaluation of such letters: he distils from them the accusations and clues which, in his huge bureaucratic war of paper, he passes on to government departments or to the competent authorities. In this he is helped by his phenomenal memory: Wiesenthal is able to quote telephone numbers which he may have happened to see on a visiting card two years before. He can list the participants in huge functions, one by one, and he can add what colour suit each wore. Although he writes up to twenty letters a day, and receives more than that number, he can, years later, quote key passages from them and indicate roughly where that letter may be found in a file. At the same time he gives the impression of being untidy: on his desk, and in his office generally, a chaos of newspaper cuttings, books, photocopies and letters reigns – a chaos no secretary has ever been able to contain. Nevertheless, he expects his staff to put their hands on a document in a second, and he is enraged when they stand helpless in front of mountains of paper: he reaches into them twice and the right document is in his hand.

If there is anything about him that fits the cliché of the demonic 'hunter' then it is this ability – which is also the only secret of his success as an investigator. After all, dossiers such as Wiesenthal's – in greater detail and greater volume – are kept by all appropriate authorities. But whereas there they are managed by trained criminal investigation officials, Wiesenthal's 'agents' are laymen: as a rule he hires them from among his acquaintances. If a friend tells him of a student who would like to earn a little extra money during the summer, Wiesenthal hires him. He also found his secretary through an advertisement.

The image of the 'intelligence centre' with its attached 'network of agents' compares to reality rather like the homicide department of Scotland Yard to a local police station. But whereas the files in official archives are dead, they are alive in Wiesenthal's office. 'Archives are like something in the freezer,' he says, 'You can't use them unless they're thawed out.'

The facts stored in Wiesenthal's head are in continuous interaction. If some retired teacher from New York reports in a letter how a man, whom his comrades called Günther, had opened fire on a train of deportees, then Wiesenthal remembers that after the war there was a tent camp of neo-Nazis in which one Günther had boasted of his experiences in the east. When Wiesenthal reads the name of an SS man who was a guard at Buchenwald, then he remembers that he heard the same name ten years earlier in a trial concerned with shootings in Lvov. A man's civilian occupation, his origins in a particular region, his accent mentioned by someone – all these stick in Wiesenthal's memory for years. And, just like a computer, he can call them up at any time.

This permanent readiness of recall means that the horror is not relegated, as it is with most people (and increasingly also with victims), to a remote recess of the mind, but is always at the forefront, at the painful boundary of consciousness. Wiesenthal possesses what is usually called a photographic memory: he is a man who cannot forget. And just as a small electrical imbalance can sometimes cause a computer program to run itself spontaneously, so it occasionally happens that all the horrific images in Wiesenthal's mind combine into a film whose automatic unrolling he can scarcely bear. He screams in his sleep, to this day.

Wiesenthal has neither the ability nor the wish to expunge what he has experienced or what he knows. His memory still reproduces with their original clarity the features of those who were waiting for their death, the features of those who dropped into the graves, and himself among them.

People who call on Wiesenthal in his office in order to tell him about their own horrors frequently make the astonishing discovery that, after all these years, he is not dulled: he cannot listen to stories of past sufferings without shedding tears. That too is one of the secrets of his success: he does not process 'cases' or 'files', but he experiences those life stories as he works on them. Eyewitnesses who turned to the authorities after the war and 'made a statement' bear witness at Wiesenthal's office. They – not infrequently even former Nazis – talk themselves free of a burden that has grown and been repressed over decades. It can happen that he spends a whole day with a man who tells him things which are totally irrelevant to any kind of investigation. Or that, to the relief of them both, he cries with him.

Wiesenthal does not enjoy stirring up the past; it gives him pain. Even after more than forty years he cannot, as some can, push aside the visions of death, or forget them like bad dreams. He has to have them ever-present, like a self-established concentration camp. While others suppress their memories, he conjures up his own: he has an envelope full of the most terrible photographs that he was able to obtain from those days, and he looks at them again and again. 'Because then I know what I am living for.'

Psychoanalysts might say that he is a person who seeks painful experiences. But that is probably true of all those who, throughout history, have made the sufferings of others their own.

2

To the Pit and Back

By mid-July 1944 the Soviets had advanced close to Lvov. We could hear
the din of battle in the concentration camp: every night just before eleven
o'clock the bombardment of the city began, and it became so fierce that
the SS men fled from their watchtowers to take cover.

The relatively fit ones amongst us therefore decided to attempt an escape.
We settled on the night of 16 July. As expected, the bombardment began
at eleven, and under cover of darkness we left our hut. I could scarcely
stand, I was so weak. I was probably able to move only because Lola was
guiding me. Lola was a Jew, but she had a sister who was regarded as a
Pole, and it was at their flat that I had hidden along with her and her
brother-in-law Josef Busch. We had then been discovered and taken back
to the Janowska camp, the one from which I had escaped in 1943.

Now we were groping our way through the darkness, one behind the
other, with Lola holding my hand to make sure I didn't fall behind. It
seemed to me to take an eternity to get to the barbed-wire fence. We were
by then a fairly substantial group, but no one saw or heard us because the
roar of the guns blotted out all other sounds, and the SS men, even those
still on the towers, were taking cover. The men doing duty behind the
lines were not necessarily the bravest of the brave.

One of us, I think it was Moldauer, cut a hole in the fence with a pair
of pincers, just about big enough for someone to get through. It would
have been wiser to spend a little longer cutting and have a bigger opening,
but our nerves were not up to it. As it was, we could only crawl through

the narrow gap one by one. Lola was number eleven and I was to follow her through the fence: she would give me a hand. But that was not to happen. The guards had spotted us and opened fire. 'Run, run!' I called out to Lola and the others who were already outside the fence, then I mustered what strength I had to get back to my hut as quickly as possible.

When the bombardment was over we were fetched out from our huts. We had to fall in for parade in two ranks, to be counted: on the ground between our ranks the SS placed two of our companions who had been shot dead while escaping. Together with them we numbered twenty-seven. Within a few hours, we felt convinced, we would be twenty-seven corpses.

We were the last prisoners in the camp, which was about to be dissolved. The guards, too, had been greatly reduced, but even so there were twice as many SS in the camp as prisoners. Their rifles at the ready, they led us to the tube – a corridor bounded on both sides by barbed-wire fences, at the end of which were the 'pits': those mass graves which the prisoners had to dig for themselves, to tumble into them backwards as they were shot.

Perhaps I was lucky to be experiencing the situation for the second time. Once before, a little more than a year earlier, I had stood in a line in front of just such a pit, when someone had suddenly called out my name and I was taken out of the line: chief inspector Kohlrautz of the eastern railway repair shop had commandeered me for painting work and thereby called me back to life. (I have described the event in my book *The Murderers Among Us*.) Now I was standing in such a line again. Some had collapsed and were crouching by the edge of the pit – partly from weakness and partly from fear. A few were crying.

Years after the war Isak Lehmann, who had then stood in that line along with me, told me that I had comforted the crying. They should stop being sad, I am reported to have told them; we might not live much longer but the war was won. Won by us. Perhaps I used other bombastic words as well. I cannot myself recall any such speech and was surprised by Lehmann's story after the war. Maybe my thoughts were somewhere quite different while I was speaking. With my wife – of whose whereabouts I knew nothing, or even whether she was still alive. Maybe it wasn't me speaking, but something coming from my lips mechanically, the way one mechanically mumbles a prayer in church and feels secure.

The SS men were standing there with their rifles at the ready; any moment now a superior officer would arrive and give the order to fire. We were not surprised to be kept waiting for hours. Life in the concentration camps was one continuous wait. Organization was always unbelievably inefficient. There was only one thing a Jew could be certain of in the camps of the Third Reich: at the end of the waiting was death.

By then it was ten in the morning. We were no longer standing but lying down. The SS did not object, much as a man condemned to death is permitted to smoke a final cigarette under the gallows. The SS men, too, had sat down, making themselves comfortable at the edge of the grave which already contained hundreds, scantily covered by a thin layer of earth, from which, here and there, a leg or an arm protruded. I don't know what feelings we experienced as Hauptsturmführer Warzog approached. Maybe we were even pleased: now he would give orders to fire, and this state between life and death would come to an end. Perhaps fear flooded us like a rush of blood to the head and made us insensitive. I can no longer tell. Fate is merciful and grants those sentenced to death a state of detachment, of alienation from oneself, almost of unconsciousness. Or perhaps that isn't correct either: perhaps these moments carry so much fear that subsequently we repress all memory of them, that, with our present thoughts and feelings on the matter, we avoid even brushing against the thoughts and emotions of those seconds. Warzog would say 'Fire!', and we would simultaneously be consumed in the fire of our fear and be extinguished.

'The SS Police Chief of Galicia, Katzmann,' Warzog said, 'has decided to make you a present of your lives. You will now return to the camp and you will leave it together with the German contingent. Before we blow up our stores and camp facilities, to prevent them falling into Russian hands, each one of you may take with him whatever he wants. You will need food for the long journey ahead of us.'

We thought we were going mad. Perhaps, we feared (or hoped), we were mad already. Perhaps we had only imagined all this – the way through the tube, the wait by the edge of the grave, perhaps the whole camp, and the whole era, was just a hallucination. Or else we were dead and there was life after death, when we might fantasize that we had been saved. I was walking back not along the camp street, but I was reeling, quite beyond myself, through something totally unreal, something spinning about me, dissolving, reassembling, approaching and slipping away, as if I were drunk. Sometimes I had the impression of seeing myself from outside and no longer being myself.

Somehow we managed to get up the hill on which the camp stood. We stumbled into the food store, now wide open, and, as if under hypnosis, obeyed the order to take something for ourselves. I took a large tin box from a shelf and with it stumbled back towards my hut. Next to me walked a man who had grabbed a loaf of bread, and another was clutching a cabbage-head to his chest. These two, evidently, had found their way back to reality more quickly than me.

Suddenly an SS man came walking towards us. He was slim and young and wore his cap rakishly over one ear, which lent him an air of daredevilry.

'Well now, what goodies have we in there?' he asking, pointing to my tin. I opened it and looked down on a heap of colourful boiled sweets. The SS man told me to put the tin on the ground. He too had been carrying something – a petrol can. He opened it slowly, savouring every second, and poured about half a litre of its contents into my tin, saying, 'I want them to taste really nice for you.' Then I knew that I was back in the real world.

I had seen that SS man in the camp several times before. He was thought to be a Sudeten German, and his name was Ritschek. He was conspicuous through invariably having an Alsatian dog with him, whom he would encourage to attack half-starved prisoners. For people like him it must have been a source of colossal irritation that we were reprieved that morning. His type regarded this as a sign of weakness – which it probably was – and could not reconcile themselves to the fact that we evidently now had the status of human beings and no longer of Jews whom one might shoot without another thought, as one might shoot at a squirrel trying to climb a tree. When he couldn't kill, Ritschek was missing out on something.

A few hours later I was standing in front of my hut and saw him again. He was in a small group that was moving towards us. In front of him walked a man, a woman and a child. We thought he would be taking them to our hut, but he took them past us and disappeared behind the kitchen. Then a few shots rang out, and Ritschek returned on his own. He was walking just as he always did: he had shot three squirrels. Those shot were a Jewish couple with their child, who had been hidden by a Polish family. Somebody had betrayed them, and while the Russians were marching into Lvov, the three were brought to the camp by the regular police. Ritschek saw to the rest.

Nearly twenty years later I was going through a list with Prosecutor Rolf Sichting of the Public Prosecutor's Office in Stuttgart; this was a list of SS men who had served in the ghetto and the camp in Lvov. One name leaped out at me: 'Viktor Ritschek,' it said on one of the sheets, 'Sudeten German.'

I would have given a lot to find him. We immediately approached the Sudeten German Association of Karlsbad (Karlovy Vary) and district – the association of expelled Sudeten Germans, now in West Germany – without success. A year later Rolf Sichting heard that Ritschek's mother was living in Germany and that he himself was reputed to have gone to a Scandinavian country. The old lady was found and questioned. However, as might have been expected, it yielded no result.

Eventually I flew to Sweden myself with a photograph of Ritschek and, along with friends, combed the telephone directories of the major towns – again in vain. Swedish papers carried reports on Ritschek and pointed out that he was dog-mad and would certainly own an Alsatian. This brought us clues leading to several innocent owners of Alsatian dogs; Ritschek was not among them.

Nevertheless, I don't know on what grounds, I am convinced that Ritschek is still alive and that he is living under a false name somewhere in Sweden. I probably want him to be alive – because I hope to find him. To find him and see his face: the face of a man that doesn't change at all after he has shot dead three human beings for whom the gates of freedom would have opened within a few days.

3

Liberation and Calling

I wouldn't have recognized him in the street. But then forty years had passed since our brief encounter, in Mauthausen. He, too, would have walked past me without another glance if he hadn't, from time to time, seen my picture in the newspaper.

'I have often told my children about you,' he now said, almost shyly, just as, all that time ago, I had addressed my first words to him; 'I told them how you were brought to me at Mauthausen. I can still see you standing before me, a skeleton supported by two men, a skeleton on which hung a striped uniform. You spoke with your eyes.'

I too suddenly remembered how my eyes were then. I saw them for the first time when a fragment of a mirror fell into my hands: my face was no more than a bony triangle around them, with skin stretched tight and a mouth that was an open wound.

'He won't survive,' I heard the interpreter say to the American officers, but I was determined to survive, I was determined to speak out. Why else had I staggered all the way from my hut and, totally exhausted, entered the office of the American camp commandant, the room from which, only a few days before, the German camp commandant Ziereis had reigned. Two prisoners had to support me on my way and now one of them, a doctor, was holding me to stop me keeling over forwards. A chair was pushed under me and I was carefully set down on it – holding me up was child's play, I weighed a mere 110 pounds – and my arms were placed on the table in front of me.

Having struggled for breath for a minute, I was able to speak: 'I was beaten.'

'By whom?'

'By a block clerk.'

'An SS man?'

'No, a prisoner.'

The American officer before me regarded me uncomprehendingly: this man went through hell, he can scarcely stand up he's so weak, and he struggles up this hill to complain about a few blows. Blows not even from a Nazi. He didn't understand: it was just because the Third Reich had collapsed three days before that these blows hurt. Because I was determined never again – never again – to let myself be beaten by another person.

Now, forty years on, I was facing him again. In Los Angeles a banquet was given in honour of the liberators of 1945, and Colonel Richard Seibel had been invited as the American camp commandant and I as a representative of the prisoners of Mauthausen.

Then, in 1945, I would scarcely have dared to touch his hand, except possibly to kiss it. Now we embraced each other.

Colonel Richard Seibel had ordered the Polish block clerk to be brought before him and this had given me the assurance that right and justice were once more supreme on earth. Without being aware of it, he contributed significantly to my recapturing the meaning of my life: to help restore justice by bringing to trial those who had humiliated, tortured and murdered my companions in the ghettos and my fellow prisoners in the concentration camps.

It had not been a sudden decision, more of a slow process. Although our guards had fled or been taken prisoner, we were still living in the camp and were still watching people die. Added to those who died because they were beyond help were those who died because they were being helped: the Americans distributed canned lard and corned beef with which our metabolism, attuned to 400 calories a day, could not cope. The starving pounced on the food – now, finally, they could eat their fill – and they died at the gate of paradise, having managed to survive hell.

New graves had to be dug. From my bunk I watched through the window as American soldiers escorted a group of civilians – captured Nazis – into the camp and ordered them to bury the dead. And now, all of a sudden, they were unable to face the horror, they refused to touch the naked corpses, they put on gloves, they could not bear the stench of decay which hung over the whole camp. For years they had lived in close proximity to this camp, smelling the sickly odour of the crematoria; they had seen columns of emaciated figures moving off to work, they had listened in the local tap-rooms to drunk SS men boasting of their murders. Yet now they tried, during their midday break, to walk over to us and speak to us: they had known nothing of all this, they swore; they had joined the party only because they'd been compelled to; deep down they had always rejected Hitler. One of them announced proudly that he'd known for months that the local priest was listening to the British radio – yet he had not denounced him. Given another year the man would have been a resistance fighter.

For the first time in my life I saw what enormous cowards these people were; how, instead of dealing with their guilt, they tried to deny it, to suppress it so far that in the end they couldn't see it themselves. We didn't feel like talking to these people, but we realized one thing: the Germans and the Austrians would not simply acknowledge with shame what we had experienced – they would dispute it. Every one of us survivors was a witness and had the duty to bear witness. Most of all a surviving Jew. The realization that I had remained alive while so many others – better ones, cleverer ones, more decent ones – had died, at some moments almost seemed to me an offence against justice: I could restore the balance only by ensuring that the dead received justice.

I therefore approached Colonel Seibel and requested him to let me sit, as a guest, in that office in which the Americans were trying to solve the well-nigh insoluble problem of 'war crimes'. Most of the officers working there were very young. They were speechless in the face of what they saw, and helpless in the attempt to assign responsibility and guilt. Some of them hardly knew the difference between an SS man and a soldier. But they were trying to learn the difference. With the methods of a state founded on law they proceeded to analyse the state founded on total lawlessness: they investigated, verified, considered objections and filed statements. That was a slow and cumbersome procedure, and many of the worst criminals and greatest liars probably slipped through the net – but it re-established confidence in the rule of law. I feel that I owe a debt of gratitude to every one of those young officers.

When I'd been sitting there for many hours, just listening, one of them addressed me and asked about my profession and my family; then he obviously wanted to say something nice to me. 'First of all we're sending you to a nursing home, where you'll recuperate, and then you'll go back home to Poland and will build houses again.'

'Home?' I asked, putting the question to myself. Where was home? What did the concept mean? Family, friends, a house, relations? None of these existed for me any longer. None of them was alive, there wasn't even a cemetery where I might shed tears. I carry the tombstones of my family and my friends within me, and they will remain part of me as long as I live. Poland to me was one gigantic ruin. Can one live in, or with, such ruins? The houses I built have all collapsed with the rest. People like me, uprooted and torn from all ties to life, need no houses.

'I don't think I shall ever build houses again,' I said slowly, and at that instant I realized that I would never return to the profession I'd been trained for. I realized that I had a calling: to live on for the dead who were within me. I would try anything to work for the War Crimes Unit.

*

A lorry had brought a load of clothes from Linz. They had been unloaded in one of the huts. The things had come from the stocks of the Nazi Welfare Organization and were destined for the 'Werewolf', a German partisan group set up as a last-ditch attempt to reverse the Nazi defeat. Now they were to be our first civilian clothes. The things I chose were all right for length but not for girth. My trousers were so wide that another person could have fitted into them with me. Fortunately I found a discarded belt, so that I was able to fit them round my waist in numerous pleats.

On my way to the clothes hut I saw something flashing in the grass; I bent down. It was a fragment of a mirror: in it I could just about see my eyes and part of my nose. They were the eyes Colonel Seibel remembered. A few months earlier I had drawn them a few times; I tried to record, with the stub of a pencil on some scrap of paper, what my face was like: an upside-down triangle with the eyes forming the base and the chin the apex. I had not then seen myself – we had no mirrors – but I had probed my head with my fingers and had looked at the faces of my fellow inmates: they all had the same eyes.

Now I was able to regard myself at leisure for the first time, and I have rarely been so shocked by a face. No one seeing this face would want me sitting in his office, I thought; they'd throw me out at the War Crimes Unit. I must give my skin a healthier colour. They ought not think that I am close to death; they must see that I am alive.

The following day, when I had collected my food, I saw that someone had thrown away a piece of red paper in which something had been wrapped. There was no wind and I able to pick it up without an effort. The next morning, as I was rubbing my face with it in front of my mirror fragment, the man on the next bunk watched me. He was a Belgian, waiting for a repatriation transport for invalids, and he didn't know if he'd live to see it.

'Getting ready to go courting?' he asked.

'I don't know if the girl will have me,' I replied, glad to be able to tell someone about my plans. 'I want to report for the War Crimes Unit.'

The Belgian didn't even know such a thing existed, but when I'd explained to him what went on there he felt a similar satisfaction to mine,

'Yes, you go and do that for the lot of us, for the living and for the dead,' he said, and I could see from his expression that he wasn't sure how long he'd be one of the living or how soon he'd be one of the dead.

'You'll get well again, Albert,' I said. 'You have a family who'll look after you. You must give me your address before you leave. I'll certainly come and visit you.'

Albert didn't believe me but he attempted a smile. 'All right. But now you'd better stop this masquerading, you can't show yourself like this. Go and wash your face.'

He was right. I went over to the bucket and tried to wash those red blotches off again. I only succeeded partially, and some traces remained.

'Wiesenthal, what's happened to you? Has someone struck you? You're all red in the face and under your chin.'

Embarrassed, I stood in Lieutenant Mann's office, where I was hoping once more to listen to the questioning of former SS men. 'No, nobody's struck me, it's only a stain and it'll be gone by tomorrow. Have you got a few minutes for me?'

'Yes, in half an hour.'

For the past ten days I had even owned a handkerchief. I wet it and began to rub my cheeks and neck with it. Then I focused my attention on an SS man who was brought in by two military policemen. In spite of his protests they refused to take off his handcuffs.

'Come into my office, Herr Wiesenthal,' I heard the lieutenant say. 'What was it you wished to see me about?'

'Well, you liberated me, you saved my life. But I don't know what to do with my life. I have no one for whom or with whom I want to live. Now that I've seen what you're doing here in this office I'd like to participate. That could be a task which would lend some meaning to my life. I spent four years in various concentration camps, in ghettos, and in Gestapo prisons. I've seen a lot and I have a good memory. I can help you find the criminals, put the right questions to them, interrogate them. I don't expect any pay – I want to do it to justify my own survival.'

I had summoned all my strength to convince the lieutenant. But he asked me just one question: 'How much do you weigh?'

'A hundred and thirty pounds,' I lied.

'You don't look it. I don't want to offend you, but first of all you've got to regain your strength.' He smiled at me to make the refusal less painful.

'May I come back?'

'Yes.'

'What I'm seeing here restores my health a lot faster than any medication. I can't get enough of it. Can you believe that?'

'Yes, I can believe that. But why don't you write down what you know? It'll do you good.'

'Write a letter, you mean?'

'If you like.'

'Whom shall I address it to?'

'To my boss, the commandant of this camp, Colonel Seibel.'

Now I had a task. In the way that I used to map out a construction plan in the past, I now approached my letter. First of all I sketched it out in my mind, to clarify my ideas. This letter was to contain as much information on every person as I could find in my memory. I realized that, given the kind of people I had resolved to describe, everything could be of importance. For instance, I had memorized the exact address of a railwayman who had shot dead an old woman before my eyes. He had written it, in the workshop where I had worked, on a package he was sending home, and I had watched him. But there were other criminals, too, on whom I had at least some fragmentary information as to where they came from. There were a few camp officials or prisoners who had contact with SS men and therefore knew something about them – all that I had stored in my memory. In the ghetto, too, people often knew where their guards came from. During those four years on the verge of death I had memorized a great many things. Now the time had come to recall it all and put it down on paper.

So I sat outside my hut in the sun, with pencil and paper on my knees, and from memory jotted down names and facts. I set aside several sheets for each camp, in order that all the data referring to the same subject should be grouped together. On the basis of this stack of sheets I then began to write the letter proper: it contained the names of ninety-one men who had to be brought to trial if my need for justice was to be satisfied.

Three days later the letter was finished. It was written in Polish, and of course there was no copy because I had no carbon paper, and I don't even know if the thought of making a copy then occurred to me. Years later, when my letter was found in the National Archives of Washington, I was able to establish that it had been correctly translated.

When I called on Lieutenant Mann a few days later he knew about my list. 'May I join you now?' I asked.

'Of course,' he said. 'You've been with us for a long time already.'

4

The Encounter

At the beginning of 1947 the provincial government of Upper Austria provided me with an office in a hut at Goethestrasse 63, in Linz. My neighbour was a certain Dr Wasyl Stroncickij, who, in two rooms, was setting up an organization for Ukrainian refugees. He introduced himself to me at once and told me that he had lived as a doctor in the small town of Mosty Wielkie and there had fallen foul of the Germans. They sent him first to Lvov, then to Auschwitz and finally to Mauthausen–Ebensee. In all he'd spent over three and a half years in concentration camps.

The conversation stuck in my mind because I had never before met a Ukrainian political prisoner. Generally speaking, the Ukrainians had shown remarkable agility in running to the Germans and collaborating with them. The Ukrainian police in particular had played a disastrous role in Galicia following the entry of the German troops at the end of June and the beginning of July 1941. The bulk of these men had previously served in the Soviet militia, because when the Soviets took possession of the territory in 1939 they relied mainly on the Ukrainian population which consisted of farm labourers, peasants and workers, and therefore appeared to have the right ideological prerequisites. But when the Soviets had to withdraw again it took scarcely twenty-four hours before the same militiamen offered their services to the new Nazi rulers and became their most loyal assistants.

Admittedly there were also a certain number of Ukrainian nationalists who had opposed the Soviets. But that stance was now likewise driving them into the arms of the Germans, who, they hoped, would set up for them a state of their own. Evidently there had been behind-the-scenes contacts, because they knew a long time before the German surprise attack against the Soviet Union that something was in the air. Thus most of them succeeded in escaping in good time to the German-occupied part of Poland. Subsequently they returned to their homeland alongside the Germans and took their revenge against the Communists.

The Jews, who represented the upper stratum in that region, were hated in any case. A few days before the German invasion of 22 June 1941 there were some broadcasts in Ukrainian which combined the announcement of Galicia's imminent liberation with this appeal: 'Welcome us not with flowers but with severed Jewish heads.'

Often identified only by a yellow-and-blue armband and scantily armed by the Germans, the Ukrainian police auxiliaries in Galicia operated as the vanguard of the German troops and the SS. Their task, which they performed with enthusiasm, was to corral Jews and members of the Polish intelligentsia, and to hand them over, ready packaged, to the Nazis for annihilation.

This generally close connection between Ukrainians and Germans made a Ukrainian concentration camp inmate an exception. If Ukrainians were sent to a camp it was generally only because they had offended against one of the economic laws – for instance, if they were caught illicitly slaughtering animals or distilling vodka. But a Ukrainian political prisoner was something special, and I decided to talk to Dr Stroncickij about his personal story when an opportunity arose.

That opportunity was to arise soon – though in a rather roundabout way. I was visited one day by a couple, Adolf and Antonie Weiler. The two were searching for surviving relations and wished to inspect the lists of refugees which we were receiving at our office from all parts of liberated Europe. As a matter of routine we inquired how they had lived through and survived the Nazi period, and whether they could remember the names of any of their tormentors.

It turned out that the couple, just like Stroncickij, came from Mosty Wielkie. In all some 1500 Jews had lived in that little Polish town. When the Russians marched in in 1939 they appointed a Ukrainian mayor and put him in charge of the local Ukrainian militia, who distinguished themselves by their hatred of the Jews. Anticipating, as it were, the policy of the Germans, the militiamen made extensive arrests for the Soviets, including equally among them Ukrainian nationalists, Poles and Jews. When the German attack came on 22 June the Soviets had no time to take with them the people they had locked up. So they simply killed them. Thousands of detainees were shot dead in their cells by the retreating Soviets. This gave rise to one of the craziest accusations of that period:

among the strongly anti-Semitic population the rumour was spread by the Ukrainian nationalists that all Jews were Bolsheviks and all Bolsheviks were Jews. Hence it was the Jews who were really to blame for the atrocities committed by the Soviets.

All the Germans needed to do was to exploit this climate of opinion. It is said that after their arrival they gave the Ukrainians free rein, for three days, to 'deal' with the Jews. Strangely enough, the mayor who had been installed by the Soviets and had later vanished now reappeared and was once more, this time by the Germans, installed as mayor: 'A certain Dr Stroncickij, one of the worst Jew-baiters.'

Naturally I pricked up my ears at the mention of this name. I requested the Weilers to tell me everything they knew about that man. It exceeded my worst expectations: Stroncickij, Adolf Weiler reported, had not only allowed the Ukrainian police to run amok but had himself taken part in their atrocities. 'We have been told that he had his police drive dozens of Jews out of their homes, to be taken to a nearby patch of woodland known as Babka,' he said. 'There they had to dig trenches and take up position, in a straight row, in front of it. The Ukrainians kept firing until all of them lay in their grave. It was said that when he came back from the wood Stroncickij was spattered all over with blood.'

Assuming that this blood-spattered Stroncickij was in fact my Stroncickij – which seemed to me highly probable given the unusual name and also because my instinct told me so – how then had he landed in a German concentration camp?

The Weilers were able to solve this mystery too. The Germans had set up a major store of captured equipment at Mosty Wielkie, to which the weapons left behind by the Soviets during their hasty retreat were brought from all over the district. The town commandant of Mosty Wielkie, who was also responsible for the store of captured weapons, was an Austrian Oberleutnant by the name of Kroupa. He was one of those men who demonstrated that it was possible even for a German soldier to behave decently – not by any suicidal piece of heroism but by prudence and, at the crucial moment, cool nerves and imagination. Kroupa simply would not tolerate any mistreatment of the Jews working at the arms store. A German ordinance made it obligatory for Jews to perform this kind of forced labour, and Kroupa took the view that they must therefore also receive adequate nourishment and medical attention. In point of fact, the Oberleutnant went further: when he learned that the forced labour men were being harassed and struck by their SS or Ukrainian escorts on their way to and from the arms store, he at once put an end to it. In doing so he referred to the law according to which even forced labourers were – in theory – to be treated correctly.

Stroncickij hated Kroupa for this. Where he himself had powers of command – or arrogated them to himself – he cut a swathe through the Jewish population. He had the Ukrainian militia spead out and arrest all the elderly, retired Jews they could get hold of and take them to a wooden building which adjoined a (likewise wooden) synagogue. Then the synagogue along with the little building was set on fire. When the Russians returned in 1944 they found the charred skeletons in the debris.

All the Jews, though given a temporary lease of life, realized that they could save themselves only by escaping. But few were able to do so. Among them were the Weilers, who managed to make their way to Lvov and hide there. There they learned, from others, who had escaped, of how the clash between Stroncickij and Kroupa had developed: Stroncickij had been so furious at the town commandant's pro-Jewish attitude that he denounced him to his superior for 'favouring Jews'. He was also said to have written a letter to the new governor of Galicia, Dr Lasch, requesting him at long last to arrange for Mosty Wielkie to be 'cleansed of Jews'.

An inquiry had actually been started against Kroupa. But the Ober-leutnant did not lose his nerve. His task, he defended himself, was to administer the weapons store as efficiently as possible, ensuring that all usable material, especially arms, was sorted and reconditioned as swiftly as possible. For that he needed his Jewish workforce, and he needed them in good health and for a prolonged period, because any new labour had to be trained. It was just because his work was of importance to the war that he inevitably had to attach importance to proper treatment of the Jews.

The Wehrmacht commission of inquiry was satisfied with this answer – another example that it was possible for members of the German armed forces to act either way. The commission could equally well have believed Stroncickij and sentenced Kroupa. I think it entirely possible that some members of the commission were well aware that Kroupa was trying to spare the Jews – that sort of information would always spread within the Wehrmacht – and that, ultimately, they condoned his attitude.

At any rate, Kroupa was acquitted and was now determined to get rid of Stroncickij. Three days after returning to his office he invited Stroncickij for a 'conciliatory chat'. Stroncickij arrived, entered the room in some embarrassment and waited to be asked to sit down. Only the two men were present, but apparently Kroupa later related the incident to his numerous friends with shining eyes. He slapped Stroncickij's face, twice and noisily, then tore off his own epaulettes and two buttons from his tunic and rang for his orderly. 'This man,' Kroupa screamed, 'has physically attacked me, he's torn my uniform, and moreover he's insulted Germany and the Führer.' Orderlies immediately arrested Stroncickij, who was handed over to the Gestapo in Lvov and presumably then sent to the Lvov concentration camp.

'The whole story spread through the population like wildfire. Everyone who hated the Germans had heard it. It actually became a legend, and quite possibly it was embroidered here and there,' Adolf Weiler concluded. 'But its nucleus is obviously true.'

'Would you recognise Stroncickij now?' I asked.

'Of course. Unfortuntely we met him often enough. And this wasn't so long ago.'

My secretary, Weissmann, who had been present throughout the conversation and had taken notes, now typed out the couple's statement. He read it to them and the Weilers added their signatures. Since their arrival roughly an hour and a half had elapsed: it was now about eleven o'clock in the morning. On my desk I had a list of telephone numbers, including those of the national refugee organizations. I dialled that of the Ukrainian organization and in a calm voice requested Dr Stroncickij to come round to my office for a moment, I had something to show him. Stroncickij said he'd be with me in five minutes.

Meanwhile I asked the Weilers to withdraw to the next room and keep quiet there while they waited. I'd call them when the moment came.

Thus, for the second time in his life, Stroncickij unsuspectingly entered a room where a shock was awaiting him. 'You did say you were from Mosty Wielkie?' I asked him. 'Could you perhaps help me by telling me what happened to the Jews there?'

'Unfortunately that's something I know nothing about,' Stroncickij replied. 'The Nazis picked me up as early as March '42 and interned me in the Lvov concentration camp. Then they dragged me to Auschwitz and Mauthausen. All told I spent nearly four years in their camps.'

'Why didn't you return home after the war?' I inquired.

Stroncickij had an answer ready for that one too. 'Back to Galicia? But the Bolsheviks are there now, and they're no better than the Nazis.'

At that moment I made a sign to Weissmann. He opened the door to the next room and the Weilers walked in.

'Herr Doktor, you didn't catch us!' Adolf Weiler said.

Stroncickij just stared at him, stunned, and kept silent.

'We got away from you,' Weiler continued, 'and so did young Gleicher. He told us how things developed in Mosty Wielkie. And why you really found yourself in a concentration camp. We know the whole story about Kroupa.'

Then Stroncickij lost his self-control. 'What, Gleicher told you that? When I personally let him go free? So that's his gratitude! He'd have been dead if I hadn't . . .'

Stroncickij's last hope of dismissing the witnesses against him as liars and slanderers was gone. I telephoned the Linz police, informed the officer of the confrontation and handed over to them the signed testimony of the witnesses. An hour later Dr Stroncickij was in custody. And the following day the *Linzer Tagblatt* carried a long article on the 'sensational arrest'.

What gave me particular pleasure was that the report also underlined the courageous and humane behaviour of Oberleutnant Kroupa. I determined to seek out Kroupa to thank him for what he had done and to offer him my help in case he needed it. He is one of those people who make it possible for me, after all that has happened, to continue living in Austria: when one talks about Oberleutnant Waldheim, one should talk about that other Oberleutnant as well.

At the same time, the Stroncickij is one of several cases that should bring down, by a peg or two, the self-righteousness of the Americans when they deal with the past. Three days after his arrest Stroncickij was again a free man and sitting in his office. He didn't deny himself the pleasure of telling me so in person. The testimony of the Weilers, he informed me in a mocking voice, was of no importance, because the Americans wouldn't give it the slightest credence.

I couldn't understand that. The witnesses' statements were both specific and precise. They could not possibly be brushed aside. I therefore went to see the head of the CIC (Counter Intelligence Corps) in Linz, an organization with which I had good relations, since immediately after the war I had worked within it.

'How could you release Stroncickij again?' I asked.

But the man displayed no wish to discuss the matter: Stroncickij, he said, was not a case for the CIC. He was an important source of information for another American department, which was in Harrachstrasse 16. The officer concerned was a Major Bromberg; he alone could provide information.

I went to see Bromberg, who was prepared for my arrival – the CIC had obviously warned him. It was clear to me that Bromberg was heading an intelligence unit and that Stroncickij was one of his information sources. About that time various Americans had repeatedly been turning up in the refugee camps, asking questions about different localities and conditions in the east. None of us at first understood what these questions were aimed at. Stroncickij obviously had cottoned on very quickly.

'You arrested Stroncickij and I released him again,' Bromberg received me with a smile, as if this were the most natural thing in the world.

'Herr Major, we have statements by witnesses to the effect that this man committed an unknown number of murders – with his own hands.'

'That may well be,' Bromberg answered, 'but my task is the

collection of information; who supplies me with it is no concern of mine.'

This remark made Bromberg feel enormously superior, today we might say 'cool': as a man who puts the higher interests of the state above childishly naive ideas of justice, because he is in possession of wisdom and information which are simply beyond the unsuspecting, haggard Jew before him.

I have often asked myself in what way Stroncickij could have been useful to the Americans: after all, he had spent most of the war in camps and not at the eastern front. And there were certainly better sources of information available from the camps than him. Presumably Stroncickij had managed, as he had done with the Russians and subsequently with the Germans, to present himself in the right light: as a man willing and able to discharge any job for his taskmasters. In this case, for instance, to set up a catchment committee for Ukrainians and there to collect information from Ukrainians who really knew something. But that task, too, might have been accomplished equally well, in my opinion, by any decent person, and moreover out of anti-Communist conviction. But there is evidently something like sympathy on the part of all apparatchiks for all other apparatchiks: to Bromberg Stroncickij radiated both obedience and efficiency. Compared to his organizational usefulness, his inclination to kill people was evidently irrelevant.

I could do no more than complain to a friend in the CIC about the brush-off I had received from Bromberg. 'I know how much you people contributed to the winning of the war,' I told him, 'and I know that none of us would have survived if you hadn't liberated us. For that I shall be eternally grateful to you. But I simply cannot understand that, after such a short while, you are prepared to protect a mass murderer merely because he can be useful to you in some way or other. Believe me, he cannot possibly supply enough information to you to undo the damage he caused: if you shake hands with someone who has blood on his hands you stain yourself too.'

My friend couldn't, and didn't wish to, contradict me to any great extent. 'Yesterday's allies,' he said, 'just aren't allies any longer. You'll see how quickly things change. The Germans are needed against the Russians. Good Germans alone are too few.' But, as if to refute his own arguments, he gave me an address to turn to: there was a department in a château in Gmunden which outranked Bromberg. I should take my story to them; maybe I would meet with some understanding.

In point of fact the gentlemen in Gmunden were exceedingly polite and exceedingly friendly. After I had passed several sentries, Austrian police as well as American, I was received by a very pleasant young man who evidently felt he had to be nice to me and therefore invited me to lunch.

'Thank you,' I said, 'but I don't feel like eating. What I need is your help to ensure that justice prevails.'

The young man wasn't in the least put out. He willingly listened while I recounted the Stroncickij case from beginning to end – including my conversation with Bromberg.

Then I waited for a reaction. That too was friendly and held out some hope: they would look into Stroncickij. That was the last I heard from the Americans on the matter.

After my return, I wanted to console myself by at least finding Ober-leutnant Kroupa. I got hold of all the available telephone directories, and my staff fished out all the Kroupas and phoned them. At one number, in Korneuburg in Lower Austria, a female voice answered. 'Unfortunately you cannot talk to my husband,' she said. 'He's still a prisoner of war in the Soviet Union.'

I wrote a letter to the Soviet High Commissioner, General Sviridov, who was simultaneously the Soviet representative on the Allied Council in Austria. I set out Kroupa's merits and concluded with the request that the man might be released as soon as possible. I never received a reply.

Stroncickij is no doubt living in the USA or in Canada with a new identity provided for him by the Americans. We were at the beginning of the Cold War and the Allies had new priorities.

5

Operation Sacher

Towards the end of 1947 I received a telephone call from the head of the Security Directorate for Upper Austria, Ministerialrat Ruppertsberger. He said that an official would come to see me and that I was to give him information about an SS Sturmbannführer by the name of Viktor Naegeler. The next day I had another telephone call, this one from Mr Ettinger of the CIC. He too wished to know about Naegeler. This pattern was soon repeated: shortly after the Security Directorate had inquired about a certain Josef Urban and CIC wanted to know details about Josef Urban.

It was obvious that something big was happening, something played out between the Austrians and the American occupying power, and evidently concerned with former Nazis. But not so much with war criminals, as with people who were important now. Otherwise there wouldn't be so much excitement.

Ministerialrat Ruppertsberger already possessed a number of little pieces for his mosaic. He knew, for instance, that the regional Nazi party chief of Styria, Dr Siegfried Uiberreither, equipped with false papers, had got away via Italy to South America or the Middle East. And he also knew that in mid-1947 a number of identity cards had disappeared from the Vienna state printing shop. The serial numbers of these identity cards were known, and it was reasonable to suppose that they played a part in Uiberreither's escape. But that, meanwhile, was just a suspicion lacking all proof.

One fine day, however, a Nazi district chief with a past as an 'Illegal' (a Nazi party member prior to the *Anschluss*) was arrested. He produced an identity card with the number of one of the stolen cards. The police then put him through a tough interrogation. They pretended that other people with false identity cards had also been arrested and that they had already confessed. On the third day of detention they got him to 'sing'.

It was in this connection that the name of the Graz industrialist Theodor Soucek first came up. Not until much later would the state police identify him as the head of a many-tentacled underground Nazi organization. Like the PLO it appeared in various guises, possessing a 'military' and a political branch. The political branch called itself SORBE (the European Social Order Movement) and hoped to gain political influence once more for Nazism. It was then, in 1947, that the Nazis were beginning to be hopeful again: they sensed the tensions between the Allies and believed – not without some justification – that they might drive an even deeper wedge between them. Above all, they proceeded from the assumption – again not without some justification – that following the withdrawal of the occupying powers they might once more become a political factor in the country. After all, there were 660,000 'ex-Nazis' registered in Austria as having been members of the Nazi party, the SS or the SA (the Storm Troopers or 'Brownshirts'). If one included their families this represented a very substantial voter potential. Meanwhile, of course, Nazis were deprived of the vote by law. They were in a kind of political illegality which they hoped to make use of by training cadres for the future. Once conditions had changed, this élite would establish and lead a neo-Nazi party.

The 'military' branch of Soucek's organization, on the other hand, was helping the former Nazi bigwigs to escape from Allied internment camps, especially from the British camp at Wolfsberg and the American camp at Glasenbach. Soucek had contacts with access not only to identity cards but also to passports. Ruppertsberger's suspicions were to prove correct: the wanted regional chief Uiberreither had come by his false papers through these channels.

The number of persons then trying to escape was fairly large, because in the immediate post-war period there were special laws concerning Nazis, and even the Austrian judiciary was taking its duties relatively seriously. Basically there were wanted lists for two categories of people: those who had worked with the Gestapo, in the ghettos or in the concentration camps, and would therefore be facing charges of murder, and those who, by virtue of their position in the Nazi party or another Nazi organization, had helped to bring about the so-called *Anschluss* and would, in consequence, be facing charges of high treason.

This latter group included all the 'illegals' – those who had joined the Nazi party prior to the *Anschluss*. The principal characteristic of an illegal was a party membership number below 6,600,000 – this being the serial number issued on 13 March 1938. Any number lower than this was regarded as proof of illegality and hence of high treason. Not always justly so: as in all periods of upheaval there were opportunists who, after the *Anschluss*, applied for and obtained a lower number. As a rule it was enough to produce two witnesses who would confirm that these people had been so highly illegal that they didn't even wish to risk formally joining the illegal movement – though in their hearts they had long been on the Nazis' side.

In a country where you can even buy low number plates for motor cars this resulted almost invariably in the acquisition of low party membership numbers which not only lent prestige to the bearer but also ensured for him preferential treatment in the allocation of Jewish assets and in the Aryanization of Jewish real estate, flats and shops. After 1945 these people then found themselves trapped: now they had to convince the authorities that in reality they were never illegals but had obtained their low party numbers retrospectively, by fraud. For that they again needed two-witnesses – so-called de-Nazification witnesses – sometimes the same witnesses as the first time around.

All these complicated proceedings, with often grave consequences – sentence in a high treason case was followed by forfeiture of property – required a considerable number of people with juridical and financial expertise, not to mention the requirements of those wanted for charges of mass murder. Soucek's Nazi underground organization therefore had a dual function: it was not only the production line of the party of tomorrow but also the principal service centre for the party of yesterday.

For all these tasks it needed money. Ministerialrat Ruppertsberger's staff knew that the Nazis had that money, but where it came from was as much of a mystery as Theodor Soucek's role. At that moment the state police received a confidential tip-off: it concerned the companion of a French officer, a lady with the sonorous name of Marion de Costa. Her real name was Maria Apfalter and she came from Solbad Hall. During the Nazi era she had played an obscure role between German and French counter-espionage, and at the end of the war she unambiguously joined the French side. Thus it came about that Maria Apfalter was permitted to travel to Switzerland and back every week in the French compartment of the Mozart express, and was thereby out of reach of the Austrian criminal police. One day, however, as she was getting off the train, she was arrested at the station. Her luggage was found to contain a large amount of money and an enormous parcel of saccharin. It was this saccharin that gave the further actions of the state police the code name 'Operation Sacher'.

Under interrogation Maria Apfalter confessed to acting on behalf of her brother, a former senior SS officer, and that the sweetener, then much in demand, was to have been sold on the black market in the Resselpark in the centre of Vienna. It turned out that the organization of ex-Nazis operated a whole series of illegal businesses like this. Sewing needles were sold, through black-market dealers, to Yugoslavia, and in Salzburg the police arrested a man who was supplying the Russians with smuggled ball-bearings from Germany. The revenue from all these transactions flowed into a treasury administered, according to Marion de Costa's evidence, by a certain Amon Göth in Graz. Amon Göth was a friend of Theodor Soucek's.

Göth was arrested and exhaustively questioned. At last a clearer picture of the escape organization emerged. If one took a map of Austria and drew on it the escape routes of wanted Nazi criminals, a pattern emerged which looked like a spider's net. The spider himself sat in Graz, and his threads radiated to Linz, Salzburg, Innsbruck and Vienna, branching out into Vorarlberg, Italy and Germany. Along these routes were 'staging posts', where the 'needy' could identify themselves by passwords in order to be furnished with fresh papers and new identities. From those staging posts group transports went into the frontier areas, where, finally, local guides infiltrated the wanted men into Italy or Switzerland.

Police agents throughout Upper Austria spread out and began to put various meeting places under surveillance. The biggest fish went into the net of Linz criminal police. On its staff were some especially capable, anti-fascist-minded young officers who discharged their duties with both conviction and originality. One of them was Leo Maier, the future Austrian observer at the Eichmann trial, who retired a few years ago as a colonel of police. He has used his experiences of those early years in Linz in writing crime and spy thrillers. And that, in fact, was the style in which things were happening. The Linz agents staked out a café continually entered by rather shady characters who, subsequently, were not to be discovered among the guests and who could not be seen leaving the café either.

Maier (who meanwhile has become a good friend of mine) drew my attention to this curious café. I sat in it for hours on several occasions but did not observe anything out of the ordinary.

The Linz police were more successful. One evening, shortly before closing time, agents stormed the place, discovered a staircase to the base-ment, broke down a bolted door, and in the basement found a fully equipped printing shop. Alongside freshly manufactured personal papers they discovered some of the identity cards stolen from Vienna as well as the official rubber stamps of police authorities and district governors' offices. The 'manager', a Dr Hugo Rössner, was arrested. Shortly after-wards Theodor Soucek was likewise put under arrest.

A series of further arrests followed, including that of my two 'acquaintances' Viktor Naegeler and Josef Urban. Naegeler was one of the 'ideologists' of the group. He was sentenced, but shortly afterwards managed to escape to West Germany, where no doubt he found good friends. The Urban case was more delicate. I discovered that he had been working in Budapest as a member of Department VI of the SS intelligence service. This didn't surprise me at all. What did shock me was that he was now evidently enjoying equally good relations with the American intelligence service. To my mind, he has always only served his old comrades.

Ministerialrat Ruppelsberger invited me to be present during the interrogation of Urban, who, in consequence, felt it necessary to show off. 'I behaved decently to the Jews,' he declared. 'Why don't you ask Rezsö Kastner – he was my contact.'

Kastner at that time was a senior government official in Israel, and Urban evidently thought that this disclosure would embarrass me. I did, in point of fact, feel obliged to write a letter to Kastner, requesting him to tell me whether he was even acquainted with Urban. (To be on the safe side I enclosed a photograph of Josef Urban.) Kastner did not answer. Two years later there was the 'Kastner affair' in Israel: a certain Grünwald had claimed that during the war Kastner had been a Nazi collaborator. Kastner sued, and the matter came to court. I informed the judge of what Urban had told me, and Kastner was asked why he hadn't replied to my letter. He said he hadn't found time to do so. Grünwald lost the case, but – and this is surely significant – was given only a nominal fine of one Israeli pound. A few years later Kastner was assassinated by a member of an Israeli underground group.

That, for the time being, was the clearest aspect of the Urban case. His role on the American ex-Nazi and neo-Nazi scene, however, remained obscure. The protective hand of the Americans evidently hovered above him to the end. They clearly had a liking for former members of Department VI; they had also hired SS Obersturmbannführer Wilhelm Höttl, who lives as a retired headmaster in Bad Aussee to this day. Both Urban and Höttl had conned the Americans into believing that they still had the same agents in the Balkans as when they were officers of the Nazi intelligence service. This was subsequently revealed as a huge bluff – but in the late forties it was very useful, at least for those two men.

In all, no fewer than two hundred people in Theodor Soucek's circle were arrested at the time – among them such disparate people as the second chief of the Riga ghetto, Eduard Roschmann, who was responsible for the deaths of approximately 35,000 Jews (and to whom I have devoted a separate chapter in this book) and the future Austrian Socialist Party Minister of the Interior, Otto Rösch. Rösch, a teacher at the Napola in Trainskirchen and a member of the Nazi party, was active in the welfare organization in Graz. When he was arrested a locked trunk was discovered in his flat, which was found to contain identity papers and various lists. Rösch denied any knowledge of the contents of the trunk – it had been given to him, he claimed, by an unknown person for safekeeping. After eight months' detention on remand he was acquitted through lack of evidence.

Rosa Jochmann, a former inmate of the Ravensbrück concentration camp and a fighter for Austria's freedom, emphatically supported him. Rösch, who came from a Social Democratic family, she stated, had been infiltrated into the Nazi scene by the then Minister of the Interior, the Socialist Oskar Helmer, in order to recruit members for a fourth political party, yet to be founded. Such an attempt was in fact made, and may be understood due to the political circumstances of the post-war period, when the Social Democrats were clearly lagging behind the Conservatives in their bid for Nazi votes. While the impact of the war was still fresh the Social Democrats had coined the slogan 'Nazis to Siberia', and although registered Nazis did not have a vote, they still had relatives – brothers, sisters, spouses, parents – and they mainly voted against the Social Democrats, hence for the Conservative Austrian People's Party.

Subsequently the Social Democrats repaired this tactical mistake by vigorously urging that ex-Nazis be restored their right to vote. Simultaneously they offered them well-paid jobs as economic managers in the nationalized industries, because they had few people qualified for this in their own ranks. Even so the Austrian People's Party maintained a small lead. That was when Minister of the Interior Helmer conceived the idea of encouraging those ex-Nazis who were not to be won over directly to set up a new party. The idea was that such a party would rob the Austrian People's Party of its Nazis, and would split the bourgeois camp generally. As a result the Socialist Party would clearly become the strongest party in the country. Obviously this strategy made sense only if the future force were to maintain good relations with the Socialists and therefore make a credible coalition partner. The person chosen to help implement this concept was Otto Rösch.

I have later talked to him repeatedly about the discussions and events of those days, and I am inclined to believe that he was infiltrated into Soucek's organization for this purpose only, and that he never really served it. Nevertheless a somewhat delicate situation arose during Rösch's term as minister: as Minister of the Interior he was the superior of some of the officials who arrested him in 1948. Apart from that, it is only fair to say that he was an outstanding portfolio minister, whose competence and energy vastly surpassed that of his predecessors, and that he acted with particular decisiveness to curb neo-Nazi tendencies.

However, we who in 1947 operated against Soucek and co. have often asked ourselves if Rösch realized what a dangerous game he had let himself in for. Soucek's organization did not just manufacture papers for incriminated SS men; it was also supposed to be making identity cards available to members of the former Vlasov army. The Vlasov army was composed of Russians who had joined the German forces because, at first, they saw the Germans as liberators who would free them from the Communist yoke. Many of these Russians, some of whom had brought their families along with them, had thus found themselves in Allied captivity and were now, on the basis of a British–Soviet agreement, being handed over to the Soviet Union. There they were all executed without trial. In the British POW compounds in Carinthia there were numerous Vlasov army members who preferred suicide in the icy Drau river.

As these circumstances were becoming known and as protests against the action by the British gathered momentum, the remaining Vlasov men were brought together with numerous Nazis at the Wolfsberg detention camp. Soucek's organization succeeded in getting the Russians out of the internment camp, declaring them refugees and channelling them into Germany.

This did not remain hidden from Soviet headquarters in Baden for long, as the network of Soviet agents had long before spread into the British, French and American zones. It had been known for some time that a major Nazi underground organization was in the process of being established. But the Soviets didn't dream of passing their knowledge on to the Austrian authorities or to the Allies, because to them nothing could have been more welcome than the growth of 'revanchist and neo-Nazi' cells. They supported those cells to the best of their ability. In the Russian POW camps the Soviet secret service had succeeded, by means of so-called 'anti-fa' classes, in converting a number of former Wehrmacht members, and making faithful Communists out of faithful Nazis. These people, in a sense, left one church in order to be received into another, and now made ideal Soviet agents inside Theodor Soucek's organization. They enthusiastically helped to set up Nazi cells in order to promote the final victory of Communism. What was wanted was a vigorous Nazi organization in order to pillory democratic Austria. Operation Sacher foiled that strategy.

Theodor Soucek, Amon Göth and Hugo Rössner were sentenced to death under the law prohibiting ex-Nazis from engaging in renewed political activity. The death sentence was subsequently reduced to life imprisonment, which ran for precisely three years – and then the three men were pardoned. Their organization was completely smashed by the state police. This was a heavy blow, and the only one, against the principal escape organization, whose name I was not to discover until later: Odessa.

6

Odessa

The people around Theodor Soucek undoubtedly played an important part in the escape of former Nazi bigwigs. But considering that there were many thousands who needed to get away after the war, and that these people were not safe until they had reached either an Arab country or one in South America, it was obvious that Soucek's organization could be no more than a part of a much larger whole.

As early as 1947 I had begun to enter on maps the details of all escape routes known to me, and in so doing I found that a network of staging posts emerged similar to that in Austria and Germany. The escape routes invariably ran through particular German towns – Bremen, Frankfurt, Augsburg, Stuttgart and Munich – to converge in Memmingen, a small medieval town in the Bavarian Allgäu. There they divided again. One route continued to Lindau on Lake Constance, where it divided once more, to lead either to Bregenz in Austria or into Switzerland. The main route, however, lay from Memmingen to Innsbruck, and thence over the Brenner Pass into Italy. Later I discovered that the Nazis called this north–south route the 'B–B' axis, meaning the link from Bremen to the Italian port of Bari. From there the escape routes continued to Spain, to various Arab countries, or, predominantly, to South America.

In all these countries the fugitives needed papers, and we knew from several cases that they evidently had no difficulty in obtaining forged documents. Nor did they seem to have any problems about establishing a new livelihood: the top-ranking ones, at least, immediately had substantial financial resources at their disposal wherever they arrived, sufficient to enable them to set up businesses, become partners in major enterprises, and, if necessary, bribe the authorities.

It was obvious that a secret organization of considerable magnitude, drive and exceptional wealth was at work here. At least certain preparations for such an organization must have been put in hand during the final years of the war: once the war was over the Nazis would have found it difficult to transfer such vast sums of money out of Germany. No doubt, as usually happens in history, the leaders responsible for the war were the first to transfer their loot abroad.

One day in the spring of 1946 an American officer brought a big rucksack to our office and from it produced a dark blue envelope which, he reported, he had taken off a Colonel Keitel in the SS internment camp at Ebensee, near the famous Austrian spa of Bad Ischl. Like the Americans, I only glanced through the documents cursorily at the time; they did not relate to Nazi murderers but to money. Not until much later was I to realize that if one followed the trail of money one might track down a murderer. At the time, however, the records were more of a curiosity to me.

The strangest document was the protocol of a secret conference of top German businessmen, held at the Maison Rouge hotel in Strasbourg in August 1944. Unbeknownst to Himmler and Hitler, who still believed in final victory, a number of industrialists and financiers had met there, realizing that the war – which for so long had earned them great profits – was now lost: the coal baron Emil Kirdorf, the steel magnate Fritz Thyssen, Georg von Schnitzler of IG Farben, Gustav Krupp von Bohlen und Halbach, and the Cologne banker Kurt von Schroeder. All of them, having been among the first to turn to Hitler in 1933, were now also among the first to turn away from him. Even if Nazism were to survive – which all those at the conference hoped – it would be Nazism without Hitler. The chairman of the conference made the following statement, one for which the man in the street would have been sentenced to death for undermining the war effort: 'The battle of France is lost for Germany; henceforth German industry must adjust to the fact that the war can no longer be won and that, in consequence, steps have to be taken for a post-war economic campaign. To this end every industrialist must seek and establish contact and links with foreign firms; but each one for himself and without attracting suspicion to himself. In the sphere of financial policy, moreover, the ground will have to be prepared for taking up large-scale credits after the war. On top of all this, however, industrialists must also be prepared to finance the party, which will be compelled to go underground.'

In actual fact, German industrialists had long begun to gradually transfer their money, giving preference to accounts in Switzerland and in Spain, from where, however, even then, large amounts were being transferred to Argentina. Some of these money movements were camouflaged by the establishment of fictitious firms; others made use of private individuals as blinds. Thus, many years later, I talked to the widow of a former SS Obersturmbannführer, who told me a strange story. In the autumn of 1944, six months before the end of the war, senior SS officers had approached her husband and demanded that he tell them the number of his account at the Dresdner Bank and give them two signatures on blank pieces of paper. After the war, when all banks were placed under Allied control and trustees were appointed for the administration of all Nazi assets, the Obersturmbannführer was informed, to his amazement, that two accounts existed in his name: one to the tune of 12,000 and the other to that of 2.6 million Marks. The 12,000 Marks were the SS man's own money, while the 2.6 million had evidently been paid in by his superiors.

In this particular case their plan misfired, because one way or another the money was labelled Nazi assets. But it may be assumed that in countless other instances the Nazi bigwigs succeeded in transferring large amounts in this way. On the other hand, it would not be surprising if the participants in the Strasbourg conference were worried lest their cover men, especially if they were abroad, decided to keep the money for themselves. For that reason records were made of such transactions, and it was decided to conceal them 'in watertight containers in various Alpine lakes'.

If only I had shown more interest in those documents then – if I hadn't just read them but drawn the logical conclusions from them – I would have arrived much sooner at the conviction that a major escape organization must exist. After all, the protocol of the Strasbourg conference contained this passage: 'The party leadership is aware that, following the defeat of Germany, some of her best-known leaders may have to face trial as war criminals. Steps have therefore been taken to lodge the less prominent party leaders as "technical experts" in various German enterprises. The party is prepared to lend large sums of money to industrialists to enable every one of them to set up a secret post-war organization abroad, but as collateral it demands that the industrialists make available to it existing financial resources abroad, so that a strong German Reich may re-emerge after the defeat.'

This document is exceedingly interesting in two respects: for one thing it confirms that the Nazi party evidently had at its disposal enormous financial assets, comparable to the reserves of major industrial firms; for another, it suggests that, in contrast to industry, it had not yet transferred those funds abroad.

But where did the party get so much money? The answer is simple: the Nazis were not only murderers but robbers. This realization seems to me important, especially as in Germany and Austria there is a certain tendency to regard the mass murders as motivated by insanity. In reality it was never just a case of ensuring the hegemony of the Nordic race on the European continent; there was always the lure of the art treasures which might be stolen from Germany's neighbours. And it was never just a case of exterminating the Jewish race, but always also one of Aryanizing Jewish assets, plundering Jewish homes, and prising gold from the teeth of Jews after they had been gassed.

The Nazi leaders stole like magpies. Some idea of the amounts may be gained from the fact that in Salzburg the former ADC to Martin Bormann, a Dr von Hummel, was arrested as he was trying to do a bunk carrying gold to the value of five million dollars. A few miles to the east, near the schloss of Fuschl, once the property of Ribbentrop (and now an elegant hotel), a peasant found a crate containing quite a few pounds of gold coins, which, being an honest man, he took to the police. And a few dozen miles even further east, in the Aussee district, the most surprising amounts of gold coins have cropped up from time to time – except they are not necessarily handed in.

The area around Aussee, in the northwestern corner of Styria, had been dubbed the 'Alpine redoubt' by Goebbels, and many top Nazis did in fact seem to believe to the very end that it would be possible to 'hibernate' there. About Christmas 1944 they began to set up their families there and send their looted possessions by the crateful. At the beginning of 1944 some 18,000 people had lived in that neighbourhood; by the end of the war the number had risen to roughly 80,000. Even Nazi collaborators from Romania, Hungary and Slovakia sought refuge in the magnificent wooden houses of the Aussee district, and were proud to be living in close proximity to their bosses. Thus the head of the SS Reich Security Directorate, Ernst Kaltenbrunner, moved into a house in Altaussee, and Adolf Eichmann turned up with members of his Department IV B4 and straightaway stored twenty-two iron-clad boxes there, presumably containing documents and gold. The boxes attracted more attention than Eichmann himself, and it was they that made it possible subsequently to find his trail.

In its methodical way the SS, from March 1945, made records of the assets brought into the region. Only one of these records has fallen into American hands: it listed the assets of the Reich Security Directorate brought to Altaussee from Berlin by Ernst Kaltenbrunner: 111 pounds of gold bars, fifty crates with gold coins and gold objects, each crate weighing 222 pounds, as well as two million US dollars, two million Swiss francs, five crates of precious stones and jewelry, and a stamp collection valued at no less than five million Gold Marks.

In the early days of May 1945 a special department of the Reichsbank, which administered booty from concentration camps, sent several crates of 'dental gold' to Aussee. And stored in the Altaussee salt mine were the art treasures pillaged from all over Europe. If discovery threatened, the Nazis intended to blow up these priceless cultural treasures – paintings by the greatest masters stolen from the major museums in France, Italy, Belgium and Holland – and blame the Allies for this act of barbarism. However, members of the Resistance got wind of the plan and succeeded in foiling it.

When the 'Alpine redout' fell on 9 May 1945 – Major Ralph Pierson took it with just five American soldiers in one tank and one jeep – the Nazi bigwigs were desperately retrieving the treasures which they had hidden all over the place or, according to rumour, sunk in the 900-foot-deep Lake Toplitz, and removing them to some safe place. Frau Christl Kerry, an elderly lady from Vienna who owned a house in Altaussee, told me that once in the middle of the night she heard some digging in her garden. She was afraid to do anything, but when she looked out of the window in the morning she saw a number of large square holes in the ground, from which crates or trunks had evidently been removed. A peasant, Josef Pucherl, found two steel boxes with 10,167 gold coins inside under a refuse heap.

To this day boxes are being fished out of Lake Toplitz, although the legendary gold treasure of the SS has never been found – only a huge quantity of forged British pound notes.

This is not to say that the gold treasure did not exist, but it suggests that those who knew its hiding place retrieved and removed it in good time. Only individual efforts have become known. Thus as early as 1946 two unknown men went to the shore of Lake Toplitz and fished out a wooden crate with printing plates for forging dollar bills, and in June 1950 a group of French divers lifted twelve steel boxes from the lake at Altaussee. Not until much later did the Americans discover that the alleged Frenchmen (who had produced French identity papers) had in fact been Germans.

Some of the treasure-hunters appear to have paid with their lives for what they knew or suspected. In a gully in the nearby Totes Gebirge mountains the bodies of two former members of a German naval research station on Lake Toplitz were found. In 1955 another German, who also worked there, was found dead at the base of a cliff, and on the evening of 5 October 1963 a young man from Munich, Alfred Egner, was drowned in a diving attempt for which he had been hired by two fellow countrymen. One of the two was a former SS leader by the name of Freiberger, who had worked as a German agent in Switzerland during the war; the other was a Dr Schmidt, who had got into trouble with the West German authorities in 1962 for illicit dealing in gold coins. In Alfred Egner's wallet, which was found in his clothes on the bank, were gold coins dating from 1905.

It may well be supposed that the real gold treasure was not sunk in Lake Toplitz at all. While its unusual depth would certainly have ensured safety, there would, at the same time, have been the enormous risk of the sunken crates never being found again. In the neighbourhood, at any rate, there is talk to this day of buried treasure; the lake may have become the focus of public interest because of the romantic nature of that theory. All in all, the fortune which the Nazis managed to hide and stow away is estimated at roughly four billion Gold Marks.

Who was able to dispose of these monies, whose signature authorized the withdrawal of funds from accounts in Switzerland, Spain or Argentina – these are some of the as yet unresolved secrets of the Third Reich. It is said that six lists exist, two of them in the keeping of well-known banking institutions. Two more may well have been held by the people who in 1947 set about creating the greatest escape organization in world history.

*

By mere chance I learned of the existence of that organization at the very start. During the Nuremberg trials I made the acquaintance of a former member of German counter-espionage, who had been recommended to me by American friends and who evidently still had sufficient contact with his former comrades to be *au courant*.

'How did the big Nazis manage to disappear?' I asked him.

'Have you ever heard of Odessa?' he countered my question.

'A pretty town,' I observed, a little nonplussed.

During the next four hours Hans (which is what I propose to call him) enlightened me about Odessa, the 'Organization Der Ehemaligen SS-Angehörigen' (Organization of Ex-Members of the SS). It was only set up in 1946, when a number of top Nazis were already in prison camp or penitentiaries. Somehow they succeeded in making contact with old comrades who were still free, and 'aid committees' were formed for prisoners' welfare. Under this humanitarian cover the committees conveyed letters, established contact with old comrades and, most important, raised money. Everything was done quite officially under the eyes of the unsuspecting Allies, who believed that even Nazis must be granted the benefits of a humanitarian society. The aid committees were promoted in particular by the Catholic Church, which suddenly remembered its humanitarian duties. Although during the Nazi period it had not done much for prisoners and virtually nothing for concentration-camp inmates, it was now evidently trying to make up for its omissions by looking after the inmates of POW camps.

In many instances, however, the assistance of the Church went far beyond the mere toleration of aid committees and actually amounted to abetting criminals: the most important escape route, the so-called 'monastery route' between Austria and Italy, came into being. Roman Catholic priests, especially Franciscans, helped Odessa channel its fugitives from one monastery to the next, until they were received by the Caritas organization in Rome. Best known was a monastery on Via Sicilia in Rome, a monastery under the control of the Franciscans, which became a veritable transit camp for Nazi criminals. The man who organized this hideout was no less than a bishop and came from Graz: in his memoirs Alois Hudal subsequently boasted of the many top people from the Third Reich to whom he had been able to render 'humanitarian aid'.

It is difficult to guess the motives of these priests. Many no doubt acted from a misunderstood Christian love of one's neighbour – some of them, indeed, may have done the same for Jews under Nazi rule. The fact that of Rome's 8000 Jews 4000 survived the Third Reich is certainly due, above all, to the Church. Most of them had been living in monasteries, and a few dozen had actually been admitted into the Vatican. It seems to me probable that the Church was divided: into priests and members of the religious orders who had recognized Hitler as the Antichrist and therefore practised Christian charity, and those who viewed the Nazis as a power of order in the struggle against the decline of morality and Bolshevism. The former probably helped the Jews during the war, and the latter hid the Nazis when it was over.

While initially most fugitives used the Brenner–Bari route, the main link later ran between Bremen and Rome or Bremen and Genoa. At roughly every 25 miles staging posts were set up, organized as a rule by three people who, for their part, only knew the next two staging posts. The fugitives were passed on anonymously, as it were, and it was evidently easy to cross the various demarcation lines which at the time ran across Austria and Germany. The American forces newspaper *Stars and Stripes*, for instance, was transported by German civilian employees of the US army on trucks down the autobahn from Munich to Salzburg. As a rule these transports were simply waved through at the frontier because it was known what they were; very occasionally a military policeman would glance under the tarpaulin and would see there piles of batched newspapers. What he didn't see were the men crouching behind the papers, holding their breath to escape being heard; what he didn't know was that the truck driver belonged to Odessa. This particular escape route was subsequently cut because of a report I made to CIC in Salzburg, and the truck driver was arrested. But a dozen other routes remained open.

I am aware of only one operation which was similarly successful in channelling a large number of fugitives across Austria into Italy and there getting them aboard a ship: the illegal transports of Bricha (the Hebrew word for 'escape'), by means of which Jewish refugees got to Palestine. Occasionally both organizations even used the same staging posts: there was a small inn near Merano, where illegal Nazi transports and illegal Jewish transports spent the night together without knowing about each other. The Jews were secreted on the first floor and the Nazis on the ground floor. Both groups had been told: 'Don't move whatever happens!'

Odessa, however, had at its disposal a second, far less dangerous, escape route. This ran across Vorarlberg and profited from the casualness of the French occupation forces. As, in view of the beauty of their mother tongue, the French are in principle opposed to learning any other language, the French occupying officials had no clue what was happening around them. Thus Vorarlberg, in the triangle between Austria, Germany and Switzerland, became the Eldorado of fugitives from all parts of Germany. From Bregenz they effortlessly got across the Swiss frontier. Sometimes no doubt the Austrian and Swiss police turned a blind eye, and sometimes the fugitives had valid frontier passes: Odessa men were still, or again, working in all possible authorities and departments and evidently stole the required documents and rubber stamps.

Particularly astounding was the brazenness with which Nazis directly offered their services to the occupation armies. There seems to be a certain type of person who inspires confidence in officers: the haircut, the way of clicking one's heels, the readiness to lower one's head immediately in obedience – these presumably signal a certain kinship of souls. The Americans in particular had an incredible talent for being taken in by tall, blond, blue-eyed Germans, simply because they looked exactly like American officers in the cinema (whereas real American officers are, at least just as often, short, dark and of Italian descent). Quite recently the Office of Special Investigation revealed how many Nazis had found immediate re-employment as agents for the CIA after the war, merely because they were able to display the anti-Communism drilled into them under Hitler and to claim a detailed acquaintance with the east. In return for that, the Americans were willing to disregard the fact that these same people had previously served Adolf Hitler and that frequently their hands were still stained with fresh blood. It is just because I revere the Americans (and, God knows, have no sympathy for the Communists) that I find this misjudgement incomprehensible: Communists are bad, but Nazis are worse.

I often think that the Americans are repeating the mistake they made then in Austria and Germany in their present Latin American policy: there too, time and again, they place their trust in the worst kind of Fascists, merely because they show off their anti-Communism and declare that they like free trade and Coca-Cola. The Nazi criminals after the war all liked free trade and Coca-Cola – but this did not change their vile nature in the least.

One of this type who immediately adjusted to the new age used the cover name of Haddad Said and was one of the most successful escape helpers. Later to become a respected Austrian businessman, he was then travelling on a Syrian passport, organizing transports from Munich or Lindau to Bregenz. All who travelled with him had valid frontier passes. From Bregenz they crossed the Swiss frontier, only a few miles away, and there they boarded the first train to Zürich or Geneva, to fly on to the Middle East or South America.

I discussed these matters at length with an Austrian police officer serving in Bregenz, but he thought not much could be done about it: 'These people's papers are in order, for the most part they are in transit, and we're relieved when they're out of the country.'

'And what are the French doing?' I enquired.

'Nothing,' the officer said angrily.

I was subsequently able to discover who was hiding behind the pseudonym of Haddad Said: he was a former SS Hauptsturmführer and one of the leading lights in Odessa. He made his fortune by providing pretty holiday homes on Spain's Costa Brava for former SS leaders and party bigwigs. And for those who would find even Spain too hot to hold them, he obtained villas in Uruguay.

The more I discovered about the activities of Odessa the better I understood why it remained hidden from the Allies for so long. This was a Nazi enterprise run by professionals – former 'illegals', members of the Security Service, former agents, men who had proved their worth and distinguished themselves in the administration of the Third Reich. Just as they had organized mass murder to perfection, so did they perfectly organize the escape of the murderers.

In the course of my researches I eventually came across a man who, more than anyone else, had demonstrated his talents in both these spheres: SS Obersturmbannführer Walter Rauff.

7

The Pro

Mass murder, as we all know, was viewed by the Nazis – with German thoroughness – as an industrial problem. The traditional method of shooting soon proved too inefficient. The cost of, at least, one bullet per person was too high in relation to the turnover, and face-to-face murder, moreover, required qualified specialists. Time and again the victims would panic, and in such circumstances untrained personnel were often found to be unable to cope with the stress. There was excessive consumption of alcohol during on-duty hours, and a number of intensively employed murderers committed suicide. Otto Ohlendorf, the head of Special Squad D, one of those murder branches set up in the east behind the lines, tried to solve the problem by issuing orders that 'no one person should shoot any other one person dead.' Instead, 'several men should fire simultaneously so that there should be no personal responsibility.' 'Some squad leaders', Ohlendorf later explained at his trial, 'demanded that the victims lie flat on the ground, to be killed by a bullet in the back of their necks. But this method did not meet with my approval.' Questioned why he did not 'approve', Ohlendorf stated factually: 'Because it was too much of a psychological stress for the victims and for the executioners.'

A method had therefore to be found that would be more cost-effective and avoid stressing the executioners. The appropriate innovation was supplied by medical specialists. In euthanasia experiments at special institutions such as Hartheim, Hadamar and Sonnenberg, the use of gas had proved effective. It ensured a substantially bigger yield of corpses at reduced costs, and it was less of a stress on doctors and nurses than other forms of killing.

Meanwhile the extension of the death market required a transition from a few small stationary gas chambers to mobile units which could be employed everywhere. Possibly even before ready-to-pour concrete was invented, the German inventive genius hit upon the production of ready-to-bury corpses. Concrete mixers, mounted on trucks and driven by the truck engine, are an elegant answer to a whole series of economic requirements: mixing can be done not only at one stationary spot but anywhere; travel time is not additional to mixing time; and the concrete can be tipped straight into the pit where it belongs. The invention of the gas truck represents a similarly elegant solution to the problem of mobile extermination of Jews: murder was no longer tied to a particular location but could be performed anywhere; the driving time was not additional to the killing time; and the corpses could be tipped straight into the pits where they belonged. Just as the engine of a concrete mixer truck simultaneously drives the mixing drum, so the engine of the gas truck had a dual purpose in that the exhaust fumes could be channelled into the truck's body, where the people locked up would slowly choke to death.

In the Nuremberg courtroom Ohlendorf explained to his judges the 'advantages' of the death truck in brief and impressive words: 'It all looked very harmless, so there was no panic when the victims were loaded. It was possible to load the trucks at an appropriate distance from the most convenient site, which served for both the execution and the burial of those who had been shot or hanged; and there was no excessive stress for the truck driver or his mate, as the engine noise drowned the cries of the dying.'

What Ohlendorf was praising was not his own invention but that of his friend, SS Obersturmbannführer Walter Rauff, born in 1906 and by profession a naval officer. However, because of an affair with a girl student, he was dismissed from the navy by a court of honour. This proved to be a leg-up in his career: Reinhard Heydrich, the head of the Reich Security Directorate, had also been kicked out of the navy for a similar business and thus, when he met Rauff in 1939, he was instantly attracted to him. He made the cashiered lieutenant-commander his head of Department IID for technical matters.

In this capacity Rauff, in continuous and intensive co-operation with the head of the motor vehicle department of the Security Directorate, SS-Führer Friedrich Pradel, developed the gas truck. Although the preliminary studies by euthanasia institutions provided a starting point, the problem of costs had not been sufficiently borne in mind. There the corpses had been produced by chemically pure carbon monoxide, which had to be stored in steel cylinders which were much too expensive. Rauff and Pradel therefore resorted to pilot experiments with exhaust fumes, which admittedly did not ensure such rapid or certain death but which were substantially cheaper. And if some small child, owing to its relatively large heart–lung capacity, occasionally survived, then such a malfunction could easily be remedied by the driver with his rifle-butt.

The facility of rapid unloading was another important requirement. A working party specially charged with this problem came up with the idea of fitting a 'rapid discharge device': they calculated the time that might be saved if the fifty to seventy corpses could be unloaded by a tipping mechanism.

The manufacture of airtight special superstructures was entrusted to the firm of Gaubschat in Berlin (whose entire correspondence with Rauff has been preserved for us). A special team, subordinate to Rauff, was responsible for continual improvements. Thus one 'Just' in a letter of 5 June 1942 proposed to his boss a number of technical modifications which would make it possible to squeeze in more than just nine or ten persons per square metre of vehicle space. The next sentence has to be read three times to be believed: 'Since October 1941, for instance,' Just wrote, '97,000 were processed in the three trucks in use without any faults appearing in the vehicles.'

I first read that sentence some time about the end of the 1940s or the beginning of the 1950s, when I was studying a bundle of documents from the Nuremberg trials. By chance – the kind of chance I regard as a disposition of fate – I was often in Italy at the time, following the trail of the governor of Galicia, Dr Otto Wächter. Wächter had evidently succeeded in escaping via Italy, and now I learned that the organization which had helped him was headed by an SS Obersturmbannführer by the name of Rauff: the head of research and development for the gas trucks was also the head of Odessa. Rauff was especially suited to his task, as he knew his way about Italy. Towards the end of 1942 he had been instructed by Himmler and Kaltenbrunner (who became his new boss after Heydrich's death) to ship the Jews of Tunisia over to Italy and to apportion them from there to various extermination camps. To this end Rauff was appointed SS police chief of Tunisia and he promised his boss 3000 new victims. Reputedly, however, he allowed himself to be bought off with a large gift of gold; at any rate he supplied only 120.

After Rommel had lost the battle of El Alamein, Rauff had to leave Tunisia; he moved first to Rome and later became SS police chief of Milan. When, following the fall of Mussolini, the Germans virtually took over Italy, Rauff made use of the opportunity to establish contacts for the future: the German bishop in Rome, Alois Hudal, introduced him into sympathetic

Church circles. This proved exceedingly useful, for Rauff was taken prisoner at the end of the war and put in a POW camp near Rimini; however, Hudal and co., thanks to their position, soon got him out. Bishop Hudal accommodated Rauff privately in Milan, and there the inventor of the gas truck began to organize the so-called 'Roman route' for his comrades. What made the camouflage of this enterprise easier was the political background at that time: the seizure of power in eastern Europe by Communist or semi-Communist regimes. Throughout the former Nazi satellites – in Slovakia, Hungary and Croatia – mass arrests were being conducted by the new rulers, the first victims being the former Fascists, from the Slovak Hlinka Guards to the Hungarian Arrow Cross. As these men were without exception good Catholics, the Vatican established aid missions for them (which it had failed to do for the victims of Nazi persecution). Through Bishop Hudal Rauff now established links with those aid missions and made sure that his comrades were not forgotten.

The fugitives had no papers, and provisional identity cards were therefore issued to them with the aid of the Vatican and the Red Cross. Next, the Vatican arranged South American visas for them, especially for Argentina. Until their departure these fugitives from justice were mostly accommodated in religious houses, such as the Franciscan monastery on Via Sicilia in Rome. Embarcation was from Bari or Genoa. Frequently there were refugee passports ready for them, obtained from the Red Cross by a secretary of Archbishop Giuseppe Siri. Transportation from Italy to South America was then arranged by Caritas, who evidently failed to notice that a substantial number of its refugees didn't come from Croatia, Slovakia or Hungary at all.

In addition to Church sympathy, however, an organization like that needed money. Providing that money was one of Walter Rauff's most essential tasks. He made use of a man who had also ended up in Italy after the war: Friedrich Schwendt. Schwendt was living at Schloss Labers near Merano in the South Tyrol and had almost unlimited funds at his disposal. How he came by them I have described in earlier books. In the course of her multi-front war Germany, of course, ran out of money – whereupon Himmler, within the framework of Operation Bernard, ordered colossal quantities of counterfeit money to be printed. On the one hand these forged pounds (of which several cratefuls were subsequently found in Lake Toplitz) were designed to damage the British currency, and on the other the Nazis succeeded in exchanging them for real money, thereby obtaining hard currency. These were probably the most perfect forgeries ever produced.

It so happened that Heydrich (and Kaltenbrunner after him), as head of the Reich Security Directorate, was also the head of Interpol, founded by Austria in 1923. (One of the consequences of this was that after the war there were a number of big Nazis in Interpol, who, instead of searching for their wanted comrades, covered up for them.) During the war Interpol provided Heydrich, and later Kaltenbrunner, with access to the records of the best banknote forgers. The Nazis assembled an élite of them in the Sachsenhausen concentration camp, and subsequently in the Redl corner of Upper Austria, and charged them with the production of counterfeit pound notes. They were so perfect that after the war the British had to withdraw all notes of that denomination and produce a new issue.

Friedrich Schwendt was the man chosen by the SS to exchange the forged notes for real foreign currency. He succeeded in this task, and it would seem as though he didn't necessarily account for every penny, because after the war he was an enormously rich man.

Rauff knew Schwendt's past history and seems to have paid a very forthright visit to his comrade: he pointed out that the old comrades would not readily understand how one of them was holding court in a castle while they were in prison camps or hiding in monasteries. At any rate, Schwendt subsequently handed over huge amounts of money to Rauff and also transferred major sums to South America. He eventually finished up there himself: in Santiago, Chile, he set up a business and was also in partnership with Klaus Barbie.

Rauff himself stayed on in Italy until 1949. On one occasion he was detained by Italian partisans but he was probably able to buy back his freedom: it is said that he handed over to the partisans a section of the archives of the Fascist Party of Italy, which he had got hold of after the fall of Mussolini. Nevertheless, the place was beginning to get too hot for him.

At the beginning of 1954 I received information that he had settled in Quito in Ecuador. I even had his post-office box number, but that didn't help me: Rauff didn't collect his mail himself, and later he found a postal official who rented a box for him, collected his mail and forwarded it. Because, by then, Rauff had long ago left Ecuador and was living in Chile. There he was the owner, or at least part-owner, of a tinned food factory, and he lived in Puntas Arenas.

In 1955 he applied to West Germany for authorization for his old-age pension. After the Eichmann trial, however, the Germans had begun to process Nazi crimes as thoroughly as they had once been committed. When in 1960 I was able to inform the public prosecutor's office of Rauff's address, they were all keyed up for action. His case was immediately assigned to the prosecuting authority of Hanover, which was supplied with all the necessary evidence by the Central Office in Ludwigsburg. He was able, therefore, as early as 1963, to address a well-founded extradition application to Chile. Its central piece was the letter about the '97,000 processed persons'. In addition there was a statement by his subordinate Pradel and the records of the Gaubschat car and truck body factory.

But Rauff was lucky: under the Chilean statute of limitations murder charges cannot be brought after fifteen years, and when the Supreme Court in Santiago dealt with the case eighteen years had elapsed. By three votes to two the application for extradition was rejected. A judge from Hanover, who went to Chile to interrogate Rauff in the action against Pradel, returned with the conviction that it would only be possible to get hold of the Obersturmbannführer if a different regime came to power in Chile.

Eight years later just that happened: the socialist Salvador Allende became head of State. On 21 August I handed over to the Chilean ambassador in Vienna, Professor Benadava, a letter to Allende, drawing his attention to the Rauff case. Allende replied very cordially but pointed to the difficulty of reopening a case when the Supreme Court had already handed down a judgement. I requested Allende to examine the possibility of having Rauff, who was not yet a Chilean citizen, deported: we might be able to proceed against him in a country with a more favourable legislation. But before Allende could answer my second letter there was a coup and Allende lost his life.

In 1975 Walter Rauff moved from Puntas Arenas to Los Posos 7243, Las Condes, in Santiago. He set up a new firm, called Neptuna Sociedada de Navegazao, and acquired a new post-office box, No. 14120. To this post box I possessed a special kind of key: a friend of mine, a German, had gained Rauff's confidence to such an extent that he was able to copy his letters. In consequence I am in possession of a substantial quantity of correspondence by the former escape organizer. Sometimes the oddest things are reported to me: Himmler's personal ADC, Karl Wolff, working with a ghost-writer named Heidemann (from *Stern* magazine), wished to write a book about the war period and in this connection had asked Rauff for expert help. He had in the meantime become a prominent figure. For years my bulletins and reports had made him famous, and now the political opposition was taking him up. There were big stories in illustrated magazines, claiming that he had operated as an advisor to the Chilean secret police Dina. As if they needed him.

In 1983 I was received by President Reagan, who asked if he could do anything for me. I requested help in the Rauff case. Reagan did inform the State Department, which asked us to make our entire file on Rauff available to them. Unfortunately the outcome was nil.

A conversation with Chancellor Kohl – though I didn't find out until later – proved more successful. I mentioned the Rauff case to him too, and he mentioned that he would talk to his Ministry of Justice to see if a new extradition application might not be made.

I realized that it would be necessary, above all, to create a climate in which Pinochet would find it difficult to reject a renewed application. The Simon Wiesenthal Center in Los Angeles launched a large-scale signature campaign: in 100,000 postcards from the USA President Pinochet was asked to expel Rauff.

This at least kept Rauff's name before the public – though it didn't achieve anything else. We had to find another way of appealing directly to the Chilean government, and to argue that it would help the country's image if Rauff was extradited. For a while I even considered making contact with Pinochet's son who, under a different name, works in a Chilean diplomatic mission in the USA. The Dean of our Center, Rabbi Hier, however, believed that it would be more useful to talk to Chile's consul general in Los Angeles, with whom he was personally acquainted and who might have more receptive ears.

In a way he was correct. Although the consul general remained fairly impressed by my argument that Rauff's extradition would help Chile's image, he showed great interest in a slight exaggeration which I permitted myself: I thought it conceivable, I said to him, that many decent people in the USA might decide on an economic boycott of Chile if Pinochet continued to show the world that the constructor of the gas truck in which 97,000 Jews were 'processed' was a welcome guest in his country. Moreover, the circumstances that the President's son was working in the USA under another name would not necessarily enhance Pinochet's image among the Americans.

These, evidently, were better arguments than my reference to the dead: the very next day the consul general handed our Center a copy of a telegram from General Sinclair, the chief of staff of Pinochet's office, to the effect that West Germany should reapply for Rauff's extradition.

I got in touch at once with public prosecutor Landgraf in Hanover and informed him of the new development. He had in fact already prepared a new warrant of arrest in response to the intervention by Chancellor Kohl. This was issued on 21 February 1984 and soon translated into Spanish; on 16 May it was to be taken to Santiago by courier, along with an application for extradition.

Two days before the courier's departure, on 14 May, the news arrived that Rauff had died of heart failure. At his funeral in Santiago his friends from all over South America honoured him at the graveside by raising their hands in the Hitler salute. There were still quite a lot of them, but some of the best known were absent: the commandant of the Riga ghetto, Eduard Roschmann; the gas chamber supervisor of Sobibor, Gustav Wagner; and his close friend, the commandant of the Treblinka extermination camp, Franz Stangl. Adolf Eichmann, too, was no longer among the mourners. All these men had been helped by Rauff to escape, but they all made mistakes. And I had exploited these mistakes.

8

The Search for Eichmann

Adolf Eichmann's mistake was his family sentiment: he wanted to keep in touch with his wife, he wanted to take part in family festivities, he wanted to have his children around. He was an utterly bourgeois, an utterly normal, almost in fact a socially adjusted, person. That he had the death of six million Jews on his conscience was due not to any criminal character but, on the contrary, to his readiness to be totally absorbed in a common task, giving it all his ability and all his effort: he would have similarly had six million gypsies gassed if there had been that many. Or six million left-handers. And if Hitler had commanded him not to kill the Jews but instead ship them to Palestine to enable a Jewish state to be created there, he would have done that as well. He was not driven by blood lust.

That, exactly was his crucial qualification. People who kill from a confusion of emotions – from a serious neurotic disturbance if not from mental sickness – are unsuitable for teamwork. They are not suitable for membership in an organization because sooner or later they direct their aggression inwards and against one another. This is precisely the difference between amateur crime, as experienced in most European countries, and the professional crime of the Mafia in the USA: the members of the 'family' are sufficiently social to get along with one another. The leaders organize the murder – they don't soil their own hands. For that they have their killers, among whom are occasionally found those deviant sadists which, in our imagination, represent the prototype of the murderer. But even these hit-men cannot be so disturbed that they would kill in a frenzy, for the sake of mere murdering. That would be too great a risk for the group.

The Nazi murder machine was similarly constructed: its key positions were held by people who regarded murder purely as an organizational problem. The sadists only came into their own at a much lower level. And even there they were the exception rather than the rule: an SS man murdering through sheer delight in murder was in danger of being disciplined. (I shall describe such an instance in Chapter 32.)

The characteristic trait of the individual murderer is the perversion of his emotional life. Eichmann's characteristic trait was an intact emotional life in everything concerning his personal sphere, and utter lack of emotion where his 'task' was concerned. Only this kind is capable of mass murder.

None of this was clear to me when I first heard his name immediately after the war. I was then searching for 'individual murderers': I wanted to find the men who humiliated, beat up and shot people dead in front of my own eyes. Ritschek was the prototype of the SS man I was hunting then – not yet Eichmann. Nor was it at first realized how significant his role had been. The first list of war criminals published by the Jewish Agency gave him without his first name: 'High Official of Gestapo HQ, Department of Jewish Affairs' was what it said, and not until my boss in the OSS, Captain O'Meara, told me that Eichmann had been 'the head of the Gestapo department responsible for Jews' did I enter his name in my notebook.

The OSS office in Linz was on Landstrasse 36. I myself was living just a couple of houses down the street, as a lodger. One evening, as I was once again bent over my lists, Frau Sturm, my landlady, walked in and, as usual, looked over my shoulder. 'Eichmann,' she said. 'That must have been the SS General Eichmann who was in command of the Jews. Did you know that his parents live here, in this street, just a few houses along, at number 32?'

That was my first specific clue, and if I had pursued it consistently Eichmann would probably have been arrested then, immediately after the war. That would have saved us a great deal of trouble, and yet it would have been disadvantageous: the Eichmann trial would have been lost among the many war criminal trials then taking place. He would certainly have been executed – but it is highly doubtful whether his part in the extermination of the Jews would really have been uncovered. Presumably one would have contented oneself with the evidence of a few witnesses, for the archive material which we possess today was then still scattered across half of Europe.

From that point of view my omission was fortunate. I was not personally present when two members of the OSS searched the Eichmann family house the following day. Eichmann's father stated that his son had been with the SS and had not returned from the war. The last news he'd had from him had come from Prague some months earlier. In reality Eichmann had not been in Prague for some time, but in Altaussee in the Salzkammergut: it had been agreed that the Austrian leaders of the Third Reich should all congregate there in the 'Alpine redoubt', and Eichmann didn't see the slightest reason why he should not go. Right to the last moment he was doing his duty. He didn't realize that men like Kaltenbrunner no longer wanted to have anything to do with him. Besides, he was longing to see his wife. She had rented a place in Altaussee, Fischerndorf 8, and it was an open secret in the village that her husband had come back to see her.

By then I had quite good contacts within the Nazi scene, and one of my staff was given a useful tip-off. Strictly speaking, I need only have taken a jeep and two soldiers, and Eichmann would have found himself under arrest. Instead we turned to the CIC, which resided in the immediate neighbourhood of Altaussee, and they in turn approached the Austrian gendarmerie. Two gendarmes fanned out and made for house number 38 instead of house number 8. But the way matters stood in that area, they stumbled on another war criminal in the process: at Fischerndorf 38 an SS Hauptsturmführer, Anton Burger,* was hiding out. A major arsenal of weapons was confiscated and he was locked up.

After that the Americans went to number 8 for themselves. But, once again, they did not find Eichmann; only a Frau Veronika Liebl, who claimed to be the 'former' Frau Eichmann. She had been divorced from him in Prague in March 1945, she stated, and had resumed her maiden name. Since then she had not seen him. On 15 April she had come to Altaussee, where she had first stayed at the Seehotel, next at the Parkhotel, and had only then rented the house in Fischerndorf because, after all, she had to accommodate her three children – Klaus, Dieter and Horst.

By then I had become suspicious. I went to Altaussee myself and talked to Frau Maria Bucher, the proprietress of the Parkhotel. She gave free vent to her anger: not only had Frau Liebl stayed there but also her husband, who'd arrived in full SS uniform. One night he'd broken open her husband's locked wardrobe and simply helped himself to one of his suits. Without a single word, without any payment. Surely that was not the behaviour one expected of a proper guest.

* Anton Burger was a member of Eichmann's staff and deputy commandant of the Terezín ghetto. He was responsible for a number of crimes in Austria, Czechoslovakia and Greece. After his arrest he was taken to the American internment camp at Glasenbach. There I was able to interrogate him about Eichmann once more, in the presence of an American captain. He confirmed that he had seen him in Altaussee on 4 May. On 18 June 1947 Burger escaped from Glasenbach; but I uncovered his trail again in 1949 and he was arrested a second time by the Austrian police. However, he succeeded in escaping from prison in Vienna. I was able to follow his trail until 1956. After that it was lost in West Germany.

We confronted Frau Eichmann-Liebl with that statement, but she stuck to hers: she hadn't seen her husband since her divorce in Prague. The only point that was correct was that Eichmann had last served in Prague, except that his headquarters had meanwhile moved on to Budějovice and thence to Austria.

At any rate, Eichmann was now placed on the Austrian wanted list, and his importance was slowly emerging. Again and again his name cropped up in the documents of the Nuremberg trials. It was clear that deportation orders had come from him and that he had been the person principally responsible for the functioning of the whole extermination machinery. I spent an entire week in Nuremberg, doing nothing but studying correspondence: how he had applied for money for the construction of further gas chambers, how he had commented on various methods of extermination or discussed deportation problems. Slowly a personal picture of Adolf Eichmann was building up in me. It wasn't yet the picture of the murder official sitting behind his desk, adding columns of figures, but it was the picture of a mass murderer. I realized that the search for him was infinitely more important than anything I had done so far.

That was the moment when the public began to link my name with Eichmann's. In Linz I was called the 'Eichmann Wiesenthal' and I was beginning to be swamped with information. But I was clumsy then and still unable to separate promising tip-offs from self-advertising ones. The only thing which my colleague Manus Diamant got hold of then was a photograph of Eichmann dating back to 1934; Diamant had persuaded Eichmann's former girlfriend in Linz to part with it. We added it to his warrant for arrest.

Now our wanted man had a face. There were no other photos of Eichmann. His father asserted that, as a matter of principle, Adolf had refused to be photographed. At first we didn't believe that, but it turned out to be the truth. Eichmann was evidently aware that he was doing something that might, at some time or other, expose him to prosecution. In this respect, too, he was like the boss of a gang of professional criminals: he wished to remain as little known as possible. If he talked about his work at all, then it was only to his own kind. In the autumn of 1944 in Budapest, for instance, he had drawn a brief balance sheet of his success for SS Obersturmbannführer Wilhelm Höttl: 'The number of Jews killed amounts to nearly six million – but that is top secret.'

I have sometimes asked myself if Eichmann had ever discussed such figures with his wife or his children. And how they would have reacted to them. How Frau Veronika Eichmann-Liebl could live with a man who was responsible for the death of nearly as many people as the total population of Austria. If she thought the charges against him were wicked defamation or if, on the contrary, she thought that the murder of the Jews was something to his credit? Probably neither one nor the other; most likely she was convinced that her husband had done no more than 'his duty'. What duty it was would have been a matter of indifference to Frau Eichmann. Otherwise I can't explain why she did what she was doing: she fought for Eichmann's escape to remain successful, and for being able to live with him again. By pretending that he had died.

Towards the end of 1947 I received information through an American friend that Frau Veronika Liebl had applied to the district court in Bad Ischl for her divorced husband to be declared dead 'in the interest of the children'. Austrian and German courts were at that time being flooded with such applications. Thousands of women whose husbands had not returned needed such a declaration in order to receive a pension for themselves or their children, and in order to marry again. The courts handled such applications as routine matters because they knew that there was no way of verification. It was essentially a matter of letting the women have their wish.

I realized what it would mean if Eichmann too were declared dead: his name would be crossed off the wanted lists and any official search by the authorities would come to an end. We decided that my American friend Stevens, the head of the Bad Ischl CIC, should talk to the judge. The judge willingly supplied the information he had: a certain Karl Lukas, resident in Prague, Mollicarstrasse 22, had declared on oath that he had witnessed Eichmann being shot dead in the fighting for Prague on 30 April 1945. Stevens explained to the court that this 'dead person' was one of the most wanted Nazi criminals, and the judge was prepared to delay the processing of the case.

I had researches made in Prague and I soon discovered that Karl Lukas was married to Maria Lukas, whose maiden name had been Maria Liebl and who was Veronika Liebl's sister. I passed this information on to Stevens, who passed it on to the court: Eichmann's declaration of death was turned down.

This unspectacular move was probably my most important contribution to the Eichmann case. Where I might possibly have been a 'hunter' I had failed – first in Linz and later in Fischerndorf. But the search for Eichmann resembled a hunt only at the very beginning and the very end. In between it was a laborious compilation of more or less significant pieces of information, upon which we acted with greater or lesser skill. I was a dogged pursuer, but I was no marksman.

In the spring of 1948 I was able to reconstruct Eichmann's escape route: he had left Prague on 28 April 1945, he had reached Budějovice on 29 April and Ebensee near Bad Ischl on 1 May. There, as had been arranged among the members of his staff, they would all meet. Eichmann, however, stopped only briefly in Ebensee, for on 2 May several witnesses already identified him as being at Altaussee, where he stayed until 9 May. After that he hid out in American internment camps, where he would be less conspicuous than hiding on his own in some lonely house. Via the camp of Berndorf near Rosenheim in Upper Bavaria he got to the camp at Kemnaten and later to that at Cham in the Upper Palatinate.

A German camp official called Rudolf Scheide remembered the unremarkable inmate: in June 1945 an SS leader had come to him and requested him to enter him in the camp register under the name of Obersturmführer Eckmann, although in reality he was Obersturmführer Eichmann. 'As the name of Eichmann meant nothing to me, I intimated to him, especially at the beginning, that it was his own business what he did with his name.' Subsequently Scheide found out what the Americans associated with the name of Eichmann and on 30 June he informed the CIC. However, Adolf Eichmann was equally well informed: when his squad, which had been detailed to construction work, returned to the camp in the evening Eichmann was no longer with them. For a time he hid out somewhere in northern Germany; later he moved to an uncle in Solingen (the Eichmann family came from that area: he had only come to Linz with his father at the age of three). When British officials questioned the uncle things became too hot for Eichmann and he decided to return to where he felt safest: the Aussee district. It was the decision of a guerrilla who, when forced underground, chooses an area he is familiar with and where he can count on numerous sympathizers among the population.

There was another thing which may have lured Eichmann to Aussee: the gold he had buried there. There were several statements to the effect that, on his first appearance in May, Eichmann with several helpers had recovered twenty-two steel boxes from the Altaussee lake and taken them to the remote Blahalm, a mountain pasture area. The boxes were said to have contained not only documents but, more particularly, 'dental gold'.

Finally there was Eichmann's wife, still living at Fischerndorf 8 with her children. Although I can't prove it, I am certain that he was in touch with her throughout that period, even though the censor intercepted all letters to and from Frau Eichmann. There were so many mutual friends, and there was moreover a smoothly functioning Nazi underground organization with a well-established information system. But at the same time the breadth of this Nazi underground also represented a risk: there were a lot of SS comrades who knew where Eichmann was at any particular time. I had a colleague then who was well in with those circles. He had been a major in the German armed forces and I had succeeded in making him see that he had nothing in common with the concentration camp murderers. Those men were murderers who happened to commit their murders during a war. It was by accident that they had worn a uniform similar to that of the army. The major was willing to help me run down the murderers, if only because he wanted to exculpate the men of the Wehrmacht. But the SS continued to regard him as one of their own people, merely because he had worn a uniform too. He could talk to them, and they trustingly told him how they felt about things. It turned out that even within the SS there was a tendency now to dissociate oneself from Eichmann: even the members of a 'criminal association', as the Nuremberg verdicts described the SS, did not wish to be bracketed with the systematic murder of millions. True, there was no one who would have, so to speak, delivered Eichmann to the executioner, but they were ready enough to tell my major that he was hiding out somewhere in the surroundings of Aussee and presumably was enjoying the support of friends.

In point of fact, the headquarters of the Nazi underground movement Spinne ('Spider') where at that time in the immediate proximity of Aussee, in Gmunden. Another organization, operating in Styria, was the so-called 'Sechsgestirn' ('Constellation of Six'), with which Anton Burger – the man the gendarmes had found when they were looking for Eichmann and went to the wrong house – maintained close links. Burger was now thought to be acting as a courier between Eichmann and Sechsgestirn. Finally both Nazi cells, Spinne as well as Sechsgestirn, were included in Theodor Soucek's organization which was based at nearby Graz. Thus interlinked, these organizations formed the network on which Odessa could base itself; Odessa by then was fully operational. This network evidently gave Eichmann a sense of security greater than the fear which our 'network' could inspire in him. Thank God he underrated us a little.

On 20 December 1949 a senior Austrian police officer called on me and we discussed the situation. We were both convinced that Eichmann was hiding out somewhere in Aussee. The police officer supposed him to be in the vicinity of Grundlsee, a lake separated from the Altaussee lake by a ridge. This fitted in with an observation one of my people had passed on to me a few months earlier: there was a black Mercedes with Upper Austria plates which had been seen in the Grundlsee village and shortly afterwards at Altaussee. There it was pulled up outside Fischerndorf 8, the house occupied by Frau Eichmann. A man in a raincoat had got out, stayed briefly indoors, and left again.

The police officer evidently had an even better source of information. When he visited me again the following day he let the cat out of the bag: 'We have found out that Eichmann intends to spend New Year's Eve with his family in Altaussee. That's when we'll pick him up.' Then he invited me to take part in the operation. New Year's Eve is my birthday and I couldn't think of a better present.

But at just this decisive phase I was to make a vital mistake: I declared myself willing to bring along a young Israeli who was then, with youthful enthusiasm, working in my office and who would probably have followed me secretly if I had excluded him from the operation.

We set out on 28 December and took rooms at the Erzherzog Johann hotel in Bad Aussee. Everyone was cold and bored. I had asked my young friend not to walk about too much and, above all, not to talk to anyone, but evidently he thought this ban only concerned our operation. Instead of going for a walk he went to the bar. There he greatly impressed a number of girls by telling them that he had only arrived from Israel a short time ago.

On 31 December I met my friend from the police. He had brought six men with him, who were all to be posted near Fischerndorf 8 in order to intercept Eichmann in the street, as we didn't have a search warrant. Until then the police officers sat in various local bars keeping their ears open.

It was bitterly cold and we too wanted to warm ourselves with a cup of hot tea at our hotel. I opened the door to the restaurant and found a lively company there. The local youth were listening to my Israeli's accounts of the heroic actions of the Israeli army.

The police officer barely managed to restrain his fury: 'If word gets about that a young Israeli is in the vicinity it is quite possible...'

'It's gone ten o'clock,' I said. 'Nothing can go wrong now.'

'Let's hope so,' he replied grimly.

We left the hotel and sought the nearest police officer, who was obediently sitting over a glass of beer in a tavern. 'They're all talking about the Israeli who's come to Bad Aussee,' he said.

My companion looked at me as a professional mountain guide might after he'd been crazy enough to take a few amateurs on a climb and then noticed that they are wearing plimsolls instead of mountain boots. For a while I cursed the young Israeli, and then I cursed myself.

By then it was eleven, and if Eichmann wanted to be with his family at midnight he should shortly be leaving Grundlsee. We waited and waited. At last a plain-clothes man arrived – a man we had posted to Grundlsee – and whispered something to the officer. He listened in silence and then asked him to repeat his report so that I too could hear it. 'At half past eleven,' the officer said slowly and clearly, as if charging me, 'two men appeared on the road from Grundlsee. It was rather dark but I could make them out against the light background of the snow. They were only about a hundred and fifty yards away from me – I was hiding behind the trees by the road. Suddenly another man came from the direction of Grundlsee and called out something to them. They stopped, talked to him, and immediately all three ran back the way they'd come.'

The police officer tried to console me: it was by no means certain that my assistant's actions had led to Eichmann being warned. Anyway, having discovered Eichmann was progress of a kind. He would leave two men behind; they were sure to track him down. But I knew that all that was only politeness. For the police officer it was a professional defeat, for me it was a human catastrophe.

A week later I was informed that the search for Eichmann had been called off: he had disappeared from the Aussee neighbourhood.

During the next few years I heard only rumours and gossip about him in the gutter press. He had been seen in Cairo, it was claimed; he met old comrades in Damascus; he was setting up a German legion of Arabs. None of this seemed to me very likely: a man who refused even to be photographed would hardly make enough noise to attract newspaper attention.

In any case, the world's real interest was focused on other matters: the Cold War was at its peak and in Korea had turned into a hot war. In Europe the Americans realized that West Germany would be at least as important an ally as Britain or France – and possibly a more reliable one. The erstwhile adversaries were being wooed, and even in American films they were no longer being portrayed as murderous monsters but as gallant officers who merely had the rotten luck to be in the service of a madman. Against this background the picture of Adolf Eichmann was fading. If I tried to talk about him to my American friends they would reply a little wearily: 'We've got other problems.'

At the beginning of 1951 I learned from a former member of German counter-espionage, who had friends in Odessa, a few rather vague assumptions about Eichmann's escape: he had been channelled to Rome by a Croat committee, using the 'monastary route', and had arrived there in the late summer of 1950. The committee was headed by followers of the head of the Croat collaborationist government, Ante Pavelić. In Rome Eichmann had presumably been hiding out in a monastery. 'There he was probably given a Vatican passport, which he needed if he wanted a visa for a South American country.'

The final part of this piece of information was undoubtedly the most important. Americans and Israelis then held the view that Eichmann had moved to the Middle East. But my friend was convinced that he was in South America. The Odessa transports had nearly all gone to Brazil or Argentina. This seemed to me the most likely destination.

My only hope of discovering further details was once again based on Eichmann's family sentiment: he was bound to try to make contact with his family in Altaussee and to bring them over eventually. I settled down to a prolonged wait. But I was to hear about him suddenly in a totally different way.

In the autumn of 1951 there appeared in my office a slim man in his forties, immaculately dressed and with immaculate manners – he almost clicked his heels as he briefly bowed to me, and produced his visiting card. He was Heinrich von Klimrod and represented the Vienna group of former SS men, who had long followed my activities with interest and admiration. The man was obviously trying to establish an atmosphere of 'a talk between equals'. We were all professionals, he said; it was, in a manner of speaking, just an accident that we stood on different sides, but, in a certain higher sense, what we had in common was more important. 'Your interests and ours meet at one point. You want to find Eichmann to bring him to justice. We want Eichmann's gold. It seems to me that a mutually beneficial cooperation might be arranged.'

Now that really was the most natural thing in the world: the immaculate gentlemen with their immaculate manners wanted the gold which Eichmann's henchmen had prised from the teeth of murdered Jews. To this end they were even prepared to cooperate with a Jew and to surrender their former colleague to him. He, as it were, had already done his job – the dirty job which Herr von Klimrod had been spared. Now the two of us, between us, might come to a gentleman's agreement. 'We know a lot about Eichmann's escape. We know that two priests, Father Weber and Father Benedetti, helped him. We know the Capuchin monastery where he hid out. Although Eichmann's present name is unknown to us, we have many comrades in South America who might help us. Well then, is it a deal?'

I think that to this day Herr von Klimrod still does not understand how I could refuse his offer. Although he repeatedly referred to my idealism when he noticed that I wasn't rising to his 'we're both professionals' bait, he didn't understand that idealism does not justify any means. I might have been prepared to give him money of my own in order to get at Eichmann with his help – but to let him have the gold out of the mouths of my murdered brethren would have been like desecration of the dead. But 'desecration' or 'shame' presumably were not part of his conceptual vocabulary. He left my office totally baffled.

About six months later I was again contacted in connection with Eichmann. An acquaintance from Altaussee told me that Frau Eichmann-Liebl had disappeared along with her sons. She had taken the children out of school in the middle of term, although they would not have been accepted at any other Austrian or German school without a leaving certificate. The rent for the house continued to be paid, and none of the contents had been removed, as would have been the case if they had just moved house. The neighbourhood immediately suspected the truth: Frau Eichmann was about to do a bunk. Presumably to South America; according to rumour, to Brazil.

My crucial piece of information came from an elderly Austrian baron whose acquaintance I had made at the stamp collector's club. One day he invited me to his house to show me his collection. On that occasion our talk turned to the Nazi period. He had been a member of counter-espionage under Admiral Canaris and, because of his Catholic-monarchist views, had always been sceptical of the Nazis. When I told him what I had been doing all these years he got up and said: 'I think I may have something for you.' He walked over to a stack of books and papers and pulled out a blue airmail envelope. 'This is a letter from an army comrade,' he said. 'He's living in Buenos Aires and is now an instructor with President Perón. We've kept up a correspondence, and in one of my letters I once asked him if he'd come across any mutual acquaintances. His answer will interest you.' With these words he held out the letter to me and with his finger pointed to the final paragraph. I gasped as I read it: 'I saw that miserable swine Eichmann, the one who was in charge of the Jews, he's living near Buenos Aires and works for a water plant.'

I realized that I had come to the end of my private facilities. In Perón's Argentina the Nazis exercised considerable power; they were the organizers of the Argentinian army, experts in Argentinian industrialization, and their money added to the liquidity of Argentinian banks. Eichmann could feel secure in Argentina. As an adversary I was now too lightweight for him.

I consulted the Israeli consul in Vienna, Arie Eschel, who invited me to compile a report for the World Jewish Congress, listing all my information. This report was virtually identical to my own Eichmann file. It began with what I had discovered about Eichmann's personality and concluded with the baron's tip-off. I also enclosed samples of his handwriting and the photograph we had of him.

I sent one copy of the report to Dr Nahum Goldmann, the President of the World Jewish Congress, and another to the Israeli consulate in Vienna. From Israel there was no reply at all. From New York, at least, I received a letter after two months: a rabbi named Kalmanowitz informed me, on Goldmann's behalf, that he had received the material, but he would like to have Eichmann's precise address in Buenos Aires. I replied that I would gladly send someone to Argentina if the travelling costs and five hundred dollars' worth of expenses could be taken care of by them. Rabbi Kalmanowitz wrote back to say that there was no money; besides, Dr Goldmann had been informed by the FBI that Eichmann was in Damascus, in Syria, a country which would certainly not extradite him, as the murder of Jews was not considered a criminal offence there.

American Jews at that time probably had other worries. The Israelis no longer had any interest in Eichmann; they had to fight for their lives against Nasser. The Americans were no longer interested in Eichmann because of the Cold War against the Soviet Union. I feel that, along with a few other like-minded fools, I was quite alone. In March 1954 I closed down the Documentation Center, tidily packed all the files in boxes and sent them to the Yad Vashem archive in Jerusalem. The only file I kept was the Eichmann file. I honestly don't know why, because I had in truth given up.

Five years later, on 22 April 1959, I was, as always, reading the Linz daily, *Oberösterreichische Nachrichten*. On the back page there was a big notice announcing the death of Frau Maria Eichmann (Adolf Eichmann's stepmother), with the names of the mourning relatives underneath. I began to read them as a matter of course. Then I froze: I had come across the name Vera Eichmann. People don't lie in these notices: Veronika Liebl had resumed the name which she evidently regarded as her only legitimate one. Wherever she was living now, she was Frau Adolf Eichmann.

I sent one of my people to Frau Eichmann's mother, who seemed to regard a half-truth as the best form of concealment. She stated that her daughter had married a man called 'Klems' or 'Klemt' in South America. I sent this piece of information to Israel, and the Israelis were able to verify it: Frau Eichmann, I was informed a short while later, was cohabiting with a German. The Israelis also knew his name: 'Ricardo Klement'.

On the strength of the death notice it was obvious to me that the German could only be Adolf Eichmann. In that case Eichmann's sons must also be with their parents in Buenos Aires. An inquiry to the German embassy confirmed my assumption: they were registered there under their real names (an embassy official later told me that no one could have known that they were the sons of the notorious Adolf Eichmann.)

All we needed now was a way of identifying Ricardo Klement with some degree of certainty as Adolf Eichmann. Our chance came with another death notice: in February 1960 Eichmann's father died, and once again *Oberösterreichische Nachrichten* carried a black-framed announcement, signed again by a Vera Eichmann, daughter-in-law.

The Eichmanns' family feeling evidently made them blind to danger. For an instant I even indulged in the hope that Adolf Eichmann himself would come over for the funeral. I hired two press photographers and requested them, while hiding behind a gravestone or a tree, to take pictures with a tele-lens of every member of the cortège. That same evening the photos were on my desk: they showed a number of men who resembled Adolf Eichmann – his brothers Emil, Robert, Otto and Friedrich. Otto, Friedrich and Robert were already known to me. Emil, whom I hadn't seen before, had come from Frankfurt. Adolf Eichmann was absent.

But their incredible family likeness gave me an idea. I fished out the old photograph of Eichmann which we extracted from his Linz girlfriend, and compared it with the photos of his brothers. And there was indeed one which might have been young Adolf Eichmann thirty years on – his brother Otto. That, presumably, was the reason why time and again people claimed to have seen Eichmann in all kinds of places where he quite certainly had not been: they had mistaken his brother for him. Anyone with Otto Eichmann's photograph in his hands would be able to identify Adolf Eichmann – even if he now called himself Ricardo Klement.

The Israeli embassy thereupon informed me that two young Israelis would call on me. Very soon afterwards they turned up in Linz in a great hurry, pocketed all my funeral snaps and instantly departed. On Monday, 23 May 1960, David Ben Gurion told the Israeli Knesset that Adolf Eichmann had been seized and was in Israeli custody. The following day I received a telegram from Yad Vashem: 'Warmest congratulations on your brilliant success.'

What then was the real success of the hunting down of Eichmann? It reminded the world of the tragedy of the Jews at the time when it seemed to be being repressed and forgotten. After the Eichmann trial, no one could doubt any longer the extent of the tragedy. It was Eichmann's evidence that destroyed the fairy tale that Auschwitz was just a lie. The Eichmann trial, moreover, substantially enhanced our knowledge of the Nazi murder machinery and its principal operators. Since then the world has been familiar with the concept of the 'murderer at his desk': we now know that fanatical, near-pathological sadism is not necessary for millions of people to be murdered; that all that is needed is dutiful obedience to some 'leader'; that mass murderers need not be – indeed should not be – asocial types; that large-scale murder in fact presupposes a socially integrated murderer.

During the Eichmann trial I was sitting next to an American journalist – I think his name was Golden – when the judge asked the accused if he pleaded guilty. Eichmann answered: 'No.'

'Strictly speaking, the judge should ask him that question six million times,' I said to my neighbour. I later found this phrase repeated in a whole string of American newspapers – because, in shorthand form, it encapsulates the problem of these trials. Unfortunately, it is hardly ever possible to present the murder of millions emotionally in such a way that it will be understood by people as a perfectly specific individual murder committed millions of times.

In Austria – as everywhere in the world – there were at one time prolonged arguments about the purpose of criminal law. The Minister of Justice Christian Broda, to whom I am devoting a later chapter in this

book, took the view that a humane criminal law could aim only at resocialization. On that basis Adolf Eichmann need not have been sentenced.
He was fully integrated into Argentinian society – he was working, he was
living within a well-ordered family framework, and he was a good father
to his children. It was unlikely that he would ever again send Jews to gas
chambers. Why then, Broda was asked in a television discussion, was
Eichmann sentenced, if criminal law aimed solely at resocialization? The
Minister of Justice did not know what to say. If his theory had been
followed, all the Nazi murderers should have been allowed to live on in
their villas in Argentina, Brazil, Uruguay and Paraguay. At most, their
own consciences might in the end have become their prisons. Though I
doubt that this would have happened to Eichmann. Only once during his
trial, on the forty-fifth day of the proceedings, did he utter a sentence
which suggested some inner emotion: 'I must admit that today I regard
the extermination of the Jews as one of the worst crimes in the history of
mankind. But what's done is done, and we must now do everything in our
power to prevent it happening again.' Whether this sentence was meant
sincerely or whether it was suggested to him by his counsel in the hope of
averting a death sentence, I don't know.

Nevertheless one has to be grateful for those words. After all, the
commandant of the Treblinka extermination camp, in a trial in West
Germany, tried to arouse some pity by telling the court that he had been
compelled to gas the Jews because otherwise there wouldn't have been
enough room in the camp. That man was Franz Stangl. The way in which
I found him says something about the 'conscience' of former SS men.

9

What's a Corpse Worth?

Franz Stangl was one of the most prominent Nazi criminals to escape with Odessa's help to South America, where he hoped to start a new life. I first came across his name on a list of decorations presented to senior SS officers. Against his entry was a pencilled note: 'Top secret – for psychological stress'. Translated from Nazi terminology this meant that the commandant of Treblinka received his decoration for special merits in the performance of mass murder.

I would question that his work has caused him any particular 'psychological stess'. When eventually, in May 1970, he was standing trial, he explained to the judge what had really caused him stress: some days he had been sent as many as 18,000 people at a time for extermination, yet it had been his duty to return all the railway wagons empty. He simply had no choice but to kill the people; there just wasn't the room to accommodate them.

This justification is fittingly illustrated by a document which the chief of 'Operation Reinhard', Odilo Globocnik, sent to the Reich Security Directorate. This listed all the items which the administrators of the extermination camps at Treblinka, Sobibor and Belzec had sent back to Berlin between 1 October 1942 and 2 August 1943. I quote:

> 25 goods trucks female hair
> 248 goods trucks articles of clothing
> 100 goods trucks shoes

22 goods trucks underwear
46 goods trucks medicines
254 goods trucks rugs and blankets
400 goods trucks various articles of daily use
2,800,000 US dollars
 400,000 pounds sterling
 12,000,000 Soviet roubles
140,000,000 Polish zloty
 400,000 gold watches
 145,000 kg gold wedding rings
  4,000 carats diamonds, each in excess of 2 carats
120,000,000 zloty in various gold coins
several thousand pearl necklaces

signed
Odilo Globocnik

The Nazis were not just murderers; they were robbers and murderers.

Towards the end of 1943 there were no victims left in the region: Poland was 'cleansed of Jews'. And just as the godfathers of Mafia families get rid of their hit-men when they no longer need them, in order to remove the last witnesses of their atrocities, so the 'godfathers' of the Third Reich decided to rid themselves of their extermination experts. Franz Stangl was sent to the Yugoslav front, where the chances of survival would be slight, as Tito's partisans were not taking any prisoners. The man who, in the Treblinka crematoria, had burnt 800,000 human beings was himself to be 'burnt'. But Stangl was one of the few who returned. Shortly after the end of the war he was back with his children and his wife, a worker in a children's home, in Wels.

He made little effort to hide because this would probably have made him more conspicuous. As a former SS Hauptsturmführer, however, he was soon subject to 'automatic arrest' by the Americans and was taken to the Marcus W. Orr internment camp at Glasenbach near Salzburg. He kept silent about the fact that he had been commandant of Treblinka, and during the two years he spent at Glasenbach this was not discovered. In 1947, however, the situation suddenly turned critical for Stangl: the Austrian authorities had found his name on the staff list of Schloss Hartheim.

Hartheim is an old Renaissance castle, not far from the Mauthausen concentration camp in Upper Austria, and it had been – along with Hadamar near Limburg, Sonnenstein in Saxony, and Schloss Grafenegg in Brandenburg – one of the four 'sanatoria' where the Third Reich developed mass murder. They started with a programme for 'the liquidation of life not worthy of life'; this was under the medical supervision of Dr Werner not worthy of life'; this was under the medical supervision of Dr Werner Heyde, professor of psychiatry at the University of Würzburg. (Heyde, responsible for the death of a least 100,000 people, was arrested in 1962 under the name of Dr Savade and committed suicide.)

When, nowadays, I again hear physicians discussing euthanasia, and when they call it 'mercy killing', horror grips me: an academic degree is unfortunately no guarantee against psychopathic or sadistic behaviour, as was amply proved by the medical staff of Schloss Hartheim. There, too, it was first of all the 'incurably sick', next the mentally disturbed, the mentally retarded, and the very old. Soon anybody with any kind of disability was 'not worthy of life'.

Even then the life-and-death decision was, as it were, regulated by law: the 'T4 experts' had medical records sent to them by hospitals and, on that basis, formed their opinion. A cross at the bottom of the file meant death. A special unit rounded up the patients earmarked for euthanasia and took them to the nearest 'sanatorium'. There they were put to death, initially by the injection of poison.

But that was only the prelude. As the Third Reich made an all-out effort to solve the organizational problem of the murder of the Jews, Heydrich realized that the euthanasia sanatoria represented ideal teaching, training and experimental centres. Hartheim and Hadamar might run pilot experiments for what was subsequently to be applied on an industrial scale at Treblinka and Auschwitz. The laboratory was in the cellar of the schloss and was linked with a small crematorium. It was here that the commandant of Hartheim, Captain Christian Wirth, first had people killed by poison gas. Their death throes were timed with a stopwatch and photographed, and the pictures were sent to Berlin. I later met the person who had been compelled to take those photos. That was how I discovered the story of Hartheim.

In 1941 Captain Wirth was transferred and his successor was a certain Franz Stangl. Although the Austrian authorities did not then have any precise information about the function of Hartheim, Stangl was put on an arrest list and had to move from the American internment camp to the detention prison at the Linz provincial court. In those days the detainees had to help with the clearing of debris and the restoration of bombed buildings. Stangl was assigned to a working party along with men charged only with minor offences; hence supervision was not particularly strict. On the evening of 30 April he failed to return to prison, though nobody noticed that he was missing. When it was noticed, no one was greatly upset. And as no American authority was notified, it was only much later that I learned that Stangl was no longer under lock and key. When I checked out his family I was informed by neighbours that Frau Stangl, along with her daughters, had left Austria for an unknown destination on 6 May 1949.

Subsequently, at his trial, Stangl gave a rough outline of how he escaped. While still at Glasenbach he'd been told that the main thing was to get to Rome. There an ecclesiastical centre would help him. Protestants were to turn to *Praeses* Heinemann: Catholics would find asylum with Bishop Alois Hudal. This information was to prove correct. Hudal obtained a Red Cross passport for Stangl, and the Collegium Germanicum of the German seminary found him a job until the continuation of his journey.

In his memoirs, *Römische Tagebücher* (*Roman Diaries*), published in Graz in 1976, Hudal declared himself happy that he had been able, after 1945, to devote his entire work to former followers of Nazism and Fascism, especially to so-called 'war criminals' and that, by means of false identity papers, he had snatched not a few of them from their tormentors by enabling them to flee to happier lands.

Stangl's 'happier land' was Syria. Six weeks after his escape Stangl was in Damascus and began arranging for his wife and daughters to follow him. Frau Stangl chose the route through Switzerland. In Bern she was given visas for Syria and disappeared.

In the meantime details about the Treblinka extermination camp had become known, and Franz Stangl became one of the most wanted Nazi criminals. Naturally there was not the slightest risk of his being extradited: the Syrians regarded his kind as soulmates and as experts in the struggle against Israel. Had Stangl stayed in Syria, he would no doubt be safe to this day, just like his colleague Alois Brunner. But when Eichmann was seized in Argentina in 1960 the submerged Nazi murderers became jittery. No one believed himself safe where he was. There was the additional worry that no one then knew precisely who had kidnapped Eichmann. As this operation ran counter, formally, to international law, the Israeli government took the line that they had nothing to do with it. Thus, when shortly after the seizure of Eichmann I was invited by Yad Vashem to talk about my part in tracking him down, I was earnestly instructed by the director of Yad Vashem, Dr Kubovy, not to mention on any account that my whole correspondence had gone through the Israeli embassy or that Israeli intelligence had played a part. I faithfully obeyed, and never mentioned Israeli intelligence by as much as a single word. This evidently so angered the head of the Israeli secret service, Isser Harel, that when he published his memoirs in 1971 he likewise made no mention of my work.

But I am digressing. Then, in the spring of 1960, the mystery surrounding the capture of Eichmann gave rise to all kinds of speculation in the international press – including one suggestion in a German magazine, that Eichmann had been brought to Israel by pro-Israeli members of the Muslim Druze tribe, who lived close to the Israeli frontier. The story was an invention from beginning to end, but it was probably enough to alarm Stangl. At any rate, I learned from a German journalist that he had left Damascus rather precipitately. I fished his card out of my card index and replaced 'Damascus' by 'whereabouts unknown'.

In December 1956 I gave a press conference in Vienna about the murder schools of Hartheim, Hadamar, Sonnenstein and Grafenegg. I told the journalists about the link between these euthanasia institutions and mass extermination in the concentration camps: the staff who had learned to live with the stench of cremated corpses at those institutions were, almost without exception, promoted to leading posts in the extermination camps. As an instance of such a career I mentioned Franz Stangl.

A month later an evil-looking, unkempt type called on me at my office; he didn't manage to look me in the eye even for an instant during our conversation. Now and again a lucky fate really makes people look what they are: my caller informed me that he'd been a member of the Gestapo. Of course he hadn't done 'anything bad' – that was the normal form for Gestapo members. 'Anyway, what could I have done? I'm one of the little ones who get the stick for everything.'

I had it on the tip of my tongue to retort that, in reality, I had been one of the little ones who'd got the stick – but as the man evidently wanted to tell me something, and as he might know something, I restrained myself.

'I read the story in the newspaper. About Franz Stangl. Because of people like him the likes of us have been getting nothing but trouble since the end of the war. Time and again I'd get a job, then after a while they'd find out about what I did, and I'd be back on the street.'

'I thought you hadn't done anything bad?'

There was a brief flash of anger in the man's eyes, but then the erstwhile tormentor recovered his obsequiousness. 'The fat cats, the Stangls and the Eichmanns, they got all the backing they needed. They were smuggled out, they got money and papers. But who'll help me? Look at my shirt, my suit. No work, no money. Can't even afford a drop of wine.'

That last statement, at least, was a lie: my visitor's breath revealed that he had enough for frequent drops of schnapps.

'Look here,' he said when I stayed silent. 'I know where Stangl is. I could help you find him. Stangl never helped me. Why should I cover up for him?' And after a short pause, during which he was watching me out of the corner of his eye, he added: 'But it will cost you something.'

I had felt from the start that this conversation would lead to money. 'How much?' I asked, remembering the man who had proposed to help me track down Adolf Eichmann if I helped him find the gold prised from the teeth of my murdered brethren.

'Twenty-five thousand dollars.'

'You might as well ask for two million. I don't have that kind of money.'

But the man was ready to bargain: 'All right, I'll make you a special price. How many Jews did Stangl do in?'

'We'll never know exactly how many people lost their lives during the time that he was commandant of Treblinka. It could have been 700,000.'

For a moment he did some calculations in his head, and his eyes, though he kept them open, were so 'closed' that my glance slid off them. Then suddenly they lit up, like the lights on some cash registers just before the bell tinkles: 'I want one cent for every dead person. Seven hundred thousand cents ... that's seven thousand dollars ... a steal of a price.'

I pressed my hands against my desk top so as not to strike him in the face, and I tried to close my eyes the way he had done a moment earlier. I didn't wish to see his features. Slowly, very slowly, I managed to regain control of myself. The commandant of Treblinka, the murderer of 700,000 Jews, was more important than this filthy man, who was now standing before me expectantly, no doubt considering whom to turn to if I declined his offer.

'You don't get a penny from me today,' I said, 'but if Stangl is arrested on the strength of your information you shall have the money.'

'What guarantee have I got that this agreement will be kept?'

'You have no guarantee, but if you don't like it get the hell out of here!'

'All right. No need to get heated. I'll tell you exactly where Stangl works. But I don't know what he calls himself today. Does our deal still stand?'

'Yes. Go ahead.'

'Not till I get an undertaking from you.'

I took out a visiting card and wrote on the back: 'I shall pay the bearer of this card the sum of seven thousand dollars if, on the strength of the information given me, Franz Stangl is arrested in Brazil.'

My visitor put the card in his wallet but was still not satisfied. He now wanted a promise, on my honour, that I would not try to find out who he was.

Franz Stangl was worth such a promise.

After these preliminaries my visitor finally produced his information: 'Stangl is working as a mechanic at the Volkswagen plant in São Paulo in Brazil.'

The information proved to be correct. It only took me a few weeks to get hold of Stangl's address. The warrant of arrest from the Linz provincial court was still valid, and Austria demanded his extradition.

For some reason or other the Brazilian police didn't want to arrest Franz Stangl until after the Carnival, but they put his house under surveillance from mid-February 1967. Two plain-clothes men, pretending to be cable layers, began to excavate trenches opposite his front door. Because it was a hot job they knocked at his door and asked for a glass of water. They used this opportunity to find out whether Stangl had any weapons at his place. That, in their mind, was part of the picture of a mass murderer. What they found instead was the home of a solid citizen with crocheted runners on the sideboard and a crucifix in the corner. They reported to their superior that Stangl would not offer armed resistance.

On 27 February the police chief of São Paulo called at the Austrian embassy in the capital to inspect the documents, now translated into Portuguese, on whose grounds Austria was demanding Stangl's arrest and extradition. Each sheet of paper represented thousands of murders.

The police chief returned to São Paulo the same day, and on the very next morning the police – without orders from above, for which they were subsequently criticized – moved in. Three police officers accompanied by a photographer went to a hospital in São Paulo, identified themselves, and requested a sister to phone the Volkswagen plant with a message for Herr Stangl that his daughter had had a road accident and was in hospital. He should come round at once.

The management of the Volkswagen plant had the message announced over the loudspeaker, and half an hour later Stangl was outside the hospital. The photographer caught his arrest in a picture that made the rounds of the world's press.

I only learned all these details later. At the time I was on my way to the USA when, during a stopover in Amsterdam, I caught Stangl's name mentioned on the radio. The news of his arrest, however, was followed by an alarming piece of information: the governor of São Paulo had reproved his police chief for failing to inform him. In any case, I would have been greatly surprised to hear that a Nazi criminal was arrested so smoothly in a South American country, and Stangl wouldn't have been the first one to buy his freedom back. Brazil had never yet extradited a Nazi criminal, and I realized that it would require the greatest public pressure to carry it off.

While still in Amsterdam I contacted my friends in many different countries and asked them to organize demonstrations by camp survivors in front of Brazilian embassies. With the Minister of Justice for North Rhine–Westphalia I discussed an additional extradition request by West Germany, and from the Poles I asked for the same request to be made by the Committee for the Investigation of Nazi Crimes. One couldn't have too many extradition demands in South America.

But it was undoubtedly the United States which could apply the greatest pressure. No sooner had I arrived in New York than I requested an audience with the former Attorney-General, Senator Robert Kennedy, and asked for his intervention. In my presence Kennedy telephoned the Brazilian ambassador to Washington and positively told him what might have been put less pleasantly: 'What's at stake is justice for enormous crimes. Brazil now has an opportunity to gain millions of friends.'

To be on the safe side, the Brazilian government decided to seize that opportunity. Under the pressure of public opinion and after countless interpellations it agreed in 1967 to West Germany's demand for extradition.

After my return to Vienna I had a call from a German notary, who had my visiting card. My friend Hermann Katz in New York, whom I had previously informed about my strange deal, transferred the seven thousand dollars.

On 13 May 1970 the long-awaited trial opened in Düsseldorf. Stangl defended himself in the way he considered truthful and correct: 'I only did my duty.' On 22 December 1970 the court passed sentence: life imprisonment. For Stangl it did not last long: he died in prison on 28 June 1971.

A short while afterwards his former best friend Gustav Wagner was to call on Stangl's widow in São Paulo and ask her to marry him. That was one of those little mistakes that made it easier for me to trace Gustav Wagner.

10

The Marriage Proposal

It happened some time in May 1978. I was on a plane between New York and Amsterdam, listlessly turning the pages of the *New York Daily News*, when a small story in it caught my eye. On 20 April, it said, a party of old Nazis at the Hotel Tyll in Italiata, São Paulo province, had celebrated the eighty-ninth anniversary of the birth of their Führer Adolf Hitler.

I tried to picture this festivity. What old Nazi would be living in Brazil without a good reason? Eleven years earlier I had succeeded in tracking down Franz Stangl, the commandant of Treblinka, in São Paulo. Was it not likely that his best friend, Gustav Wagner, was also in Brazil?

Wagner had been Stangl's right-hand man when Stangl was in command of Sobibor extermination camp and had subsequently served Stangl's successor, Kurt Franz, as deputy camp commandant. According to the stories of survivors he had been one of the most brutal sadists in that Eldorado of brutality. His enormous physical strength had made it possible for him to kill an emaciated prisoner by simply striking him in the pit of his stomach or flinging him to the ground.

We had a number of tip-offs to the effect that Wagner was in Brazil – I even possessed a copy of a Brazilian identity card – but all the official agencies declared themselves unable to find him. Now he was emerging before my mind's eye, raising his glass to his old comrades on Hitler's birthday, talking to them about the great times they'd had together, and, while they compared how many dead Jews each of them could boast of, proudly declaring: 'But I did it with my own hands – and that's more beautiful still.'

I was convinced that Wagner must have been one of those attending the curious party. Maybe some newspaper or other had taken a photograph of it – that might help me track him down.

Once before, in 1967, I had possessed a very precise idea of his where-abouts. But surveillance of someone in South America required money, and our resources were totally exhausted by the costly search for Franz Stangl. Friends who wanted to help introduced me to a Jewish millionaire who had himself been in a concentration camp and whom I might ask for money. I found the whole business rather embarrassing: I talked about every possible subject except money, until my friend kicked me under the table and I summoned up my courage. It was a matter of tracking down one of the worst concentration-camp henchmen, I said; he was living in South America and a search there was expensive. The millionaire was understanding: he pressed a cheque into my hand – for fifty dollars.

'If I could get Gustav Wagner arrested for fifty dollars I wouldn't have to come to you,' I said, rose, and made for the door. The American got up, ran after me, and spent a quarter of an hour explaining to me how many millions he'd been losing lately.

'If you are so poor I'll give you a hundred dollars,' I said, stepped into the lift and rode up to my floor. If Gustav Wagner had many enemies like this survivor then he didn't need friends.

And yet, Wagner was a man who usually aroused greater emotions than the so-called 'desk-bound murderers', whose murders always seemed like mere adding of columns of figures, even if the sum total below the line represented corpses. Wagner was a murderer as one imagines a murderer. Looking like a picture-book SS man, with huge shoulders and enormous hands, he had been assigned to Schloss Hartheim near Linz as early as 1939, to work in the 'euthanasia programme'.

Wagner had been employed as a cremator of corpses. It was in this role that he made the acquaintance of his colleague and the future commandant of Hartheim, Franz Stangl. The two became friends and remained together when, in the spring of 1942, they were called to higher things: they were to apply their Hartheim experience within the framework of 'Operation Reinhard'. Stangl became camp commandant of Sobibor; Wagner, as his top sergeant, was in charge of all 'accommodation' and later also of the gas chambers. Because of his rough manner he was regarded as particularly suited to handling the so-called 'working Jews', who had been selected from the transports so they could put their skills to the service of the SS. On the one hand this was useful and pleasant, but on the other it always irritated men like Wagner: a 'working Jew' could not simply be killed; one had to wait for him to fall ill or become weak. It was therefore necessary to remind those Jewish swine that they were alive only because of their usefulness and for a limited period, and that this changed nothing about their fundamental worthlessness. This was best achieved by beating the Jewish swine, preferably not with one's hands but by kicking them with one's feet. Even though they would sooner or later be killed anyway, no opportunity was missed for humiliating those living dead with words. Thus Dov Freiber, a witness in the Eichmann trial, recounted how the working Jews always had to march to work with a song on their lips. Twenty years later he still knew the text by heart:

> O Lord, send Moses back again
> so he may lead his Jewish clan
> away into the Promised Land.
> Command the waters to divide
> so that the piled-up waves may stand
> like rocky cliffs on either side.
> And when the Jewish pack is striding
> between the waters still dividing,
> then, Lord, command the trap to close,
> and all the world will have repose.

As the divided waters failed to do their job, Wagner took it upon himself, in as much as his power allowed. Each gas chamber had a capacity of one hundred Jews, and together with Stangl he saw to it that charging proceeded quickly and without incident. If incidents did occur nevertheless, Wagner made sure they did not diminish the daily quota of corpses: anyone breaking ranks, resisting or collapsing was killed by Wagner with his own hands. This continued unchanged even when, in the summer of 1942, Stangl was appointed commandant of the Treblinka concentration camp, where he would be able to apply his Sobibor experience on an even greater scale.

However, Stangl's successor did not have such a firm grip on Sobibor: in October 1943 there was a rebellion of 'working Jews' who realized that soon they wouldn't be needed any more and that their closed season was coming to an end. They attacked the guards, killed some of them – the deputy camp commandant Josef Niemann was also killed – and escaped into the woods. The SS immediately started a search for the escapers and actually caught some of them; they were, however, unable to prevent a few of them from regaining their freedom for good, among them a Jewish officer from the Soviet Union, who had been transferred from a POW camp to Sobibor and who had organized the uprising.

His testimony was one of the most important items of evidence against Wagner.

Shortly afterwards the camp was disbanded. The remaining inmates were shot. The German camp staff were sent to Italy, where Wagner once more met up with his friend Stangl. Together they joined a larger group which consisted entirely of men like themselves. This was no accident: Odilo Globocnik, who had meanwhile been appointed SS police chief of Trieste, did not want the men who had served him loyally for so long to fall into Allied hands and possibly confess their deeds. That was why, whenever possible, he sent men 'in possession of secrets' to a front where as a rule no prisoners were taken – to Yugoslavia, where the partisans were increasingly decimating the German army.

In this way a number of the worst murderers of Jews were in fact sent to their deaths by their own boss: Christian Wirth, inspector of the extermination camps of Treblinka, Sobibor and Belzec, was shot by the partisans, as was the commandant of Sobibor, Franz Reichleitner. Wagner and Stangl, on the other hand, were lucky. They were re-employed in a familiar sphere: on the island of Arbe near Fiume (now Rijeka) and in Abazia (now Opatija) they were to track down, assemble and take to the Sušak camp all the Jews still living there. A few were put to death while still at the Sušak camp, the rest somewhat later at the extermination camp of Riseria di San Sabba. (At that camp, incidentally, there was yet another Austrian serving: Ernst Leich, likewise detailed there by 'Operation Reinhard'. However, owing to the minimal interest shown by the Austrian judiciary, his role at Risiera has never been clarified.)

At the end of the war the Germans blew up Risiera in order to obliterate all traces of it. Wagner and Stangl fled to Austria and from then always followed the same path. Both were interned at Glasenbach and transferred to prison in Linz. Together they escaped while engaged on building work, and made their way to Bishop Hudal in Rome. Together, by way of Beirut and Damascus, they eventually got to Brazil.

Years later, when I was looking for Stangl and retraced his escape route, we received, from one of our sources, a copy of Gustav Wagner's Red Cross passport, and therefore knew what he looked like at the end of the war. Besides, his trail was not completely cold in Brazil. I was told that he travelled from one German settlement to another, without, however, stopping at any of them for any length of time. Nor was the frontier to Paraguay difficult to cross if one could produce Brazilian papers. Nevertheless, all our efforts to establish the exact whereabouts of Wagner were in vain. The police were not very cooperative: their typical reply was that they couldn't find Wagner.

The search for Stangl then rather overshadowed the search for Wagner.

But two years after Stangl's death I made the acquaintance of a married couple who had encountered Frau Stangl in São Paulo. Outraged, she related a strange encounter to them: one day, Frau Stangl told them, Gustav Wagner had appeared on her doorstep, in rags and totally dishevelled. He had expressed his condolences at her husband's death – and immediately afterwards made her a proposal of marriage. Of course she had angrily rejected him and shown him the door. Apparently Stangl had not even fully initiated his wife into the circumstances of his former life, because she made derogatory remarks to the Austrian couple not only about Wagner as a person but also about his work. 'My husband was a decent, proper man who did his duty,' she said about the work of the commandant of Treblinka; 'he never laid hands on an inmate, at most he had to shout at one of them now and again. But that Wagner was notorious and feared as a sadist. And he has the nerve to come to me and ask me to marry him.'

This odd conversation took place in the latter half of 1975. It proved to me that Wagner continued to live in Brazil, presumably in the vicinity of São Paulo, and it seemed inconceivable to me that a man like him would not have attended the Hitler celebration at the Hotel Tyll. Wagner loved parties where he could cut a fine figure and brag. He told his friends over and over again that he had taken part in the 1936 Berlin Olympics as a javelin thrower – though we have been unable to find his name in any of the reports on the games or in the Olympic register. All we knew was that he had tested his strength on emaciated, helpless prisoners, until the half-dead were dead. The Hotel Tyll event would be an opportunity for bragging.

Somehow, I thought, I must get more detailed information on that party. Chance came to my aid: on a visit to Israel I made the acquaintance of a Brazilian journalist, Mario Chimanovich, of *Jornal do Brasil*.

'Would the paper you work for have photos of that meeting at the Tyll?' I asked him.

He was fairly optimistic: the celebrations had gone on for three days and a whole string of reporters had covered them. He'd get me all the available material.

Only a few days after my return to Vienna he phoned me: he possessed not only a huge photograph showing all the guests clearly, but also an invitation complete with guest list.

I asked Mario to take the next plane for Vienna.

Feverishly I scanned the guest list – no Gustav Wagner. He might still be one of the men in the photograph – he could be using a false name. I studied the photo with a magnifying glass: no Gustav Wagner. Only one old acquaintance by the name of Manfred Roeder, a lawyer by profession and head of a neo-Nazi citizens' movement in West Germany, whom I knew of through a number of trials. (At present Roeder is in prison in Stuttgart, having been sentenced on 18 June 1982 to thirteen years' imprisonment as responsible for arson and explosive attacks which had cost two lives. In that respect he disproved the slogan under which the Hotel Tyll meeting, according to the invitations, had taken place: 'We are not the last of yesterday, we are the first of tomorrow.')

In spite of this 'find' my disappointment was boundless. I had so confidently expected Wagner to be among the guests that I regarded it as a kind of impermissible deviation of history from its predetermined course that he obviously had not been present at the Tyll. But it was just this irritation that gave me an idea: I would myself correct fate. I wasn't sure whether what I was intending was a hundred per cent kosher, whether it was quite legal. But the murder of 150,000 Jews at Sobibor and the attitude of the Brazilian authorities justified my actions to my own conscience.

'Are you prepared to help me?' I asked Mario.

'If I can.'

So as not to place the journalist in too difficult a position I didn't tell him that I was about to give him a deliberately false piece of information. From the men in the photograph I had simply picked one who had caught my eye by his enormous projecting ears. I now told Mario: 'This one is Gustav Wagner. He's showing himself quite publicly in Brazil at a celebration of Hitler's birthday and nobody is taking the slightest notice. If you write your story like this the police will now have no excuse unless they want to be the laughingstock of the world: they will have to produce Wagner. Because they know perfectly well where to find him.'

Mario cooperated: the news that I had identified the deputy commandant of Sobibor in a photograph of the Hotel Tyll festivities on Hitler's birthday appeared on the front page of *Jornol do Brasil*.

It was taken up by the radio and disseminated throughout the country. The police had no hope of remaining inactive, even though the man I had described as Wagner vigorously, and rightly, protested that it was all a mistake. Somehow they had to find Gustav Wagner.

He saved the police their work. Evidently worn down by constant flight and weary of hiding, confronted in every newspaper with a genuine 'wanted' photograph from his Red Cross Passport and his Brazilian identity card, he surrendered to the authorities.

He saw his last chance in denial: he did not deny that he had served at Sobibor, but, according to his statement, he had been concerned solely with the construction of huts, and, secondly, not a single Jew had lost his life there. But the media wouldn't let go of Wagner. In the town of Gojana, 550 miles from São Paulo, Stanislaw Szmajzner read about Wagner's arrest in the paper and from the reproduced photograph recognized one of his tormentors. Szmajzner was one of the few survivors from that camp, where he'd been sent as a boy of fourteen and where, because of his particular craftsman's skills, he had escaped the gas chamber for eighteen months. He immediately travelled to São Paulo to make himself available to the authorities as a witness. And now the two men, who had last faced each other in the camp, were facing each other at the police station.

'How are you, Gustl?' Szmajzner asked.

For a moment Wagner regarded him with bafflement, then he recognized him: 'Yes, yes, I remember you well. Surely I picked you out of the transport and saved your life.'

'That's correct,' said Szmajzner, 'but you didn't save the lives of my sister, my brothers, my mother and my father. And if you're saying that you saved my life, then you also knew that the others had to die.'

Wagner made no answer. To the authorities it was proven at least that his statement that no one had been put to death at Sobibor could not be quite correct, and that he had been in a position to decide on an inmate's life or death. The man who had opted for life in Brazil was detained pending extradition.

Meanwhile it was exceedingly unclear what country he was to be extradited to. In Austria he had been involved in the euthanasia programme; most of his crimes had been committed in Poland; he had worn a German uniform; and his victims had mainly been Jews. As a first step I notified the Israeli Minister of Justice Tamir, and Israel applied for extradition within twenty-four hours. However, they had no hope of success. In Austria there were two valid warrants of arrest out against Wagner, for his activities both at Hartheim and at Sobibor, but experience taught that the Austrians took their time about extradition applications. Although Poland filed an application for extradition, her chances were slight because in Poland Wagner would receive the death sentence, which was more than he'd get under Brazilian law (in such cases extradition is as a rule refused). Only the Düsseldorf public prosecutor's office had both well-founded evidence and a well-founded legal claim to put him on trial.

That's what we thought. In June 1979 the Supreme Federal Court of Brazil ruled that none of the extradition applications was to be met. The reason was that in the translation of the German application into Portuguese a typing mistake had crept in. Whereas the Germans had stated that limitation had been suspended as early as '1947', the Portuguese translation said '1974'. In that case murder, under Brazilian law, could no longer be prosecuted. Wagner was discharged.

The German embassy in Brazil discovered the error and immediately approached the Supreme Court to demand a revision. But there they were told to await the decision in writing. By the time it arrived at the embassy several months had elapsed and Wagner could no longer be found. The Brazilians definitively refused to extradite him.

To the Jews this refusal, coming as it did simultaneously with Brazilian recognition of the PLO, did not create a friendly impression. But Gustav Wagner once again spared the authorities work: even while in detention he had suffered severe heart attacks and had attempted suicide a few times. When eventually he left prison as a free man, after a lengthy hospital treatment, he was no longer able to profit from his freedom. For months the Brazilian papers had reported on his reign of terror at Sobibor and carried excerpts from witnesses' statements – whatever doors he knocked at, were, even in German circles, shut in his face. At the beginning of October he hanged himself at a remote farm.

I asked myself whether, in those few seconds before death, he was visited by the ghosts of the hundreds of thousands whom he had on his conscience, whether the heavy burden of guilt had crushed him. Or whether he was merely weary of being chased, of having to hide out. Like Eduard Roschmann, whom I would probably never have caught, yet who died the worst death of all: the death of a man fleeing from himself.

11

Flight from Oneself

I hadn't heard his name before but he told me he was a well-known author and several of his books had already been made into films. By way of confirmation he handed me a letter of introduction from Fred Zinnemann, the director, who told me the same thing: Mr Frederick Forsyth was a gifted writer, and would I please give him my support.

'How can I help you?' I asked.

It turned out that Forsyth knew more about me than I did about him. 'I have read your book *The Murderers Among Us*,' he said. 'You have a chapter there about the Odessa escape organization. That would make a first-rate story for a film.'

'And what do you want me to do?'

'You must supply me with the historical background. Even in a thriller everything's got to be correct. It should be so it could really have happened like that.'

I reflected for a while. I had of course repeatedly helped with book projects, but those had been serious documentaries. If I now got involved with a Nazi thriller for the entertainment industry I might wreck a lot of things. 'I am afraid I can't help you with that,' I said regretfully.

But Forsyth was not to be put off: 'I'll leave you the synopsis of my book. Read it. Perhaps you'll give me a chance after all.'

'Very well,' I said, and we agreed to meet again the next day.

In the evening I read Forsyth's story of an escaping German war criminal – and an idea occurred to me, an idea connected with one of my oldest cases, that of Eduard Roschmann. The first piece of information on him was dated 8 December 1946 and contained his personal data and a short biography: born in Graz on 25 November 1908, Roschmann had been a liquor salesman before the war, and later an employee in a Styrian brewery and distillery. He had a bad reputation, and was even then close to the Nazis. During the Third Reich his career took off: he became the second-in-command of the Riga ghetto. In this post he was responsible for the murder of at least 3800 Jews, including 800 children under the age of ten. In addition he arranged for the deportation of an indefinite number of Jews to the Auschwitz extermination camp. According to more recent testimony, dating from 1960, the total of his victims was even higher. Roschmann is held responsible for the murder of 2000 Jews who could not work, and for the organization of the notorious deportations from Dunamünde (now Daugavpils) in Latvia. If one adds the number of known deaths to the minimum number of estimated deaths, he had some 35,000 human beings on his conscience.

As with many Nazi criminals, the rumour spread shortly after the war that Roschmann had been discovered and killed, but this could not be verified. In 1947 he appeared, very much alive, at his family's place in Graz and was actually arrested. Not, however, for his crimes in Riga, but because of his membership of a neo-Nazi organization: he was a friend of Theodor Soucek and his European Social Order Movement, SORBE. And when a whole group of Soucek's old and new comrades in Graz and district were arrested, Eduard Roschmann was one of them.

At that time I was working fairly closely with the Austrian police and therefore not only learned of his arrest but was able to take some action. I informed the Americans that by mere chance the second-in-command of Riga had been nabbed, and that they had better look after him before the Austrians, as they might quite possibly do, released him again. This they did: they notified the British, in whose zone of occupation Graz was, and asked for Roschmann to be 'delivered' to them.

At first Roschmann didn't worry too much about his arrest. He believed that he was suspected 'only' of neo-Nazi activities and, anyway, he was just one of two hundred detainees. Only when a sergeant and a private of the British army stood before him one morning, in order to take him to Dachau, did he realize the danger of the situation. The sentences passed by the American military tribunal at the former concentration camp had become common knowledge among Austrian Nazi circles for their particular severity.

He was being taken by rail, and on the journey from Graz to Salzburg Roschmann had ample time to reflect on his future. When the train stopped at Hallein he asked to be allowed to go to the toilet – which should have aroused his escort's suspicion since the use of toilets is forbidden while a train is at a station. But Roschmann's British guard merely posted himself outside the door. Roschmann got out through the window on the far side from the platform and escaped into the winter night.

Although the British soldier broke down the toilet door a few minutes later and halted the train by pulling the communication cord, the train by then had travelled a few miles and a search for Roschmann's tracks in the newly fallen snow proved in vain. Roschmann subsequently related that he had lain still in the snow, in the same spot, all through the night, so as not to give himself away. Not until the next morning did he seek out a comrade, who helped him on his way. The newspapers did not report Roschmann's escape because the British didn't want to look foolish. I only learned about it when I inquired from Dachau how preparations for his trial were going. By then all hope of catching him while he was still escaping had gone.

Years later I learned that he had made his way from Hallein to a staging post for Nazi fugitives at Ostermiething on the border between Upper Austria and the province of Salzburg. By means of passwords, which the old comrades passed on to one another, he had identified himself and was kept hidden in a brickworks for a couple of weeks, until the next transport infiltrated him across the frontier into Italy. There, like nearly all his friends, he found asylum at the Franciscan monastery on Via Sicilia, enjoying the protection of Bishop Hudal. The Roman Caritas organized and paid for his emigration to Argentina, where he settled in the Villa de Mayo in Buenos Aires.

Roschmann had chosen Argentina because some relations of his wife's (a family called Vidmer) were living there, from whom he expected help. Like all Hudal fugitives, Roschmann possessed false papers: he now called himself Fritz or Frederico Wegener and under that name was employed first in the Aeros travel agency and then, together with a certain Stemmler, he managed a joinery. In 1955 he went through a ceremony of marriage with his secretary Irmtraud Schubert, although he had a wife and children back in Graz. His legal wife in Austria heard of this, by way of the Vidmer family, and notified the authorities. Thus it came about that Eduard Roschmann, alias Fritz Wegener, had a warrant of arrest on a charge of bigamy issued against him in 1959. A warrant of arrest on account of his activities in Riga was not issued until a year later.

Although time and again we received snippets of information on Roschmann, and although we knew his false name, his trail was lost. In 1958 Irmtraud Schubert left him and returned to Germany, where her marriage was declared null and void by a Hamburg court. Roschmann himself, it was said, had moved to Brazil. All efforts to track down the murderer of 35,000 Jews remained fruitless for many years.

This then, was the situation when, in the summer of 1972, Frederick Forsyth turned up at my office and confronted me with his Odessa project. The principal character of the book, and subsequently of the film, was to be a fictitious criminal by the name of Bergmann, who, hunted by me, would try to escape with the help of Odessa. The story was well written, realistic and full of suspense. It protrayed Bergmann as a hunted man who could never remain anywhere for more than a few days before resuming his flight. This gave me an idea.

'I am prepared to help you', I said to Forsyth, 'provided you give Bergmann the features of a genuine Nazi criminal. A man who actually exists, who actually got away with the help of Odessa and who now lives under a false name somewhere in South America. Of course there will be people who will accuse me of debasing myself to the level of a thriller, but I don't care if we can catch the man as a result.'

'Mr Wiesenthal, you have just written the preface to my book,' said Forsyth.

Then we both immersed ourselves in the Roschmann file.

As I had no personal knowledge of conditions in Riga or the Kaiserwald camp, I arranged for Forsyth to meet the Viennese antique dealer Fritz Deutsch, who had been deported from Vienna to Riga and had survived. He supplied the details for the book whose title had already been decided on: *The Odessa File*.

Forsyth remained in touch with me, and we discussed the individual chapters. This enabled me to plant a further time-bomb. I asked him to insert a scene which would make Roschmann lose the sympathies of his former comrades. Forsyth had his fugitive shoot dead a German officer in order to grab his place on an evacuation ship during the German retreat.

Only as far as the 'happy ending' was concerned, I was unlucky. My idea was that Bergmann should make good his escape, just as Roschmann had, because I wanted the public to go on looking for him. In the film of *The Odessa File*, however, he is caught and shot. It wasn't possible, the filmmakers told me, to present an evil criminal to the audience for two hours and then allow him to get away: people leaving the cinema must have the satisfaction that justice has prevailed in the end. I could see their point: this is the difference between life and the cinema.

It was even suggested to me that I should – for a great deal of money – play the part of myself, but I didn't want to get involved to that extent with the entertainment industry. So my part was played by the Israeli actor Schmuel Rodensky. He had to have pounds and pounds of make-up stuck on his face, and even then he still didn't look like me. As Rodensky is also a lot shorter than I am he was almost invariably shown sitting behind a desk. That desk didn't look like mine either: there was a cleared space on it for writing.

Both book and film were extraordinarily successful. *The Odessa File* was translated into seventeen languages, and the film, which premiered in New York in October 1974, was shown all over the world. And my own calculation, in some respects, turned out to be more than right: although the criminal was shot in the film, we received countless tip-offs from viewers who claimed to have recognized Roschmann somewhere or other. An American couple had spotted him at a restaurant in Santa Cruz in Bolivia, in a fairly large company of Germans. The Americans succeeded in waiting for the party to disperse, in sitting down at his table with him and offering him a glass of champagne. That glass, carefully packed, was sent to my office. 'Roschmann is alive,' the enclosed letter concluded; 'you will find his fingerprints on the glass.'

This would in fact have enabled us to identify Roschmann, as his fingerprints had been taken when he was arrested in Graz. There was just one snag about that tip-off: the man whom the American couple had identified didn't look like Eduard Roschmann but like Maximilian Schell, the actor in *The Odessa File*. As this person he was also discovered several dozen times in Germany, Austria and Switzerland. I consider it extremely lucky that no one actually tried to detain Maximilian Schell.

By then I thought that, despite all my hopes, my plan had misfired – when it suddenly produced results in a different unexpected way. It left its mark on Roschmann's old comrades in South America, and presumably on Roschmann himself. I heard about this from a German actor who, with a touring company, had been performing in the German colonies and settlements in Latin America. These performances were put on by cultural associations in West Germany by way of support for Germans abroad, and the actors were frequently accommodated in the homes of German families. This had given the company an opportunity to assess the climate of opinion then prevailing: in many homes there were pictures of Hitler, Himmler and other prominent Nazis hanging on the walls, and fugitive Nazi murderers were talked about as persecuted figures. Oddly enough these views were encountered not only among Nazis who had fled there after the war but also among pre-war German immigrants. In their minds they had idealized their German homeland and equipped it with all conceivable virtues – whatever else happened in the Third Reich they just brushed aside. 'It is unthinkable that a German would bring himself to kill women or children,' one of those elderly Germans once remarked to Hans (as I will call my actor friend); 'such a thing might happen among savages, like the ones living in the jungle here, but not in a cultured nation like ours.'

The argument that surely there had been countless trials of such crimes was dismissed with the observation that it was the victors who had sat in judgement. Newspaper reports, books and judgements would have been very different if the Germans had won the war. In a corner of the world where the worst Third Reich murderers were gathered, many Germans regarded the murder of millions of Jews as a wicked Allied – or Jewish – invention. This explains why so many fugitive Nazi criminals have found support and shelter with their – often perfectly decent – fellow countrymen. I once called Argentina the 'Cape of Last Hope', and this is just what it was: Nazi criminals could expect to find their final refuge there, and the German settlers desperately clung to the hope that the Nazis had not been criminals.

In that kind of atmosphere the charge of *The Odessa File* that Roschmann, in order to gain a place in an evacuation boat, had shot a German officer was a serious matter. 'That man's a swine,' my friend Hans was repeatedly told in German circles there, 'one can understand that he had to flee, but surely one wouldn't do that at the expense of another man.' For the women Roschmann was altogether done for: that he had been commandant of the Riga ghetto they would have forgiven, but his bigamy was evidence of a bad character. It may be assumed that Roschmann was being increasingly ostracized by his former comrades. We know for certain that, from the moment 'his' film started showing in South America and 'his' book appeared in the bookshops, he continually changed his place of residence and never stayed anywhere for more than a few weeks.

Even though Maximilian Schell does not resemble him in any way, Roschmann knew from the posters that he himself was the man. The newspaper reports which discussed the film actually discussed him. And the people who poured out of the cinemas remembered him, his escape and his crimes. What he didn't know, however, was that the tip-offs they gave us were all wrong. If anyone looked at him for more than a moment, if anyone stared at him in a restaurant, if anyone asked him to wait a moment in a shop, he was bound to fear that they were notifying the police. Any of his German friends could turn Judas at any time in order to avenge the 'murder' of a German officer. Roschmann became the hunted man portrayed in the film.

In the summer of 1977 the Argentinian police received a precise tip-off and on 1 July Roschmann was arrested at his hiding place. The German embassy immediately passed on the news to the German justice department who, a mere three days later, demanded his extradition. For the first time in relations between the two countries the Argentinians agreed to an extradition request – in the past they had always pointed out that no relevant agreement between the two countries existed. All they demanded was that the entire file be translated into Spanish and submitted within sixty days.

The news was carried in the press and abruptly changed the climate among German circles in the country: suddenly there was the fear that, if Roschmann was to be handed over so readily, others might be extradited too. But 'German circles' have some influence in Argentina: on 5 July 1977 the prison gates once more opened for Roschmann. He was discharged on condition that he never showed himself in Argentina again. The press was informed that the person detained had not been Roschmann after all, and the government issued a statement that it had by no means assured the German authorities that Roschmann would be extradited. There had merely been an assurance that the application would be studied. 'German circles' once more felt reassured.

Only Eduard Roschmann remained unreassured. On that very day he went to the bus terminal and bought a ticket to Paraguay, where, after nineteen hours, he arrived at the bus terminal in Asunción. All he carried was a small suitcase with his most important personal belongings, and in his wallet he had his Argentinian papers in the name of Frederico Wegener, which had been returned to him when he was discharged.

I have credible information from the police in Paraguay that Roschmann did not feel safe there either, not for a second. He was staying at a modest pension belonging to the De Rios family on Hurba street; he always paid his rent ten days in advance, and received neither letters nor callers. His landlords described him as insecure, nervous and introverted. He would often spend days on end in his room, reading, and had no contact with the other residents of the pension.

After only two weeks, on 25 July, he went into cardiovascular shock. Señora De Rios and her son took him to the university hospital, where he claimed to be Ramón Nahrea, from Uruguay. No sooner did he feel a little better than he left the hospital, returned to the pension on Hurba street and paid his outstanding rent. Evidently he intended to move elsewhere. But he was overtaken by another heart attack: he had to be readmitted to hospital and there he died of cardiac failure during the night of 10 August.

A Jew who during the war was in Riga and now lives in Asunción, identified Ramón Nehrea, alias Frederico Wegner, as Eduard Roschmann. Unknown men threw a bomb at his house.

A week later two Paraguayan journalists brought me the dead man's fingerprints and a photo. The picture shows a man hunted even in death, and the fingerprints were identical with those of Eduard Roschmann when he was arrested in Graz on 31 December 1947. Any error was ruled out.

There have, unfortunately, been quite a number of cases where such ambiguous identification has not been possible. The most important is that of Dr Josef Mengele. On the strength of my most recent information I doubt that he is dead.

12

The Man Reported Dead

Declarations of the deaths of Nazi war criminals are a tricky business. Nothing is easier than to stage one's own death in order to live on. Adolf Eichmann tried it, as did Dr Heyde-Savade and Gestapo chief Heinrich Müller. I have always, therefore, treated such declarations of death with extreme scepticism. And there is a psychological dimension: much as during the war we may have wished for the death of our tormentors, after the war we felt a need to track them down alive. First they must suffer their just punishment, then they can be allowed to die.

Yet the thought that a mass murderer simply lives on after the war, that he grows old and eventually passes away peacefully, is intolerable. It was probably this mechanism that, since we were certain of Hitler's death, led us to hope that his deputy, Martin Bormann, might still be alive: he, at least, was to answer for his deeds.

Bormann was credibly reported to have been seen at every possible point on the globe. Victims recognized him, former Nazis as well as neo-Nazis cheered him as their secret leader, and illustrated journals paid real fees for fake interviews with him. I myself, in the first edition of my book *The Murderers Among Us*, in 1967, devoted a special chapter to the hunt for Bormann, listing the countless pieces of information we had received by that date.

It was information on a ghost. In 1973 the public prosecutor's office in Frankfurt succeeded in identifying parts of a body whose characteristics identified it as unquestionably that of Bormann. Moreover, Bormann's companion in his escape from the Reich Chancellery bunker, Dr Stumpfenegger, was unambiguously identified. I thereupon went through our entire file of material on Bormann – nine bound folders, two thousand sheets in all – in order to discover the reason for so much false information over the years. I believe that there were four reasons:

(1) The Nazis themselves needed Bormann alive immediately after the war, for their slogan 'We'll be back'. Thus the legend arose of Bormann's escape by submarine to South America, where he was time and again reported seen until his mirage shifted to the Middle East. These rumours have still not dried up. Their basis was a radio signal from naval intelligence, found after the war, sent by Bormann on 22 April 1945 to his ADC Hummel at the Obersalzberg, reading: 'Accept suggested move übersee Süd'. It was not until sometime in the 1970s that I learned that the words 'übersee Süd' (overseas south) had nothing to do with South America but designated a railway station south of Munich.

(2) For Cold War Communist propaganda against West Germany, a 'haven of Nazism and revanchism', Bormann alive was a useful figure. This interest ended with the conclusion of the German 'eastern agreements'.

(3) Newspapers and illustrated journals throughout the world paid fantastic sums for Bormann stories. Dubious information dealers and fakers made a business out of hoodwinking journalists with sensational stories about Bormann staying at a 'jungle stronghold'. In the ceaseless rivalry the editors of *Stern* actually offered one such alleged middleman not only financial payment for an interview with Bormann but, in addition, that they would embark on anti-Israeli propaganda.

(4) Bormann had a typical run-of-the-mill face. Among every fifty Germans there would be at least one who resembled him enough to be mistaken for him. Whenever such a German turned up in Latin America he triggered off a wave of rumours, and occasionally was even arrested, merely because he was the spitting image of Bormann as shown in a 1945 photograph. Except that the real Bormann would by then have been thirty years older.

On the basis of these reflections I am in no doubt today that the Frankfurt public prosecutor's office was correct in its view that Bormann committed suicide in Berlin during the night of 2 May 1945, when he realized that an escape attempt would have no chance of succeeding.

Just because I had been so wrong in Bormann's case I wondered for a long time whether it was proper for me now to put on record my doubts about the death of Josef Mengele. But I have come to the conclusion that there are sound, rational grounds for such doubts, even though I am aware that my irrational need to believe Mengele alive is particularly strong. Ella Lingens, the president of the Austrian Auschwitz community, who worked under him as a doctor – though herself a prisoner – once said to me: 'I believe I could today meet all the other people I encountered then without feeling the need for revenge. Of course I would want them to be punished, but only for the sake of justice, not for personal gratification. But with Mengele I would feel the need to walk into the courtroom in person in order to strangle him.'

The woman who spoke these words is now eighty and well known for her even temperament and for her great readiness to meet ex-Nazis with forgiveness and understanding. Her crucial experience of Mengele was his behaviour during the frightful typhus epidemic which spread in mid-1942 from the women's camp of Birkenau: we know now that this meningeal inflammation, which is carried by lice, on some days killed more people in the Polish camps than even the Nazis could put to death in the gas chambers. Without heart stimulants typhus can almost never be survived by a weakened person. And without a disinfectant which destroys the lice it cannot be fought.

Nevertheless the detainee doctors dared not report to Mengele that the prisoners crowding the sick bays were suffering from typhus. They realized that Mengele would instantly send every patient to the gas chambers. And although they knew that the chance of survival for a typhus case was, at best, one in ten, this was nevertheless a barrier they did not wish to overstep even in Auschwitz: they didn't want to be the ones who decided over life or death.

This resulted in a terrible conflict for the detainee doctors: by keeping silent about the presence of typhus they did not receive disinfectants, although Mengele of course knew very well what the rampant disease was. And the absence of disinfectants meant that each day the epidemic continued hundreds would die. Mengele watched it all with satisfaction: the lice were saving him a lot of work.

But then some members of the German staff fell sick. The lice did not differentiate between superior Aryan and inferior Jewish or Polish heads. SS men were also dying, although they were well-nourished and received heart stimulants: even with good medical care the disease has a high fatality rate. Mengele was compelled to take some action against typhus: he sent the entire complement of a Jewish block into the gas chambers. In consequence the block was empty and could be disinfected. Then the women from the next block, having all first been deloused, were moved into the disinfected block, and so on, until the whole of the women's camp was clear of lice. It is probable that by this action Mengele saved the lives of many thousands of non-Jewish inmates.

Ella Lingens described him as a good, professionally interested doctor of above-average intelligence. In addition to his medical degree he was also a Doctor of Philosophy from the University of Munich. His special field, which he intensively pursued at the camp, was research into twins; his incredible experiments are a matter of history. He was a fanatic; he was one of those who really believed in racial theory: he was hoping for a race of blond, blue-eyed heroes. Presumably because he himself did not in any way match up to that image. He was about five and a half feet tall, had a slight squint in his left eye and, while still in Auschwitz, was beginning to go bald. He was outraged when children were shorter than they should be. A boy reported to me that one day Mengele drove nails into a wall which enabled him rapidly to determine whether a child had reached the height prescribed for his age – if he fell short he'd be sent to the gas chambers.

In so far as Mengele murdered personally, he did so 'medically' with scrupulously clean sterile hypodermics, by injecting his patients, out of scientific interest, with carbolic acid, petrol or air. There is one account of him personally killing a child by stabbing him with a bayonet, but I think this may be based on mistaken identification. Mengele, with his sharply pressed trousers, highly polished boots and white gloves, does not seem to me the type who'd get blood on his hands: he killed by injection, he gave orders, he selected those to be killed – but he considered himself above ordinary killing. He preferred the pose of the absolute ruler over life and death, the man standing by the notorious ramp at Auschwitz, giving the thumbs-down.

What Ella Lingens reported about his selection at the sick block was typical: needless to say, all patients who were not expected to be capable of work again soon were sent into gas chambers. The detainee doctors attempted to resist by making good prognoses even for the most seriously ill. Whereupon Mengele issued the following instruction: every doctor was to make out a list of all his patients, containing diagnosis and prognosis. Presumed convalescence exceeding three weeks meant the gas chamber. Otherwise the doctor was compelled to discharge his patient as fully restored to health after the expiry of those three weeks – which for the seriously ill likewise meant certain death.

Josef Mengele was everybody's mental picture of an SS man. It would have been exceedingly valuable to have him face trial like Eichmann, with the whole world following proceedings: the public would then have realized what people looked like who implemented the orders Eichmann issued from his office desk. Eichmann, who organized the murder of the Jews because he had been ordered to do so, and Mengele, who was convinced that the Jews must be exterminated, complemented each other – they were equally necessary in order to make Auschwitz possible.

Unlike Eichmann, whose whereabouts remained unknown for a long time, Mengele's whereabouts were mostly known. In 1945 he returned from Auschwitz to his native Günzburg and until 1950 lived entirely unharassed in that little town on the Danube. About the turn of the century his father had set up a factory for agricultural machinery, which had meanwhile, under the name of 'Karl Mengele & Sons', grown into a firm of worldwide repute. After the war the firm became a half-share partner of 'Fadro Farm KG SA' in Argentina, a subsidiary company for the distribution of German tractors, so that Josef Mengele was not to feel utterly cut off even in exile. It was in 1950 that his name first cropped up in proceedings against Nazi criminals. Some of his former colleagues and subordinates, including his former SS driver, began to tell of the crimes he had participated in at Auschwitz.

This shows how chaotically the investigation of Nazi crimes was practised after the war: after all, the book *Prisoners of Fear*, in which Ella Lingens described Mengele's crimes in detail, had been in existence from the beginning of 1948. But that book was published in England, and the appropriate public prosecutor's office for Mengele was in Freiburg/Breisgau. There was as yet no Central Office for the investigation of Nazi crimes, which was set up in Ludwigsburg in 1959, and it was only by chance that incriminating evidence available to one court of law became known to another. Five years elapsed before Mengele was in serious danger of being arrested in West Germany.

Typically he got wind of it. In 1951 he fled by the Reschenpass (Resio)– Merano route to Italy, and from there, with Odessa's assistance, via Genoa to Spain and later to South America. In 1952 he arrived in Buenos Aires with a whole string of false papers, calling himself by the aristocratic name of Friedrich Edler von Breitenbach, and opened a practice.

By 1954 my friend Hermann Langbein, the secretary-general of the International Auschwitz Committee, had his address. The German authorities demanded his extradition, but the Argentinians maintained that they couldn't find him. This was repeated in 1959. Then it was one of my people who located Mengele in Buenos Aires and, on my behalf, gave his address to the German embassy: 'Virrey Ortiz 970, Vicente Popez FCNGBN Pcia de Buenos Aires'. Thereupon, at the beginning of January 1960, Bonn addressed to Buenos Airies a second urgent request for Mengele's extradition. Again the Argentinians refused: the charges against Mengele, the 'Procurador de la Nación' declared on 31 December 1959, were of a 'political' rather than a 'criminal' character.

Latin American countries did not extradite anyone for political offences. This was not only due to the sympathy which the strongmen in power there had for Germany's fascist regime, but sprang from an ancient South American tradition: because of the frequent *coups d'état* in the region politicians who were heading a country only yesterday would suddenly find themselves seeking asylum in a neighbouring country: this happened continually. The concept of political asylum, therefore, was taken very seriously by all South American governments: every president realized that tomorrow he might himself have to request asylum. That is why for a long time Latin American countries never extradited anybody. In particular the fact that someone had used bestial methods of murder would, in view of their own torture chambers, appear to them in a less harsh light. Of course, there are not only huge quantitative but at least as many qualitative differences between the brutality of Latin American dictatorships and the bestiality of the Hitlerite regime: there has never been in Latin America the quasi-industrial extermination of human beings. Nevertheless, Latin American politicians felt they could not afford to extradite a mass murderer because this might create a precedent. Mengele profited from it: at times he lived quite openly under his real name.

In September 1959 – having learned of the German extradition request – he briefly moved to Paraguay and within a week, by government decree No. 809, he acquired Paraguayan nationality as José Mengele. Then he returned to Argentina. At the same time he found it desirable to move from Buenos Aires to Baríloche in the lake region below the Andes, where many affluent ex-Nazis have their villas; from there it was but a stone's throw to the Chilean border, and if things became unsafe in Argentina he could retreat to Chile.

But Argentina continued to be safe, even under Perón's successors. The German extradition request was quietly shelved – which was ultimately why, in Eichmann's case, the Israelis decided to resort to kidnapping. The Argentinians got terribly excited about that and were anxious to demonstrate that they were perfectly willing to extradite Nazi criminals. Thus in June 1960 they suddenly issued a warrant of arrest against 'José Mengele'.

However, he was no longer there. On the day Eichmann was seized he skedaddled across the Paraguayan border. The physician from Auschwitz had friends everywhere. They served him so loyally and discreetly that on the occasion of his father's funeral he could even risk returning to Günzburg and staying there for several days at the English Young Ladies' Boarding School. Although countless people knew him, no one denounced him. Public prosecutor Rahn, then in charge of the Mengele case, declared at a press conference that the inhabitants of Günzburg had acted like a band of conspirators. Günzburg's mayor, Dr Seitz, protested – and was revealed as the Mengele family lawyer. The former mayor, Michael Zehetmeier, told a Swiss paper: 'In this town nobody will say anything, even if they know a lot.'

On such occasions I always ask myself if these people are really acting in full knowledge of the facts: whether they really know – and believe – that Mengele sent hundreds of thousands of people into the gas chambers at Auschwitz, that he had children killed merely because they were too short, that he killed thousands by sinking a hypodermic filled with poison into their hearts. If the people who saw Mengele in Günzburg really knew all these things and yet did not denounce him, then I fear that in that little town all the things that happened under Hitler could happen again.

After the funeral Mengele returned to his new home, South America. He would have preferred to live in Buenos Aires, but the warrant of his arrest against him had not yet been revoked. So he settled in the Paraguayan capital Asunción. Paraguay was good soil for old Nazis. Of a total population of roughly two million some 30,000 were of German extraction, including the president, General Alfredo Stroessner the grandson of a Bavarian cavalry officer. Although Stroessner, himself was born in Paraguay, he had great sympathy for things German: his bodyguard – like Frederick the Great's – was full of 'tall lads' and marched with the Wehrmacht's goose-step.

In July 1962 the Bonn government addressed a request to Paraguay to investigate one Dr José Mengele, resident in Asunción, Fulgenico Morena 507. A few months later an answer arrived: 'Mengele is a citizen of Paraguay and has no criminal record.'

When, on 16 July 1964, the German ambassador Eckhart Briest handed President Stroessner a new formal request for extradition, the dictator lost his temper. 'If you don't stop this,' he shouted, 'I shall break off diplomatic relations with the Federal Republic.'

That was a little rash, considering that Paraguay was just then hoping to receive a development loan to the tune of twelve million Deutschmarks from West Germany. When the magazine *Der Spiegel* learned of the clash between Briest and Stroessner, and published an account of it, the Bavarian in Paraguay felt compelled to look at the Mengele business again. For a week the fate of the Auschwitz doctor was uncertain, but he continued to live openly in Ascunción, consorting with his friends. Shortly afterwards someone daubed the German embassy building: 'Jewish embassy! Hands off Mengele! This is an order!'

President Stroessner obeyed it. Instead of surrendering Mengele it was decided that he should live in a military zone in the east of Paraguay, forbidden to foreigners. Between Puerto San Vicente, on the road from Asunción to São Paulo and the Carlos Antonio Lopez border post on the Parana river he occupied a small white hut in a clearing made by German settlers. There are only two roads leading to the remote building, and both were guarded by military patrols with orders to open fire at the approach of any unauthorized person. Mengele himself kept four heavily armed bodyguards at his own expense. The camp doctor of Auschwitz had become an internee, forced to live in a hut and deriving no advantage from the fact that armed men surrounded him in order to protect him rather than to keep him prisoner. He was cut off from the world outside.

In 1962 I learned that Mengele's wife Martha had rented a small house in Klothen near Zürich, on Schwimmbadstrasse 9, and that it was probable her husband would visit her there. I therefore requested the Swiss member of Parliament, Werner, with whom I am acquainted, to inform the Swiss police, so they could keep an eye open for Frau Mengele's visitors. A woman from such a wealthy family does not normally have to live under an airport flight path. Proximity to the airport seemed to be important. The Swiss acted on the principle that the best treatment for a headache is to cut off the head, and expelled Frau Mengele. She moved to Merano and has been living there ever since, at Via Park number 2.

Not until 1979 did I succeed, jointly with the Simon Wiesenthal Center in Los Angeles, in making Stroessner drop Mengele: the Paraguayan dictator did not want to annoy quite as many American senators as had promised me their support. To begin with, however, his authorities denied that Mengele was a Paraguayan citizen at all, but this was refuted by a statement made by a Baron Alexander von Eckstein in Frankfurt in 1961. Eckstein testified that, along with another German, a businessman called Werner Jung, he had made a statement to the effect that Mengele had already been living in Paraguay for five years, to ensure he received his citizenship on the spot. This testimony convinced the American senators and, in consequence, had to convince Stroessner as well.

In the spring of 1979 a new sheet was added to my file: I learned that Mengele's son Rolf, who is working as a corporation lawyer in a Berlin firm, was planning a trip to Brazil. If it was his intention to meet his father there, it would have been a journey to see a dead man. On 7 February 1979 Mengele was reported to have drowned on a bathing trip not far from São Paulo.

The news of Mengele's death did not reach the public until 5 June 1985, and it didn't reach me until a day later because I was at that moment flying from Amsterdam to New York. When I arrived at Kennedy airport I was surrounded by a pack of journalists who wished to know what I thought of this report. When I had cursorily informed myself about it my first reaction was rather sceptical: 'This is the seventh dead Mengele since I've been looking for him.'

Only at the hotel did I learn further details. The public prosecutor's office in Frankfurt had received a tip-off to the effect that important documents concerning Josef Mengele were to be found at the house of Hans Sedlmaier, the confidential clerk of the Mengele family firm. Senior

Public Prosecutor Klein applied to the court for a search warrant but was refused. He then appealed to a superior court, and after a few weeks' delay a search was eventually conducted. Correspondence with Brazil was found, showing that Mengele had died on 7 February 1979 and had been buried at the cemetery of Embu, São Paulo district, under the name of Wolfgang Gerhard.

The date of discovery of that correspondence is the most important argument in favour of its truth. If Mengele's death had merely been staged, then it would have been sensible to make the fact known speedily. On the other hand, it might have been sensible to stage his 'death' in 1985 in such a way as to suggest credibly that he had died as early as 1979. Just because it would look more credible.

I inquired of the German authorities whether Sedlmaier's telephone had been monitored from time to time or his mail opened. But nothing of the sort had ever been done – even though it was known that Sedlmaier was in constant touch with Mengele and had actually met him. Another of Mengele's friends and protectors was Colonel Rudel, the most highly decorated German officer, who was organizing the Paraguayan police for his friend Stroessner. He maintained contact with Sedlmaier and on one occasion met Mengele in person. I reported this connection to General Prosecutor Fritz Bauer. Dr Bauer wrote back to me, as early as 1964: 'That Herr Sedlmaier has met Josef Mengele several times in the past is known to us. That this happened again six weeks ago is new to us. Herr Sedlmaier has been questioned by the prosecutor's office on this matter; perhaps we may try something or other again.' The authorities clearly realized that Sedlmaier was probably the most important link to Mengele.

In 1971 the Frankfurt investigating judge, von Glasenapp, who was in charge of the Mengele case, travelled all over the world in order to update his Mengele dossier. In this connection he also questioned Sedlmaier. But Sedlmaier gave nothing away: he had seen Mengele and spoken to him only once, in 1961, at the airport in Buenos Aires. That, as the prosecutor's office was bound to know, was an untruth. But the investigating judge made a mistake: he forgot to put Sedlmaier on oath for his evidence. And although certain services which Sedlmaier might have performed for Mengele in the past had infringed the law, they could not, under the German Statute of limitations, be prosecuted after a lapse of five years. The judiciary was unable to get at Sedlmaier. Nevertheless, I assumed that in the circumstances they would not let him out of their sight even for a moment, and it was with that in mind that I informed Neal Shaer of the American Office of Special Investigations, when he visited me in 1984: 'The key to Mengele is Sedlmaier, but he is no doubt being watched by the Frankfurt prosecutor's office.'

The man in the street invariably believes that public prosecutors would act in at least approximately the same way as every amateur detective would. But after more than forty years' experience I really should have known that this is a fallacy. I certainly thought it suspicious that Sedlmaier, of all people, should have been the one from whose correspondence the authorities learned about Mengele's death. The whole sequence – confidential tip-off, house search, news of Mengele's death – struck me as just a little too perfect.

At that point, however, the forensic doctors stepped into the limelight. The body of 'Wolfgang Gerhard' at the Embu cemetery had been exhumed and several acknowledged experts were asked their opinion: Ellis Kerry, professor of forensic anthropology at the University of Maryland, and Lowell Levine, an expert on dental comparison who had participated in the autopsy of John F. Kennedy. Ali Hameli is head of the forensic medicine laboratory in Delaware; Clyde Snow is a forensic anthropologist at the University of Oklahoma; John Fitzpatrick is chief of the radiology department of Cook County Hospital in Chicago and Leslie Lukash belongs to the US Marshal Service, a police authority brought in on the Mengele case. In addition three specialists from West Germany and a number of specialists from Brazil participated in the autopsy of the dead man from Embu.

Mengele, according to the letters found at Sedlmaier's house, had lost his life on a bathing trip with a family called Bossert. The Bosserts came from Austria; Herr Bossert was a former member of the SS. However, according to his report, he had not been present at the crucial moment. His wife, on the other hand, who had also walked ahead a little way, had suddenly heard Mengele cry for help: she had run back and had seen the old man struggling in the nearby lake, drowning. Although she had managed to drag him ashore he was already dead. Frau Bossert had then, in the course of the ensuing night, organized both a coffin and flowers for the deceased.

There was an incident at the funeral. The director of the cemetery intended, as was customary, to open the coffin briefly – but he was prevented from doing so by those present. The Brazilian police subsequently questioned Frau Bossert, as well as a family called Stammer, with whom Mengele had previously lived. Among other things they wanted to know how Mengele had come by the name 'Wolfgang Gerhard'. The answer seemed plausible. Wolfgang Gerhard was an Austrian, like the Bosserts, and out of conviction had wanted to help Mengele. So, when he himself was returning home to Austria, he had left him his identity card. Admittedly he was Mengele's junior by sixteen years. That was why the cemetery director had been stopped from opening the coffin; he might have noticed the discrepancy in age. Wolfgang Gerhard died in Graz shortly afterwards, in circumstances which have not been entirely cleared up.

Everything the Bossert and Stammer families related was just possible, even though somewhat unusual: why should Mengele, then nearly seventy, bathe in a lake while his friends had gone on ahead? How did Frau Bossert manage to recover the dead man from the water? If Mengele had been close to the bank, possibly still within his depth, it was hard to understand how he could have drowned, unless of course he had suffered a heart attack. But if he was far enough out from the bank to drown, how then did Frau Bossert get the dead man ashore?

However, all these doubts were swept away by the unequivocal findings of the commission of experts: on the strength of a comparison of the skeleton with medical data on Mengele made available by the German judiciary, it could be assumed, 'with a probability bordering on certainty' that the dead man from Embu was in fact Josef Mengele. Brazil thereupon declared Mengele dead in an official statement. Admittedly, some doubts persisted here and there, especially among his former victims, but I regarded these as a result of the psychological mechanism mentioned earlier and I took the view that the judgement of such a highly qualified commission of experts had to be accepted.

Maybe I myself fell victim to a psychological mechanism: having wrongly doubted Bormann's death I didn't wish to doubt Mengele's wrongly as well. Even a number of letters from persons claiming to have seen the allegedly dead Mengele in Paraguay, alive and well, could not shake my belief: the dead Bormann had similarly been seen by several dozen witnesses over the years.

The public prosecutor's office in Frankfurt received letters similar to mine, and Senior Public Prosecutor Klein, who didn't go through the same Bormann experience as me, was more impressed by them than I was. When I asked him when Mengele would be declared dead he declined to give a definitive answer: reports were still coming in that Mengele was alive, and until these were disproved Mengele could not be declared dead. Among other things a woman dentist had been in touch with him, ready to prove by her records that Mengele had been treated by her as recently as April 1979, that is, two months after his alleged death. The Brazilian police had dismissed her statement as an ego-trip, but it would have been interesting to hear the dentist's arguments.

I myself at that time was still firmly convinced that Mengele's death was unshakeably established. Until I learned of the following incident: in 1982, that is, three years after Mengele's alleged death, Karl-Heinz Mengele, Mengele's nephew and stepson (Mengele's second marriage was to the widow of his brother, the mother of Karl-Heinz), and Mengele's intimate friend Dr Hans Sedlmaier, had a meeting with Dr Hans Münch, the

Auschwitz camp doctor and a friend of Mengele's. In 1947 Münch, along with several SS leaders, had been charged in a Cracow court with crimes committed at Auschwitz but he alone had been acquitted. The questions which Karl-Heinz Mengele and Hans Sedlmaier discussed with Münch, however, touched only indirectly on that court case: what they wanted to know was whether Josef Mengele, supposing he surrendered to a court, would be charged with his experiments or with participation in selecting persons to be put to death.

What I am writing about is not a rumour. Münch as well as Karl-Heinz Mengele and Sedlmaier were questioned with regard to that conversation and had to admit that it had taken place, although they attempted to play it down as a theoretical discussion. Such 'toying with ideas' is of course possible – but would the busy head of a large enterprise, moreover accompanied by Hans Sedlmaier, travel to meet Dr Hans Münch, whom neither had ever met before, merely in order to discuss hypothetical questions with him?

My mistrust thus aroused, I once again studied the expert opinions and witnesses' statements in connection with 'Wolfgang Gerhard's' death, and more particularly I looked into the criticism which had even been directed at the finding of the commission of experts. The journalist Ben Abraham from São Paulo, in his book *The Mengele Dossier*, had listed a number of details which had not then been taken seriously but which should now be viewed in a fresh light. In particular, there was a hole which the medical men found in the dead man's jaw. The experts suggested that it might have been caused by a nail in the coffin. The American consul general in São Paulo, sometime professor of dentistry at Washington University, believed that Mengele or his dentists might have probed with a needle in the dental canal concerned, and a perforation could have resulted. The nail-in-the-coffin theory, at any rate, did not strike me as very plausible, considering the usual position of a body and the location of the nails.

Another of Ben Abraham's objections concerns Mengele's height: according to the German SS files he was 1.74 metres tall, including no doubt the hair on his head and the skin on the soles of his feet. The height of the skeleton is exactly 1.74 metres, even though the intervertebral discs had gone, as had his hair and skin. On the other hand, of course, there is no telling how accurately the SS measured its men.

Finally, there was a curious feature about the interment. When the presumed Mengele died he had papers on him, made out to a man of fifty-two. Mengele would have been sixty-eight on 7 February 1979. That, according to the Bosserts, was why the coffin had not been opened in front of the cemetery director. However, the dead man, according to custom, had been fully dressed before the burial. No remains of any clothing, however, not even of buttons or shoes, were found upon exhumation of the body.

There are some further inconsistencies in Frau Bossert's testimony, concerning the time after Mengele's bathing incident. It is amazing that Frau Bossert should have succeeded, in the time span between the evening of the death and the morning of 'Wolfgang Gerhard's' funeral – that is, within a few hours – in getting hold of a coffin and even flowers, even though she had to do her travelling by bus.

These, admittedly, are merely some curious aspects which would not normally shake the finding of so many experts. Nor can I assert that they were wrong – but I do think the conversation between Hans Sedlmaier, Karl-Heinz Mengele and Dr Münch is a serious piece of circumstantial evidence. 'It suggests a living Mengele rather than a dead one,' I said to Senior Public Prosecutor Klein, and he has not contradicted this view.

For the time being, at any rate, Josef Mengele is unlikely to be declared dead. This means that I shall continue my search for him and that I shall again study thoroughly any tip-offs I may receive about his appearance in Paraguay. I believe in the importance of a court on this earth putting the question to him: 'How can you reconcile what you have done with the Hippocratic oath, which makes it your duty to help people?'

13

The Hippocratic Oath

'How can you reconcile all that's happening here with the Hippocratic oath?' the detainee doctor Ella Lingens once asked the camp physician Dr Rohde in the face of the smoking crematoria of Auschwitz–Birkenau. Rohde's reply was: if someone suffers from a festering appendix you've got to cut that appendix out even if it hurts, for otherwise the patient would die. 'The Jews are the festering appendix of Europe.'

Whenever in the course of my work I have met doctors who were Nazi criminals, they have always been fanatics. The Eichmann type, who would have been just as ready to release the Jews to Madagascar as to gas them, depending on the Führer's orders, is scarcely imaginable as a doctor. Because anyone who has chosen the medical profession is, as a rule, driven by an ambition to help others. It takes a strong psychological impulse to make that ambition turn into its opposite and to make a physician, who would normally try to save a patient weakened by sickness with an injection, turn into a murderer who kills with an injection.

But this has happened astonishingly often. Physicians played a considerable role in the death machinery of the Third Reich. Not only did they make the selection of victims in the concentration camps, but almost invariably they were ready to commit individual murder. Within the framework of the programme for liquidating 'life not worthy of life', they would provide the 'scientific basis', give expert opinions, and in 'sanatoriums' such as Hartheim or Hadamar personally participate in murder. But unbelievable things were happening at less notorious

psychiatric hospitals too, such as the Steinhof in Vienna, where Dr
Hans Gross, who is still working to this day as a forensic psychiatrist, was
responsible for killing hundreds of disabled children with a hypodermic
needle. To fight as a doctor against death and simultaneously to bring
death seem to be more mentally compatible than one might think. I was
reminded of this when I read that the utterly respectable and dedicated
professor Julius Hackethal advocates the 'mercy killing' of incurably ill
patients. For him this is undoubtedly an act of mercy: the patient would
be spared his pain and the physician the sight of that pain. Yet for me,
quite apart from all the legal problems of this new form of euthanasia,
Hackethal's attitude is incomprehensible. Surely it means ultimately that
he himself must be able to hand his patient a lethal pill or administer a
lethal injection.

We all have, I believe, an inhibition against such a deed that is both
acquired and inborn. Even though we realize that in the immediate case it
would probably be of benefit to the patient, we are, I should like to believe,
unable, exactly because of that inhibition, to give the injection. Professor
Hackethal trusts himself and his colleagues to overcome that inhibition.
That frightens me. Though I do not want to compare the two situations,
the same argument was used by the doctors of the Third Reich: that the
physician must kill in accordance with his professional ethics in order to
prevent something worse – the Judaification of Germany or the spread of
inherited diseases.

It frightens me – now as it did then – that so many physicians regard
these arguments as worthy of discussion. No other profession (with the
exception of teachers, who, of course, were under pressure and wished to
keep their jobs in state schools) was quite so addicted to Nazism: nearly
50 per cent of all physicians in Germany after 1933, and in Austria after
1938, were members of the Nazi party. This may have been partly due to
the fact that the medical profession in Germany and Austria was particularly
non-political. A doctor is, as it were, expected not to descend to the level
of politics, to remain above ordinary things. At the same time, society
allows him – to this day – the position of a 'God in white'. Many hospitals
are as strictly hierarchical as military organizations – the chief surgeon at
the top and the patient at the very bottom. This encourages a sense of
being one of the elect: if God in heaven decides over life and death, why
not also the 'God in white'?

Finally, the patient–doctor relationship is, by its nature, one in which
the patient is at the mercy of the doctor, who represents omnipotence. It
is probably a psychological quality of a good physician that he radiates
great natural authority – the patient need only hear his voice or feel his
hand to believe that he is on the way to recovery. This attraction which

the profession holds for authoritarian characters – I am using this term in an entirely positive sense – could be a further reason why so many doctors in the Third Reich were willing to place their authority in the service of death. The concept of 'healthy' in itself contains a certain danger, in as much as everything else is categorized as 'sick'. Overestimation of health, which comes naturally to a doctor, may easily lead him to overestimate the danger of sickness – as can be seen now, again, in the debate on AIDS. The Third Reich practised the most extreme form of 'health' by trying to eliminate all alleged diseases. And 'alien' Jewish blood was simply regarded as diseased.

What I am going to say now is even more delicate, and I would ask physicians reading this book not to take it as an affront – but I believe that there is a certain affinity between the powerful wish to save people from death and the wish to send them to their death. We know this from depth psychology, which has studied, in particular, the surgical profession: a surgeon must be able to cut into the flesh of a living person. This requires a very slight inclination to sadism, of which the person concerned is not even aware. I don't want to condemn that inclination, and on the contrary I'm asserting that it is of great social value: instead of hurting someone (which, on the basis of that inclination, the doctor might be capable of) he helps him. We know that our society would probably not function without this kind of thing happening all the time: police officers almost invariably have an above-average interest in criminal behaviour, psychiatrists must feel some kinship with the mentally ill, and no doubt I myself pursue my activities because of a particular psychological structure. I do not, therefore, mean any offence when I say that a slight tendency towards sadism may be found a bit more frequently among medical men than among others. The frightful thing about the Third Reich was that it created conditions in which such psychological inclinations redounded not to the advantage but to the disadvantage of human beings. Doctors who might have made excellent surgeons cut off patients' limbs while they were alive; doctors who presumably had a perfectly rational interest in research on twins ran tests to discover whether twins reacted differently to hot needles being driven into their bodies. Doctors whose operative skills could have been of great value in cases of uterine cancer applied these skills to performing hysterectomies on healthy women. The physician's necessary interest in the progress of a disease became the ghoulish interest of the Hartheim doctors in the agony of people being gassed.

During my internment at Mauthausen I repeatedly heard about a doctor who seemed a particularly striking illustration of this problem: when he was no longer the camp physician of Mauthausen, Dr Aribert Heim, as a frontline medical officer, saved the lives of numerous servicemen. In

Mauthausen, on the other hand, a prisoner, attached to him as an operating theatre assistant, had this experience. A transport of Jewish internees had just arrived from Holland. The SS doctor inspected the younger men, made them open their mouths and apparently examined their teeth. In the end he chose two of them and asked them to make themselves available for a small, harmless operative intervention. In return they would be given their freedom. The two chosen men, believing they had drawn a lucky number, trustingly followed the doctor into the prisoners' compound, undressed, and while one of them waited the other lay down on the operating table.

The doctor opened up the anaethetized man's chest and abdomen in order, as he said, to study the internal organs 'in vivo': 'This is the first time that I can see in a live person how his stomach works.' In front of the eyes of his flabbergasted assistant Dr Heim then picked up his scalpel and, just as if he were dissecting a corpse, cut out one organ after another. After he had cut out the heart as well he had the body pushed aside and called for the second patient. With him, too, like an excellent student anxious to demonstrate his skill, he neatly laid bare the organs and then, with a swift cut, removed them. This time, however, he remembered that the young man's oral cavity had also interested him, and so he extracted a tooth. After that he extinguished the last remnants of life, if any were left in the body, by an injection into the heart. His appetite now stimulated, the doctor then with his own hands cut the heads off both bodies and sent the bloody, mutilated corpses to be incinerated in the crematorium. Only the skulls, he requested, should be kept aside, carefully boiled and cleared of all soft tissue: he would like to keep them as a souvenir. One of the two skulls, the one with the complete set of teeth, subsequently sat on the SS doctor's desk. He was said to have made a colleague a present of the other.

No less ghoulish is the case of a boy of twelve who, having been put on the operating table, realized with greater perspicacity than most adults that he was to be killed. With folded hands he prayed aloud and in his prayer said goodbye to his parents. Dr Heim listened to him attentively and then, as if convincing a child of the need for a tonsillectomy, he began to explain to him in a friendly voice why the Jews must die: they were the cause of all misfortune in the world and, above all, of this war. Having thus lectured his victim on the moral justification for his execution he killed the boy by injecting poison into his heart.

When, years after this incident, I was myself taken to the Mauthausen death block to die there, the older prisoners were still talking about that doctor's practices: they remembered him for his height. I was not to discover his name until very much later: Aribert Heim came from Radkersburg in Styria, where he was born on 28 June 1914, the son of a gendarmerie inspector. The family – Heim had an elder brother and two sisters – subsequently moved to Graz, and Aribert Heim joined the Nazi party as early as 1935, as an 'illegal'. His medical studies at Graz university prepared him in every respect for his future 'activity'. In 1938 the university senate only just managed to shelve a proposal for renaming it 'Adolf Hitler University', and soon all professors, assistants and other staff were fired if they did not make a clear political declaration. At the faculty of law a 'race law seminar' was introduced; the theological faculty was disbanded; the medical faculty was extended by an SS medical academy which, under the leadership of SS Obersturmführer Hans Kaether, was to impart not only medical knowledge but also military discipline and, above all, Nazi principles. Kaether's ADC, Dr Ding – also known as Ding-Schuler – subsequently became camp physician at the Buchenwald concentration camp, where he performed typhus experiments on prisoners. His work enabled him to keep the SS medical academy – and also, in part, the anatomical department – supplied with prepared medical specimens, demonstration items and, above all, bodies for dissection practice. In May 1945 the university still had a stock of forty-four bodies, prisoners killed at the Buchenwald concentration camp.

This then was the medical training Aribert Heim received. As for his work in the concentration camp, Heim saw that as an advanced training course since, as a future medical officer with the fighting forces, he would frequently have to perform emergency operations and amputate the limbs of wounded men. It was, so to speak, in line with his sense of duty that he should prepare himself adequately by amputating the arms and legs of healthy prisoners or removing their organs while they were alive.

Dr Heim – and this is the most ghoulish aspect of this affair – might well have returned from the war as a good army doctor with an unblemished reputation. A man of whom his comrades would have said that he saved the lives of many of them by his personal dedication and skill. In Dr Heim's life there were only those short phases in the Buchenwald and Mauthausen concentration camps during which, one is tempted to say, by chance, he found an opportunity for giving vent, as though in a frenzy, to a latent bestiality and an obvious tendency to sadism. Apart from that we find him as the medical officer to the SS special reserve in Prague, to the élite SS division known as the *Leibstandarte Adolf Hitler*, and to SS Division North. For a while he was also chief medical officer at SS general headquarters. His record lists service in Denmark, Holland, Hungary, Yugoslavia, Bohemia, Romania, Belgium and France. He was arrested on 25 April 1945 as 'SS Captain and Medical Officer' of the SS Mountain Division North, but he was evidently so inconspicuous that he was released again in 1947.

In 1948 Dr Heim turned up as a gynaecological specialist in Mannheim and there married a colleague. Where he acquired this qualification is unclear. The couple moved to Baden-Baden, where they opened a practice; this obviously flourished, as in 1958 Aribert Heim purchased a residential block in Berlin, in the Tiergarten district, with thirty-four apartments yielding six thousand Deutschmarks a month.

The mills of justice grind exceeding slow. Not until 1962 was a warrant of arrest issued against Heim on the strength of numerous statements by witnesses. On 13 September the police rang his front doorbell in Baden-Baden. But Dr Heim was no longer there. He had been warned by someone – to this day unknown – and had made off.

From the evidence which I exchanged with the provincial crime police in Stuttgart, especially from the death records painstakingly kept by Heim himself, it emerges that during his 'work' in Mauthausen about 540 people lost their lives. But Dr Heim was alive. For years he lived on the revenue from his Berlin-Tiergarten block – quite officially, represented by the Heidelberg tax consultants' firm of Paul Barth and by Frankfurt attorney Fritz Steinacker, who, until Mengele's alleged death, had also been Mengele's lawyer. The administration of the apartment block was in the hands of Johann Eckert of the reputable firm of Droste. Every month, with the cooperation of that circle of discreet and informed representatives, Frau Hilde Barth, Aribert Heim's married sister in Buchschlag near Frankfurt, collected the rent of the building at Tile-Wardenberg-Strasse 28 and passed it on to her brother. Attempts by police to gain information from her, or from Heim's other sister in Graz, on the wanted man's whereabouts prove, as might be expected, unsuccessful: as close relatives the two women were entitled to refuse to give a statement. Whether this right to keep silent extends to all the other persons involved might be worth a juridical study in some depth.

In 1977 I began my attempts to break open the Heim case from the financial side. Here the tax laws seemed helpful: the money, after all, was being transferred to Frau Barth, and if she did not pass it on to her brother she herself would have to pay tax on it. From this it followed that she must be able to prove to the tax inspector that she actually passed on the money to her brother. Moreover, as I saw it, the tax inspector was entitled to demand that Aribert Heim present himself in person, in order to lay to rest the suspicion that he was no longer alive and that his sister was merely evading her income tax by referring to him.

The Berlin tax office acted on my suggestion, which I had asked friends to convey to someone at the top, and, in line with the law, demanded that Frau Barth prove the existence of her brother and that Heim present himself at the office. But instead of Aribert Heim his tax consultant appeared, producing a tax return signed by Dr Heim. When the tax office questioned the genuineness of the signature, attorney Steinacker provided a tape recording of Dr Heim's voice. Both gentlemen regarded this as within their professional duties.

On October 1978 I wrote a letter to the then Minister of Justice of West Germany, Dr Jochen Vogel, drawing his attention to the fundamental problem in this case. Of course a tax consultant and an attorney were normally entitled to keep confidential anything concerning their client. But surely – at least in my reading of the law – this applied only when they represented him as an attorney or under tax law. But in this case there was no longer any question of normal representation: the gentlemen involved, by their collusion, were enabling Aribert Heim to evade justice by ensuring the financing of his life underground. 'One is forcibly reminded', I wrote, 'of a parallel with the lawyers of the Bader-Meinhof gang. They were accused of supporting a criminal organization and of having knowledge of the whereabouts of the criminals who had gone underground. Now surely the SS, at least that part of it active in the concentration camps, was also a criminal organization, and Dr Heim as camp physician was a member of that organization, which committed incomparably greater crimes than the Bader-Meinhof gang.' I therefore viewed Dr Steinacker's actions as a continuous endeavour to obstruct the course of justice.

On 5 April 1979 I lodged a complaint against Dr Steinacker with the Frankfurt Chamber of Lawyers, and a day later I applied to the public prosecutor's office for criminal proceedings to be brought against him. But the crimes of the SS evidently do not weigh as heavily in West Germany as the crimes of the Baader-Meinhof gang: in August we were notified that the case had been dropped.

I saw one more chance. I knew that the Four-Power Statute, which continues to be valid in Berlin, allows for persons guilty of crimes during the Nazi period to have fines imposed on them. I therefore lodged a complaint with the Berlin tribunal, which on 13 June 1979 had just resumed its work after an interval of eight years. When a number of testimonies about Heim's activity had been read and a number of witnesses heard in person, the chairman of the judges, Dr Wolfgang Neesmann, concluded that Heim had committed the offences he was charged with and in committing them had acted with murderous intent. On these grounds the tribunal sentenced him to a fine of 510,000 Deutsch-marks. Payment was covered by a mortgage on the apartment block on Tile-Wardenburg-Strasse. Dr Steinacker appealed, but his appeal was dismissed. Since then Dr Heim has been cut off from his source of income.

Although, among other things, the television programme 'File XY –

Unsolved' broadcast a report on him, his whereabouts are unknown to this day. It may be assumed that he had put by enough to enjoy his golden years in comfort.

14

The Doctor and
the Dead

This chapter, too, is about a doctor. One who, until as recently as 1985, has lived as a respected man in a small town in Austria and practised there for three decades. He didn't commit any crimes during the war, and what makes up this story does not fall foul of the law. In his case it wasn't even a matter of discovering a crime (the crime has long been known) but of giving a dignified burial to fourteen Dutch resistance fighters, executed by an SS firing squad on 26 May 1944. Their families wanted to exhume their bodies and transfer them to a cemetery.

But no one knew precisely where they were buried. All that was known was that the execution had taken place somewhere in the so-called Drunen dunes between s'-Hertogenbosch and Tilburg in the Dutch province of Brabant. The man in charge of the operation had been a certain Herbert Funk, who came from the regular police and had been taken on by the SS as an Obersturmbannführer. In this operation, however, he had been in command not of an SS unit but of a squad of German police in Tilburg. After the war he was sentenced to only ten years' imprisonment, because he had not ordered the execution himself but had put it into effect upon higher orders.

One might have thought that these ten years would have given him pause for reflection and made him see the error of his ways. But Funk remained exactly the man he had always been: when family members of the men shot in the dunes came to him to ask where they should dig for the remains of their relations, he turned them out of his house. He was, he declared, bound to secrecy, and the oath he had sworn to the Führer forbade him to disclose any information.

The inhabitants of Tilburg, where most of the shot resistance fighters came from, did not give up. From the files they discovered that a police surgeon had been brought in after the execution to confirm the death of the men. The doctor's name was Ernst Zartl, and he came from Austria. Our office was asked to look for him, which was not difficult as the register of the Austrian Chamber of Medicine showed Dr Zartl to be resident and practising at Hohenau-on-March in Lower Austria.

Christian van Hombergh, a furniture dealer from Tilburg who had made it his personal business to discover the burial place of his fellow-countrymen, on the strength of my information got in touch by telephone with Zartl's listed address. The call, however, was taken not by Dr Zartl but by his wife. Her information did not sound very promising: her husband didn't talk about 'these things', not to anyone. Then she hung up.

Van Hombergh next tried a letter. He explained to the doctor that he had no intention of dragging him into any kind of proceedings and that he was interested solely in providing a worthy grave for the dead. His letter was never answered.

Van Hombergh decided to telephone Dr Zartl once more, on 10 October 1977. I have kept the shorthand record of the conversation in my files.

Hombergh: I wrote a letter to you a few weeks ago, and I am now calling to ask if I may visit you.
Dr Zartl: I have no reason to talk to you about the matter. If you wish to talk to me I would ask you to phone the gendarmerie commandant in Hohenau, to find out when he is free to be present at this conversation.
Hombergh: Yes, gladly, but I don't need any police ...
Dr Zartl: But I need them, because I won't deal with you or talk about matters which are thirty or thirty-five years old, especially not with you as a Dutchman who are violating the UN Charter by still keeping three comrades of ours in prison, men who have done nothing but their duty. I have nothing to say to you, except, if you like, in the presence of the state police.
Hombergh: But, Herr Doktor ...
Dr Zartl: Look here, don't get worked up, I have nothing to say to you.
Hombergh: Surely I wrote a polite letter to you.
Dr Zartl: Surely, whether the letter was polite or not, I have my reasons for talking to you only in the presence of the Austrian police, now that the Dutch have had the nerve to send me all kinds of threatening letters which, as a former German officer, mean nothing to me and do not scare me. I am very sorry. If you like you can ring up the superintendent of the Hohenau gendarmerie, and tell him

when you feel like coming. In his presence I will talk to you about it. You know that among the shot men there were also bank robbers, in fact all kinds of criminal elements, who had nothing to do with the Dutch liberation struggle.

Hombergh: Can it be someone other than the gendarmerie? Can it be an attorney?

Dr Zartl: No, only the gendarmerie. I'll have nothing to do with an attorney. I have been in touch about this Dutch business with the Austrian state police and the gendarmerie. I'm not interested in any private attorney.

Hombergh: That's a pity . . .

Dr Zartl: Not for me. I don't wish to have any contact with you except through the Austrian state police or the Austrian gendarmerie.

Hombergh: Certainly, if that's what you wish it shall be done that way. I just don't understand why you're reacting so harshly to my polite letter.

Dr Zartl: Why I'm doing that? Of course. I have passed on to the state police letters from Dutchmen threatening to murder me. That's all in the hands of the state police, if you want to know. You can inquire there.

Hombergh: But mine, surely, was not a threatening letter.

Dr Zartl: You are a stranger to me, and you don't interest me. And I have no interest in talking to you, except through the police. And privately I would advise you to request your people to release those three, Kotälla, Fischer and the one from Fünten, who were exempted from a pardon in spite of a UN resolution, and when these three German officers have been freed, only then will I talk to the Dutch about the things which happened.

Hombergh: Surely, Herr Doktor, as a medical man you don't identify with criminals . . .

Dr Zartl: Why do I identify with them? Because I'd be a villain if, as a former officer, I didn't identify with those three who did their duty in Holland the same as me. And I can only tell you, about that man Kotälla, who was in charge of the Amersfort camp: why don't you go and ask for the Tongens, the shoe manufacturer's twins? He let them all go free. And this hasn't come out at any trial.

Hombergh: Yes, but the man did frightful things.

Dr Zartl: Yes, the Dutch also did frightful things.

Hombergh: But surely not yourself . . .

Dr Zartl: You listen to me. I could tell you things about the withdrawal of the German troops, when eight soldiers were killed anyway in Utrecht by gangs of Dutch murderers. You'd better understand. That's enough. Goodbye. (Hangs up.)

That was the shorthand record. From the attached personal file I see that Dr Ernst Zartl, born in 1915, had been a party member as an 'illegal' and had actually served a short prison term for it. In 1942 he was an SS Hauptsturmführer and member of the Vienna SS Medical Association. But all that might be dismissed as the youthful sins of a deluded man.

What I could not understand, and cannot understand to this day, is that a man with a university education – that is, a man to whom thought is not totally strange – could have a conversation such as this a whole thirty-two years after Hitler's death: men who had sent over 100,000 Jews to Auschwitz and hence to their certain death were to him still soldiers doing their duty. If the mass murderers were released, he would then help the executed resistance men to find a proper grave.

I wrote to the president of the Austrian Chamber of Medicine, chief surgeon Dr Richard Piaty, a man who had himself been persecuted during the Nazi period, asking him to help me. Dr Piaty replied at length and said what any person of normal sensitivity must feel: Dr Zartl, he wrote, was under an obligation, not as a medical man on professional grounds but on wider humanitarian grounds, to pass on his knowledge about the burial place of the executed men to their families. He had no sympathy for his linking the release of convicted criminals with this piece of information. However, the assurance did not lead to Dr Zartl being struck off the register.

A final attempt was subsequently made by a member of the German army, Günther Brabeck. He wrote to Dr Zartl, telling him how fairly the Dutch public had behaved towards him after the war and how he had been helped to find the graves of German soldiers. Zartl did not reply to this letter and in 1985 took his knowledge with him to the grave.

15

Another Doctor

I owe my knowledge of the following incident, which again involved a number of doctors, to Ella Lingens. A woman colleague of Dr Lingens, Adelheid Hautval, had been sent to Auschwitz for having favoured Jews and was assigned to Block 10, where the gynaecologist Dr Clauberg, a hunchbacked dwarf, was conducting his sterilization experiments. Hautval – in the middle of Auschwitz and in the face of an SS doctor – refused to perform such operations. This caused such amazement that the camp medical officer, Dr Wirtz, was sent for. He, too, stared at Hautval in disbelief.

'What do you mean, you don't want to operate on healthy people?' he asked the doctor. 'Don't you know that there are differences between people – these here are Jews, whom you're to operate on.'

Hautval looked him up and down and calmly replied, 'Oh yes, I know that there are differences between people. Like the difference between you and me.'

Wirtz turned as white as chalk, ran from the room and slammed the door behind him.

Hautval was sentenced to death. Someone crossed her name off the death list, and in the general chaos she managed to survive.

16

Did Hitler Have Syphilis?

A struggle for a healthy nation, together with a healthy national awareness, is probably typical of many totalitarian regimes. But the intensity with which the Third Reich pursued it is rather striking, especially as Hitler was personally involved with it. This was no longer a deification of the 'healthy' but a pathological hatred of anything 'sick', which the man from Braunau then felt entitled to destroy.

The question strongly arises of what that hatred sprang from, and whether, or how, it was connected with Hitler's hatred of the Jews, whom he regarded as the cancer of mankind.

In psychologically well-constructed thrillers there is almost invariably a simple explanation: the phantom which kills one disabled person after another is always revealed, at the end of the film, as a disabled person himself, a sick person trying to conceal his sickness from the world. This film-plot explanation of Hitler's actions is found also in the work of several historians: the British historian Alan Bullock (now Lord Bullock), in his book *Hitler: A Study of Tyranny*, proceeds from the thesis that the young Hitler had been infected with syphilis by a prostitute.

It is possible, however, that the very simplicity, plausibility and film-story character of this explanation militates against its credibility: historians dislike being associated with such cheap 'theories'.

Although indications that Hitler may have been infected with syphilis have long existed, little has been done so far to verify them – in my opinion because those involved were all inhibited by psychological mechanisms.

The old Nazis, who might have contributed something to the clarification of the question, bridled at the image of a syphilitic paranoiac as the greatest leader of all time: this would have besmirched their idol. But opposition from the victims and opponents of Nazism has been at least as strong: they are afraid that an enormously complex pattern of events might suddenly be reduced to the pathological degeneration of a single individual instead of being seen as the sickness of a whole society. I, as least, can see no other reason why the question of whether or not Hitler had syphilis has received so little attention from serious historical researchers.

I came upon that question in the mid-1960s, more or less by accident. After a lecture I was sitting with the Munich city councillor Herr Fackler and the conversation was about Hitler's personality. And Fackler, in a matter-of-fact manner that surprised me, called Hitler a 'syphilitic'. When I asked him how he had arrived at that diagnosis, Fackler told me he was acquainted with Ernst Hanfstaengl, who had been a close friend of Hitler's in the twenties. Hanfstaengl had told him about Hitler's syphilis. His story was astonishingly detailed: during the First World War, when Hitler was stationed in Flanders, he had very nearly – according to Hanfstaengl – faced a court martial for 'self-disablement', the term then used for syphilitic infection which, in certain circumstances, led to exemption from active service. Hitler, however, had succeeded in proving that his syphilis was of an earlier date, and thus had been spared a trial.

At the time I didn't attach any particular importance to this account, which is also mentioned in Hanfstaengl's memoirs, in spite of its circumstantial nature. This may have been due to the psychological mechanism I mentioned above. I also remembered that for a time it had been fashionable to present all great rulers, from Napoleon to Lenin, as syphilitics.

Towards the end of the sixties, however, I had a visit from Dr Edmund Ronald, a physician living in Portugal who was married to a Viennese woman, the daughter of an old friend of mine, and he too mentioned Hitler's syphilis to me. Ronald, also, had surprisingly precise grounds for that suspicion: while working at the Scandinavian Hospital in Seattle, in the USA, he had, towards the end of 1952 or at the beginning of 1953, made the acquaintance of a young Austrian doctor from Graz, who told him that his father had treated Hitler for syphilis. Some time after 1938 German agents had turned up at his father's practice and had confiscated all index cards and medical records concerning the patient Adolf Hitler. The Austrian doctor also claimed to have learned from his father details about the origin of Hitler's syphilis: prior to the First World War he had been infected in Vienna by a Jewish prostitute.

Dr Ronald thereupon conducted some researches on his own initiative, and these produced further information: it appears that in the twenties Hitler consulted Professor Spiethof, the Jena specialist in venereal diseases. It was also significant that, as early as *Mein Kampf*, Hitler stressed the particular importance of the fight against venereal disease.

The matter seemed important enough to me to talk about it to Albert Speer. Although Speer had not heard anything about this suspected syphilis, he remembered that Hitler's entire entourage had been surprised when Hitler appointed Professor Morell to be his personal physician. Morell was a specialist in skin and venereal diseases. (When he assumed his post with Hitler the plate on his house, describing him as such, had to be removed.)

Dr Ronald pointed out to me that the mysterious death of Hitler's niece Geli Raubal might also be plausibly explained by the syphilis theory. It had been widely surmised that there was a sexual relationship between the two; if Hitler had actually suffered from syphilis it could be that Geli Raubal was infected and took her own life, or else that she was shot dead to stop her from talking.

Moreover, everything that is officially known about Hitler's psychological and physical health fits in with the syphilis theory: it would explain why he avoided women; the trembling of his right hand would be entirely in line with the clinical picture of syphilis, though it may have been caused equally by the necessary medication. Finally, of course, Hitler's paranoid illusions and his progressive loss of reality would be in line with a later stage of the disease.

I discussed the syphilis theory with Professor Maser, undoubtedly the greatest expert on Hitler's life, to discover what he thought of it. Maser had of course read Hanfstaengl's memoirs but did not attach a great deal of credibility to them.

I myself, who know a lot less about Adolf Hitler's life, must be even warier of passing judgement. Of course it is possible that Hanfstaengl was fantasizing or merely presenting defamatory rumours as the truth. It is equally possible that the young Austrian doctor was merely bragging about his father's mysterious role. As a criminal investigator, however, I would say that two sources at a considerable distance from each other have nevertheless come up with clues which conform astonishingly well. Clues which, if it were a criminal case, would induce me to follow them up.

All I did was to try to find that young doctor of whom Dr Ronald (who fortunately has since died) has told me. One of my helpers found out that he had taken his degree in Graz in 1952 and immediately afterwards had emigrated to the United States. However, all efforts to locate him there were in vain. But closer investigations in Graz might offer some hope of success. Instead of purchasing fake Hitler diaries a German magazine might invest some money and professional effort in this kind of research. Although the history books would not need rewriting in any way, they would be richer by one piece of information.

17

Plastic Surgery

One day in May 1971 I was roused from my sleep at two in the morning by a telephone call. Drowsily I picked up the receiver, a long-distance operator came on, and a female voice said: 'Herr Wiesenthal, we have an urgent call from New York. Shall I put them through? I know you have a secret number but the caller in New York said it was most urgent and asked us to call at once, he said it was enormously important.'

'Very well,' I said; 'now you've woken me you might as well connect me.'

On the other end of the line was a man who introduced himself as a doctor and director of a hospital in New York. To my short question: 'Where's the fire?' he replied with a long nervous preamble: 'Please excuse me, Mr Wiesenthal, I know it must be the middle of the night where you are, I'm sorry if I woke you up, but I have a problem. The matter seems very important to me. I really did think for hours whether or not to call you.'

'Please go ahead and tell me,' I interrupted his flood of words.

'Yesterday a man arrived at our hospital from Argentina. He is fifty-eight years old and German – you know, a typical German with that particular haircut. I've seen it before; I was an American officer in Germany.'

'So?'

'The man wants us to perform a cosmetic operation on his face. You ought to know that we specialize in cosmetic surgery.'

'You are to make the German more beautiful?'

'That's what he asks me to do.'

'So where's the problem?'

'I'm convinced that the man is a Nazi who wants to change his appearance in order to hide his identity. I consulted with an assistant at my hospital, who's a Jew like myself, and asked him what to do. He shares my opinion that what I'm doing now carries a great risk. If anyone discovers that I, as a doctor, have passed this kind of information on to you it could cost me not only my job at this hospital but even my licence as a doctor. I struggled with the problem one whole night, and then reduced it to the question: "Am I first of all a doctor, or am I first of all a Jew?"'

'And who won?'

'I called you.'

I assured the excited caller that he needn't have the slightest anxieties about me. My informers were as safe with me as with their father confessor.*

The doctor thereupon gave me the full name of his patient – let's call him Adolf Berger – as well as his date of birth, passport number and address. His passport had been issued at Santa Rosa Calamuchita. At the mention of this locality I jumped, for this little Argentinian town had been mentioned to me repeatedly as a hideout of German Nazi criminals. Allegedly it even housed airmen from the notorious 'Condor Legion' who were responsible for the bombing of the Spanish town of Guernica. I tried to conceal my excitement and asked how long the patient was expected to remain in hospital.

'Eight or ten days.'

'That's not enough. I think we'll need a little more time.'

'Very well, then he'll have to stay longer – and it'll cost him a little more.'

I gave the doctor my private number, so he could get hold of me at any time without going through operators, and assured him for the millionth time that he needn't worry about me. No one would learn where I received this or any other information.

'I have a wife and two children,' he implored me and hung up.

The following morning I went to the office even earlier than usual. The story had excited me so much I hardly slept. On my desk there was a pile of inquiries which had to be answered, I dictated a number of letters, but my mind wasn't really on them. At eleven in the morning came a call from New York. A female voice wanted to speak to Simon Wiesenthal. When I said that was me, the words just tumbled out of her: 'I am a nurse, an

---

*I wouldn't like to break this promise even now, which is why I have changed all details which would allow conclusions to be drawn as to the identity of the person concerned. In particular, 'Adolf Berger' does not come from Santa Rosa Calamuchita.

American Indian. I'm working at a hospital here that specializes in plastic surgery. I have a Jewish friend who gave me your telephone number. I think you should know that we have a man at our hospital who's waiting for facial surgery. I only know his name; it's "Berger", and he is a German ... I had to tell you, but please don't give me away. I've been working here several years and I like this place. If it came out that I've passed on information about patients it'd cost me my job.'

I made my voice sound excited so the nurse shouldn't suspect that her information was no news to me, expressed some outrage at the brazenness with which those bastards again ventured to show themselves in New York, thanked her for her information and reassured her that no one would learn anything from me.

Until then I never seriously believed that the Nazis would submit to plastic surgery in order to cover their tracks. Such operations – at least without unreasonable risk – couldn't be performed at any jungle hospital, as I have repeatedly been assured. But if they are performed professionally at a qualified hospital there are too many people in the know. Besides, this was 1971, twenty-five years after the end of the war; countless men living under false names had been arrested, and not one of them had shown signs of surgical intervention (other than medically necessary operations). As, however, the idea of facial surgery is rather fascinating – if only because of the many crime films on the subject – I have repeatedly discussed the possibility with the Ludwigsburg people. They too didn't know of any Nazi who had shown signs of such an operation. On the other hand, of course, the ones who submitted to facial surgery may as a consequence have escaped identification and arrest.

During the many years that I was searching for Eichmann I had repeatedly been informed that he had had his face changed – which subsequently turned out to be nonsense – and I therefore began to collect information on 'beauty clinics' and similar institutions. I knew of large hospitals in São Paulo and Buenos Aires, but there was no indication that they were frequented by Germans of 'possible Nazi age'. I wondered therefore why the German Adolf Berger had chosen to come to New York to acquire a new face. After all, there were nearly two million Jews in that city, including a substantial number of survivors from the Nazi period. The risk of being recognized was substantially higher for him there than in South America. But one should not necessarily assume that Nazis act logically.

I was again reminded of Santa Rosa de Calamuchita, which so many Nazis had made their home. Only recently I learned from an obituary notice in the paper that a man by the name of Ludolf von Alversleben had died there – he had committed monstrous crimes in Poland and in the Crimea. Might not Adolf Berger be likewise living there?

At that time I had a collaborator in Argentina by the name of Harry, a former attorney. We had arranged that if ever I wanted to pass on some information to him I would divide it in two: the second part I would phone to his office number, and the first part two hours later to his private number. This I now did and asked Harry to help: I gave him the name of the German, his address in Santa Rosa, but I didn't tell him where he was at present. Harry or one of his friends was to collect information in the most discreet way possible.

Two days later the New York surgeon again telephoned me, to ask if I had taken all the necessary steps. He had thoroughly examined the man and explained to him that his hospitalization might take a little longer than envisaged. He would operate in two days' time and, as he jokingly assured me, would 'certainly not turn him into a beauty.'

Four days passed and the suspense became almost unbearable. Instead of Harry the surgeon rang again: the operation had been done. He had learned that a blonde lady, looking typically German, was visiting the patient. He had instructed the nurse to tell her the patient needed a lot of rest and had to stay at the hospital for a while. Nevertheless, he'd like to know at last what I intended to do.

I didn't even know myself. The following day I rang Harry in Buenos Aires. The connection was particularly bad and each of us only caught fragments of what the other was saying. Harry was clearly surprised to find me so interested in Adolf Berger. He would send me his collaborator's report the next day, as the telephone lines were so bad. This puzzled me. Even though Harry didn't know the details of the case it was nevertheless astonishing that he regarded Berger as so uninteresting that he entrusted his report to the slow mails. Perhaps he really was just small fry.

I phoned the surgeon in New York in order to play down the matter a little. Well, I said to him, we have decided to tackle the case only after Berger's return home, so that neither you nor your hospital will be involved in any way. Your reputation should not be jeopardized by any actions of ours.

He was relieved. 'God bless you,' he said at least five times. 'You've taken a load off my chest. On the one hand it was very important to me to talk to you about this matter – after all, some distant relations of my wife were murdered by the Nazis – but on the other hand it would have been an enormous risk, suppose the police had come to the hospital and had arrested a patient, possibly in front of the press ... God bless you for sparing me that.'

Three days later an express letter arrived from Buenos Aires. I read it expectantly – and had to sit down, otherwise I would have collapsed with surprise. Harry's friends had discovered that Adolf Berger of Santa Rosa de Calamuchita was a German Jew. He had emigrated to Argentina with his family in the 1930s and was living in Santa Rosa, totally assimilated, among the other Germans. He was a consultant to a firm, a widower with no children. Acquaintances of his reported that he had met a young German woman whom he wanted to marry.

A few months later I was in New York and phoned the surgeon, who was anxious to know how the story had ended. I told him that his patient was an entirely unimportant person, of whom we couldn't even say whether he'd been a member of the Nazi party. His wish for facial surgery had apparently been prompted by the blonde young lady who'd visited him at the hospital. And since we had now broken professional medical secrecy so often, I requested him to show me a photo of his patient. He showed me two, one before and one after the operation. I was unable to see a great deal of difference. Evidently the 'Jew' within the surgeon had come out on top.

I am sorry that Adolf Berger was only slightly beautified for a lot of money. And I am determined definitely to put aside the fairy tale of plastic surgery on former Nazi bigwigs. Anyway, it is unfortunately only the exception that German Nazi criminals look like 'German Nazi criminals'. Only very rarely can you read a man's soul from his features. And the Americans have exactly the same problem as the Austrian and German public in recognizing the beasts of the past in the respectable men and women of today. This was strikingly demonstrated to me by my biggest case in the USA.

18

One of the Nicest Women We Know

It was the last day of my stay in Israel in January 1964. I was sitting on the terrace of the Café Roval in Tel Aviv, trying to soak up as much as possible of the warm sunshine and not to think of the wintry cold that was awaiting me back in Vienna. Any moment now my friend Zeev Porath, with whom I'd studied architecture in Lvov and who was now deputy chief architect of Tel Aviv, would arrive. We'd talk about our time as fellow students and about what our wives and children were now doing – the time span between then and now would stay outside the conversation.

I was turning the pages of a magazine which I'd bought on my way to the café: Zeev seemed to be late. Just then I heard an announcement over the loudspeaker: 'Telephone for Mr Wiesenthal!' As I rose to go to the telephone the café patrons became aware of me. Some of them recognized me, rose to their feet and applauded as I passed them. In Vienna, too, café patrons had risen in the past – in order to spit at my feet. Zeev was on the line. He'd suddenly had to stand in for a colleague at a building conference and was unable to come. We postponed our meeting to the evening and I walked back to my table to pick up my paper and pay. But I couldn't find my place: I was looking out for an empty table but now they were all occupied. Finally I caught sight of my magazine lying on the table just as I had left it, and I walked over to collect it. The three ladies who were sitting there had evidently thought the table was free.

'Excuse me, may I just pick up my paper,' I said, and was about to move away.

But one of the three ladies got up and answered me in Polish: 'We must apologize for simply sitting down at your table. But when we heard your name on the loudspeaker we wanted to talk to you. All three of us were in Majdanek. So we thought we should ask you. You must know what happened to Kobyla?'

'Kobyla' is the Polish word for a mare, and I had no idea what the lady meant.

'Forgive me, we always think everybody must know who Kobyla was. We called her that because she was always kicking the women in the camp. Her real name was Hermine Braunsteiner and she was an Austrian. She was the worst of them all.'

The woman suddenly became terribly excited. She was about forty, and her experiences had not passed her by without leaving their traces on her features. Red blotches had formed on her cheeks and along her neck, and her breath was rapid and panting. 'I'll never forget that child, the child ... a small child, you know ... The man had it on his back. I mean, he had a rucksack on his back and one couldn't see what was inside. By sheer chance he came close to the Braunsteiner woman. She always had a whip with her when a new transport arrived. She lashed out with it wildly and hit the rucksack. At that moment we heard cries and sobs coming from it. She ordered the pack to be opened at once, a child emerged. We were quite close and could see its face: it was very upset and tore itself loose from the man, who tried to hold it, and ran off. But Kobyla ran after it, grabbed it hard so it screamed, and fired a bullet through ...'

The woman was unable to continue. Tears were running down her face, and the other two women were also crying. Even when one has spent several years in a concentration camp and believes oneself inured to all atrocities, almost immune, there are nevertheless experiences which have burnt themselves like fire on to one's memory. 'I believe that if they place shards on my eyes when I die, as is our custom, my dead eyes will still see that child's face,' she continued, sounding as if she had to apologize that 'after so many years' she still thought of that child murdered before her eyes. We, the victims, have to apologize for not being able to forget.

The women were now all talking at once, as if a dam had burst. 'When a transport arrived, the children were always immediately picked out to be killed, the lorries to take them to the gas chambers were standing by. The mothers wanted to hang on to their children, but Hermine wouldn't let them. She tore them apart. Then the women had to climb up on to the lorries by themselves, and Hermine flung up their children after them, like pieces of luggage. Mostly she did this along with Alice. Alice was an aristocrat, the picture-book SS woman, five feet eight inches tall, blonde, beautiful. Her speciality was young girls: she

In 1923, in my home village of Buczacz, I was photographed in the centre of a troop of Jewish boy scouts whose leader I was. Only one survived the Holocaust.

In 1936 I married Cyla Muller, with whom I had been in love since school. We lived happily until August 1939, when the Hitler–Stalin pact was signed, and Poland was partitioned. On 29 June 1941 Lvov, which had until then been under Soviet domination, fell into German hands.

With Cyla in 1946, finally reunited after the long years of hardship and separation.

'The SS police chief of Galicia, Katzmann, has decided to make you a present of your lives,' announced Warzog (*left*), the commandant of Janowska camp, on 18 July 1944, as we waited for the moment of death. (*On the right*, his deputy, Wilhaus.)

May 25, 1945.

To the U.S. Camp Commander,

Camp Mauthausen.

Sir,-

Having spent a number of years in thirteen Nazi concentration camps, including Mauthausen from which I was liberated by the American forces on May 5th and where I still am staying at the present, and desirous to be of help to the U.S. authorities in their effort to bring the Nazi criminals to account, I take the liberty of submitting the following:

1. As all of the camps where I was confined are located in the zones taken by the Soviet armies, it is my conviction that those responsible for the atrocities committed therein by the SS men are not to be found in the eastern parts of Europe but should be sought either in Southern or Western Germany.

2. I am enclosing a brief list of those whom I have seen in these various camps and whom I can recognize on sight. Many of these have caused incalgulable sufferings to myself as well as to my fellow inmates. Many of these I have personally seen commit murder phantastic both in number and method. As shown, some of them had either their homes or relatives living in localities now under Allied occupation.

3. With all of the members of my family and of my nearest relatives killed by the Nazis, I am asking of your kindness to place me at the disposal of the U.S. authorities investigating war crimes. Although I am a Polish citizen and would like to return to my homestead, I feel that the crimes of those men are of such magnitude, that no effort can be spared to apprehend them. I also feel that it is my duty to offer my services either for the purpose of furnishing the description of their misdeeds or as an eyewitness in case identification is needed.

4. To furnish you with the personal data regarding my person, a brief curriculum vitae is attached.

Respectfully,

/s/ Ing. Wiesenthal Szymon
Szymon Wiesenthal
(Camp Mauthausen, 127371).

SECRET

DECLASSIFIED
NND 750114
By _____ NARS, Date _____

209

Twenty days after the liberation of Mauthausen, I wrote a letter to the American camp commander to offer him my services in the hunt for Nazi criminals. This is an English translation of the letter I wrote in Polish.

A guided tour of Mauthausen camp. *Left*, the SS Reichsführer Heinrich Himmler; *right*, Ernst Kaltenbrunner, head of the SS Reich Security Directorate.

Franz Novak, the 'stationmaster of death', who provided the trains which, week after week, carried Jews to Auschwitz, despite the scarcity of transport which affected the fighting forces. Sentenced after the war to nine years in prison, he was freed six years later for 'good behaviour'.

In Vienna, in 1958, assisting in a trial of Nazi criminals. As a rule I have avoided attending these trials as a spectator, because the judges immediately accuse me of trying to influence the witnesses.

In 1983, the Simon Wiesenthal Center in Los Angeles launched a huge campaign to force Chile to extradite Walter Rauff (*left*). He was the inventor of the 'gas trucks', in which Jews were asphyxiated by exhaust fumes. These trucks, one of which is shown here, were painted with a red cross, which led the victims to believe that they were being taken to medical stations, and so scenes of panic were avoided.

The villa of Laber, near Merano, where Friedrich Schwendt lived after the war. Entrusted by the SS with the task of disposing of a batch of counterfeit British pound notes which Himmler had ordered made, he became quite wealthy. Later he sought refuge in Chile, where he worked alongside Klaus Barbie.

Dear President Pinochet,

Walter Rauff, the German Nazi inventor and supervisor of the mobile gas vans is responsible for the murder of 250,000 Jews during WW II. Yet this criminal lives openly in Chile. Due to a legal technicality he has avoided extradition.

Mr. Pinochet, what can we say to younger generations when this murderer has not spent one day in jail? In the name of Humanity, Justice, and Chile's good name, we join in the Simon Wiesenthal Center's International Campaign for Justice in demanding that you immediately expel Rauff.

FROM:
Name _____
Address _____
City _____
State _____ Zip _____
Country _____

Air Mail
Postage Required
U.S. 28¢
Canada 64¢

AIR MAIL

TO:
Presidente Augusto Pinochet
Palacio de la Moneda
Santiago, Chile

The guard Ritschek took pleasure in setting his German shepherd on the inmates of the Lvov-Janowska concentration camp. I am convinced that he is still alive today, and without doubt in Sweden. Unfortunately, all my investigations have so far come to nothing.

A freight document for five wagonloads of prisoners sent from Treblinka to Sobibor. (Gross weight 25,000 kg.)

In 1949, three anonymous
passengers took the air on
the bridge while waiting to
disembark in Argentina. In
the middle is Adolf
Eichmann.

In November 1959, the
Israeli ambassador in
Vienna informed me that my
help in the Eichmann affair
was greatly appreciated in
his country: 'His wife,' he
added, 'behaved as if
Eichmann was no longer
alive, and remarried a
German citizen . . .' I was
able to prove that this
'second husband', one
Ricardo Klement, was none
other than Eichmann
himself.

AMBASSADE D'ISRAËL
4050/ בכ.

שגרירות ישראל

Wien, den 10. November 1959

Herrn
Ing. Simon Wiesenthal
L i n z
Raimundstrasse 39/III

Sehr geehrter Herr Wiesenthal,

Ich danke Ihnen bestens fuer den interessanten
Bericht.

Als ich in Israel war, fuehrte ich Unterredungen
in Angelegenheit Eichmann und unsere Leute dort brachten zum
Ausdruck, wie sehr sie Ihre Hilfe in der Sache schaetzten.

Gemaess den letzten Meldungen, die sich bei
ihnen befinden, ist die Familie Eichmann in Argentinien.
Seine Frau tut so, als ob Eichmann nicht mehr am Leben waere.
Sie hat sich sogar wieder verheiratet und zwar mit einem
deutschen Buerger. Jedoch alle Anzeichen weisen darauf hin,
dass die Heirat fiktiv ist, um "den Feind zu verwirren".

Herzliche Gruesse sendet Ihnen

Ihr

Y. Sahar
Botschafter

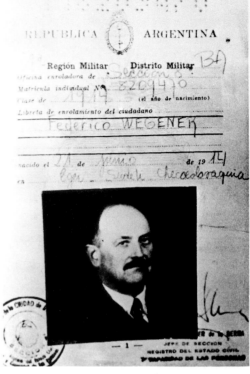

Gustav Wagner, deputy commandant of Treblinka in 1944, before the odyssey which took him to Brazil via Bayreuth and Damascus. Arrested then released by the Brazilian police in 1979, forsaken by all his friends, he hanged himself in October 1980.

Edward Roschmann, the second-in-command of the Riga ghetto, unwittingly became the star of a novel and a film, in which he died ... *Below*, his Nazi file photograph. *Above*, twenty years older, on his Argentinian identity card, under the name Federico Wegener.

Hyg.-bakt. Unters.-Stelle
der Waffen-SS, Südost

29. JUN. 1944

Auschwitz OS., am 29. Juni 1944.

Anliegend wird übersandt:

4 6 1774 / VIII / 50

(12-jähriges Kind)

Material: Kopf einer Leiche entnommen am

zu untersuchen auf Histologische Schnitte

Name, Vorname:

Dienstgrad, Einheit: siehe Anlage

Klinische Diagnose:

Anschrift der einsendenden Dienststelle: H.-Krankenbau
Zigeunerlager Auschwitz II, B II e

Bemerkungen: Der 1. Lagerarzt
K.L. Auschwitz II

Mengele

SS-Hauptsturmführer.

A form signed by Josef Mengele, detailing
the shipment of the head of a twelve-year-
old child, provided by the gypsy camp at
Auschwitz, to the histological research
laboratory.

Doctor Aribert Heim performed the most
terrible experiments on the inmates at
Mauthausen camp. He was never
captured.

struck them with her whip right across their faces, preferably across their eyes . . .'

'The Orlowsky woman,' flashed through my mind. I myself had known, in the Cracow-Plaszow camp, a camp guard who struck young girls with her whip in exactly the same way the women from Majdanek were describing. Her name was von Orlowsky and she was an aristocrat. Anyone who'd seen her wield her whip once would have that image imprinted forever on his mind: she enjoyed whipping, as if she derived her confidence from the humiliation of those she beat – with no reason and no sense: intimidated, emaciated young girls, who had often become completely apathetic from being on a transport for a week on end, girls who didn't even try to resist when they were taken to the gas chambers. The Orlowsky woman's lashes were to teach them that they hadn't simply come to die, but to die in humiliation.

'Her name was von Orlowsky,' said one of the three women. 'We shall never forget her.'

Nor will I.

Along with a third warder, whom the women called 'bloody Brigitta', Alice von Orlowsky and Hermine Braunsteiner must have had a reign of terror at the women's camp of Majdanek, such as one cannot picture even in nightmares. Of course it was by no means a case of all women guards being beasts on principle. Many had been assigned to camps more or less by chance and were coping with the horror they saw by becoming totally dulled: they treated the inmates like objects which had to be unloaded, stowed away in huts or sorted out on to lorries with the least possible fuss. Any upheaval in this procedure by some not quite predictable reaction – a woman not wanting to let go of her child, sisters clutching each other on the way to their death – was a source of irritation, in much the same way as a conveyor belt stoppage jeopardizes the attainment of a production target. Then the guards would kick or strike, because that was the simplest form of keeping the extermination machinery going. They hit out, much as a shepherd hits out at sheep straggling too far behind the flock or running too slowly through a gate, but these women did not hit because they enjoyed hitting.

Unlike Orlowsky and Braunsteiner. In them the concentration camp had evidently uncovered latent sadistic inclinations, which these women then indulged like addicts. That a woman – who might herself be a mother, or maybe was a mother – could fling a small child through the air like a sack, striking it with a whip across the eyes, firing a bullet right into its face, all this is so unimaginable that at times I am myself incapable of believing it. I know it is true – because I have seen similar things with my own eyes, because it is documented in countless statements by witnesses, laid down in books – and yet it takes a personal confrontation, even in my case, for my intellectual knowledge to become emotional belief in the reality of what I know to be true.

Only my encounter with these three former inmates made Majdanek – about which I had read numerous books and which was mentioned in any number of my files – a reality for me. And even then, typically, I repressed the enormous significance the name of this camp held for me: my wife Cyla had been earmarked for one of the transports to Majdanek. She only escaped that hell by a miracle.

Cyla at the time was hiding out, under the false name of Kowalska, at the home of my friend Szczepanski, a graduate engineer, in Lublin; she was not registered at that address and her papers were forged. One day an order was issued to the effect that all unregistered persons living in a household had to write their names on a slip of paper to be fastened on the door of the apartment. Concierges were instructed to notify the Gestapo of these names, and two days later the people thus registered had to present themselves at Gestapo headquarters. One would run an enormous risk, in a building where everyone knew how many people were living in an apartment, by not putting one's name on the list: one would become automatically suspect and probably denounced by some collaborator. On the other hand, it was at least as much of a risk to enter one's name and to hope that false papers would keep one safe. At any rate, nearly a thousand people streamed to Gestapo headquarters to register. Their names were called up, the people were registered and questioned. All day long, until six in the evening. By then some forty people were left: the Gestapo – precise as German authorities were apt to be even in that madness – sent them home at the end of the day, instructing them to come back in the morning when working hours began again. My wife was among those forty. All the rest were deported to the Majdanek concentration camp by lorries arriving at half-hourly intervals.

Cyla, who heard about it, escaped that very night to Lvov, where we used to live, and eventually, with the help of the Polish underground with whom I had a contact, found a new hiding place in Warsaw. 'If office hours had been a quarter of an hour longer,' I was now thinking, 'the Gestapo would have loaded her on one of those lorries, and she would have been greeted at Majdanek by Hermine Braunsteiner with a whip in her jackboot.'

It was late. The January sun had lost its warmth, and we sat there shivering, trying to cope with our memories. The drinks the waiter had brought us stood untouched on the table.

'From every one of my journeys I return home with new names, the way other people bring back a souvenir,' I said to the three women in parting. 'From this journey it will be the name of Hermine Braunsteiner.'

Back in Vienna I fished out from our archives all existing data on the

Majdanek camp. This is what it revealed: a month after the German surprise attack on the Soviet Union the Reichsführer SS, Heinrich Himmler, was in Lublin. He conceived the idea of having a camp built near the city, for 20–50,000 detainees. He instructed the SS and police district chief, the Carinthian Odilo Globocnik, to set up such a camp. But Globocnik had more ambitious plans: he wanted to set up a camp for roughly 150,000 slave labourers to be employed in the SS clothing and armament works. In addition, his camp was to accommodate approximately 100,000 Russian prisoners of war.

But there were not enough building materials for such a gigantic project, and he had to content himself with a first phase of accommodation for about 50,000 prisoners. The huge camp compound covered seven and a half acres and was surrounded by a double barbed-wire fence, electrified and supplemented by eighteen guard towers. There were seven gas chambers: two near the camp entrance, four near the bath house and one by the crematorium, very near the area where the women and children were held.

In 1944 Soviet troops liberated about a thousand prisoners whom the Nazis had not been able to move away. 150,000 people had lost their lives in Majdanek.

The first Majdanek trial started as early as 27 November 1944, in Lublin, and went on for eight days. Eighty out of the 1300 members of the SS who had belonged to the camp staff were convicted. Hermine Braunsteiner was not among them. But then I found her, to my surprise, in our list of people sentenced in Austria for Nazi crimes: in 1948 Hermine Braunsteiner had been arrested in Villach, in Carinthia, and put on trial in Vienna. From old newspapers, which had carried brief accounts of the proceedings, I learned that she had been sentenced to a mere three years' imprisonment for slapping, kicking and whipping female detainees at the Ravensbrück concentration camp. Her activity at Majdanek was mentioned only casually and there were no specific testimonies about it. That was all that was to be learned from the reports. But at least I knew that Braunsteiner came from Vienna, and I assumed that, having served her term, she would have returned to her native city.

But I couldn't find her. At the registration office we were informed that since 1946 Hermine Braunsteiner had no longer been registered at her former address of Kahlenbergstrasse 44, Vienna 19. But there might still be neighbours who had known her and her family circumstances, and who might even know where she had moved to. So I set out for Kahlenbergstrasse, a delightful steep street on the outskirts of the city, where the vineyards rise up to the Vienna Woods.

I didn't think it would be advisable to go straight to number 44 and ask about her there. Instead I chose a nearby house and rang the bell. A man opened the door. I asked him if he had known a Fräulein Braunsteiner who had lived next door and if he could possibly tell me where I might find her. But as I uttered the name Braunsteiner he scowled. 'Get the hell out of here,' he grunted, and slammed the door in my face.

I had better luck at a house across the street. In response to my knocking a friendly elderly woman opened the door and willingly answered my question: 'Of course I knew the girl. Won't you come in? What would you like to know about her? Are you from the press?'

I could not repay this friendly welcome with a lie and therefore told her truthfully: 'No, I'm not from the press. I am interested in Fräulein Braunsteiner because she was on trial.'

'Ah yes, the poor thing,' the woman resumed our conversation. 'I heard about it, of course, and also that she was convicted. There were all kinds of stuff in the papers, about how she was said to have treated the women in the camp. I can't really believe it of her. On the other hand, a lot of witnesses said she really did. I knew her parents, they were a strict Catholic family. When she was a little girl I always saw her with her sister, as they went to church on Sundays, prettily dressed ...' She fell silent and was lost in her memories, almost forgetting my presence. Gently I brought her back into the present and asked her to tell me about Hermine Braunsteiner.

The family hadn't been particularly well off and at the age of fourteen or fifteen the Braunsteiner girl had had to go into service with a cattle dealer, just for her board and lodgings, nothing much in the way of pay. Her sister had gone to Holland as a domestic servant, and so she too tried, with her first savings, to go to Holland because she hoped she'd get a better job there. But nothing came of it: she was stopped at the frontier and sent back. 'Why, I can't remember any longer,' the old lady went on, becoming ever more trusting. 'A relative of hers then told me during the war that Hermine was working as a prison warder in Germany and that she was well. In 1943 she turned up once in Vienna. I didn't see her but my neighbours told me that she had tried to visit me. Unfortunately I wasn't in. The neighbours at first didn't recognize her because she was wearing a kind of military uniform. And after the war, yes, I saw her once then; she came to see me but she didn't like it in Vienna. "There's nothing to eat here," she said. "I'll go to my relations in Carinthia." And that's where she was arrested by the police. Perhaps she is back in Carinthia, now that she's served her sentence. She's got a lot of relations there.'

Suddenly, with an inimitably elegant movement, a cat landed on my lap, a beautiful black and white animal with silkily gleaming fur and green eyes, which settled down comfortably on my knees and let me stroke it.

'Now that's very unusual, for my Minka to come up to a stranger and let him stroke her. Normally she makes herself scarce as soon as someone comes whom she doesn't know very well. But then I don't have many visitors. My Minka is my only company. As for the people in the building, I have hardly any contact with them. My husband is long dead, and my two boys haven't come back from the war. Reported missing, you know, and so one keeps hoping. Miracles do still happen, don't they?'

The old lady looked at me questioningly; she wanted me to confirm her belief in miracles, and so I nodded reassuringly. 'Yes, miracles do happen. I found my wife again . . . months after the war.'

The old lady was so glad to have found a listener that she continued to tell me about her granddaughter, who had lived with her for a while and who was now roughly the same age 'as Hermine was then'. Hermine Braunsteiner, who had fired into the face of a child, had remained, for this old lady, a nice girl from the neighbourhood, one she compared to her own granddaughter. If I had told her what the three women in Tel Aviv had reported about her, she wouldn't have believed me. It would have seemed to her just as unthinkable as the suggestion that the cat on my lap was in reality a fierce beast of prey.

'Can you tell me the name of Fräulein Braunsteiner's relations in Carinthia and where they live?' I asked her before leaving. She willingly wrote both down on a piece of paper which I pocketed. At that moment the cat took fright and jumped off my lap.

I had obviously made a good deal of progess. An acquaintance of mine who lived in Graz and often had business in Carinthia was to keep his eyes open for Hermine Braunsteiner, discreetly, and let me know. The attempt was a failure. The Braunsteiner woman had not been seen anywhere and was not registered with the police. There was now only the possibility of making direct contact with her relations, under some pretext or other. I needed someone suitable for such an assignment, someone who wouldn't immediately, by his behaviour or appearance, arouse suspicion in the no doubt 'nationally minded' Carinthian family, someone whom they might in fact regard as someone of their own kind.

I already had someone in mind: Richard, as I propose to call him, was about twenty-four, had studied international trade and was employed in an electronics firm in Vienna. He was a strikingly handsome young man, the kind mothers would like for their son-in-law; my secretary, with a mixture of humour and secret admiration, had nicknamed him Apollo. But that wasn't the reason why I had chosen him; the reason was that he came from a background which – as he cannot deny to this day – was more than just 'national'. 'I come from an anti-Semitic family,' he had confessed to me at our very first meeting. 'I want you to know this from me, rather than learning it from someone else. When I was still a child I often heard my parents say that the Jews ought to go to Palestine and live among their own kind there. My father, in particular, didn't have a good word to say for the Jews. But you must believe me that he never approved of these mass murders. During the latter years of the war he often talked about it to my mother, and she told me, "Your father didn't like Jews – he had this dislike from his childhood – but he cannot understand that people were locked up in camps and sent to their deaths." I myself never had a chance to talk to my father about it, because he was killed in action in 1944. But I am certain that, if he were alive today, he'd approve of my offering to work for you. I don't want you to think that my father was a bad man.'

No, I do not believe it. I know how much the background against which a person grows up can mould him. I know how – especially in Austria – people who have probably never seen a Jew, let alone come to know him more closely, have grown up with anti-Semitism as with the Ten Commandments. Anti-Jewish prejudice is something one doesn't even think about, let alone discuss, one is so certain of it. Whether a person who has grown up like this is 'good' or 'evil' is revealed only when he is confronted with the reality of the persecution of Jews. He is then able, within the limits of what is feasible for him, to accept that persecution or begin to reflect on it. If he is a decent person then this reflection will lead to a rejection of anti-Semitism. No one can be blamed for having grown up as an anti-Semite: the question is whether, faced with SS men loading Jews on to lorries or crowding them into cattle trucks, he remains one.

Richard, too, as the son of a prejudiced father, had these two options: to identify himself blindly with what he remembered of his father's opinions or, in view of all that has meanwhile become known of the Nazi period, to reflect and to form an opinion of his own. In the course of my work I have come across numerous sons of such fathers, young men who have accomplished just that, and their achievement in utterly and profoundly rejecting Nazism weighs more heavily than its rejection by the son of a resistance fighter. The latter is a matter of course; the former is a moral achievement.

The Eichmann trial played an important part in this: even people too young to have gone through the wave of revelations after the war now had an opportunity, through this trial, to be informed. Anyone who, after the Eichmann trial, still doubts that millions of Jews were deported and gassed is fighting his own better knowledge, which ought to have become his conscience. Richard was one of many who came to my office then and spontaneously offered me their help: 'I want to do something, no matter what. There must be some way to make good at least a little bit of what happened then.' They do exist. People like Richard give people like me the assurance that there was a purpose in surviving and in remaining in Austria.

I should have liked to give every one of them some assignment, if only to show that I understood and accepted what was behind their offer. Some of them worked at my office for a time, some did minor jobs for me, making inquiries at registration offices or simply taking our office mail to the post. In most cases we lost sight of each other after a while, because as a rule I need professionals for my work, people used to searching for other people. But in this particular instance, the Hermine Braunsteiner case, an amateur like Richard might be just the man. A visit to Carinthia for him would be like a return to his past, one in which he knew his way about even though he had put it firmly behind him.

'You said you wanted to help me,' I received him when he appeared a mere hour after my telephone call.

'I'll do anything I can,' he answered.

He would probably have been prepared to be infiltrated into the ranch of some former Nazi bigwig in South America. But this task, though not dangerous, was tricky enough. Richard was to take a room in the village where Hermine Braunsteiner's relations were living and make contact with them. A well-tried method for such operations was to say one happened to have relations of the same name, and could the families be possibly related? 'When you've succeeded in getting on more or less friendly terms with those people you casually mention in conversation that you have an uncle who'd had a court case because of his past in the Third Reich and who'd been innocently convicted. On no account are you to start asking questions about Hermine Braunsteiner. The most important thing is never to rush things but always to wait for what people will tell you.'

Having taken some leave from his firm, Richard came once more to my office to say goodbye, then he disappeared into Carinthia. I was beginning to be concerned when, nine days after his departure, he turned up again. I only needed to look at his face to know he'd been successful.

'I did everything just as you told me,' he began his story which, in the end, took all of two hours. 'On the third day I went to the house which had been pointed out to me as belonging to the family. I knocked and an elderly lady opened the door, and I produced my story of my relations in Salzburg province, who had the same name. The woman said at once that there could be no connection – she had no relations in Salzburg – and I was afraid she'd close the door in my face. "Maybe your husband knows something about it," I quickly improvised, trying to look as relaxed as possible. The woman scrutinized me with great reserve but I evidently looked harmless to her, and so she asked me in. I chatted calmly about being here on holiday, and how much I liked her native area, and so on.

Just then a young man of my own age entered the room and shook hands with me. He evidently liked me on first sight. We chatted easily and I asked him out to dinner at the inn.'

The following day Richard was invited to lunch at the family's home, and this was repeated during the next few days. But only on his fourth visit did he learn anything about Hermine Braunsteiner. As I had advised him, he came out with his story of the poor uncle who'd been sentenced to five years' imprisonment although he was innocent: just because vindictive people envied him the paintings he'd brought back from France they had invented all kinds of atrocities, and the court had convicted him despite his desperate protestations of innocence.

The story had its effect. 'The very same thing happened to a woman relative of mine,' his hostess said, suddenly loquacious. 'She was sentenced just because as a guard in a prison she'd slapped the faces of a few gypsy women. But happily that's over. Five years ago she married an American and is now living in Halifax in Canada.'

More difficult had been the problem of establishing Hermine Braunsteiner's present name. On a walk with the son of the house, with whom he'd become quite friendly, Richard had returned to the lunch-table conversation.

'Of course you'll go and see your relative in Canada some day?'

'That would be nice, but it would cost a lot of money.'

'Canada has always been my dream,' Richard was acting the globetrotter. 'Wonderfully wild and untouched scenery. Maybe I'll have saved up enough in a year or two to go there. In that case I might look up your relative and give her your good wishes.'

'Her name's Ryan now and she lives in Halifax.'

Richard assumed that in Canada, as in Austria, people had to register their address, so that it should be easy to find Mrs Ryan. In line with my urgent instructions he contained his curiosity and asked no further questions.

'I hope you're satisfied with me.'

I replied to his largely rhetorical question with a far from rhetorical, 'Yes, very.'

But that was only the preamble to a talk which seemed to be more important to Richard than what we'd just spoken about. 'Do you know, Herr Wiesenthal,' he said almost hastily, as if afraid I might now have lost interest in him, 'do you know why I am so anxious for you to be satisfied with my work, for you to see that a person like me can do some good?'

I looked at him questioningly because I had doubted him a lot less than he seemed to doubt himself. Or rather, it was a deep doubt about his father that had corroded him for years, a doubt he had been unable to cope with or even to utter.

'I told you that my father was an anti-Semite, even though he did not want the extermination of the Jews. Last night, immediately on my return from Carinthia, I told my mother what I had done for you. Then she told me a story which seemed to me the most wonderful reward. You know of course, she said, that your father wasn't too fond of Jews. But when he was a soldier in the east, during the war, he experienced something frightful. He had been forbidden to talk to anybody about it, but shortly before he was killed, on his last leave from the front, he made a few hints to me. "You know," he said, "I'm worried by a question that I can't get rid of and that I can't answer: to whom should I apologize for all my verbal insults to the Jews? Our unit was detailed for sealing-off measures and I saw with my own eyes what they led to. None of you will ever be able to forgive me for that."' Tears gleamed in Richard's eyes.

'You can forgive him,' I said and put my hand on his. We remained sitting like this for a long time.

I made contact with a friend in Toronto, an Auschwitz survivor, and in rough outline informed him about the Braunsteiner case. I told him she was now living in Halifax and asked him to establish the exact address for us. Three weeks later, in the latter half of June 1964, the awaited answer arrived: 'Braunsteiner-Ryan no longer lives in Halifax. She has moved to the United States and lives at 5211 72nd Street, Maspet, Queens, N.Y. That is the address to which her mail is forwarded from Halifax.'

That, one might have thought, would have concluded the Braunsteiner case. In reality it was only the beginning. During the nineteen years since the war there had not been a single Nazi war crimes trial in the USA and nobody had ever been extradited to another country for such crimes. Even so, the legal situation looked favourable: if Hermine Braunsteiner-Ryan had meanwhile become a US citizen (and only in that case would she enjoy the protection of the USA) then she must have answered the immigration authorities' question about previous sentences. If she had mentioned her conviction in Vienna this would undoubtedly have been a reason for refusing her US citizenship; if, as I assumed, she had concealed it, this would be a reason for stripping her of it.

In order to find out about such a complex problem in a foreign country the best course is to turn not to an official but to a journalist. In this particular case it was Clyde Farnsworth, the Vienna correspondent of the *New York Times* who, a few months earlier, had published a lengthy article about me in the weekly supplement of his paper, entitled 'The Sleuth with Six Million Clients'.

'Who would be right for the Hermine Braunsteiner case?' I asked him, having told him the full story. 'Because I cannot imagine that you will rest content with having that woman living in your country unmolested.'

'I'm only a newspaperman,' Farnsworth replied, 'and I know no more than you do about these legal matters. All I know is that the press is a power in the USA. If you can prove what you've just told me and I write an article about it, the pressure of public opinion will put the proper authorities into action. Write down for me everything that woman is charged with. We'll send a reporter to her, and then a story will be published – with your accusations and her justification.'

A mere ten days later, on 14 June 1964, the Braunsteiner story appeared in the *New York Times* under the title 'Former Nazi Camp Guard Is Now a Housewife in Queens' and caused an enormous stir. The reporter Joseph Leyland had called on Mrs Braunsteiner-Ryan at the address supplied by me – she was in the process of repainting her apartment in soft shades of mauve and yellow – and confronted her with the accusations I had collected. Her first reaction, recorded by him verbatim, was: 'I've suffered enough. You keep talking on the radio about peace, I have a claim to be left in peace too. Is this never going to end? After all, I only did my duty and I have already served my sentence of three years in prison. Can you imagine,' she asked the reporter, 'what that means: to be in prison for three years? And I was only in Majdanek for one year. After the war I was interned by the British, but they soon had to release me because there was nothing against me.'

Hermine Braunsteiner's husband, a building worker with the first name of Russell, defended his wife with American hyperbole: 'She's the best woman in the world, she wouldn't hurt a fly!' he didn't know (or pretended not to know) that his wife had served a three-year prison sentence after the war. He knew nothing about her work in the Majdanek or Ravensbrück camps; she had told him she'd been a guard in a penal institution during the Nazi period. For his wife to have committed any kind of crime was unthinkable to him.

Which it was equally to all the acquaintances and neighbours of the Ryans. Mrs Ryan was described as particularly pleasant, and excellent wife, and invariably helpful to a stranger who might be in need of anything. When she'd moved into the neighbourhood she had called on all her neighbours to introduce herself and she'd not allowed that contact to break off since. The woman who was a beast to the survivors of Majdanek was, to the housewives of 72nd Street, 'one of the nicest women we know'.

This is a very frequent phenomenon and has a variety of explanations. One of them is that SS guards were portrayed, after the war, in a way that in reality described only a few of them – perverted beasts, always with a whip in their shaft boots, ready to strike the face of any prisoner crossing

their path. Such warders certainly existed, and they created the image of
the concentration camp guard in the minds of both the inmates and the
public. Yet these sadists, according to information from the level-headed
Dr Ella Lingens, president of the Austrian Auschwitz community,
accounted for no more than 10 per cent of the camp staff. The remaining
90 per cent were average people, remarkable only for their extreme insen-
sitivity, which might have been congenital or might have been acquired in
the camps as a kind of psychological self-defence. These people committed
crimes only under the exceptional conditions of the Third Reich, and even
then less out of a personal urge than as a result of external circumstances.
Once the nightmare was over, once they had taken off their uniforms, they
put aside their crimes with it and, for the world around them, reverted to
what they had been before the war: totally unremarkable. If they had then
been pleasant, helpful people, good to their husbands and children, they
were just the same now. If someone who knew them heard that they had
whipped women and children in a camp, he would think it just as unlikely
as that he himself might commit such atrocities. We do not like people
capable of such crimes to be indistinguishable from ourselves.

Hermine Braunsteiner, of course, was not one of those average people.
From all I knew about her from the camp, she was one of that 10 per cent
of almost pathological sadists. Even in Majdanek it was not normal to fire
into the face of a small child who ran away. Hermine Braunsteiner's psyche
must always have contained a massive dose of aggression, and it couldn't
have simply disappeared on her return to normal life. Or could it? Is it
conceivable that people can totally expend their damned-up sadism at
a certain time in their lives, afterwards behave amiably, and without
aggressiveness? Or, vice versa, is it possible that the aggression which,
under the perverse conditions of a concentration camp, manifested itself
as sadism, manifests itself as cordiality to other people the moment the
person concerned lives under human conditions? Or is there such a thing
as normal schizophrenia, when a person can contain two sides – an evil,
sadistic one and a good, helpful one – without them overlapping at one
single point? When, in a manner of speaking, he is two people, one who
can step on a girl's face with his jackboot, while the other offers a sweet to
the neighbour's daughter?

I don't know if our knowledge of the human psyche will ever be advanced
enough to explain such phenomena credibly. And although it might be
useful to be able to do just that, I do not, ultimately, consider it that
important: any criminal act has some ultimate explanation in the criminal's
psyche. But this doesn't make the action any better. We have to go
by actions. Against Hermine Braunsteiner there were the statements of
numerous credible witnesses, to the effect that she beat, whipped, kicked

and murdered. This cannot be altered by the equally credible statements of countless neighbours that she was the nicest woman on the street.

That was also how the overwhelming majority of the American public saw it. The *New York Times* story was the talk of New York. Prior to publication the newspaper had approached the Immigration and Naturalization Service and discovered that Mrs Braunsteiner-Ryan had immigrated on 14 April 1959 and five years later, on 15 January 1963, had acquired American citizenship. It was clear, therefore, that she must have made false statements about her past. A reporter from the *New York Herald Tribune* asked the INS director, P. A. Esperdy, the very day after publication, what the Service intended to do about it. Esperdy replied that there were some fifty cases a year concerned with revocation of US citizenship, but it was in fact revoked in only about two.

In no way were the American authorities up to the task the Braunsteiner case was facing them with. It was recalled that, as long ago as the 1950s, the Soviet Union and its satellites had demanded the extradition of Nazis living in the United States, and that all these cases had been swamped by the propaganda of the Cold War. Quite a few Americans had been convinced that such accusations were untruths invented by the Communists.

But the American press did not let go. It kept pestering the INS with the question of what it was doing in the Braunsteiner case. In order to placate the public it was announced that the INS had requested Austria to supply the evidence on which Mrs Ryan had been sentenced in 1949. This was factual enough, but it was unnecessary: for Mrs Ryan to be stripped of her citizenship it would have been enough to establish – and there was no doubt about that – that she had concealed her conviction from the immigration authorities. But the bureaucrats weren't content with such a simple procedure: they were anxious to show how objective they had meanwhile become with regard to the Nazi period as well.

Mr Russell Ryan instructed the attorney Leo Barry to represent his wife, and the family was assured that the case would drag on for years. He would raise a fundamental matter: whether it was acceptable that an American family should be torn asunder by the expulsion of the wife. Such is the meticulous care which a constitutional state practises even with those who are responsible for the deportation – and the death – of millions.

I was of the opinion that, as a former Austrian, Hermine Braunsteiner had to be extradited to Austria and therefore suggested that the public prosecutor's office in Graz, which was investigating events in Majdanek, should now also hear witnesses against Mrs Braunsteiner. It was to be three years before public prosecutor Flick left for Israel to take up my suggestion.

Meanwhile we were sending out photographs of the Braunsteiner woman to every victims' association we knew of, and soon we were receiving witnesses' reports from a great variety of countries – even one from South Africa. The street where the Ryans lived became the scene of demonstrations, mainly by young people, but also by people curious to see how a woman accused of such terrible crimes now lived. A few hotheads manufactured a bomb, but set it off in front of the wrong house, so that the home of some totally uninvolved person was wrecked.

The American consul in Vienna, Mr Longo, called at my office and brought a list of witnesses who gave evidence in the Braunsteiner trial in 1949. I was to find out where they were now, because he'd been instructed to interrogate them anew. Naturally we helped him, even though we couldn't see the point of it. After all, this wasn't a matter of bringing the Braunsteiner woman to trial in the USA for her offences in the past, but of revoking her US citizenship. And for that it was sufficient that she had lied on oath. Nevertheless, at Mr Longo's request, we brought two witnesses from Yugoslavia to Vienna, where they made statements in 1968. Two witnesses were also questioned at the US embassy in Warsaw.

However, not until 22 August 1968 – four years after the case was opened – did the US Department of Justice apply to the INS for the revocation of Mrs Braunsteiner-Ryan's citizenship. And not until another three years later, on 28 September 1971, was she actually stripped of her citizenship by Chief Justice Jakob Mischler of the Brooklyn Federal District Court.

Before 1971 was out the German Ministry of Justice transmitted to the US Department of Justice, through diplomatic channels, a 300-page application for extradition. Shortly afterwards the Polish news agency PAP announced that Poland, too, had applied for extradition on the grounds that Braunsteiner's crimes had been committed on Polish territory and that her victims had predominantly been Polish citizens.

On 21 March 1973 Braunsteiner-Ryan was taken into pre-extradition detention and her attorney, who had hoped by repeated appeals to drag out the case for years, had to abandon all further manoeuvres at his client's request. Hermine Braunsteiner was so terrified at the thought of being extradited to Poland that she declared herself agreeable to extradition to West Germany.

Only Braunsteiner's American husband continued, undismayed, to collect written statements from neighbours and acquaintances in Queens, which all portrayed Mrs Ryan as a blameless, reserved and friendly person. But this signature campaign was unable to halt the course of developments: on 6 August 1973 Hermine Braunsteiner was expelled from the USA and, escorted by German police officers, taken by Lufthansa to the Federal Republic.

On 26 November 1975, almost exactly thirty years to the day after the first Majdanek trial in Lublin, the trial opened in Düsseldorf of ten male and five female members of the camp staff. By mid-1962 the Central Office of the provincial judiciary in Ludwigsburg had identified 232 persons suspected of murder in Majdanek. By the end of 1968 the total was 350. I was given a similar figure by Regional Court Counsellor Schwedersky in Düsseldorf in 1971; but now, in 1975, he pointed out that only thirty-two were suspected of murder, and three of them had since died. In the end only fifteen had to face trial. They were headed by Hermann Hackmann, commandant of a protective custody camp, who had shortly after the war been sentenced by an American tribunal to death, subsequently commuted to life imprisonment, and who in 1955 had been pardoned and released. The three principal women defendants were Hildegard Lechert, called 'bloody Brigitta' by her victims, Alice von Orlowsky – who died during the trial – and Hermine Ryan, known as Kobyla, 'the mare'.

The presiding judge was Günther Boden. The prosecution was represented by two public prosecutors, and there were two defence counsel available for each defendant, men who had figured in earlier Nazi trials. Dr Wolfgang Scheffler was appointed as a historical expert; the defence counsel vigorously protested against him because in his book *Judenverfolgung im Dritten Reich* ('Persecution of Jews in the Third Reich') he had referred to the 'brutality of the SS' and was therefore, they claimed, prejudiced. Even more important, in the view of Dr Ludwig Bock, Hildegard Lechert's counsel, was the fact that Dr Scheffler had received his degree under a Jewish professor in Berlin: this was bound to make him utterly biased.

Dr Bock had attracted my attention in the past, when he defended H. Pal, a man under strong suspicion of mass murder in Czortków (Poland) during a trial in Mannheim. For this purpose he travelled, along with the court, to Israel because the witnesses included some people too frail to undertake the journey to Germany. There he created a sensation: Dr Bock rejected the Israeli judge, who, together with the public prosecutors from Germany, heard the witnesses, on the grounds that he was a Jew and therefore biased in principle. The Documentation Center lodged a complaint against Dr Bock both with the office of the prosecutor general and with the chamber of lawyers. The attorney excused himself and his precedure by claiming that he had been asked to do so by his client and continued to be a respected member of his profession.

During the Majdanek trial Dr Bock rejected the court in its totality on grounds of bias, because parts of the indictment had been published by *Der Spiegel* even before the opening of the trial. A different criminal bench had to examine the rejection of this petition: the trial was delayed by two months. Similarly fatuous objections were produced continually.

In addition, defence witnesses from the ranks of the SS were paraded in full force. By their 'thoroughness' quite a number of SS criminals made it impossible for the courts to convict them of their crimes: after all, where are there written documents or commemorative photographs of murders? In the end even people suspected of participation in the crimes about which they were to give evidence, were heard as 'witnesses'. Their testimony had the same weight as the testimony of an ex-inmate, even though the judge, before questioning them, had to instruct them that they could decline to give evidence if by doing so they would incriminate themselves.

Some of the SS witnesses acted upon this suggestion. But most of them tried to 'talk down' the charges as best they could. What they all had in common – with one single exception – was a poor memory. There was, for instance, a witness who, as chief of the dog handler squad, was responsible for cordoning off a number of meadows on 3 November 1943. That day has gone down in history under the cynical title of 'harvest festival': 15,000 Jewish women, men and children were shot on a single day. But the witness, just like his colleagues, couldn't remember anything.

Only one admitted to having heard firing and screaming all day long – but he 'hadn't given the noise another thought'. Asked what he had been thinking about, the man answered: 'My leave.'

These hearings of 'witnesses' occupied days, weeks and months. As the recollections of the SS witnesses were so obviously characterized by conveniently poor memories, public interest in the hearings was slight. The press seats were hardly occupied and the media had nothing to report.

This picture changed only when the first witness for the prosecution was called. He was the sixty-eight-year-old Polish physician Dr Jan Nowak. He had been in Majdanek for twenty-six months, having been transferred there from Auschwitz, and had witnessed the construction of the camp. He reported that all 10,000 Jews who had arrived at Majdanek on the first few transports had to lie in the open for months, dying of frostbite and exposure. Of the 5000 Soviet prisoners of war who had to help with the construction of the camp, a mere thirty-five survived.

Henryka Ostrowska from Poland was the next witness. She had been deported to Majdanek from Warsaw and she described how, as a new arrival, she had been warned particularly against two wardresses – Hermine Braunsteiner and Hildegard Lechert. Like Dr Nowak before her, the witness Ostrowska described the selection of women and children from the Warsaw ghetto, conducted by the camp physician Dr Blanke. The Braunsteiner woman had then reselected from the women spared by Dr Blanke: she sent more of them into the gas as a 'voluntary extra'.

The witness was so upset by the sight of her former tormentors that her voice gave out during her evidence and she couldn't utter another word. The judge had to adjourn the hearing and the physician in attendance gave Ostrowka a sedative. Because she knew German, she stated, she had been made to work in the equipment room. Stored there along with blankets, bedlinen, crates and sacks of human hair, were also those Cyclon-B canisters, with a skull and crossbones on them, which were used for gassing. From the gas chambers, which were camouflaged as bath houses, so-called 'runners' would arrive to whom, on orders from her boss, she handed over the Cyclon-B canisters. A few times, likewise on orders from her boss, she had to carry those canisters to the 'bath house' herself and would be given the appropriate receipt for them.

At this point in her evidence Dr Mundorf, one of Hermine Braunsteiner's two defence counsel, intervened. He demanded that the witness be informed that by this testimony she was incriminating herself, and shortly after her evidence defence counsel Dr Bock demanded that the witness be arrested and not permitted to return to Warsaw. As she handed over Cyclon-B canisters for the gas chambers, she was under strong suspicion of having been an accessory to murder.

This monstrosity, which was publicized throughout the world, directed public interest back to the Majdanek trial for a few days. Soon, however, the monotony of horror predominated: people can take in, and possibly even emotionally digest, the account of two, three, or perhaps a hundred murders – but faced with thousands of murders the mind becomes as dulled as those of the funtionaries and victims at the time. Horror becomes a matter of course.

According to the documentation, no fewer than 250 witnesses were to be heard. The timetable envisaged that half were to be heard during the first nine months. This schedule, however, had been so upset by the constant disruptive manoeuvres of the defence that at the end of the first nine months no more than sixteen witnesses had given evidence. For those witnesses who had come from Israel, Poland and the USA the trial meant enormous stress. They suffered not only in confronting their erstwhile tormentors, but time and again had to endure the most incredible provocations by the defence. Thus, when a witness referred to the unbearable stench of burning corpses hanging over the camp, Dr Mundorf demanded that experts in both human and veterinary medicine be called, to decide whether the stench of burnt animal cadavers could be distinguished from that of burnt human corpses. The court was obliged to examine this submission, too, before rejecting it with a detailed justification.

The Majdanek trial dragged on for five years before, in January 1981, the final speeches began. Dr Mundorf, pleading on behalf of Hermine

Braunsteiner-Ryan, argued that his client had come to Majdanek because
she had been looking for an 'easy and secure job' – anyway, he asked for
acquittal on insufficient evidence. On 30 June 1981 sentence was
announced. Hermine Ryan, the only remaining defendant, was sentenced
to life imprisonment. She received the verdict stiffly and blankly. Only
later, when the meaning of the sentence began to sink in, was she overtaken
by self-pity, producing a handkerchief and wiping tears from her eyes.
Throughout the five years of the trial not a single word of remorse had
come from her lips, nor a word of pity for the victims of Majdanek.

Her husband, Russell Ryan, who was among the spectators in the
courtroom, commented on the verdict: 'I am disappointed. I expected an
acquittal.' Equally disappointed were some eighty American right-wing
and neo-Nazi organizations. At the time that Hermine Ryan was extradited
they had set up a Hermine Ryan Defense Fund, and in their journals,
notably the *Liberty Bell*, they had applied for donations. The publisher of
the *Liberty Bell*, George P. Diez, is said to have raised such a substantial
sum that her $17,000 bail was paid in advance, allowing Hermine Ryan to
go through the initial phase of her trial as a free woman. She was also
promised that Dr Böhler, professor of law at Cologne University, was
willing to give an expert opinion that the German court was not competent
to conduct her trial. (Usually things were the reverse with complaints that
foreign courts were arrogating to themselves the right to try Germans or
Austrians.) But this effort by the American neo-Nazis was also a case of
love's labour's lost. The court's judgement on Hermine Braunsteiner-Ryan
was declared valid and she is at present serving her sentence.

Diez and co. have meanwhile turned to new purposes: in Georgia a
Patriotic Legal Fund was established, to raise money for the defence of
Nazi collaborators living in North America. A number of proceedings
against these collaborators (aimed at deporting them from the USA) are
now in progress; some have been deported, while others, such as Archbishop Viorel Trifa, Fedorenko and Demjanjuk, have been extradited to
stand trial.

19

Moral Duties Have No Terms

The Braunsteiner case led to a prolonged correspondence in early 1965 between me and the then Senator and future Attorney General Robert Kennedy. I had first requested him to speed up the proceedings for revoking her US citizenship, and afterwards I drew his attention to the problems which stemmed from the fact that many Nazi murderers who had gone underground in the United States (as elsewhere in the world) would never have to answer for their crimes. The statute of limitations in West Germany was about to expire. I had been preparing a book to argue against this expiry of legal responsibility, and requested Kennedy to contribute to it. He replied with a telegram which consisted of only five words: 'Moral duties have no terms.'

Yet such terms were in fact envisaged by Austrian and German legislation: on 8 May 1965 the limitation on all Nazi crimes was to have expired in Germany, and on 29 June 1965 in Austria. As in many other European countries the limit for murder charges was twenty years – due to the fact that, as a rule, one could not be detained in prison for longer than that. In Britain, the USA and Canada there was no statute of limitation for murder or being an accessory to murder, but these countries were irrelevant with regard to Nazi crimes. It had been assumed that this span of time would suffice to bring the crimes of the Nazi period to justice. Reality, however, disproved this assumption: the still unsolved crimes known to me at that time would themselves have kept hundreds of courts busy.

There were a number of reasons for this: first of all the enormous scope of the crimes. In eastern Europe there was scarcely a spot where the Germans had not committed some crime. In the post-war chaos it took several years for those massacres even to be recorded, and then the witnesses' statements would lie in some local archive, with no one knowing about them. The political and social disruption of post-war Europe virtually ruled out any purposeful communication, let alone cooperation. Added to this, the Nazis had done everything in their power to hush up their crimes: the notorious exhumation squads were digging up corpses again and incinerating them, incriminating documents were being destroyed and sometimes entire buildings blown up. Whereas 'normal' murderers are totally isolated, the Nazi murderers had an entire state apparatus available for planning their escape: money was transferred abroad, and soon Odessa saw to it that the fugitives found safe hiding places and false papers. That kind of support would be enjoyed by a 'normal' murderer only if he belonged to the Mafia, and, as we know, the detection rate for Mafia murders is extremely low.

During the first few years after the war, with the impact of what the liberators had seen in the concentration camps still fresh, investigations were very intensive; by 1948, however, they had largely flagged. The Berlin blockade also led to a mental block for the Allied leaders: suddenly they came to the realization that they had to go easy on Nazi criminals in order to enlist the Germans for the Cold War. After Stalin's death, in particular, western propaganda directed public attention mainly towards the crimes committed under his rule. Many Austrians and Germans exploited this as a welcome opportunity for offsetting the crimes of the Nazis against those of Stalin, by equating the great famine following collectivization with the conveyor-belt mass murder of the Third Reich, and deportation to inhospitable forced-labour camps with deportation to extermination camps, i.e. camps set up for the specific purpose of extermination. More and more frequently I would encounter, both in personal conversation and in newspaper articles, the kind of view which went: 'People who are themselves responsible for so many crimes against millions of people in the Soviet Union (for instance, they let thousands die in the construction of the White Sea Canal) do not have the moral right to sit in judgement on Germans in Nuremberg. They ought to be in court themselves. Especially as crimes against humanity and violation of human rights in the Soviet Union are not nearly at an end yet.'

In fact there was only one Soviet crime which approximates in its 'quality' to the quality of the Nazi murders: the murder of 4000 Polish officers at Katyn. I have therefore worked all my life to clear up this murder too. Yet even so it is obscene to quote the 4000 dead of Katyn in the same breath as the dead millions of Auschwitz, Sobibor or Treblinka. Although of course there was that ghoulish order to murder those 4000 Poles, there has never been a Soviet decision to exterminate all Poles. Moreover, there are quantitive differences which turn into qualitative ones: 4000 corpses – that was the production quota of every single company of the First SS Infantry Brigade which followed the German troops on their advance into the Soviet Union, a quota sometimes achieved in a single day. I write this as one who has for decades been condemning the crimes of the Soviet leadership and who, as a result, has been the target of furious attacks by the eastern bloc countries. Even though they are the two greatest monsters in world history, it is unacceptable to equate Stalin's criminality with Hitler's. Stalin at least did not practise the systematic conveyor-belt extermination of entire peoples.

The beneficiaries of this attempted equation were the Nazi murderers. Throughout the period of the Cold War the search for them practically came to a halt, proceedings in progress were suspended, and the few trials which did take place resulted, with increasing frequency, in acquittals. Only the Eichmann trial – hence its particular importance – put an end to this state of affairs. Not until 1960 was the search for Nazis seriously resumed.

By 1965, however, it would have become pointless. I possess a photocopy of a letter in which a Nazi, who'd found a hiding place in South America, announces to his family that he will return as soon as the term for prosecution expires. At the beginning of November 1964 the government of West Germany declared that it was not prepared to extend the term. A flood of protests from within the country and from abroad made little impression on German government circles.

I travelled to Bonn to see Minister of Justice Bucher, hoping to convince him that Nazi genocide had to be viewed differently from a murder by some perverted individual who, at worst, might have killed twenty people. Not only were the figures beyond comparison but the situation of the murderer, too, was entirely different: the old-style murderer was an outcast who, as a rule, had to cower in some hiding place and only rarely was able to enjoy the fruits of his crime. The murderers of the Nazi period, however, were living with false papers among their own kind in villas on the coasts of Latin America, enjoying the wealth of their victims. It was intolerable to believe that after 1965 many of them should be able to shake off their last remnants of fear.

Minister Bucher listened to me patiently. His personal assistant had equipped him for our talk with a series of documents, but these concerned not so much the legal problems as West Germany's efforts at restitution. The Minister referred to 'billions of Deutschmarks' spent on victims so far –' and this process is not subject to a time limit.'

It was once more a case of us simply not speaking the same language. 'Herr Minister,' I said, interrupting him, 'the murderer of my mother and the murderers of many of my relations and friends have not been found yet. I don't even know their names. I am addressing the Minister of Justice, not the Finance Minister. I recognize the Federal Republic's financial efforts, but surely they cannot be a substitute for efforts to achieve justice. I have come to you with a very specific question; what happens after 8 May 1965?'

Bucher's reply was, 'That's not for me to decide. That's a matter for the federal government or for Parliament.'

I realized that a fight would be necessary. I wrote a letter to 369 public figures, mainly in West Germany and Austria, asking them to tell me what they thought of the limitation. Ninety per cent of them answered, and these 90 per cent were against expiry. They included Ingeborg Bachmann, Fritz Hochwälder, Erich Kästner and Golo Mann. From their comments I put together a book entitled *Term Expiry? 200 Public Figures Say No*, which was published by Europäische Verlagsanstalt at the beginning of 1965 and which I prefaced with Robert Kennedy's motto: 'Moral Duties Have No Terms'. I believe that it did something to help change the climate. The Austrian government decided to abolish the limitation on the prosecution of murder, and Germany resolved to extend the term until 1979.

The Central Office for the investigation of Nazi crimes in Ludwigsburg thereupon vigorously tried to catch up on the mass of evidence. All European countries which had been occupied by the Nazis were requested to hand over what information they had, especially lists of names of Nazi criminals still wanted. In France, the German federal government even appointed an attorney to ensure that sentences passed by military tribunals *in absentia* were enforced. I am convinced that West Germany was honestly trying to catch up on the crimes of the past, but on principle I was against that new time limit: there cannot be, on principle, any limitation on justice. Moreover, the practical problems had once again been underrated: the eastern bloc, in particular, had still not computerized its archives and continued to refuse to make them available to the West German judiciary. East Germany left hundreds of West German requests for legal assistance unanswered. It was still not possible to establish the links between place of crime, criminals and witnesses. This meant, of course, that time bombs continued to tick away, over there, and that no one could predict when or how they might blow up.

I have always been convinced that people would acknowledge the correctness of a decent view if only it was put clearly before them, almost like sales material, appealing equally to their intellect and their emotions. Thus

I spoke to a lot of young Germans then, and performed the following mental experiment with them: 'Just imagine that someone decided to exterminate all Germans, justifying this with the events of the past two centuries: the Germans started two world wars, they murdered millions of human beings, they aimed at world rule. There would in fact be as many reasons for being anti-German as there are for being anti-Jewish. And now imagine that there was a political constellation in which the proposal to exterminate the Germans met with interest and understanding. Would you then believe that the murder of the German people should be subject to a statute of limitations? Separate the problem, for once, from the murder of the Jews – it is genocide that I am concerned with. Is it not a disgrace that even genocide planned and executed in cold blood has usually been punished less severely than single murder, when it should in fact be the reverse. Genocide is the crime that threatens humanity most. We should view it as a crime with a quality of its own, a crime we must fight with the strongest means at our disposal. While, on humanitarian grounds, there may be a case for a time limit on individual murder, the same humanitarian grounds should make us reject it for genocide.'

Sometimes, of course, a visual signal is stronger than any argument. In 1978, therefore, along with the newly established Simon Wiesenthal Center in Los Angeles, I launched a postcard campaign which was to be strikingly successful. The postcard we sent out showed an SS man between two hanged camp inmates, with a third prisoner lying on the ground in front of him, face down. An American soldier had discovered this photgraph in one of the private quarters he'd been billeted in and brought it to my office. On the back of the card I had the following text printed: 'This murderer is not yet found! He, along with thousands of Nazi criminals, is still a free man; some of them under false names. They are waiting for 31 December 1979, when the limitation on their crimes will have expired. Crimes against humanity must not become exempt from prosecution! This is a moral obligation, a memento for future generations.' Underneath there was a space for the name and address of the sender. The card was addressed to 'Federal Chancellor Schmidt, Bonn, Federal Republic of Germany.' In all we had 40,000 cards printed in Vienna, of which thousands reached their addresses. Thousands of cards in reply were received from Holland, Israel, Belgium and, above all, the USA.

At the same time I undertook journeys through widely different countries in order to lecture against a statute of limitations and to mobilize some MPs with whom I was personally acquainted, such as Greville Janner and Winston Churchill (the grandson of the legendary Prime Minister) in London. On my return from London I was invited to address the European Press Union jointly with the Studiengesellschaft für Zeitprobleme (Association for the Study of Contemporary Problems). Among my audience were also some eighty members of the German Bundestag. My talk was followed by a lively discussion. A few Christian Social Union Deputies came up to me to tell me I had convinced them with my arguments – but the parliamentary CSU had decided that Deputies must vote in the Bundestag in favour of the limitation. When I asked what I could do against it, I was advised to speak to the leader of the parliamentary party, Friedrich Zimmermann, or to the party chairman Franz Josef Strauss in person.

My friend Axel Springer actually arranged an audience for me with the Bavarian Minister President. The date was Friday, 13 March, three weeks before the vote. Our conversation began heatedly, because each of us was convinced his argument was correct. But in the course of nearly two hours of argument and counter-argument a new way of looking at it emerged: I succeeded in making Franz Josef Strauss see that it was primarily the eastern bloc that would benefit from limitation. All the eastern bloc countries, having in the past torpedoed the efforts of the West German judiciary and held back their own documents, would come out, the day after the expiry of the time limit, with 'newly discovered' evidence about more or less prominent West German figures and brand the Federal Republic a 'haven of Fascism', where Nazis didn't have to answer for their crimes. This seemed to Strauss to have considerable substance and he promised he would inform his parliamentary party about our talk on the following Monday.

I left Franz Josef Strauss with the firm impression that he would allow his party colleagues to vote according to their consciences and not under a party whip. The vote was taken on 3 July: with a majority of 255 against 222 the German Bundestag decided to rescind the statute of limitation for murder and accessory to murder. Eleven of the votes against limitation came from Strauss's CSU.

20

The Reluctant Murderer

The eastern bloc's attempts to portray West Germany as a haven of neo-Nazism and a paradise for Nazi criminals hit full force with the Cold War. The motive was obvious: by claiming that they had to protect eastern Europe against German revanchism, the Soviets justified their military presence in the countries they had subjected. East Germany was a special case. On the one hand, any wish for reunification had to be stifled with particular vigour; on the other hand, it too had been part of Hitlerite Germany. The East German Communists therefore made special efforts to prove that the worst Nazi criminals were in West Germany, and moreover in key positions of power. Probably the most important case raised by those efforts was the 'Oberländer case'.

When in 1943 the Germans discovered the mass graves of those 4000 Polish officers executed in the spring of 1940 by Stalin's henchmen, with shots in the back of the neck, they began to reflect on the mass graves which they themselves had left behind. Ever since Stalingrad the German armies had been in retreat, and they had to expect that the pursuing Red Army would come across the countless pits of corpses which marked German progress through the Ukraine and Belorussia. A special unit was therefore set up, designated '1005', whose task it was to find the largest mass graves, dig up the bodies again and burn them. Standartenführer Blobel, in command of the unit, discharged his task in the usual manner: prisoners were used for the exhumation work and, when they had finished their job, were shot.

On this model a 1005 unit was set up in Lvov: with the aid of prisoners from the Janowska concentration camp they were to dig up the mass graves in the camp itself as well as in the surroundings of Lvov. On 8 October 1943 this squad came across a grave which has gone down in history: it contained the bodies of thirty-eight Lvov University professors and their families. On top were the bodies of the two Ukrainian policemen who had carried out the shooting. They had been shot by the SS as soon as they had completed their 'work', so the wouldn't tell any tales. (Leon Wells, a survivor of the 1005 squad who now lives in the USA, has described these events in his book *The Death Brigade*.)

The murder of the Lvov professors – it happened on 4 July 1941 – has interested historians, research institutes, the media, and in particular politicians. Like the murder of Jews or gypsies, this too was a form of extermination based not on any individual trait but simply on membership of a certain group: the extermination of the Polish intelligentsia had been a priority objective of German policy ever since they occupied Polish territories in 1939. Under the cynical heading of 'Aktion AB' (Allgemeine Befriedung: general pacification) SS Gruppenführer Bruno Streckenbach had since the spring of 1940 organized the murder of some 5000 university people, artists and intellectuals. (At the time a colonel in the NKVD – now the KGB – was attached as Soviet liaison officer to the Governor General of Poland, Hans Frank; he can scarcely have been unaware of Operation AB. It was matched by the simultaneous mass shootings of Polish officers by the Soviets at Katyn.) Because the Germans were reluctant to declare the Poles outcasts like the Jews or gypsies, at least officially, the executions were preceded by sham trials ending in mass sentences for all kinds of fictitious offences, from abetting the enemy to espionage.

Investigations into the events at Lvov were conducted in Poland and East Germany shortly after the war, and in 1958 the alleged culprit was announced in a sensational manner: he was Dr Theodor Oberländer, a minister in Adenauer's government. After a trial held in East Berlin *in absentia*, Oberländer was sentenced on 29 April 1960 to life imprisonment. He was found guilty of having personally ordered and directed the execution of the professors. His case became an integral part of the propaganda campaign waged during the Cold War: that a man like that should have risen to ministerial rank under Adenauer was proof that Fascists and revanchists had long been in power again in West Germany.

I had a particular interest in the matter as the murdered men included several whom I had personally known, such as Professor Minkiewicz, whose lectures I'd attended as part of my engineering studies, and Professor Boy-Zelenski, a physician and author revered by us all.

During the preparations for the Lvov trial in 1963 I was in close touch with the Stuttgart public prosecutor's office and had frequent opportunities of discussing the Oberländer issue with the man in charge, Chief Public Prosecutor Rolf Sichting. Even then we had some doubts about the East Berlin version. Although it was true that Oberländer had been in Lvov at the time in question, he was not a member of the SS but a Wehrmacht officer in command of a Ukrainian auxiliary unit called 'Nachtigall' ('Nightingale'). As, according to all our information, the murder of the professors had been carried out under the command of the SS, we couldn't see any connection with Oberländer. As a matter of fact, proceedings started against him in Hamburg were dropped on these very grounds: there was no evidence that the shooting of the Lvov professors could be blamed on Dr Theodor Oberländer.

Nevertheless, there is always some suspicion that such a discontinuation of proceedings may be politically motivated: the judiciary might have been reluctant to find a former minister in Adenauer's government guilty of murder. Although the investigation provided no basis for such an assumption, this did not impress the East German propaganda machine. For them Oberländer remained the murderer of the professors.

Our investigations led us to a different trail. In the course of my researches I came up against a Polish aid committee which had looked after the arrested Polish intellectuals until their execution. The Governor General of Poland had tolerated this aid committee, which was under Church patronage, because the Poles were being sentenced *pro forma* in official trials. The association was acting on a purely humanitarian basis, but the Gestapo regarded its members – for once not without justification – as an association of potential opponents, who should be thinned out from time to time. Thus on 12 May 1942 one of the activists in the association, Dr Carolina Lanckoronska, a member of the Polish nobility and linked through marriage with the Italian nobility, was arrested by the Gestapo. Hans Krüger, the Gestapo chief of Stanisławów, personally interrogated her in order to discover possible contacts with resistance groups or partisan units. When Countess Lanckoronska kept stubbornly silent Krüger became increasingly furious: if she didn't finally talk, he threatened, he would hand her over to his colleague Kutschmann. He'd have ways to make her talk. She'd better not believe that as a Pole she enjoyed any protection; Kutschmann had 'dealt with' the whole body of professors in Lvov without worrying about them being Poles. No reason why she shouldn't know, she wouldn't be leaving this prison alive anyway.

For once Krüger was mistaken. As a result of intervention by her Italian relations – the then Crown Princess of Italy personally approached Himmler – Countess Lanckoronska was transferred from Stanisławów to Lvov, where she was actually questioned by Gestapo commissar Walter

Kutschmann. But the interrogation took a different turn from Krüger's prediction. When Dr Lanckoronska told Kutschmann what Krüger had said about him, Kutschmann had a record made and reported his superior for breach of security. Krüger was summoned to Berlin and had to answer for himself. Countess Lanckoronska was, in a manner of speaking, pardoned, and instead of being shot was 'merely' sent to the Ravensbrück concentration camp, from where she was liberated by the Red Cross a few months before the end of the war. It seems that, upon Himmler's orders, his deputy Ernst Kaltenbrunner had arranged her release – he submitted the letter he had written to the Red Cross as a document in his defence at the Nuremberg trials.

In April 1967 the so-called Stanisławów trial took place in Münster, Westphalia, in which Hans Krüger was charged with the murder of thousands of Jews. Countess Lanckoronska faced her tormentor as one of the principle witnesses for the prosecution. Following a year-long trial Krüger was sentenced to life imprisonment for multiple murder – in all, the extermination of about 120,000 Jews.

The documents of that trial revealed how responsibility for the shooting of the Lvov professors was shared out. The person in command was SS Brigadeführer Dr Eberhard Schöngart, who had arrived in Lvov on 2 July 1941 with 230 SS men as the advance unit of the commander-in-chief of the security police. The order which Schöngart brought with him from Berlin called for the arrest and execution of all members of the Polish intelligentsia. A list was already in existence: it had been compiled by Ukrainian deserters. Schöngart's men merely had to collect the professors and their families from their homes and assemble them. He had taken them to the Abrahamowicz school, and during the night of 3 July a squad of five ethnic German SS men and two Ukrainian police auxiliaries was formed to carry out the executions. The firing squad was commanded by SS Untersturmführer Dr Walter Kutschmann.

At five in the morning on 4 July 1941 the arrested professors, their wives and their children were taken to the Wulecka hills, the Ukrainian police auxiliaries dug a pit, and Kutschmann gave the order for the execution. As the entire operation was classified 'top secret' the two Ukrainian police auxiliaries were also shot. The exhumation squad subsequently found them lying on top of the mound of corpses.

However, all attempts to induce Hans Krüger, who was in detention in Münster, to name his fellow culprits were in vain. Although, on the strength of instructions from the public prosecutor's office, he was being interrogated about Walter Kutschmann, he refused to make any specific statement. And one of the witnesses in the Oberländer proceedings in Hamburg, Max Draheim, a senior police officer who had witnessed the execution of the

Polish professors, knew only that the ethnic German policemen had been commanded by an SS Untersturmführer – he couldn't recall his name.

There was another of Kutschmann's superiors who could give evidence on Kutschmann's activity: Hermann Müller, the principal defendant in the so-called Tarnopol trial. Müller testified that Kutschmann had been in charge of the operation against the Jews in Brzezany and, from mid-1942, had been head of the Jewish department in Drohobycz. But he was unable to provide information on events in Lvov, and so they remained shadowy.

A few years later we received a witness's deposition to the effect that Kutschmann had personally shot dead a young Jewish girl in Drohobycz. At the time this seemed to us to be a side-track – I had become so accustomed in my work to think almost invariably in hundreds of dead – but in the event this murder turned out to be the only one with which the German judiciary chose to concern itself in greater detail.

Kutschmann can be shown to have left Poland in 1944 – his SS unit was sent to France. From there he deserted to Spain shortly before the end of the war and was thus placed by the SS on its own 'wanted' list. From a CV which Kutschmann himself compiled in 1940 it emerges that he was well acquainted with Spain: as early as 1937 he had joined Franco's Moroccan Legion. There he was seriously wounded in the thigh by machine-gun fire, which left him with a scar that would play a part in the future. In view of his linguistic skills he was subsequently sent as an interpreter to the German consulate in Cadiz. There he first came into contact with the Gestapo and applied for enrolment. On 1 March he was detailed to Leipzig as a cadet commissar, and was trained there at the officers' school of the security police.

It was not surprising that he chose Spain as the first stop on his escape. Nor was it surprising that he was in a hurry to go underground. He knew what he had to expect if his activities in Lvov ever came out. Franco's Spain was a relatively safe place for a Nazi criminal. It is true that Franco only sympathized with Hitler during the war, and did not support his policy of exterminating the Jews. But the links between the two Fascist regimes were enough to create a certain feeling of comradeship after the war: one didn't let one's former allies down. The more harmless refugees were granted asylum; those who were strongly incriminated found a hiding place.

Among the latter was Otto Skorzeny, who became famous in 1943 for liberating Mussolini. This was to play a vital part in our story. In 1966 a man called at my office to tell me of a strange experience he'd had on holiday in Spain. He had been invited to a club which was frequented mainly by Germans, including a number of elderly gentlemen who all described themselves as friends or acquaintances of Skorzeny's – which they probably were. At an advanced hour, reminiscing as usual about their SS pasts, the talk turned to one Kutschmann: he'd been a coward and had deserted shortly before the end of the war. Now the fellow was pretending to be a priest, was using the name of Pedro Ricardo Olmo and wanted to be one of their crowd. But he'd made a mistake there; they wouldn't have anything to do with deserters. For a while, the holidaymaker in Spain related, they had even considered 'punishing' Olmo-Kutschmann for his desertion. But Otto Skorzeny had objected: 'We don't sentence people for what they did before 1945!'

My visitor told me this story because he wanted to draw my attention to that strange circle of friends. He had no idea that it was Kutschmann who interested me most – after all, we had been unsuccessfully searching for him for years. Initial inquiries established that Olmo-Kutschmann had already left Spain – no doubt the place was getting too hot for him. I thought he would most probably have chosen the route of many other ex-SS men, to Argentina, where German and Spanish would be equally useful to him.

We then had a helper in Buenos Aires, 'Harry', who had excellent contacts with all possible people, firms and institutions in Argentina. In the absence of specific facts to support my suspicion I didn't rate our chances of success very highly, but I passed the information on to Harry and settled down for a lengthy wait. Instead I received a letter from Harry soon thereafter, informing me that he was attending an international Jewish conference in Strasbourg and would like to talk to me then.

What he told me surprised my wildest expectations: Kutschmann was ours. An electrical dealer from among Harry's acquaintances had told him that in the electrical firm of Osram he had dealt with a man who was unmistakably German, as his Spanish was heavily marked with a Teutonic accent. Questioned about his accent, the alleged Argentinian called Pedro Ricardo Olmo explained that his mother had been German and they had only spoken German at home. That's why he had never lost his accent.

That was a particularly stupid excuse and we had no doubt that this was the man we wanted. The problem was proving it. How does one prove that a man called Pedro Ricardo Olmo is the same man called Walter Kutschmann? I got hold of a photograph from Kutschmann's SS dossier and sent it to Harry in Buenos Aires. He passed it on to his friend, the electrical dealer, and he was certain: this was the man who had given his name as Olmo. A little later Harry had his address as well. Kutschmann, with his sister, was living in Buenos Aires and was employed by Osram as head of publicity.

The next task was to mobilize the public prosecutor's office in West Germany. As Kutschmann's last place of residence in Germany had been

Berlin, we sent our dossier – by then it was November 1974 – to the prosecutor's office there. Then began the usual wait. When I hadn't heard anything for a lengthy period of time I made an inquiry and was told that another attempt had been made to question Max Draheim: the German police officer who had been an eyewitness to the Lvov massacre and who remembered the officer commanding the squad but not his name. However, the officials who intended to show Draheim the photograph of Kutschmann were too late: the old gentleman had recently died.

In February 1975 I was informed that Kutschmann had been granted Argentinian citizenship under his false name. This complicated the business. Public prosecutor Stief, with whom I'd made contact, informed me by a letter dated 8 April that a request for extradition addressed to Argentina had no prospect of success. The Peronist Fascists nurtured brotherly feelings for Hitler's Fascists.

But I was not prepared to give up so easily. If nothing could be done against Kutschmann through the judiciary, I would try to root him out by other means and lure him out of hiding. I invited a journalist from *Vision*, a magazine widely read both in South America and in the United States, and told him what I knew about Kutschmann. Under the pretext of interviewing him about cooperation between the USA and Argentina in the field of electrification, the man from *Vision* succeeded in taking the first up-to-date photo of Kutschmann, and shortly afterwards the magazine ran several pages on his story.

On 28 June 1975 Kutschmann was arrested in Buenos Aires – though he was released again the following day. The background of both these moves remains obscure. The firm of Osram immediately dismissed Kutschmann – one of its directors came from Munich specially to see me and assure me how much they regretted having employed the man. Kutschmann, alias Olmo, thought it best to leave Buenos Aires. Journalists following his trail discovered him at the nearby spa of Miamare, where he declared that he'd been obliged to flee because Wiesenthal's agents had been on his heels in order to kidnap him. Unfortunately he overestimated me: I had to depend on the German authorities.

About that time, in May 1975, the Minister of Justice of Baden-Württemberg, Dr Bender, undertook a journey to Poland. He was accompanied by Dr Adalbert Rückerl, the head of the Central Office of the *Land* judiciary in Ludwigsburg, my long-time friend, who was to search for documents in the Polish archives. On this occasion Rückerl also spoke to the director of the Polish Central Commission for the Investigation of Nazi Crimes, Professor Czesław Pilichowski, who made a sensational and courageous statement: the Polish investigations had proved that Dr Theodor Oberländer could not be held responsible for the murder of the Lvov professors.

When, on his return to West Germany, Rückerl published this statement, it led to a mighty row between Poland and East Germany. The East German judiciary, having sentenced Oberländer to life imprisonment *in absentia*, was rightly concerned about a total loss of face. The East German government pestered their Polish comrades to induce Pilichowski to retract his exoneration of Oberländer. This, of course, would hardly have been possible, even if Pilichowski had agreed, as there were no fewer than three witnesses to his statement: Rückerl, Dr Bender, his press officer, and an official from the German embassy in Warsaw.

I seized on the controversy between East Berlin and Warsaw to urge Kutschmann's extradition at a press conference: if he were put on trial the murder of the Lvov professors might be finally cleared up.

In July 1975 the Senator for Justice in Berlin, Hermann Oxford, requested the Bonn government to take steps to ensure Kutschmann's extradition. The Vice-President of the Internationale de Resistance, Marie Madeline Fourcade, likewise voiced her 'urgent interest' in the clarification of the case. But even these interventions failed to produce any tangible results. I thereupon tried through friends in Argentina to intervene with the Argentinian government. A delegation of concentration camp survivors called on Minister of the Interior Alberto Rocamora and demanded Kutschmann's arrest. In vain. The Argentinians would make no move against a man for whom there was not even a German extradition request in existence.

Certainly the German hesitation about requesting Kutschmann's extradition was hard to understand. The official justification was that no relevant agreement existed between the two countries. But this could not be the real reason, since in a number of cases West Germany had succeeded in having economic and other criminals extradited from Argentina. Even if the Argentinians, out of sympathy for the representatives of Fascist regimes, were to refuse to extradite Kutschmann, it was surely worth a try. If it didn't come off, no harm would have been done. Kutschmann was already aware that we were on his track, hence an extradition request would not in itself have alerted him or led him to flee.

Why then did the German authorities remain inactive? From a few clues I have put together my own theory about it: Kutschmann, if extradicted, would have to face trial in West Berlin. His trial was bound to cover above all, along with his crimes in Brzezany and the murder of the young girl in Drohobycz, the massacre of the Lvov professors. And this would have been at a distance, as the crow flies, of only a mile or two from the East Berlin court which had condemned Oberländer to life imprisonment for the murder of those same Lvov professors. The East German judiciary would feel compelled to defend Kutschmann in order to uphold

Oberländer's conviction. The consequence might well be a confrontation not only between West and East Berlin, but between East and West Germany generally. And in view of the sensitive 'transit traffic' to and from Berlin – that, at least, is the theory I put together – West Germany had no wish to provoke such a confrontation.

At any rate, everything was moving towards a quiet burial of the Kutschmann case. First the Polish authorities issued an official statement to the effect that Oberländer was by no means cleared. And towards the end of August public prosecutor Stief informed me that the warrant of arrest for Kutschmann had to be withdrawn because, as a result of an amendment to the law, he had reached the term of limitation (this was because Berlin had wanted him not for murder but only as an accessory to murder, the commanding officer being evidently regarded as less guilty than the execution squad). Somewhat at odds with this, I was assured that there continued to be interest in Kutschmann's extradition, although it was not being requested since the Argentinian regime would anyway not grant it.

Eight years in all were to pass before a new development arose in the Kutschmann case: the Falklands war swept away the generals' regime in Argentina, and the country got a democratically elected head of state in Raul Alfonsín. The head of the South American section of the Anti-Defamation League, Rabbi Morton Rosenthal, thereupon requested an audience in order to draw the president's attention to the Kutschmann case. Simultaneously, my friend Eliot Welles, head of the Nazi crimes department of the Anti-Defamation League in the USA, declared himself willing, on his trip to Europe, to call on the public prosecutor's office in Berlin and establish whether, in view of the new situation in Argentina, it was at last prepared to make a request for Kutschmann's extradition. A little later Berlin inquired if I had Kutschmann's new address. I sent it to them, along with his telephone number, and a short while afterwards I handed to a Berlin prosecutor the original photographs taken in Kutschmann's office by the *Vision* reporter in 1975.

The public prosecutor's office took the view that it could charge Kutschmann only with the murder of the girl of sixteen, because this charge alone was sufficiently attested by witnesses. I didn't mind – so long as the extradition request was lodged and Kutschmann came to Germany.

In November 1984, twenty years after I first concerned myself with him, 'Pedro Ricardo Olmo' was arrested at his sister's home in Buenos Aires – and strenuously insisted that he had absolutely nothing to do with the wanted Walter Kutschmann. He stuck to his denial even when he was informed that the priest Pedro Ricardo Olmo, whose papers and identity he had appropriated, had died as long ago as 1969. Thereupon one of my friends telephoned the investigating judge in Buenos Aires with an obscene suggestion: 'Get Kutschmann to drop his trousers. Then you'll see the scars of the two bullets he stopped in the fighting in Spain.' Whether at that Pedro Ricardo Olmo was willing to admit that he was Kutschmann, I don't know. In view of his poor health he was released from jail and taken to hospital. On 30 August 1985 he died of cardiac arrest.

The eastern bloc will no doubt stick to its claim that Theodor Oberländer is the murderer of the Lvov professors.

21

Treacherous Language

The Communists believe they have an exclusive claim to anti-Fascism. This is partly due to historical reasons: of all political theories Hitler most fiercely fought against 'Bolshevism', and, conversely, the Communists in France, Germany and Austria probably offered the strongest resistance to the Nazis – at least in relation to their percentage of the population. Even so it is astonishing that the comrades have managed totally to dismiss from their memories the friendship treaty between Hitler and Stalin, although it was rather more than a non-aggression pact: Stalin's bridal present to Hitler was a number of Austrian and German Jews who were Communists.

Nevertheless, there is no doubt that a disproportionate number of Communists were locked up in concentration camps, or that they played a special part there: they were the only ones capable of setting up something like a political organization, and in consequence they occupied a disproportionate number of camp posts and were more able to help their party comrades. Communists therefore had a somewhat better chance of surviving Hitler's concentration camps.

If only for this reason they dominated the organizations of former concentration camp inmates after the war. Moreover, these camps had predominantly been in Poland, and as one in every five Poles had been at least temporarily detained, these camp communities played a special role in Polish political life. One consequence of this was that the major concentration camp organizations enjoyed political, and indeed also financial, support from the Polish state, which thus gained a kind of patronage over them. The camp organizations repaid this by political resolutions of an unmistakably left-wing character. They saw the danger of Fascism and neo-Nazism only where the Communists wished to see it – in West Germany and occasionally, through West German infection, in Austria. 'Anti-Fascism' became a solid component of Communist propaganda.

Not even an event like the Eichmann trial escaped such propaganda manoeuvres. In April 1961, immediately before the opening of proceedings, Dr Friedrich Kaul, an observer sent by East Germany, called a press conference at which he 'unmasked' the following conspiracy between West Germany and Israel: the only reason why Ben Gurion and Konrad Adenauer had agreed to make Eichmann stand trial was that it would make it possible to ignore all those other Nazis and war criminals who occupied positions in West Germany.

Some people believe that such remarks are best ignored – they condemn themselves. I don't share this view: even though nobody among the lawyers and journalists there believed such nonsense, young people in Austria and Germany were then eagerly lapping up that kind of stuff. They enjoyed linking the political establishment of West Germany with Nazism, and deriving from this a justification for overthrowing it. I therefore considered it necessary to react to Kaul immediately and publicly. 'Could you explain why East Germany is not paying any compensation to the victims of Nazism?' I asked him. 'Not only does it not pay any compensation to the victims, but it likewise pays no compensation for the huge assets stolen by the Nazis from all kinds of countries. Surely no one can maintain that these assets were brought only to the territory of what is presently West Germany?'

Kaul was evidently familiar with these arguments because his standard reply was pat: 'Our restitution consists in the fact that former Nazis cannot hold any kind of position in our country.'

Again I try to picture how that sentence might work on young left-wingers in Germany and Austria. Yes, they would say, East Germany may not have the money to buy indulgences for past sins, but instead it is truly atoning for the past by not giving Nazis any opportunities. I realized that people like Kaul should not be allowed to resort to generalities: they had to be confronted with specific facts. 'I have come across names like that of Major-General Lensky,' I said. 'Lensky was an assessor in the trials of the men of 20 July* – now he is a highly decorated member of the East German People's Chamber.'

---

*On 20 July 1944 a group of senior German officers – mainly aristocrats – mounted an abortive attempt on Hitler's life. They were tried by a 'Peoples' Court' and hanged from meat hooks.

Kaul realized that he was on slippery ground and tried another evasion: he would discuss all that with me privately after the press conference. But when I insisted on an answer he resorted to a bombastic outburst: 'The only democratic state which honours the victims of Auschwitz', he shouted into the hall, 'is East Germany.'

'You should at least keep the memory of the dead of Auschwitz out of your political propaganda,' I retorted.

Kaul flushed to the roots of his hair, waved his arms and gave the impression of working up to a heart attack. The press conference was broken off and, from the Communist propaganda point of view, ended in failure: the journalists wrote about my charges against East Germany rather than about Kaul's charges against West Germany.

Roughly seven years later, on 6 September 1968, I held a press conference myself at the Concordia Press Club in Vienna, to which I should have liked to have invited Dr Kaul. 'The reason why I have asked you here today, as representatives of the public', I began my address to about fifty foreign journalists, 'is, in view of the past concerns of our Documentation Center, somewhat unusual. This time it is not a case of renewing charges against hidden Nazi criminals or of demanding punishment for newly discovered Nazi crimes from lethargic authorities. Instead we think the time has come to cast light – with similar documentation – on alarming international developments, and to reveal connections which might invite historians and politicians to some very serious reflections and comparisons.'

The alarming 'international developments' I was alluding to were, on the one hand, the Prague Spring, which a few weeks previously had been terminated by Russian tanks, and on the other the Six-Day War in which Israeli tanks had, a year before, once more defended the independence of the Jewish state. Both events had triggered off a Communist propaganda campaign conducted on a very broad front throughout the eastern bloc press. With more or less the same arguments the Arabs were being defended and the Israelis damned while, at the same time, being held responsible for events in Czechoslovakia. 'In Prague Zionism is in power,' the official daily of the East German Communist Party *Neues Deutschland*, commented on Alexander Dubček and his friends. A friend of mine had underlined this sentence for me in red, and simultaneously supplied its model: 'In Prague Jewry is in power,' *Völkischer Beobachter* had written in 1939 in justification of Czechoslovakia's occupation by German troops.

This made me prick up my ears. I had a whole series of East German newspapers sent to me, and I read them with a care which their quality certainly didn't merit. The arguments they put forward differed not at all from those in the Polish or Soviet press – except in their terminology. The East German press used expressions, concepts and ideological models which were reminiscent not so much of *Pravda* as of *Völkischer Beobachter*, *Der Stürmer* and *Das Schwarze Korps*. A little experiment in textual analysis invariably led to the same result: if in the commentaries of the East German papers one replaced the word 'Israeli' by 'Jew' and instead of 'progressive forces' put 'National Socialism', one was all of a sudden faced with a product of Goebbel's propaganda ministry. That was no mere accident, and after four months of the most intensive research I was able to present to the press something which engendered considerable excitement for months to come. 'The Same Language – First for Hitler, Now for Ulbricht' was the title of a dossier prepared by us, which showed that no fewer than thirty-nine people who, as Nazi party members, held influential posts, were now wielding at least the same kind of influence in the press, radio and propaganda centres of East Germany. Thus the press secretary of the Ulbricht government then was one Kurt Blecha, who had reached that high position effortlessly although he could boast of a low membership number in the Nazi party. In the Department of Agitation and Propaganda there was a certain Herr Horst Dressler-Anders, who had joined the Nazi party as early as 1929. He was the founder of Nazi radio and was one of those who decided what came under the heading of degenerate art. The editor-in-chief of the East Berlin newspaper *Deutsche Aussenpolitik*, Herr Aust, had also been a Nazi, as had another leading figure on that paper, Minister Kegel, who had been in Warsaw in 1939 as a correspondent of *Breslauer Neueste Nachrichten* and had even then enjoyed diplomatic status – it may be assumed that he had need of it. Finally there was a staff member of *Deutsche Aussenpolitik* by the name of Herbert Kröger, who had earned his spurs with the SS and at the central office of the Security Service.

Immediately prior to the press conference I had folders prepared which my secretary distributed among the journalists present. In these they found, along with plain party members, SS men, SA leaders, Gestapo informers, members of propaganda companies, employees of Hitler's radio, of *Das Schwarze Korps* and *Völkischer Beobachter*, officials of the propaganda ministry and of the SS race and settlement office, as well as the notorious Condor Legion. All of them were now occupying important positions in East Germany – in the editorial office of *Neues Deutschland* and *Deutsche Aussenpolitik* they formed their own Nazis cliques – and they decorated themselves with high orders of the worker and peasant state. One of Hitler's former war correspondents, Wilhelm Stieler, had risen to be a city councillor in Leipzig, and I took the liberty of quoting a striking sentence from his past: 'Our Tiger tanks are squashing the Asian subhumans like bedbugs.'

I was, moreover, able to tell the journalists about a number of personal experiences. East Germany, as a matter of principle, did not reply to inquiries concerning Nazi criminals. Even if they had been named and tracked down by my Center or by the West German authorities, they would refuse to question them under the mutual legal assistance procedure. On one occasion we investigated a member of the Totenkopf-Standarte (an SS elite unit) which had been stationed in the Lublin ghetto – he turned out to be a People's Chamber Deputy. Another Deputy had, as an assessor in the Nazi People's Court trials, passed sentences of death. And in the Central Committee there was a man who had been employed in the commandant's office of the Sachsenhausen concentration camp.

In order to produce our evidence we had worked through some 600 names. Our list did not, and does not, claim to be anything like complete; it was more by way of a spot check: if you shone light into a certain sphere of East German public life – in this case the press and the radio – then this was what you found. I hardly think that a similar analysis of the police force, the intelligence service or the military would turn out differently.

Needless to say, the same kind of thing is happening continually also in West Germany: the *Stern* boss Henry Nannen has a past as a Nazi propaganda man. Werner Höfer quite recently had to resign as moderator of the *Frühschoppen* television programme because he couldn't remember a series of rather sickening Nazi articles, and I myself have in vain battled against a Dr Heinrich Tötter who had been in charge of a German occupation newspaper in Belgium and has since become press chief of the German civil servants' association. But I had to admit that none of these men after the war ever relapsed into the terminology of the Hitler period, and that West Germany has frequently taken up, or at least discussed, such cases on its own initiative.

The East German press, on the other hand, did not react at all. When, about six months after my press conference, Albert Norden, a member of their Politburo, was asked what he had to say to my collection of documents, he answered with a formula which, coming from any West German politician, he would have condemned as a 'dangerous playing down': 'All these people have changed and today are good loyal citizens of East Germany. In our country everyone can find work on the strength of his abilities.' Former Nazis in other countries evidently cannot have changed.

The only Communist to react publicly to our documents was now no longer a Communist. 'The bounds of freedom should not be transgressed under socialism either,' said Ernst Fischer, the reformist Marxist thinker from Vienna. 'Anti-Semitism must remain outlawed.' Shortly afterwards Fischer drew his conclusion: he publicly described the 'policy' by which Soviet tanks had put an end to the 'rule of Zionism' in Prague as 'tank Communism', and resigned from the Communist party.

22

The Murder of
Trotsky

When Soviet tanks were replacing the Prague Spring with a new ice age, countless Czech refugees sought asylum in Vienna. Among them was a woman from Prague, Klara D., who had for quite some time been a secretary to the Czechoslovak President Novotný. In that capacity she had participated on his behalf in various meetings which he was unable to attend himself, taken down in shorthand every word, and then subsequently made a transcript for him.

According to her recollection, Novotný in 1963 had her attend a meeting of the commission which was to decide on the rehabilitation of people who, in the late 1940s had been arrested, sentenced and expelled from the Communist Party for alleged anti-party activities. Virtually all the members of the commission were more or less strongly in favour not only of rehabilitating everyone who had then been innocently convicted, but also of accepting them back into the Party. Only one participant vehemently opposed that solution: the Central Committee member (and formerly also a candidate member of the Politburo) Bruno Köhler. He behaved as if these were his personal verdicts which were to be revised. The fact that the trials had been based on invented charges seemed to be of no interest to him. When the other members of the commission stuck to their opinions and argued with increasing heat, a sensational event took place. One of the most highly respected members of the commission stepped up close to Köhler and hurled at him a sentence which Klara D., because of its mysterious nature, wrote down word for word: 'If a person like you, who during the war – when you allegedly were in Gestapo detention in Paris – behaved as we now know you did, is allowed to sit in the Central Committee today, then surely the innocent can be readmitted to the Party.'

These words got Köhler so excited that he had to fight for breath. A few members of the commission now suddenly took his side; the others were shouting at him in undisguised fury. There was a real scuffle, and several members of the commission slapped each other's faces. Someone shouted that Köhler, along with Ulbricht, had also denounced decent and innocent comrades in the Soviet Union. Köhler turned white with rage, but said less than anyone else. When the meeting returned to the subject under discussion Köhler gave in. It was decided that the rehabilitated people would be readmitted to the Party.

Klara D. typed out the minutes of the meeting in the usual way, literally quoting the shouting matches, according to instructions and took the papers to the president. A few hours later Novotný rang through and requested her to destroy all records of the meeting. The matter was no longer topical and the quarrel irrelevant as Köhler had eventually given in.

Klara D. told me the story because she assumed that in Paris Köhler had not in fact been a prisoner of the Gestapo but a Gestapo agent – maybe, she thought, I could confirm that suspicion.

Bruno Köhler's name was well known to me. He was one of the leading Stalinists in Czechoslovakia, and unlike Klara D. I knew precisely why he had so strenuously opposed the rehabilitation of the victims of the show trials: this vicious anti-Semite had played an important backstage part in preparing the trials against Slánský, London, Löbl and others. He was regarded as a liaison man between the Soviet and Czechoslovak secret services.

Following my conversation with Klara D. I looked up his name in the *Biographical Handbook of the ČSSR* (published by V. R. Lerche in Munich) and there found the following biographical data: born 1900 in Neustadt, attended state school until the age of fourteen, became a printer's apprentice and later a soldier. In 1918 still a Social Democrat, he went over to the Communists in 1921 and was a delegate to the Third Comintern Congress. In 1926 and 1927 he attended the party school in Moscow, in 1935 he became a Communist Deputy in the Czechoslovak parliament and simultaneously a member of the Comintern executive. In 1930 he had to leave Czechoslovakia in a hurry; he emigrated to France but was caught there by the Nazis and arrested. Then there was a strange leap: in 1941 Köhler was suddenly in the USA, but by the end of the year he was in Moscow, where he edited *Československé Listy*. From 1945 to 1947 he was a liaison man between the Soviet and Czechoslovak Communist Parties. In 1947 he returned to Prague. In 1949 he was head of the personnel department, in 1952 head of the first department of the Central Committee; in 1953 he became its Secretary. In 1960 he became a Deputy of the National Assembly and in 1961 a candidate member of the Politburo. In a word: a picture-book Communist career in which there was only one mysterious feature: a stay in the USA immediately after detention by the Gestapo.

I decided to discuss the matter with Vilém Kahan. Kahan, too, was a refugee from the events of 1968, but I had known him for some time and in various conversations had learned to appreciate his precise knowledge of Czechoslovak internal affairs. In Prague he had been the secretary, advisor and friend of Josef Smrkovský who, as Chairman of the National Assembly, had been one of the leading figures of the Prague Spring. But while Smrkovský decided to remain in the country after the Russian invasion, he advised Kahan to go abroad. At any rate, Vilém Kahan was one of those who attended the above-mentioned meeting: he had been arrested and imprisoned once before, and no one could tell how the latest Czechoslovak leadership would deal with his rehabilitation.

I asked Kahan to come to my office and told him of the strange information I'd been given about Hugo Köhler, without disclosing my source. But Vilém Kahan was fully in the picture; indeed he knew considerably more about Köhler than Klara D. did. In particular, he was acquainted with his life story after his emigration to Paris. Köhler, he told me, had not been arrested by the Nazis but by the French, as early as 1939. When the Germans occupied France the French had as a rule released political prisoners who might be at risk. But Köhler had the bad luck that, at his prison, this operation was delayed, so that he fell into the hands of the German occupation forces. 'But then', Kahan told me, 'they suddenly released him on the basis of a Soviet intervention, and he went to Lisbon, and from there to Mexico.'

Thus my theory that Köhler had collaborated with the Gestapo dissolved into thin air. Even the fact that he had been released in response to Soviet intervention was not necessarily unusual. I recalled a conversation with Alexander Weissberg-Cybulski, who told me that after the Hitler-Stalin pact he had been released from a Soviet prison in exchange for Communists in Hitler's prisons. It was possible that the same had happened in 1940 to a prisoner of the Germans in Paris.

But what had Köhler been doing in Mexico? When Kahan told me I was surprised that the name of the country had not immediately triggered off the right associations in my own mind. 'Don't you know?' he said in a low voice but with evident gratification that I clearly didn't. 'To anyone who knows anything about it, Köhler was the man who organized Leon Trotsky's assassination in Mexico. From there he crossed into the United

States and in 1941 returned to Moscow as a worthy comrade. He was a close confidant of Beria [for many years the GPU [Secret Police] chief and for a short period head of the party].' Now that the penny had dropped a chain of associations started in my mind: I remembered that Trotsky's assassin, Ramón Mercader, having served his twenty years' imprisonment, did not remain in Mexico but moved, not to Moscow, but to Prague. 'Yes, it happened just as you think,' Kahan confirmed my surmise. 'He went to Bruno Köhler, who organized a flat for him, a state pension and Czech citizenship. When the Prague Spring dawned Mercader moved to Moscow.'

Mainly for the sake of order I subsequently verified whether this was compatible with what we knew of the Nazi's actions in Paris. At first glance it was suspicious that Köhler should have been in Gestapo detention so early: officially the Gestapo only moved into Paris some time after the Wehrmacht's entry. But closer study of the evidence cleared up this detail as well: at the time of the *Anschluss* and when the Germans moved into Poland, the SS and Gestapo had always moved in along with the German army. This had led to protests by the generals, and in the French campaign the German High Command had issued orders for the SS and the Gestapo to move in well after the fighting forces. Hence the general impression that the Gestapo did not arrive in Paris until some time after 14 June 1940, the day of the surrender of Paris. But appearances are deceptive. Himmler had not accepted being 'downgraded' by the generals and had set up a unit of twenty specially trained Gestapo men who, wearing the uniform of the secret field police, were, in a manner of speaking, infiltrated into the Wehrmacht and arrived in Paris on 14 June. The very next day they called at police headquarters and commandeered all files relating to German refugees, Communists or prominent anti-Nazis.

It was therefore entirely probable that the Köhler file was found very quickly and that he became an object of an exchange deal under the Hitler–Stalin pact. Finally my researches revealed that Köhler had in fact entered the USA from Mexico in early January 1941. Whatever I discovered matched Kahan's account.

According to Kahan, his comrades had subsequently always been afraid of Köhler. Even the members of the Czechoslovak Central Committee lived in permanent fear of him, and when that body was newly elected under Dubček, Smrkovský did all he could to prevent Köhler being re-elected. It was known what a man like Köhler was capable of.

In the meantime a few things have changed in the eastern bloc. For the first time, Mikhail Gorbachev uttered Trotsky's name in an official speech without following it with a tirade of execrations. It has become conceivable that this – intellectually probably the most important – Communist leader will be rehabilitated, and it may now even be possible in the Soviet Union to ask how his assassination actually came about. *Glasnost* appears to have erupted. Yet the fate of another great man, who likewise became a victim of Stalin, is still taboo: to this day the Soviet Union claims not to know what has happened to Raoul Wallenberg.

23

The Wallenberg Case

The letter was dated 29 March 1971 and came from Stockholm. A desperate mother asked me to help her in her search for her missing son: 'I have read with great admiration the book published about you by Joseph Wechsberg in 1967, describing your work in tracking down Nazi criminals ... I have reflected on what possibilities there may still exist of clarifying what happened to my son after the time when, according to witnesses, he was still alive. I have asked myself whether you might find it possible, using your far-flung network of contacts, to discover any information ...' In the slightly awkward German of a Swede who believed she had to introduce herself, the letter continued: 'The undersigned Mai von Dardel is the mother of the Swedish Legation Secretary in Budapest, Raoul Wallenberg, who was instructed by the Swedish government in 1944 at the request of the Americans, to conduct an operation to save the Jews in Hungary and who subsequently succeeded, under great difficulties and dangers, in saving thousands of Jews from the Nazis' claws. In 1945 he was taken prisoner by the Soviet authorities and moved to the Soviet Union, from where he has not yet returned.'

On 17 January 1945 Raoul Wallenberg had been sent by the Russians from Budapest to Debrecen, in order to put his case to Marshal Malinovsky at the headquarters of the Soviet zone of occupation. From that day on no direct news had been received from him. However, his mother could not believe that he was dead, or perhaps like mothers everywhere did not want to believe it. 'Over the past few years there have been repeated Swedish inquiries about my son,' the letter continued, 'but the Soviet government initially denied any knowledge. Then, in 1957, they claimed that he had died in the Lubianka prison in Moscow on 17 July 1947. Yet a number of persons who have returned from Soviet prisons have testified to having been in touch with him after 17 July 1947. The last information about him dates from 1961: then the Soviet doctor Myasnikov told a colleague that Raoul was in a psychiatric institution.'

That was all Mrs von Dardel knew about the whereabouts of her son, and she was now asking me to help her. She realized that normally I was concerned with tracking down Nazi criminals; however, she wrote almost apologetically, there might be a justification for making an exception in the case of her son. Raoul, she observed modestly, had surely protected many persecuted people against criminals. Evidently thinking that this was still not enough, she enclosed a letter from Dr Chaim Arie, the director of a hospital in Bersheva in Israel. The hospital bears the name 'Raoul Wallenberg' and was built with donations from Hungarian Jews who had been saved by her son.

Until then I had concerned myself only cursorily with the Wallenberg case. Of course I had read a number of publications, including a little book written by my friend, the historian Josef Wulf, and I knew that there was a committee in Stockholm which had made it its business to clear up his disappearance. But that was all. There were no clues for an investigation. In my reply to Wallenberg's mother I asked her, above all, to let me have all the statements by former Soviet detainees referring to her son. She thereupon sent me the testimony of a man who, so he said, had communicated with Wallenberg in prison by tapping signals. But that statement was several years old.

I turned to my former colleague Moshe Leder, who had only recently emigrated to Israel and there had taken on a position in the Russian-language service of the Israeli radio 'Kol Israel'. I asked him to put out a report on Wallenberg. As the transmission was also being listened to in the Soviet Union there was a chance that one of the many Jews who had been in Stalin's prisons might remember the Swede. The Wallenberg story was broadcast on 15 April 1971, and I was at least able to report to his mother that I had taken some steps.

I realized that a case such as this could be cleared up only if it became known worldwide. I therefore started a Raoul Wallenberg file, even though it contained practically no material, and put it on top of my desk, over-flowing as it was with files. Whenever journalists called on me to ask what cases I was working on at the moment, I would point to the Wallenberg folder, and although these journalists as a rule had an above-average interest in the Nazi period, it turned out that hardly any of the twenty who called on me had ever heard of Wallenberg. I therefore told the pressmen everything that I had in the meantime read about the man, and this was reflected in a number of articles. Moshe Leder did his part in his broadcasts: twice a month Kol Israel broadcast information on Wallenberg in order to keep the case topical.

As for myself, I wanted in particular to be quite clear on what Professor Myasnikov really knew about Wallenberg. Myasnikov, at a medical congress in Moscow, had passed his information on to Professor Nana Schwarz, and I decided to travel to Sweden to talk to her. As a family friend she had long been connected with the Wallenberg case and also had personal contacts in the Soviet Union as, after the war, she had been physician to the Soviet embassy. At the family's request she had first made inquiries about Wallenberg in 1946 and brought his parents reassuring news: he was under the protection of the Soviet government and would soon return home. This she had been told by Madame Kollontay, the Soviet ambassador. But he did not return.

In 1947 Albert Einstein wrote a letter to Stalin, requesting him to look into the fate of this heroic man. Stalin replied that unfortunately he knew nothing about Wallenberg's whereabouts.

The American government had also concerned itself with the matter: after all, Wallenberg had been asked by the Americans to undertake his mission for the War Refugee Board, by going to Budapest as legation secretary. Although the Americans could not then take any direct steps in Hungary in view of the political situation at the time (there was no peace treaty yet), they wanted the Swedes to intervene with the Soviets on their behalf. But because of their good bilateral relations with the Soviet Union the Swedes, time and again, declined to do so.

All this I learned from Professor Schwarz: I didn't want to repeat steps which had already been taken unsuccessfully. It turned out that the professor had been most successful on her personal initiative. At a medical congress in Moscow in 1961 she met Professor Myasnikov, whom she knew from past congresses, and asked him routinely if he knew anything about Raoul Wallenberg's fate. His answer shocked her: 'Wallenberg is in one of our institutions for the mentally ill.'

Professor Schwarz was so upset by this information that she left the congress, returned to Stockholm, and there alerted both Wallenberg's family and the foreign ministry. When she tried to return to the congress the following day she was refused a visa.

In response to urgent inquiries by the Swedish foreign ministry the Soviets declared that they had looked into the matter, and that Professor Myasnikov denied ever having made such a remark. Sweden thereupon demanded, through her ambassador Gunnar Jarring, that Professor

Schwarz should be confronted with Professor Myasnikov, and after a few weeks the Soviets agreed. Those few minutes remained forever engraved on Professor Schwarz's mind: Myasnikov sat opposite her, dropping his head, and avoided looking her in the eyes even once. Mechanically he said that there must have been a misunderstanding – she probably had not understood him properly because they were speaking German. 'Dear colleague,' Professor Schwarz had replied, 'we discussed the most complex medical problems in German and understood one another very well. This was a very simple question, to which you gave me a very simple answer. And are you now suggesting that I didn't understand you or that you didn't understand me?' But Myasnikov was not prepared to discuss the matter, and Ambassador Jarring, who had arranged for the confrontation in the presence of an official of the Soviet foreign ministry, did not permit any further argument either.

Although my conversation with Professor Schwarz was exceedingly instructive, as well as impressive – she is a remarkable woman – it did not in the least advance my work. I had to publicize the Wallenberg story if I wanted to succeed. So I reported on it in the bulletin which we publish every year and send out to more than 20,000 people all over the world. Anyone with any information at all on Wallenberg was to contact us.

The most important piece of information came from my immediate neighbourhood. One day a letter arrived from a Viennese doctor, by the name of Menahem Melzer, who offered to see me in connection with the Wallenberg case. I visited him that same evening and listened to his story. Melzer had been a member of the Austrian Communist party. In the early 1930s he had gone to the Soviet Union as a young doctor in order to help with the 'building of Communism' and had found himself in the midst of the great purges under Stalin. The secret police were indiscriminately arresting all kinds of people whom Stalin in his paranoia saw as his enemies – including, in particular, loyal European Communists who had been the best friends of the Soviet system. Melzer was able to work out when his own turn would come and decided to flee within the country: he volunteered to go to Siberia as a doctor. After the war he was promoted to be chief of a health department which, among other things, supervised the forced labour camps in the Vorkuta region. There was a particularly exposed camp there, by the name of Khal'mer-Yu, whose inmates were employed in the construction of the Pechora dam. Many of the prisoners were physically so weakened that they had to be temporarily transferred to an auxiliary camp to regain their strength. Dr Melzer came to this auxiliary camp in the summer of 1948; and, along with two other doctors, he was to decide to what extent the inmates were once more fit for work. To this end the men had to line up naked behind a bench on which their papers were lying, to avoid wasting time with a lot of questions.

'There I suddenly saw the name Raoul Wallenberg,' Dr Melzer related; 'I remember it quite clearly because I thought someone had written the name wrongly: it must have been Paul not Raoul.' Melzer drew the attention of the prisoner, who looked like a German, to this mistake, but the man answered that his name really was Raoul and that this was a Scandinavian first name. When Melzer observed that he had never come across that strange name, the Swede said to him that surely he must have heard of Amundsen, whose first name was Roald, which sounded even stranger than Raoul. 'It is because of this conversation that the whole incident stuck in my mind,' Dr Melzer said, 'and when I was reading about the Wallenberg case in your bulletin I felt I had to get in touch with you.'

Dr Melzer had an adventurous life behind him. Not only had he accidentally come across Raoul Wallenberg in Siberia, but he had also met his wife there. As a Jew she had been deported from Riga to the Ravensbrück concentration camp and had there been liberated by the Russians. But like a lot of ex-prisoners she was immediately locked up again by the Soviets because, allegedly, she had collaborated with the Fascists. Thus she got to Siberia, where Dr Melzer met her. When she had served her five years' detention the two got married and Melzer tried to get out of Russia. His parents had lost their lives, but from the Red Cross he learned that his sister had survived and had settled in Belgium. He got in touch with her and in his letters he conveyed to her, in disguised language, that he wanted to leave the Soviet Union with his family.

Chance would have it that a big international musical congress was held in Moscow in 1951, to which the Belgian Queen Mother Elisabeth – a great music lover – was invited. Melzer's sister approached her with a request for help, and this help was given in a manner one hardly dares record in a book because every reader must think it a piece of fiction. During the congress the Queen Mother met Joseph Stalin, and when a few polite words had been exchanged the absolute ruler over the Soviet Union asked her: 'Is there anything I can do for you?' The Queen Mother said yes. She gave him Melzer's address and stated plainly: 'I should like to take this man and his family back to Belgium with me.'

'That same night,' Melzer told me, 'there was suddenly a loud knocking at my door. It was the secret police. We were given one hour to pack our most important belongings, we were taken to a plane which was waiting for us, and we were flown to Moscow. From the airport we were driven with flashing blue lights to the Queen Mother's special train, and with her we travelled to Belgium.' It had taken an episode so unbelievable in the history of Stalinist persecution for Dr Menahem Melzer to sit facing me now and tell me about Raoul Wallenberg.

I immediately informed Ministerial Counsellor Danielsson of the Swedish Ministry of the Interior about this unexpected turn. Danielsson came to Vienna, and in order to make sure that there was no mistaken identity we showed Dr Melzer a number of photographs of different men, interspersed with which there were two of Wallenberg, one a profile and the other full face. Melzer identified Wallenberg from the profile photo. His statement was again placed on record and attested by the Swedish embassy in Vienna. From his work diary, which in view of his unusual departure the doctor was able to bring with him, along with all his other papers, it emerged that his encounter with Wallenberg had taken place in the summer of 1948 – a year after his official death.

I now began to study the older statements by witnesses – especially those by a Herr Mulle and a Herr Rehekampf, which seemed especially credible because they tallied although the two men had never met. Mulle testified that in 1956 a Swede had been held in an isolation ward of the prison hospital in Vladimir. Although he hadn't seen him personally, a Georgian called Goge Beridze had seen him. Rehekampf had likewise named the Vladimir prison hospital and, even more precisely, referred to a Swedish diplomat. To clear my mind on the subject I inquired from Ministerial Counsellor Danielsson how many Swedes, to the knowledge of the Swedish Ministry of the Interior, had been held in the Soviet Union. Including Raoul Wallenberg there had been four; three of them, however, had returned from Russia in the early 1950s. There was therefore little doubt that Mulle and Rehekampf had indeed been in Vladimir prison with Raoul Wallenberg. Then there was the Swiss citizen Emil Brugge, who claimed to have communicated with Raoul Wallenberg in the Vladimir prison by tapping signals. And finally there was the French Major Gouazé, who, during his detention in the Soviet Union, had been asked by another prisoner to pass on news of Wallenberg to the French embassy. That message, too, mentioned Vladimir prison.

There existed therefore a number of weighty pieces of evidence showing the Soviets had deliberately misinformed the Swedes about Wallenberg. But the Swedes evidently had no wish to believe that. When Danielsson put these statements to the Swedish foreign minister and pointed out that they clashed with the information given by the Soviets, the minister was outraged: 'I hope you aren't suggesting that Soviet foreign minister Vyshinsky is a liar?'

A statement which was taken a little more seriously was that of a certain Adolf Cohen, who was in a Belgian prison for illegal entry into Belgium and who made a statement to the effect that at the Brygidki prison in Lvov he had repeatedly – the last time towards the end of March 1947 – spoken to Raoul Wallenberg through an open window. This account was so precise that the Deputy for the Swedish town of Nässjöe, Börg, questioned the Swedish foreign minister about it and, at any rate, involved him in a lengthy discussion.

When I tried, in 1972, to discover through the Ministry of Justice in Brussels what had become of Cohen, I was told that he was no longer in Belgium. Considering the importance of the case the Swedes had been astonishingly negligent with regard to an available witness.

On 15 January 1972 Swedish foreign minister Wickmann, while on a visit to Austria, gave a press conference at the Concordia Press Club to about 200 journalists. As I was a member of the foreign press association, I seized the opportunity to ask: 'What does the Swedish government know about Raoul Wallenberg's whereabouts in the Soviet Union?'

Wickmann consulted with the Swedish ambassador, presumably asking him who I was, and replied curtly: 'For us the Wallenberg case is closed.'

Although the man's face spoke louder than any words, I pressed on: 'How can the case be closed if the news of Wallenberg's death is questioned, and that on good grounds, not only by his family but by all who are concerned with the case?'

But Wickmann, as expected, had nothing to add to his earlier answer. I realized that no help whatever was to be expected from the Swedish government.

Just about that time I met an old acquaintance, the world-famous writer Leon Uris. I outlined the Wallenberg case to him and suggested that he might help us by writing a book about it. 'A man like Raoul Wallenberg is perhaps born only once in a century.'

Leon Uris listened to me attentively, then he objected that he was really planning to write a book about Masada.

'Masada has waited for two thousand years,' I said. 'Wallenberg cannot wait that long.'

We agreed that I should contact the Wallenberg family and put the project to them. Wallenberg's mother was delighted at the idea – but unfortunately it remained just an idea.

Even so, the Wallenberg story had become well known in the meantime. One day I had a telephone call from my friend Jules Huf, who worked in Vienna for the Dutch *Telegraaf*. 'Simon,' he said, 'there's a Russian here who knows something about Wallenberg. His name's Yuri Belov. I'll bring him over to you straight away.'

Yuri Belov reported that in 1963 he had been in one of the many Soviet camps. One day he and another prisoner were detailed to do cleaning work at the prison hospital. The other prisoner was a Hungarian, who was anxious to find out if by any chance there was a compatriot at the hospital. He did in fact find one and the two men briefly exchanged their most interesting news. The Hungarian who had been in the hospital for some time then told him that a Swede there had begun a hunger strike – whereupon he'd been transferred to a mental hospital. The Swede had been an important person: during the war he'd been in Budapest in some high position.

I deliberately did not make a record of this statement because I wanted to prevent anyone gaining the impression that I had influenced Belov with my questions. Instead I took him to the Swedish embassy: there he made an official deposition.

I was now convinced that I was on the right track and really got my teeth into the Wallenberg case – to an extent possibly equalled only by my search for Eichmann. No detail was too trivial for me, no deposition too old for re-verification. Thus I re-read the newspaper reports of a press conference given by Khrushchev in Stockholm in 1956, where he had been first assailed by questions about Wallenberg. As so often, the master of the Kremlin first reacted with a furious outburst, but then moderated himself and supplied this Solomonic information: 'Thousands of people have disappeared in our country – after so many years it is impossible to clear up the case.'

Shortly afterwards, however, in February 1957, it was apparently possible after all. Foreign minister Gromyko handed a report to the Swedish embassy, from which it emerged that Wallenberg was dead. To be on the safe side I got hold of the text of that statement. In it Gromyko referred to the notes which the head physician of the Lubianka prison, Smoltsov (no longer alive), had sent to Abakumov (the deputy of the secret service boss Beria and executed along with him in 1953), to the effect that a certain Walenberg (with only one 'l' and without first name) had died of cardiac arrest on 17 July 1947. His body, Smoltsov added, had been cremated.

I therefore questioned former Lubianka prisoners on whether bodies had been cremated there. Most of them couldn't make anything of my question, but Alexander Ginsburg (a friend of Solzhenitsyn's), who was accurately informed on conditions, was certain of his answer: for the corpses of prisoners to be burnt at Lubianka in 1947 was virtually out of the question. Although he couldn't reveal his sources to me, people who were bound to know had assured him that all prisoners who died in Lubianka prison were buried in a mass grave.

Again I passed my information on to the Swedish Ministry of the Interior. Again I pointed out that there were now a number of witnesses who had met Wallenberg after his alleged 'death'. But again my information didn't cut any ice with the Swedish authorities. And even less with the Soviet ones. It was clear to me that the Soviets would have to be put under pressure. The best way to do this was to found Wallenberg committees in as many countries as possible – above all, in the United States. There wasn't a lecture to a Jewish community or at a university when I didn't mention him. Soon I heard from Jews who had been saved by Wallenberg. Now they were able to repay him: by setting up local Wallenberg committees and by enlisting as many politicians, senators and congressmen as possible.

After all, Wallenberg's heroic actions were directly linked with an American operation: when the mass murder of the Jews became known, at least in rough outline, in 1944, President Roosevelt issued an order that the War Refugee Board should do all it could to save at least the Hungarian Jews for whom the 'final solution' had only just begun. But as the USA was in a state of war with Hungary someone from a neutral country would have to act as an intermediary. The American ambassador in Sweden, Herschel Johnson, approached a young man, Raoul Wallenberg, with whom he was personally acquainted and asked him if he would undertake this dangerous task. Wallenberg accepted. His work is a memorial also to President Roosevelt as well.

Among the Jews he saved was Congressman Thomas Lantos from California and his wife Agnette – they both became members of the Californian Wallenberg committee. A Swede, Mrs Lena Kaplan, became the president of the Wallenberg committee in New York, which was also joined by the wife of Senator Dan Moynihan. It was my intention to set up a World Committee for the Discovery of the Truth about Raoul Wallenberg and to win over for it as many famous figures as possible, in the hope of eventually making some impression on the Soviet leadership. Wallenberg's mother, with whom I was in constant touch, suggested to me three Swedes of international repute: the Nobel Prize winner Hannes Allgren, Premier Tage Erlander and the initiator of all Wallenberg investigations Professor Nana Schwarz. On the occasion of the thirtieth anniversary of the attempt on Hitler's life the Union of Resistance Fighters, whose vice-president I am, decided to propose to the Norwegian parliament that Raoul Wallenberg be nominated for the Nobel Peace Prize. The President of the Internationale, Albert Guérisse, to that end obtained the agreement of Nobel Prize winner René Cassin. But nothing could be done in Oslo until we possessed indisputable proof that Raoul Wallenberg was still alive. Unless something was done soon he certainly wouldn't be alive.

In 1975 I wrote to Senator Henry Jackson, asking him to make Wallenberg's release the subject of American–Soviet negotiations. Elizabeth Taylor, who was then married to Senator John Warner, gave a dinner in my honour at her home, to which some fifty senators including Henry Jackson were invited. Thus I had the opportunity, throughout a whole dinner, to talk to him about the Wallenberg case.

In October 1975, when I was elected a member, and two years later the president, of the Sakharov Hearings I had another opportunity for championing the case of Raoul Wallenberg. The case was now so well known that I decided to write a letter to Brezhnev. Wallenberg's mother drafted the letter in July 1977 and we jointly released it to the press. But we had overrated Brezhnev's sensitivity.

I have time and again asked myself if the Swedish government had really done everything in its power to clear up the matter. And the answer I have arrived at, regrettably, is that it has not. As far as I can judge, the reason was to be found in the political situation. For one thing, the Swedes have a fundamental interest in living in untroubled harmony with their super-powerful neighbour to the east. For another, the mostly Social Democratic governments depend on Communist support in parliament. Finally, it even seems as though the Wallenberg family – one of the wealthiest in Sweden, with extensive business interests with the Soviet Union – had been in agreement with the policy of not pushing too hard. The Wallenberg case was being conducted with a certain noble restraint – an attitude I sensed in particular on the part of the head of the family, Markus Wallenberg.

I was hoping, finally, to establish in Paris that international Wallenberg committee that I'd had in mind all the time. Nobel Prize winner René Cassin, the father of the human rights convention, was prepared to cooperate; I also succeeded in enlisting Arthur Goldberg, the former American Attorney General and future US representative at the United Nations. Not, however, Markus Wallenberg. When I had informed him that such a committee would need an office with at least one secretary, which I found myself unable to finance, he asked me to let him have a detailed paper – and I never heard from him again.

I therefore once more tried to stimulate public interest. In 1981 we staged an international Wallenberg Hearing in Stockholm, the participants in which included Greville Janner, the president of the Board of British Jews, and Prosecutor General Gideon Hausner, the prosecutor in the Eichmann case. 'This is not an anti-Soviet conference,' I said as I opened the meeting. 'We have not come here to change the Soviet regime. But we want to free an innocent man from undeserved imprisonment, a man to whom thousands owe their lives.' When journalists thereupon asked if one could really assume that a man arrested in 1945 was still alive, I replied, without consulting the others: 'Raoul Wallenberg will be alive until the Soviets supply us with credible proof of his death.' Here was the formulation of the principle from which this conference and all Wallenberg committees were to proceed. This was no longer a matter of Wallenberg alone, but of the system of concealment of the truth by the Soviet Union.

Unfortunately the popularity of the case now also brought the self-seekers into play: one witness claimed that Wallenberg was in the top-security wing of the Irkutsk prison, another reported that Wallenberg had been sighted on Wrangel Island beyond the Arctic Circle, and finally an Israeli claimed to have telephoned her father in Moscow who had just been released from prison and who, according to her, had said: 'My three years are nothing, there's a Swede here who's been in prison for over thirty years.' I flew to Israel twice to check on statements of this nature – nothing ever came of them.

Basically it was now no longer a case of proving that Wallenberg had survived his official 'death' – that proof had long been furnished – it was a case of compelling the Soviet Union to confess. If need be, to confess to murder.

Lena Kaplan of the New York Wallenberg committee made sure that American diplomats visiting the Soviet Union invariably raised the Wallenberg case. And one day an idea cropped up of how one might get to Brezhnev in person: Lena Kaplan requested the well-known American multi-millionaire Armand Hammer, who had been a friend of Lenin's and had at all times enjoyed excellent relations with the Soviet leadership of the day, to raise the Wallenberg case with the Soviet party boss. Brezhnev listened to him but remarked that he had never before heard Wallenberg's name. But he promised to inform himself and let Hammer know next time he visited the Soviet Union. Some hope, therefore, flared up briefly. But the cold shower followed shortly afterwards: when Hammer saw him the next time, Brezhnev told him he had inquired of Gromyko and learned from him that Wallenberg had died in 1947.

In the meantime my friend Tom Lantos had found a way of making it possible for the US government to intervene directly in the Wallenberg case: in conjunction with a number of congressmen and senators he arranged for Wallenberg to be granted honorary US citizenship. The whole business became a minor state ceremony: Ronald Reagan and Vice-President George Bush invited Raoul Wallenberg's brother and sister, Mr and Mrs Lantos and myself to a ceremony, at which the American president put into words what was in the minds of us all: long before the USA was able to honour Raoul Wallenberg, his work within the framework of an American institution had honoured the USA. From then on the United States was able officially to act on behalf of its honorary citizen Raoul Wallenberg.

Yet the Soviet Union preferred not to enter into discussions at all. The regimes changed – Brezhnev was followed by Andropov, and Andropov by Chernenko – but the silence remained the same. Only with Gorbachev did hope arise again, after decades, that the Soviet Union might remedy this part of its past by coming out with the truth. Especially if Raoul

Wallenberg was found to be no longer among the living, it was important for the truth to be known. Historical truth is valuable in itself. Only a regime which admits to historical truth can learn from the past. Why, we must discover, did the Soviets arrest Wallenberg in the first place? Why did they initially admit but later deny that he was imprisoned in Moscow? Why did they at first want to blame the Nazis for his disappearance and subsequently declare that he was under Soviet protection and would soon return home? Why was this announcement also retracted and finally replaced by the lie that Wallenberg had died in Moscow's Lubianka prison in July 1947? Of the many speculations made in this connection I should like to mention one which seems to me at least conceivable. It is based on Stalin's persecution mania. Just as in the so-called 'doctors' plot' he formulated the accusation that Jewish doctors were aiming to kill important members of the Politburo, he might have intended – in the midst of the Cold War – to brand Wallenberg as an American agent and make him into the key figure of a show trial. In such a trial Hungarian Jews might then have appeared, declaring that Wallenberg had helped rich Jews only so that they, out of gratitude, would then build up an American spy network. All this sounds rather far-fetched, but no idea could be too paranoid for Stalin's mania. He repeatedly tried to concoct a conspiracy by Jewish agents. In 1952, Mátyás Rákosi, himself a Jew and Stalin's man in Hungary, was forced to arrest a whole string of members of the Hungarian intelligence service who were of Jewish extraction, and to have them imprisoned along with other leading personages such as Lajos Stoeckler, Dr Balinth and the psychiatrist Dr Benedek. Colonel Abrasimov, the chief advisor to the Hungarian secret police, was said to have been instructed to prepare an appropriate show trial at which all these Jews would have been unmasked as American agents. Only Stalin's death prevented that spectacle from being staged. (Instead Abrasimov was recalled to the USSR and executed along with Beria.)

Needless to say, the fate of Hungary's Jews holds no clue to what happened to Raoul Wallenberg, but it does suggest the climate in which his case was unrolling. That he should have been consigned to the psychiatric ward of a prison hospital in order to be prepared for a show trial is no less plausible than that he was sent there because of a hunger strike.

Raoul Wallenberg long ago became a symbol. His case reflects the inhumanity of the Soviet system, but it also reflects the humanity of which an individual is capable. Nothing in the early life of young Raoul Wallenberg suggested that this man was to become a hero. When he assumed his post in Budapest he was undoubtedly willing to help – but he was also in danger of his life. While powerful states were watching the millions being murdered in self-chosen impotence, Wallenberg acted: he declared Jews to be Swedish citizens and thereby snatched them from the death machine. When in January 1945 – when everything seemed to be over and all danger past – he approached the Soviet occupation authorities with a request for food for the 25,000 under his protection, Raoul Wallenberg was arrested. Having escaped the Gestapo he lived through the end of the war in the GPU's dungeons.

Today, forty-two years later, his life has not yet run its full course. I am writing these lines in the latter half of 1987, two months after Wallenberg's seventy-fifth birthday, and I am sticking to what I said at the Wallenberg Hearing: Wallenberg will be alive until the Soviets have supplied convincing proof of his death. Mihkail Gorbachev, too, will have to be questioned about Wallenberg until he supplies an answer.

24

Andrei Sakharov

As I was completing the final corrections to this book, news reached me that the Soviet Academy of Sciences had appointed Andrei Sakharov a member of its presidium. By the time this book is published, he may well have received permission to travel to the West: I would thus be able to meet in person for the first time a man in whose name I have been permitted to make my own personal contribution to the birth of freedom in the Soviet Union, and for whose rehabilitation I have fought for thirteen years.

In my view, Andrei Sakharov is one of the greatest men of this century.

Arguably the most important physicist the Soviet Union has ever produced, he would, despite living under a Communist system, have been able to lead a comfortable, carefree life with all the advantages of a privileged class.

Instead, he took up the cause of the persecuted.

He did not cross swords with just anybody, but with the all-powerful Soviet secret police. He traced the fate of people arrested without judicial process; he supported their dependants out of his own pocket; he undertook long journeys in order to attend judicial proceedings from which in the end he was excluded on the grounds that there were no available seats in the courtroom. Above all, time and again he raised his voice, futile though it may have seemed, in favour of freedom for humanity, for peace.

No one deserves a Nobel Peace Prize more than he. Although unable to bring any specific armed conflict to conclusion, his struggle nevertheless helped create the principal prerequisites for a lasting peace: recognition of human rights.

The present trend of events in the Soviet Union would have been inconceivable without him. Though officialdom silenced him, and eventually exiled him, the Soviet apparatchiks could not escape the force of his arguments. I am convinced that even in their minds he successfully planted the seeds of a desire for change, for freedom. The fact that Gorbachev in his thinking today stands where these dissidents stood only a few years ago is ultimately due to Sakharov.

Almost equally important were the warnings he addressed to the West, which time and again displayed an alarming readiness to come to terms with conditions in the Soviet Union and indeed to play them down. Whenever Western political leaders joined forces to pursue a policy from strength, whenever they pointed to Soviet violations of human rights, they found themselves not only not encouraged by many newspapers, but on the contrary criticized as Cold Warriors, needlessly and dangerously interfering in Soviet affairs.

It was of decisive importance that Andrei Sakharov stood up at such moments and with his authority demolished Western illusions about progress towards freedom in the Soviet Union – by showing how important it was for the dissidents to have their calls for human rights supported by the West, by demonstrating that the strength of the West was regarded by ordinary people in the Soviet Union not as a danger but as a source of hope.

No one could accuse Andrei Sakharov of being a 'reactionary', nor of being a person blind to the faults of the West, or a man who had turned his back on his own country.

Sakharov spoke with the authority of a great humanist and a great patriot. So long as he was able to speak out, Russia was not lost.

It was therefore a great honour for me to be invited, in the spring of 1975, to become a member of a committee which had been set up in the West to protect Sakharov. Unlike the Wallenberg Hearings, whose purpose was merely to keep the memory of Wallenberg alive in the public mind, the Sakharov Hearings served a different purpose: to provide information on conditions in the Soviet Union.

The main theme of the first hearing, held in Copenhagen from 17–19 October 1975, was the situation in the gulags, the Soviet camps. To anyone who has ever been in a concentration camp, any camp anywhere on earth is a festering wound: if I think of a person lying on his bunk in a Soviet camp then he is at that moment my fellow inmate, and anything inflicted on him is being inflicted on me.

Everything that emerged at that hearing – the insidiousness of the secret police, the obsequiousness of the judges, the brutality of the guards – all these I knew from my own experience.

It seems that dictatorships at all times produce the same kinds of people: the same informers, the same fellow-travellers, the same sadists. Even the structure of the camp hierarchy was the same: in the gulags, too, the guard personnel used criminal convicts to harass the political prisoners.

There is just one difference between the gulags and the concentration camps, an important difference: in the gulags people were not systematically killed because they belonged to a particular race. On the other hand, membership of a certain class was there, too, something like a sentence of death. In all other respects, gulags and concentration camps were totally the same: here as well as there, detainees were used as slave labour. Here as well as there, was the kind of nutrition that must have been known to result in starvation. Here as well as there, were the same atrocious hygienic conditions, with epidemics causing men to die like flies.

Though Stalin might have argued that he had dispensed with systematic murder, nevertheless, in his unsystematic manner, he was responsible for the deaths of even more people than lost their lives in Hitler's concentration camps. In any case – and this is what earned me the lasting hatred of the Eastern bloc governments – Stalin's political heirs are the last people to whom I would grant the right to sit in judgement on the West's attitude to the criminals of the Nazi era.

I have already described the consequences I brought upon myself when, during the Eichmann trial, I said all this to the face of the East German representative, Dr Kaul: a campaign of defamation was launched against me, and faked documents were eventually manufactured against me by their secret service.

That is why I should like at this point to pay special tribute to the role of the Italian Communists. When we held the second Sakharov Hearing in Rome, from 26–29 September 1979, the Communist Party refrained from belittling our event. I presided over this and the following hearing, and at our first press conference I appealed to everybody who called himself an 'anti-Fascist' not to ignore what was happening in the Soviet Union, because it was all too similar to what happened under Hitler. Our hearing, I explained, was not directed against Communism, but was fighting for human rights – that was why a representative of the Italian Communist Party should participate as well. In fact, among our listeners I spotted the Communist Senator Terrazini, who earlier had written a contribution to my book *The Sunflower*.

The Soviet Union, of course, behaved in the familiar way. Whereas at the time of the first Sakharov Hearing it had staged an – unsuccessful – counter-demonstration, this time it resorted to journalistic attacks. When

I returned to Vienna I found an article in the Soviet paper *Trud* repeating all the accusations made against me earlier by the Polish press, when I had placed before the world public a dossier about Polish anti-Semitism.

The third Sakharov Hearing was held at the US Senate in Washington in November 1981. For one day I chaired the meeting. The subject was trade unions, or the rights of the workers in the Soviet Union. As the Communist Party takes the view that thanks to the proletarian revolution socialism has been achieved, there is no longer any need for trade unions. If nevertheless they continue to exist in name, then they are organizations of slaves rather than of workers.

Although that meeting revealed crucial problems besetting the Soviet economy, the kind that are nowadays discussed by everybody, the American press in particular hardly reported the discussions, presumably because the Sakharov Hearings were seen as support for the policy of the American establishment.

By contrast, the next Sakharov Hearings, in Lisbon and London, were highly successful. Because of illness I was unable to take part in the Lisbon meeting; I was however in charge of the hearing in London, and the entire press as well as the European media reported it. Sakharov admittedly had to suffer for it in his own country: he was banished to Gorky, and when he went out his flat was ransacked, his telephone was cut off, his notes were stolen. Yet none of this succeeded in breaking his opposition: Sakharov's words could not be banished.

In November 1984 the Simon Wiesenthal Center in Los Angeles gave a dinner in honour of Sakharov and his wife Yelena Bonner, a dinner which took place without the two principal figures but which was attended by their children Tatiana and Efreym Yankelevich and Alexei Semenov. President Reagan, in a message of greeting, stated that there could be no clearer symbols of the striving for democracy in the Soviet Union today than Andrei Sakharov and Yelena Bonner. I myself was permitted to hand over to Sakharov's children a decoration from our Center for their parents. I feel proud in the knowledge that Andrei Sakharov accepted it.

On 11 November 1988 I was finally able – having concerned myself with his fate for over ten years – to make his personal acquaintance at the home of my friend Ronald Lauder in New York. It was a most happy moment for me, and I was pleased that Sakharov – who was of course informed about everything I had done for him – thanked me for my efforts to get him a visiting professorship for a year at the University of Vienna. The letter which the Austrian Academy of Sciences had sent to the Soviet Academy was never answered. Andrei Sakharov was also aware of the Soviet press attacks on me.

He follows the situation in his country with great attention and some expectations, but he is conscious of the limits of *glasnost* and *perestroika*. He told me that the concentration of power given to Gorbachev by the new constitution was a double-edged weapon which might open the way to a new Stalin if Gorbachev were to disappear or to be cast aside, as had happened to Khrushchev.

It is good to know that Sakharov is again living in his flat in Moscow, and that he is able to comment on all the problems of present-day Soviet society without having to pay for it with the loss of his freedom.

25

Jews and Ukrainians

When the Soviet leadership has an interest in clearing up an old crime, it displays, in contrast to the Wallenberg case, quite astonishing efficiency: Nazi criminals who are no longer living in a Communist state but have found refuge in the West are discovered by the Soviet security service in no time. An example is the following story.

In February 1971 a young man appeared at our office and asked to be allowed to talk to me at once: he was only passing through Vienna and would shortly be leaving again. Against my usual practice I agreed to see him because he seemed to be a well-balanced and serious young man. Now he was sitting opposite me, holding a bundle of partly yellowing papers in his hand: he began, a little confusingly, to tell me about their provenance. It was about his aunt, his late aunt. Her name had been Hanna Weiss, and it had always been said in the family that she was an exceedingly energetic and active woman. Once, in 1961, she had even managed to get close to Khrushchev in person. Khrushchev was then in Vienna to meet Kennedy, and Hanna Weiss accomplished what everyone would have thought impossible: in spite of his being guarded by hundreds of official and even more unofficial policemen, she managed to slip a letter into his hand. He didn't know what was in that letter. But then his aunt had died; his brother had been her executor, and among her possessions he had found a box tied up with string, which seemed to contain private things. But he'd had no time to sift through the papers, so he deposited the box for the time being with friends who, over the years, had had no cause to concern themselves with its contents. Now, on his chance visit to Vienna, they had handed the box over to him and, more for sentimental reasons than anything else, he'd rummaged through it. It contained old photographs, picture postcards, cookery recipes, personal documents – and, among them, two letters in Russian. These two letters he'd now brought to me, together with a translation.

Even the first letter, or strictly speaking the carbon copy of the letter, was unusual. Not so much because of its contents as because of its addressee. In it Frau Weiss was addressing herself directly to Nikita Khrushchev, asking him to see that justice was done. Her husband, along with several hundred Jews, had been picked up by the Ukrainian police on 12 October 1942 and taken to the so-called Rudolf Mill in Stanisławów in Poland. There they had been shot dead on the orders of a police officer called Ivan Dimitrevich Hrabatyn. Khrushchev, with his sense of justice, she asked, could help to track down Hrabatyn and have him face trial.

Even more astonishing was the second letter, clearly an official one. The Ministry of the Interior of the Soviet Union informed Frau Hanna Weiss, resident in Vienna, that upon instructions from Nikita Khrushchev it had conducted certain investigations. The sought-after Ivan Dimitrevich Hrabatyn was no longer in the Soviet Union but was living in Canada now, in London, Ontario, at 623 Hamilton Road. Both the letter and the reply were ten years old.

For a while I was speechless with admiration for the efficiency of the Soviet Ministry of the Interior – when it was a case of finding Nazi criminals in a Western country. If they happened to be living in East Germany it took longer. However, the Soviets' reasons for their letter need not concern me. My task was to ensure that Hrabatyn was in fact brought to trial – that much I owed to Hanna Weiss and to her executed husband.

That very day I wrote a letter to the Israeli police department for Nazi crimes, to inquire whether any witnesses' statements were already in existence on events in Stanisławów. Simultaneously I sent a letter to the Canadian ambassador in Vienna, Norman Berlis, drawing his attention to the charges against Hrabatyn and informing him of his presumed address. I soon received replies from both quarters. Lieutenant Liff of the Israeli police gave me the name of a Dr Liebesmann-Mikulski in Hadera, who was acquainted with events in Stanisławów, and the Canadian embassy in Vienna notified me that my information had been passed on to the proper quarters in Canada. Meanwhile I knew that Hrabatyn was no longer living in London, Ontario. One of my colleagues, who had looked for him, had, after a brief search, sent me his new address. Hrabatyn was now in Vancouver, working in a factory. This information was most useful, as Canada has no compulsory registration of domicile of the kind Austria has, and it is often enormously difficult to trace someone who has gone underground there.

After writing to further witnesses, survivors from Stanisławów now scattered all over the world, asking for their help, I handed the case over to the press on 8 March 1971. The *Vancouver Sun* carried a front-page story of the discovery of the mass murderer from the Ukraine. A reporter from the *Sun* had even tried to talk to Hrabatyn, but he had refused all interviews and merely declared that he was innocent.

The Israeli police had meanwhile, at our request, questioned four further witnesses against Hrabatyn and passed their depositions on to the Canadian embassy. Eventually we also heard from witnesses who were themselves living in Canada and who were willing to give evidence in court. From the point of view of the criminal investigation the case seemed to be wrapped up. The difficulties, as so often, were of a legal nature. Hrabatyn had been a Canadian citizen for several years. Canada had not concluded any extradition agreements with West Germany or with the Soviet Union. In that respect Canada is a better refuge for Nazi and other criminals than even certain South American countries, where one usually had to bribe officials to avoid being extradited. Up to a point the legal situation in Canada resembles that in the USA: a Canadian citizen cannot be extradited, and for him to be stripped of his citizenship requires an even lengthier process than in the USA. The government itself has to instruct a commission of inquiry to examine the charges. The commission's report has to be submitted to the government, which only then rules on the revocation of citizenship.

Because of this legal situation quite a number of people with an incriminating Nazi past have settled in Canada, with the result that in 1986 the Canadian government had to set up the so-called Deschenes Commission, specifically concerned with resident Nazi criminals. Nothing much, however, ever came of it. Thus we supplied the government with a list of 218 Ukrainian SS Officers, and so far not a single one of them has been stripped of his citizenship. And in December 1986, shortly before the Deschenes Commission completed its report, we submitted further evidence, showing that roughly 8000 members of the Ukrainian SS division 'Galicia' emigrated to Canada between 1948 and 1951. This had happened in defiance of then valid Canadian laws which, as a matter of principle, prohibited the immigration of SS men, at least until 1952. This prohibition, however, had been breached by a political move, by granting the Ukrainian SS a special status within the SS. The reason was that the 'Galicia' SS division had only been set up in September 1943, when it recorded an influx of no less than 10,000 volunteers. Admittedly this volunteering consisted simply in choosing between being sent for slave labour in

Germany or serving in the SS. Although the Ukrainians were very well aware of what SS service had consisted in the past, most men preferred it to being sent off to farms or factories in Germany. Besides, the Ukrainian SS division was not primarily to do the dirty work behind the front, but was by then urgently needed at the front itself. In 1944 it was sent into action against the Soviets and suffered a costly defeat in the Brody region.

When, pressed by the Soviet offensive, the Germans had to abandon Galicia, the role of the Ukrainian police as a law-and-order force for Galicia came to an end. But it was these police units in particular which had sullied their hands with the blood of Galician Jews; their ranks were swarming with mass murderers of the worst kind. The problem was that these dissolved police units were reorganized into new police regiments and in the autumn of 1944 integrated into the SS Division 'Galicia'. Thus a division, which by and large might be described as a combat unit, suddenly found itself riddled with mass murderers.

By the end of the war the division was in Italy, in the Rimini area, and was there taken prisoner by the British. But the British had concluded an agreement with the Soviets, under which all soldiers who originated from the territory of the Soviet Union and had entered the German services were to be handed over to the Soviet Union. These were mainly Cossacks, and they were actually handed over. The Ukrainians, on the other hand, were lucky: at the time in question Britain had not yet recognized Galicia as part of the Soviet Union, and Ukrainians already resident in Canada who had organized a 'Ukrainian Committee' learned of the fate of the prisoners interned in various camps in England, and took up their cause. As the huge country of Canada needed people, while little England, on the other hand, was glad to be rid of the prisoners, their intervention was successful. The Attlee government permitted roughly 8000 Ukrainians to emigrate to Canada, and the Canadians accepted them in defiance of the existing laws.

The Deschenes Commission was therefore in an extremely delicate situation from the start: if it found that the Ukrainians in Canada included a lot of war criminals, it would imply that the earlier readiness of the Canadian government to admit these members of the SS had been a grave mistake. The decision was therefore based on national interest: the commission simply came to the general conclusion that membership of the SS division 'Galicia' did not imply responsibility for any crimes. Those concerned therefore held their citizenship legally, and it could be revoked only in individual cases.

It would probably have been very difficult to arrive at a different decision, because surely the majority of the 8000 new Canadians were not war criminals but ordinary people forced into the war as I have described, who were happy to be able to do in Canada what they had done at home before the war: drive their cattle out to pasture and make hay. On the other hand, it is not pleasant to live with the idea that men like Ivan Dimitrevich Hrabatyn are running about free, and that the humane treatment shown to his compatriots has become for him, and the likes of him, a virtual amnesty.

Accounts will have to be settled one day also between Ukrainians and Jews. Ukrainian anti-Semitism used to be on a par with German and even with Austrian anti-Semitism. For centuries Jews and Ukrainians lived together in Galicia. The Ukrainians made up the majority, the Jews the minority. But the Jews frequently belonged to the upper levels of society, and this, quite understandably, led to social tensions. All the nations who have ever ruled over the Ukraine, whether Russians, Poles or Germans, exploited those tensions for their own ends. Whenever the Ukrainians revolted and demanded a state of their own, the rulers succeeded in diverting their aggression towards another target – the Jews. Thus, in the seventeenth century, there was a rising under Khmelnitsky, which ended in pogroms in which half a million Jews lost their lives. (Khmelnitsky is now revered in the Soviet Union as a national hero.) In 1919, in the train of the Russian Revolution, the Ukrainians once more rehearsed a rising under Ataman Petlyura – and again thousands of Jews paid for it with their lives.

During the thirties Nazi Germany was the great hope of the Ukrainian nationalists. The Third Reich, they believed, would at last help them gain their independence. Three days after the German attack against the Soviet Union a national Ukrainian government was proclaimed in Lvov. Its first offical action was a letter of homage to Adolf Hitler. But the Germans had other plans for the Ukraine – they came not as liberators but as oppressors to the region which was to give living space and labour slaves to the 'nation without space'. The Ukrainian government had a life of exactly three days; then it was dissolved by the Germans. Ukrainian nationalist sentiments were forbidden, and the occasional champion who had but recently paid homage to the Nazis was imprisoned.

Nevertheless, the Ukrainians suddenly were no longer the lower stratum but, because of their better relations with the Nazis, something like a 'ruling class'. Whereas in the past they had, in spite of their numbers, lived in the shadow of the Poles or the Jews, they now attained power. The Germans in particular recruited their so-called police auxiliaries from among the ranks of the Ukrainians: frequently identified only by blue-and-yellow armbands and scantily armed with German weapons, they were to ensure 'order'. Most of them had previously been members of the Soviet militia, because the Soviets, too, had used the Ukrainians in Galicia –

presumably because they belonged to the proletariat – in preference to Jews or Poles. The anti-Semitism of these simple, mostly rural, people was traditional and, in a manner of speaking, natural; they did not have to be indoctrinated. The Nazis only had to apply their German thoroughness to mobilizing and utilizing that anti-Semitism: virtually all operations against Jews were conducted by Ukrainian police auxiliaries, commanded by two or three German SS men or ordinary police.

I don't wish to claim that the entire Ukrainian population shared these anti-Semitic sentiments or approved of anti-Jewish outrages. There were, time and again, Ukrainians who knocked at the doors of their Jewish neighbours to apologize or to warn them – but anti-Semitism was so firmly entrenched that it survived beyond the war even in the minds of the Ukrainian intelligentsia. The leadership of the Ukrainian Communist party has made successful use of this anti-Semitism to deflect Ukrainians from their strivings for independence: whatever reprisals were imposed on the country by Moscow were attributed to the Jews, who allegedly were largely at the helm there. Thus a book was published under the auspices of the Ukrainian Academy of Sciences in Kiev by a certain Kichko, entitled *Jewry Unmasked*; it would have deserved a place of honour in Rosenberg's library. Ukrainian newspapers were continually publishing anti-Semitic cartoons which plagiarized cartoons from Nazi papers. Jews who managed to emigrate from the Soviet Union after the war have told me of downright ghoulish confrontations. 'Anything the Germans can do,' was a common phrase, 'we can do better. You can have another Babi-Yar any time you like.' At Babi-Yar 35,000 Jews from Kiev had been massacred before the eyes of the Ukrainian population in 1941.

Ukrainian anti-Semitism did not therefore begin with the Third Reich, nor did it end with the Third Reich – just as Austrian anti-Semitism existed long before Hitler and did not simply vanish after Hitler. But just as it is an indispensable prerequisite of Austrians' coming to terms with their past for the murderers living among them to be brought to justice, if only so the accusation of collective guilt cannot be made, so it is necessary for the Ukrainians. Men like Hrabatyn must be brought to book, no matter whether they have gone to ground in the Soviet Union or have been lucky enough to emigrate to Canada. The Deschenes Commission missed that opportunity. In all it had about 700 cases to examine, of which more than one-third came from my office. In its final report the Commission recommended that twenty of these 700 suspects be brought to trial – including Ivan Dimitrevich Hrabatyn. Except that Hrabatyn has been dead since 1980. The murder of Hanna Weiss's husband, the murder of at least 600 Jews, has gone unpunished.

26

Jews and Poles

I have myself suffered from the anti-Semitism of the Ukrainians. It was Ukrainian militiamen who first dragged me out of my home and marched me off to a place of execution. But Ukrainian anti-Semitism was embedded in both Soviet and Polish anti-Semitism, which I was aware of from my student days and found confirmed during my escape from the Nazis. When I was liberated at Mauthausen, a Polish camp clerk, the future Deputy Minister of Culture Kazimierz Rusinek, struck me across the face in the way he had been accustomed to striking Jews across the face. That is why to this day I have time and again concerned myself with the anti-Semitism of the Poles – with anti-Semitism throughout the Communist system – with the result that the Polish secret service has in turn thoroughly concerned itself with me. A lot of paper has been printed in order to libel me.

In Poland this was not very successful. But in another country it was to produce astonishing results: in Austria. When, during the debate about Friedrich Peter, Bruno Kreisky libelled me as a Gestapo informer, the Austrian Minister of the Interior, Otto Rösch, was one of his principal supporters. Otto Rösch, acquitted in a neo-Nazi trial in 1948 for lack of evidence (not for proven innocence*), persecuted me with undiminished hate, in spite of what I hope has been an impeccable attitude since. Thus, at the peak of my arguments with Kreisky, he presented to journalists a

* For this reason Rösch was not awarded compensation for his detention.

dossier from his top-secret safe, in order, as he hoped, to open their eyes about me. These were documents from post-war Poland, of which even German translations existed. Some of them were simply intemperate vili-fications, but another part, to which Rösch drew his visitors' particular attention, voiced similar suspicions to those uttered by Bruno Kreisky: it was astonishing that I had survived the war, and one had to ask oneself how this could have been possible without Nazi help. Naive journalists, at any rate, might be impressed by such documents. To those with any background at all it was instantly obvious that this was material manu-factured by the Polish intelligence service at the behest of Mieczyslaw Moczar, the notorious Polish Minister of the Interior, who, as is generally know, has long been my enemy.

I have always regarded it as my duty not only to bring to justice those who had raged against my people during the war, but equally to oppose present-day anti-Semitism wherever I found it. Poland is a country, where, unfortunately – just as in America – one encounters a deep-rooted and evidently ineradicable anti-Semitism. I myself experienced this anti-Semi-tism as a child, as a youngster and as a student, but I continued to experience it even when the Jews of Poland had already been corralled in ghettos and were being exterminated on a massive scale. Even then there were people in Poland who were saying that Hitler had done at least one good thing: he had cleansed them of the Jewish plague. Of course these were only a minority compared to the countless Poles who tried to help their Jewish compatriots and who, after all, saved my wife and me from death. But the hope that Auschwitz and Treblinka might have finally stifled anti-Semitism in Poland is unfortunately vain. From numerous Polish refugees who have come to my office since the war and have made statements about the period of the Third Reich, I found out that the Communist regime was using anti-Semitism in exactly the same way as it had been used for centuries: to divert attention from its own incompetence and its own crimes and to offer the public a scapegoat which it was only too ready to accept – the Jews.

This gives rise to a paradox. On the one hand a relatively large number of Jews rose to high office in the Communist party of Poland, and indeed they played a leading role in all Communist parties at all times – not because they have some inborn inclination towards Bolshevism, but because they represented a more or less oppressed minority everywhere in the world. The oppression they themselves were subjected to made them more responsive to the oppression of others – including the oppression of the working class in early capitalism. They saw Marxism as an ideology and a movement that would destroy all oppression, including their own. It is easy to understand, therefore, that a disproportionate number of Jews were deluded by Communism, and that, with an elite of doctors, lawyers and scientists, they played a leading part in the political life of every country, and hence also in that of the Communist countries. Moreover, membership of the ruling Communist party must have seemed to them a personal protection against persecution, or at least discrimination.

At the same time these Jewish intellectuals in the ranks of the Communist party almost invariably excited hostility among the really proletarian, usually much less well educated and much less articulate, 'Aryan' officials. There has always – whether in Poland, Russia or Austria – been hatred by 'Aryan' workers, and party functionaries, of Jewish intellectuals and ideologues. There developed a certain mental connection between Jewry and Bolshevism, a connection which was vigorously fanned by the Nazis, and not only by them. People who didn't like Jews anyway liked them even less because, allegedly, they were to blame for Bolshevism. And conversely: people who hated Communism moved on to an aversion to Jews because they appeared to be the exponents of Communist ideas.

In Poland the two effects combined. Many Poles are traditional anti-Semites, and all Poles hate Communism. This makes for a knife-edge existence for Jews in Poland to this day. Time and again there are phases when politically motivated anti-Semitism erupts or is deliberately fanned. The latter happened quite systematically in the late sixties: contrary to Soviet hopes and expectations Israel had shown itself superior to its Arab adversaries in the Six-Day War, thereby inflicting a heavy defeat on Soviet policy in that region. Israel thus became a suitable target, better even than the USA, for 'anti-imperialist' propaganda. It is difficult to say whether that propaganda was the ultimate political objective, or whether the struggle against Israel merely served the party functionaries as a pretext for action against their Jewish fellow party functionaries. One thing is certain: a lot of Jewish party functionaries were first compelled, in 1967, to sign anti-Israeli declarations; then, as soon as that was done, they were hauled before party tribunals, charged with contacts with Israel, which were 'proved' by the interception by party censors of letters to relations in Israel; and eventually they were kicked out of their party posts and out of the party – some on the basis of such proceedings and others without any proceedings. These measures were directed not only against Jewish party officials but also against Jewish university professors who were accused of subversion, and against Jewish students. They were the first to flee, and the stream of refugees grew ever greater. One gained the impression that the Communist rulers wanted to drive out what remnants of Jewry still existed in Poland after Hitler, and to make Poland finally 'cleansed of Jews'.

My aversion to Communism, as practised in the eastern bloc, is surpassed only by my aversion to Nazism. I have occasionally caught myself listening to the accounts of escaped Jewish Communist party functionaries with more than a touch of glee. 'That's what happens to people who pray in a temple and discover too late that there is no God in it,' I commented on their stories with an old Jewish saying. But I realized that I had to do something if I wished to remain true to myself. On 17 March 1969 I held a press conference at the Concordia Press Club in Vienna under the heading 'Pre-war Fascists and Nazi collaborators are now allied with anti-Semites from the ranks of the Polish Communist party'. I presented the results of months of research: a list of forty men who were heading the campaign against the Jews of Poland in speeches and publications, and of whom at least half were former Fascists. Poland's leading anti-Semite admittedly was a man who had fought against Hitler: Mieczyslaw Moczar – his real name is Nikolay Demko – had been a Communist before the war and for his opinions had been imprisoned in Poland. During the war he organized Communist partisans in the Lublin area. After the war he became head of security police in Lódź. In 1948 he was removed from the security police as a follower of Gomulka, but he continued to hold important government posts and remained a candidate member of the party Central Committee. Following the events of 1956 – the rising in Hungary and serious disturbances in Poland – he returned to the security apparatus and became Deputy Minister of the Interior. Soon, in 1957, he embarked on cleansing the apparatus under his command of persons of Jewish origin. When Gomulka returned to power he founded the so-called 'partisan group' which fought against the 'intellectuals' and 'liberals' for control of the country. 'Intellectuals' and 'liberals', to Moczar, were synonyms for Jews.

Even before the Six-Day War, in 1967, he began to prepare a major anti-Jewish operation. The war then offered him an ideal opportunity: he had reports passed to the party high-ups to the effect that Jewish party comrades and members of the army had held drinking parties to mark the Israeli victory. This doctored information did not fail to produce the desired effect on Gomulka: a number of Jewish officials were kicked out of the party. This was the start of a kind of persecution of Jews, which reached its climax in March 1968: this time Moczar used student demonstrations as an occasion for action against Jewish students and professors.

In these confrontations Moczar had an articulate comrade-in-arms: Bolesław Piasecki, member of parliament and of the praesidium of the 'National Front', which supported Moczar's national policies. In his party newspaper *Slowo Powszechne* Piasecki supported Moczar's anti-Semitic actions. But Piasecki's anti-Semitism was entirely his own. Prior to the war he was one of the founders and leaders of the ONR (Obóz Narodowo Radykalny or 'National Radical Camp') and of the radically right-wing

storm troop like-group 'Falanga'. In several Polish towns he organized storm-trooper squads which attacked Jews, especially Jewish secondary
school students, to prevent them from studying. Perhaps even more dangerous were his crudely anti-Semitic speeches and his articles in various
papers, whose tone was entirely up to *Stürmer* standards. He made no
secret of his admiration for Hitler and Nazi Germany – he introduced the
Hitler salute in the ONR. After the German invasion he tried to make
contact with the Germans in order to grab for himself a leading role in the
Fascist Poland which he hoped the Germans would set up. But they, of
course, had other plans: the Polish nation was to be kept at primary school
level and to serve the German nation as slave labour. It took Piasecki some
time to realize this, but even then it did not deflect him from his anti-Jewish
line. He founded a military organization called Narodowa Organizacja
Wojskowa which fought for a Polish nation free from foreign influences,
which would have as little as possible to do with Jews.

When the Red Army arrived in 1945 Piasecki was arrested by the
Russians and feared being sentenced to death. But he was offered a last
chance: he was to help win over Polish nationalist circles to Communism.
Piasecki was released but remained under surveillance by the NKVD, on
whose instructions he subsequently founded a periodical called *Dziś i Jutro*
('Today and Tomorrow'). Its aim: anyone still a nationalist today was to
be a Communist tomorrow. Piasecki did in fact succeed in rallying a
considerable number of pre-war Fascists from the ONR and from among
the National Democrats. The group turned into a movement of its own
under the name of 'Pax', which proclaimed itself progressive-Catholic,
thus exploiting for its purposes the Catholicism of numerous non-Com-
munist Poles. Attached to Pax was a large economic organization which
ensured a measure of financial independence for this movement and for
Piasecki. Politically, however, he remained dangling from the NKVD's
strings, a man of the regime, whose long years and wealth of experience
was available whenever the regime needed anti-Semitic propaganda.

Another man who came to the Communist party from the Fascist ONR
was Dr Czesław Pilichowski. He had managed to get admitted into the
Communist party immediately after the war; shortly afterwards, however,
he was expelled because of his Fascist past. Not until the beginning of the
sixties was he rehabilitated: upon the intervention of a Communist activist
he was readmitted to the party and in 1966 was made head of the Central
Commission for the Investigation of Nazi Crimes. This enabled him to act
like an incorrigible Nazi: he questioned the number of Jewish victims of
Nazism, accused them of collaboration with the Germans, and more or less
clearly allowed it to be understood that they were themselves responsible for
their persecution and murder.

At times it seemed to be a deliberate tactic to place anti-Semites in posts where they had to deal primarily with Jewish affairs. Thus Tadeusz Walichnowski, for many years an official in the Polish secret police, was entrusted with the control of the Bureau for Jewish Affairs in the Ministry of the Interior. There he possessed a complete list of all Jews in Poland, which he readily made available for anti-Semitic use. He became famous for his anti-Semitic articles and features in the press and on the radio. His scribblings were seriously recognized as a doctoral thesis by the University of Toruń: he was granted a degree there and was even able, subsequently, to qualify as an assistant professor after the Polish Institute for International Affairs had honoured his anti-Semitic brochures with a prize. Having distinguished himself in the anti-Semitic campaign which followed the Six-Day War, he saw his political career come to an unexpected (temporary) end in 1968: he had interested himself too closely in the intimate affairs of some of Gomulka's close friends, and publicly referred to them. This didn't do him any good at all. (Today, as director of the police academy, he only holds an administrative post.) His anti-Semitic brochures, however, were until recently still on sale, and being bought in Polish bookshops.

The worst thing, of course, was for a former concentration camp prisoner to lend himself to anti-Semitic propaganda. Into this category falls Kazimierz Rusinek, who was interned at the Mauthausen concentration camp during the war and survived there as a camp clerk. After the Six-Day War he joined a group around Moczar, became deputy minister of culture and secretary general of the resistance organization 'Zbowid'. He abused this function on 17 July 1967 in a radio address which, for its infamy, I can compare only to my being suspected of being a Gestapo spy: in Israel, Rusinek declared, over a thousand Nazi criminals from the German Wehrmacht and the SS were employed as advisors to the Israeli army – that was the only reason why the Israelis had been victorious. Two days later I requested Rusinek, in a Radio Free Europe transmission in Polish, to name me a single Nazi active in Israel; I was ready to bring that man to Poland personally. Rusinek did not reply. But I believe that even anti-Semitic Poles didn't need this exchange to realize what a fantastic lie they had been served up by Rusinek.

The careers just outlined are no more than a selection of the cases which I discussed at my press conference. The journalists had at their disposal precise evidence not only about the men named by me but also about the other thirty-five anti-Semitic functionaries in the Polish Communist party. 'I am aware,' I concluded my exposé, 'that the Polish anti-Semites will try to represent these documents as anti-Polish propaganda. After all, we had the same experience with the Nazis in West Germany: they too tried to depict any attack on Nazis as an attack on Germany and all matters German.

In our view, anti-Polish propaganda is being disseminated not by foreign countries or by the Jews, but by the Polish anti-Semites. As a person born in Poland, as one who grew up in Poland, who suffered in concentration camps alongside Poles, I regard it as my duty to demonstrate who the men responsible for this vicious campaign really are. I owe this to all those Poles who opposed Nazism and thereby perished in prisons and concentration camps. Their number is far greater than that of the anti-Semites now fighting against the Jews.'

Later I reworked our documentation into a brochure in English and German, which I prefaced by a letter from Albert Einstein to Leopold Infeld, dated 20 June 1949. In it the greatest Jewish scientist in the world pointed to the parallels between Nazi and Polish anti-Semitism, and warned against the danger arising from the continuity between Fascism and Communist anti-Semitism. Added to the documents was a letter from Ernst Fischer: 'I am well informed through friends about the shameful anti-Semitism in Poland, and I try to help as much as I can. The histories of some influential anti-Semites were not unknown to me either; much, however, of what you have discovered is new to me. That your press conference is passed over in silence in Poland doesn't surprise me; even so, they'll hear about it, and any such collection of documents represents moral support. I shouldn't like to let this occasion pass without assuring you of my deep respect for yourself and your work. We non-Jews have a double responsibility to adopt an inflexible stand against any kind of anti-Semitism.'

*

Relations between Jews and Poles have concerned me as long as I can remember, and they will concern me as long as I am able to think. Although I know that there were numerous Nazi collaborators in Poland and that the anti-Semitic sentiments of some Poles accompanied us all the way to the concentration camps, this does not excite any anti-Polish feelings in me. But it does excite a wish to do something for a better understanding between Poles and Jews. I share this wish with many of my Jewish friends who were born in Poland. One day it led us to phone three Polish friends who had fought in the Polish underground during the war: in 1943, risking their lives, they had got to England as couriers and emissaries in order to report to the Polish government-in-exile on the Jewish tragedy and to inform the world about it. We met with these people, and we agreed that the thousand-year-old history of the Jews in Poland must not end in sentiments of mutual hatred. In that spirit we drafted the following manifesto, signed jointly by three Jews and three Poles.

Manifesto

Forty years ago two flags were hoisted alongside one another on the roof of a building in the hotly contested Warsaw ghetto. One was white and blue, the other white and red. The Jewish fighters had only a few hours left of their lives when they addressed this message to the Polish nation: 'We send you our fraternal greetings from amidst the flames and the blood of the ravaged Warsaw ghetto ... The struggle being waged here is a struggle for your freedom as well as for ours. For the human, social and national honour and dignity of us all ... Long live the brotherhood of arms and the blood of fighting Poland. . . .'

That was the farewell which, tragically and movingly set the final seal on a thousand years, during which Jews and Poles lived together on Polish soil.

Forty years after the Warsaw ghetto Rising, that climax within the greatest tragedy in the history of mankind, we the undersigned see it as our moral duty not to forget the message of Masada. Three of us, during the Second World War, were representatives of the Polish underground army fighting in Poland and of the Polish government-in-exile in London. Across frontiers and front lines we carried eyewitness reports and documentary evidence of the mass extermination of the Jews as well as desperate appeals from the dying, appeals which should have stirred the conscience of an unconcerned world. The other three signatories are Jewish activists in the West, each with many years and a wealth of struggle behind him, each linked in sincere loyalty to the fate of Polish Jewry.

Of the pre-war Jewish community of three million, only a few thousand are left today. The Jewish quarters and the walls which the Nazis erected around them have since been levelled by a common enemy. Yet today a new wall is being erected to divide Poles and Jews, and on both sides of that wall there is resentment and a sense of injustice, which brings hostility and hate.

Hate is a boomerang which comes back on us all, sparing no one, powerful or weak. The harvest of hate sown in Germany's soul was Hitlerism. And the inhuman tyranny of the Soviet Union was the fruit of hate. Hate and deep resentment may arise when a whole nation or a whole community is held collectively responsible for the crimes and the sins of an individual or a minority, when responsibility is indiscriminately attributed to all people of the same nationality, religion or race. Vindictive hate is blind to the good, the beautiful and the noble in another people or in another nation. Such hate only sees what is bad and criminal.

Jews still remember the Polish anti-Semitism which began to manifest itself so strongly about the turn of the century, and they forget at the same time that broad stratum of Polish liberal intellectuals, along with the Polish working-class movement and the leading figures of Polish cultural life, who fought against it. The strongest supporters of the Jews were some of the greatest Polish writers, such as Adam Mickiewicz, Ignacy Krasicki, Bolesław Prus, Eliza Orzeszkowa, Maria Konopnicka, Andrzej Strug and others.

The Polish anti-Semites forget that, while there were few cases of outright brutality or physical violence in the independent Republic of Poland, even a Jew brought up in the Polish language and the Polish cultural tradition could never feel a fully integrated citizen. He was not only aware of the ghetto situation at the universities, he was also treated with derision and mistrust, he was a victim of boycotts and discrimination, although there was no basis for this in Polish law. The familiar epithet of 'Judaeo-Communism' forced every Jew into the role of a potential enemy of the Polish state, an agent of a foreign power. The part played by the Jews in the Kosciusko rebellion of 1794 and the revolts of 1831 and 1863 was forgotten, as also were the Jewish volunteers who, during the First World War, fought for an independent Poland in the Polish armies and in other military formations. The British historian Norman Davies, a great friend of the Poles, recently reminded the world of those Jews who in 1920–21 volunteered for the struggle against the Bolsheviks in the Polish–Russian war, but who were thrown out of the army and interned in camps. But does anyone remember that the famous article in the St Petersburg manifesto of 27 March 1917, in which the Council of Workers' and Soldiers' Delegates demanded that Poland be granted the right to absolute independence, was drafted not by a Russian but by a Polish Jew, Henryk Ehrlich, the leader of Bund, the Jewish socialist party? Communist propagandists invariably emphasize that article, but they fail to mention this fact, just as they do Ehrlich's execution on Stalin's orders during the Second World War.

The Jews for their part hold the entire Polish nation responsible for the deeds of the 'Szmalcownik' criminals, who existed in all the occupied countries and handed the Jews over to their Nazi murderers. Hate has made the Jews forget that the majority of those who survived the Holocaust outside the extermination camps owe their lives to the heroism of Poles, who risked their own lives and those of their families in order to save them, and that the incomplete list of Poles executed for sheltering Jews numbers 521 families. They forget that there are more Poles than any other nationality entered in the rolls of honour at Yad Vashem in Israel, and that a number of fighters in the Polish underground army were killed or wounded as they tried to help the fighters of the Warsaw ghetto. Hatred nowadays allows many Jewish writers and journalists to forget or underrate the work of the Council for the Help for the Jews, set up by the highest commanders in the Polish underground army. Forgotten or underrated also are the efforts of the Polish authorities in occupied Poland as well as in exile in London, who did everything in their power to draw the attention of the Western governments, and of world opinion generally, to the desperate cries for help from dying Jews.

The Poles feel that they are gravely wronged by being held responsible for the mass murder whose victims they, too, were. And the Jews feel equally offended if they are blamed for crimes committed by the Polish Communist security police during the Stalin era, when a number of senior positions within the terror machine were held by Jews. On the other hand, there is no recognition for the Poles of Jewish extraction who since 1956 have stood in the forefront of the liberation movement and are facing the threat of reprisals with courage and self-sacrifice.

The time has come to lay the ghost of mutual antagonism. It is wounding to Poles as much as to Jews, and it is especially painful to those Jews who are Polish patriots and simultaneously wish to remain loyal to their Jewish heritage and their religion. Mutual recrimination serves no useful purpose. Men of good will, both Poles and Jews, are attempting to set up a genuine dialogue and to build mutual understanding. Let us use this dialogue to discover what Poles and Jews have in common.

First of all, it is a common determination that there must never again be an attempt to totally annihilate a people. Unfortunately Poles and Jews still live under this threat, which hovers over them fatefully. Poland's geographical position makes her particularly vulnerable to the constant Soviet threat. And Israel is surrounded by a sea of hostile Arab countries which are only waiting for their opportunity to destroy the young state, a state reborn as though by a miracle after two thousand years. Only the Poles, themselves eyewitnesses of the Holocaust and themselves victims of Nazi terror during the war, can fully understand that sense of danger which fills the Jewish survivors who have returned to their promised land. A considerable proportion of the Israeli population is of Polish origin. There is a Polish language newspaper. The Polish monthly *Kultura*, published in France, and other Polish publications are read throughout Israel. Polish musical and theatrical events are invariably welcomed by the older generation of Jews in Israel, by people who still have memories of the land of their youth, of 'the little town of Belz' made immortal in Jewish songs.

Any gesture and any sign of solidarity by Poles at home or abroad with the state of Israel would do more to erase Polish–Jewish misunderstandings than volumes of apologetic and self-incriminating prose.

Poles and Jews are brothers in misfortune in the Soviet Union, where they represent two of the most fiercely persecuted minorities; both are victims of inhuman discrimination and injustice. If the Jewish diaspora, which has great influence on democrats in the West, were to extend its struggle for the right of Soviet Jews to emigrate to members of other nationalities and religions, including Poles – to all those who wish to return to their homelands – such efforts would be welcomed by Poles everywhere.

In voicing these preliminary ideas on a rapprochement between Jews and Poles we are aware of the risk of becoming a target for extremist opponents in both camps. But we shall not allow ourselves to be deflected from our endeavour, because we are firmly resolved to serve the idea of brotherhood, regardless of origin, nationality or religion, as the foundation upon which the highest values of our civilization rest. We are convinced that in this way we are best serving the cause of Poles and of Jews.

Signed by: Michael Borwicz, Joseph Lichten, Simon Wiesenthal, Jan Karski, Jerzy Lerski, Jan Nowak.

The manifesto was published in a number of Jewish newspapers. It also found its way into Polish papers – those in exile. Not all those whom we had hoped to reach have received it: there was criticism of our intention and of its execution. Nevertheless we believe we have achieved a breakthrough. More and more Polish intellectuals are getting in touch with us, wishing to add their signatures, and many are signing it in spirit.

Meanwhile official relations between Poland and Israel have begun to improve. As I was writing this chapter I received, to my great surprise, a telephone call from Warsaw: the head of the Polish Central Commission for the Investigation of Nazi Crimes, Professor Kakol, invited me to attend the anniversary of the Warsaw ghetto Rising as a guest of the Polish government. Indeed now I hold the invitation in my hands, but I believe that it is too early to accept it: I should like to await further developments in Poland.

27

Jews and Gypsies

Not only have some Poles forgotten that Poles were incarcerated in the Nazi extermination camps alongside Jews, but some Jews have forgotten that they are the survivors of a disaster that also befell another people to a scarcely lesser extent, a people to this day they view with prejudice – the gypsies. The whole world knows of the murder of six million Jews, the whole world speaks about the tragedy of the Jewish people – but hardly anybody knows that an estimated half a million gypsies likewise perished. The Nazis would just as soon have gassed six million gypsies, had there been that many. In their misfortune gypsies were on virtually the same footing as Jews.

The Nuremberg Laws, known as the 'laws for the protection of German blood', referred equally to gypsies and Jews. Sexual intercourse with a gypsy, too, was 'racial defilement', and mixed marriages between gypsies and non-gypsies were equally prohibited. After 1936, on the model of the offices for registration of Jews, there was also one for the registration of gypsies. Its records served Himmler in 1938 as the basis of his so-called 'gypsy decree', in which he ruled that all gypsies living on German Reich territory (hence also in Austria) were to be deported to the east. For the sole purpose of extermination.

To each Jewish transport going east, Eichmann's deputy, Hauptsturmführer Rolf Günther, in agreement with Alois Brunner, attached one goods truck filled with gypsies. There was an agreement between the chief of the Reich crime police, Nebe, and Eichmann to the effect that the gypsy problem was to be solved in unison with the Jewish problem by a Hauptsturmführer called Braune. The transports initially terminated in the ghettos (Warsaw, Lublin and Kielce); later there was a special gypsy camp at Auschwitz. There Mengele performed the same ghoulish experiments on gypsy children, especially on twins, as he practised on Jewish children.

Ella Lingens, who was at the women's camp of Auschwitz-Birkenau and lived close to the gypsy camp, remembers how the gypsies were sent to the gas chambers, block by block, just like the Jews. That is about all we know of the fate of the gypsies. We hardly know how they were rounded up; we hardly know what happened to their possessions; we hardly have any records of individual tragedies.

In West Germany, the Nazi records relating to the 'racial assessment' of the gypsies, which provided the basis for their deportation to the extermination camps, were after the war being administered at the University of Tübingen by the same Professor Sophie Ehrhardt who in 1942 had helped to compile them. (Following repeated suggestions by me the files were transferred to the federal archives in Koblenz in 1981.)

No attempt was ever made after the war to make a systematic record of statements by gypsy survivors. What little literature exists on the subject is incomplete, and rarely comes from gypsies but usually from Jewish fellow prisoners or historians. As for myself, it was not until the early 1960s that I began to interest myself more closely in the tragedy of the gypsies. I had been detained alongside gypsies in various camps and therefore knew about their fate, but naturally the fate of my own people was initially of greater concern to me. Only later did I begin deliberately to collect Third Reich documents relating to gypsies. Thus, on one occasion, I got hold of a whole bundle of papers dating back to 1938, dealing with questions of identification and registration of gypsies. In 1965, when a limitation on prosecutions was imminent for the first time, I sent everything I possessed to the Central Office for the investigation of Nazi crimes in Ludwigsburg, and that same year I was notified that the relevant proceedings were being prepared in Berlin against members of the Reich Security Directorate. In my book *The Murderers Among Us* I tried to outline the gypsies' fate in a special chapter, and my documents were also published in a number of important papers, such as the *New York Times*. In Holland a special research project was set up under my friend Professor Ben Sijes.

The tragedy of the gypsies, however, has never really sunk into public awareness. This was probably largely due to the fact that these dark-skinned people, who came to Europe from the depths of India, continued to be the object of old prejudices and discrimination even after the war. Administrative and police authorities, especially in West Germany,

Hermine Braunsteiner, known as 'the mare', greeted the prisoners, whip in hand, as they arrived at Majdanek.

The *New York Times* article on the Braunsteiner case.

Former Nazi Camp Guard Is Now a Housewife in Queens

By JOSEPH LELYVELD

A private investigator of Nazi war crimes has identified a Queens housewife as a guard in the death camp at Majdanek, Poland, in World War II.

The investigator was Simon Wiesenthal, who had a key role in tracing Adolf Eichmann in 1960.

The woman served a prison sentence for her activities at another concentration camp. But the Immigration and Naturalization Service here said that when she entered the United States, she denied she had ever been convicted of a crime.

The woman, the former Hermine Braunsteiner, now is an American citizen. She lives in Maspeth, Queens, with her husband, Russell Ryan.

The identification was made by Mr. Wiesenthal in letters sent from Vienna to Israeli authorities in Tel Aviv. Mrs. Ryan, at her home, readily acknowledged that she was Hermine Braunsteiner of Maidanek. She declared, however, that she had never been more than a guard and had no authority whatever.

Mrs. Ryan was doing some painting in the home she and her husband, a construction worker, recently acquired at 52-11 72d Street when she was interviewed about the report of her wartime activities.

A large-boned woman with a stern mouth and blond hair turning gray, she was wearing pink and white striped shorts with a matching sleeveless blouse.

"All I did is what guards do in camps now," she said in heavily accented English.

"On the radio all they talk is peace and freedom," she said. "All right. Then 15 or 16 years later why do they bother people?

"I was punished enough. I was in prison three years. Three years, can you imagine? And now they want something again from me?"

According to Mr. Wiesenthal, who is director of a documentation center in Vienna called the Federation of Jewish Victims of the Nazi Regime, legal proceedings are still pending against Hermine Braunsteiner in the provincial court at Graz, Austria.

Mr. Wiesenthal said she was

3 German Companies To Pay Former 'Slaves'

FRANKFURT, Germany, July 13 (AP)—Three major German concerns have agreed to compensate Jews who worked in their plants as slaves in Hitler's Germany, an organization of former concentration camp inmates announced here today.

The International Committee of the Camps said that the Krupp steel company, the Siemens-Schuckert electric company and the Aeg electric company had agreed to the compensation. Years ago the I.G. Farben chemical concern agreed to make such payments.

The amounts to be paid were not announced.

sentenced there in 1953 to three years' imprisonment as a minor offender as an overseer of the Ravensbruck concentration camp.

"Of her activity in Maidanek

only little was known," his letter said. "Except for the letter of a Polish woman, which did not figure in the Graz proceedings, nothing was known. The matter of Maidanek was not mentioned."

Mr. Wiesenthal explained that he could not say what offenses had been proved against Hermine Braunsteiner on the basis of her activities at Ravensbruck.

Released by British

Mrs. Ryan said she had spent a year at Maidanek, eight months of it in the camp infirmary with a serious illness. After the war, she said, she was held for eight months by the British and then released.

It is estimated that 1.5 million people were killed at the Maidanek camp, which was on the outskirts of Lublin in eastern Poland. About half of them were said to have been Jews.

"My wife, sir, wouldn't hurt a fly," Mr. Ryan said in a telephone conversation. "There's no more decent person on this earth. She told me this was a duty she had to perform. It was a conscriptive service.

"She was not in charge of

anything. Absolutely not, as God is my judge and your judge."

Mr. Ryan said he had never known until now that his wife had served a prison sentence or that she had been a guard in a concentration camp.

"These people are just swinging axes at random," he declared. "Didn't they ever hear the expression, 'Let the dead rest'?"

Mrs. Ryan broke into tears when she was told of the Wiesenthal letter. "This is the end," she said, crossing her small living room. "This is the end of everything for me."

Mrs. Ryan became a citizen in 1963. She entered the country in 1958. An official of the Immigration and Naturalization Service said that the fact that she had falsely sworn that she had never been convicted of a crime might be ground for a review of her citizenship. But he indicated that such reviews rarely result in the withdrawal of citizenship.

Pour la révision de la convention franco-allemande sur l'impunité de criminels de guerre condamnés en France

Par SIMON WIESENTHAL

grande
partie
npopu-
cours,
s d'un
so ré-
loublo.
n. Les
let les
or des

rsnociós
ot dont
òre fois
:oalition
décom-
8.4 %
insi dir

lectoral
. paroit
allecte
do la
lliàmo.
rlin, de-
ublique
port de
premier
Kaisen,
Illet ac-
o recui
ix libé-
mesure.

s dou
dden et
dult le
néór ua
opulaire
montrer
lu disai-
ant de
a même
ient dú
iouvenu
ns poli-
t résolu
sous le
c'est lo
lon de
la plu-
to.

— Sué-
'er, ap-
-amlrni
lui ans,
it de la
guerre
cérémo-
inistère
.F.P.)

Les gouvernements français et allemand s'efforcent actuellement de remédier à une longue négligence qui a permis à des criminels de guerre allemands, condamnés en France par contumace, de vivre librement dans leur pays, sans avoir jamais été incarcérés.

Telle est, en effet, l'une des conséquences d'un « accord d'échange » signé par la République fédérale, peu après sa fondation, avec les trois Occidentaux. Un des points de cet accord précisait que les personnes qui auraient été jugées une première fois par un tribunal allié (que ce fût le tribunal militaire international de Nuremberg ou toute autre cour militaire nationale), ne pourraient être jugées à nouveau par un tribunal allemand. De nombreux criminels de guerre, condamnés notamment par des tribunaux français à la peine de mort ou à la détention à perpétuité, ont bénéficié de cette clause.

Organisateurs des déportations

C'est le cas de Kurt Lischka, cinquante-sept ans, ex-SS-Obersturmbannführer, qui ...
... ...
... ...
... rpétuité le 18 septembre ... par le tribunal militaire ...

Même condamnation le même jour pour Herbert Hagen. Actuellement âgé de cinquante-quatre ans, il collabora jusqu'en 1940 avec Adolf Eichmann dans le service antijuif du S.D. (le service de renseignements des SS). Devenu SS-Sturmbannführer, il fut le bras droit d'Oberg, le « bourreau de Paris », chef suprême des SS pour la France. Avec Lischka, il organisa la déportation des juifs de la zone Sud. Il eut de vives altercations avec les Italiens, à qui il reprochait leur « manque de coopération ». Le 16 décembre 1942, il rédigeait cette note dont on connaît désormais la sinistre signification : « Au titre de Nacht und Nebel (Nuit et brouillard), prévoir l'arrestation d'intellectuels. »

Ce n'est que le 7 mars 1956 que le tribunal militaire de Paris condamnait à mort pour contumace l'ex-SS-Oberscharführer Ernest Henrichsohn : il avait été particulièrement difficile de réunir les preuves de ses nombreux assassinats. Âgé aujourd'hui de soixante-quatre ans, il participa à la déportation des juifs des zones Sud et Nord-Ouest, et fut l'un des responsables de la Gestapo de l'avenue Foch.

Je citerai aussi Heinz Röthke, mort au mois de mars 1966, à l'âge de cinquante-cinq ans, sans avoir jamais été inquiété. De 1942 à 1944, il avait été chargé des questions juives auprès du chef de la police de sécurité. Le 22 mars 1949, il avait bénéficié d'un acquittement devant le tribunal militaire, mais une enquête ultérieure apporta assez d'éléments pour retenir contre lui des chefs d'accusation plus graves.

En 1943, il avait remplacé Dannecker à la tête de la Gestapo en France au service antijuif 1 VJ, devenu le service 1 VB. De son état-major de 140, boulevard Haussmann, il dirigea le service central de la Gestapo de 1943 à la libération, et fut l'un des principaux organisateurs de la déportation des juifs dans la France entière.

Un paradoxe et une injustice

La justice allemande, qui poursuit l'examen d'affaires de crimes nazis en Europe, se penche à présent sur les problèmes posés par ces crimes en France.

La justice française exis ...
... ...
... ... Allemagne ... Autriche, et vivaient le plus souvent sous de faux noms.

Les enquêtes et les découvertes se multipliant, il s'avéra que de nombreux nazis ayant commis des crimes de moindre importance furent alors condamnés plus lourdement que beaucoup de ceux qui avaient commis les forfaits les plus abominables. Au contraire, des hommes qui avaient d'abord été sévèrement punis par des tribunaux alliés, mais dont les peines furent, par la suite, diminuées ou même supprimées, se trouvèrent favorisés.

Pour mettre fin à cette injustice flagrante, le procureur fédéral auprès de la Cour suprême fédérale proposa une procédure qui fut rejetée. A l'heure actuelle, la justice allemande s'emploie surtout à mettre au point avec la France une convention d'après laquelle cet « accord d'échange » pourrait être suspendu en ce qui concerne Lischka, Hagen et Heinrichsohn. Car le crime majeur de la « solution finale du problème juif » en France demeurera sans expiation tant que ces hommes ne seront pas traduits devant un tribunal.

Copyright 1967 by Opera Mundi.

● Directeur du Centre de documentation des victimes juives du nazisme, M. Wiesenthal tiendra une conférence de presse mardi, à 17 h., à « Opera Mundi », 100, avenue de l'Opéra, à l'occasion de la sortie de son livre Les assassins sont parmi nous (Stock).

On 3 October 1967, *Le Monde* printed an article by me in which I attacked the non-punishment of Nazi crimes committed on French territory.

Archiv: Dokumentationszentrum des Bundes Jüdischer Verfolgter des Naziregimes, 1010 Wien, Salztorgasse 6/IV/5

Dieser Mörder ist nicht gefunden worden! Er und tausende Nazi-Verbrecher sind noch immer auf freiem Fuß, viele unter falschem Namen. Sie warten auf den 31. Dezember 1979, an dem ihre Verbrechen verjährt sein werden.

Verbrechen gegen die Menschlichkeit dürfen nicht verjähren! Das ist eine moralische Verpflichtung und eine Mahnung für künftige Generationen.

Name:

Adresse:

Porto
S 3,—

Herrn

Bundeskanzler

Helmut Schmidt

Bonn

Bundesrepublik Deutschland

We had this photograph printed on postcards which were sent to Chancellor Helmut Schmidt in 1979, demanding that the statute of limitations on Nazi crimes be revoked.

'Jud is Jud ob mit, oder ohne Beine': 'A Jew is a Jew, with or without legs'. This is the note written by General Christiansen at the top of a letter from a Dutch Army veteran who had lost both his legs in combat.

Reinhard Heydrich, head of Interpol from 1938 to May 1942, when he was assassinated by Czech resistance fighters in Prague. In his honour the campaign to exterminate the Jews of Eastern Poland was given the name Operation Reinhard.

In 1942 Ernst Kaltenbrunner succeeded Reinhard Heydrich as head of Interpol. The organization collaborated closely with the Gestapo.

SS Brigadeführer Odilo Globocnik was in charge of Operation Reinhard. He carried out his task with remarkable thoroughness.

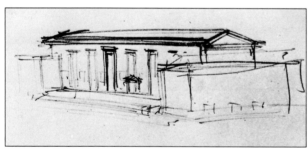

'Wiesenthal, as seen by Kreisky': This cartoon, which appeared in the magazine *profil*, illustrates the Austrian chancellor Kreisky's campaign to discredit me by portraying me as a Nazi collaborator.

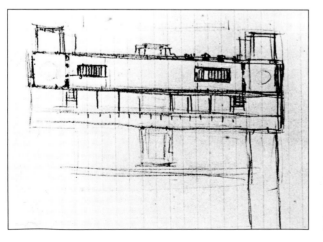

These sketches, from the hand of Hitler himself, were given to me by Albert Speer. They show the plans for a museum which would have been built in Linz, to house the works of art pillaged from all of occupied Europe. The first dates from 1938. The second, more ambitious, is from January 1943, even as German soldiers were fighting a desperate battle at the gates of Stalingrad.

Alois Brunner, the inventor of 'Jewish collaboration', was charged with repairing the extermination machine wherever it was getting rusty. He exercised his talents in Vienna, Thessalonika, Paris, Nice and finally Slovakia. After the war he found sanctuary in Egypt (the photograph, *right*, is from his false passport) and then in Syria, where he still lives.

On 30 October 1988, in Los Angeles, President and Mrs Reagan took part in a ceremony to mark my eightieth birthday, arranged by the Center which bears my name. The president made me blush when in his speech he set me among the true heroes of the twentieth century.

Paris, le 7 octobre 1988

Cher Simon Wiesenthal,

Vous êtes, chacun le sait, l'homme d'un combat.

Votre engagement a sa source en un lieu et un temps qui marqueront à jamais la conscience que l'humanité a d'elle-même.

On sait, après les camps, quel monstrueux visage peut prendre la croyance absurde en la supériorité de certains hommes sur les autres.

Des millions sont morts sans pouvoir témoigner. Ceux qui sont revenus portent en eux des blessures qu'ils savent inguérissables.

A tous nous devons de ne pas oublier afin que ce qui fut n'advienne pas à nouveau.

En ce jour anniversaire, je vous adresse, cher Simon Wiesenthal, en même temps que mes voeux personnels, le salut d'un pays décidé à rester vigilant.

A vous

François Mitterrand

François MITTERRAND

On my eightieth birthday I received messages and good wishes from many people, among them Chancellor Kohl, ex-President Carter and Henry Kissinger. This letter from the French president François Mitterrand touched me particularly.

continued to view them as 'chicken thieves', so that it seemed quite natural for Hitler to have them locked up. They were never, as the Jews were, regarded as racially persecuted, but as a particular kind of 'asocial element' who, in the Third Reich, had simply been accommodated in concentration camps instead of workhouses.

Because of this attitude the gypsies had initially been refused any kind of restitution. It took years before at least some of them were put on an equal footing with other victims. Many of them did not live to see this. The main problem was that the gypsies were mostly unaware that they had any claims to compensation. There was no organization to draw their attention to their entitlements or to assist them in the fight against bureaucratic chicanery. Only much later was an Association of Sinti and Romany (the two biggest gypsy tribes affected) set up, which eventually also held world congresses – but mostly they rated no more than a few newspaper articles.

In 1981 the German chapter of the Society for Threatened Peoples helped with the organization of the third World Congress of Sinti and Roma in Göttingen; this was attended by 300 delegates from thirty countries. Mrs Miriam Novitch of the Kibbutz of Ghetto Fighters in Israel presented a twenty-five-page documentary report on the tragedy of the gypsies, and I gave a paper on the juridical consequences of this genocide. To that end I had collected information on all criminal proceedings in Austria and Germany connected with the persecution of the gypsies, and tried to discover what had emerged from these trials. It was unbelievably little. In many criminal cases the murder of Sinti and Romany was treated, as it were, in a package together with the murder of the Jews. In most of the more specific proceedings there were too few witnesses, so many cases were dropped. For decades there had been no organization to collect or record the evidence of such witnesses.

Unfortunately, however, we Jews, including Jewish survivors of the Holocaust, have by no means shown the gypsies the understanding or sympathy to which, as brothers in misfortune, they are entitled. It was typical not only that no one bothered about 'compensation' for gypsies, but that they were disadvantaged even where legal provisions existed for making some payments to them. In Austria, for instance, there was a large fund which drew its resources from so-called 'ownerless assets'. These were assets of which no one admitted ownership after the war but which were obviously stolen property and which should, in consequence, benefit the victims. Ella Lingens told me how she had in vain fought to have the gypsies receive something from that source. Most of the officials of the Jewish community, however, took the view that ultimately only Jewish property had been confiscated – the gypsies hadn't owned anything anyway.

This may almost be true – if one looks only at absolute values. But to a gypsy the horse-drawn cart he had lost was surely worth just as much, and was just as vital to his livelihood, as his lost business was to a Jewish merchant. But gypsies remained second-class citizens.

In speeches made at concentration camps or on anniversaries no mention at all was made of the gypsies for decades; more recently a few sentences have been devoted to them. When the Central Council of Jews in Germany held a memorial ceremony in 1985 to mark the liberation of the Bergen-Belsen camp, the Central Council of Sinti and Romany asked to be given the opportunity to speak as well, seeing that their people had lost their lives in that camp too. This was rejected by the Central Council of Jews. I thereupon telephoned the then President of the Central Council Werner Nachmann (who in the meantime has got himself into a dubious light for misappropriation of restitution funds), requesting him to grant the Sinti and Romany representative at least a few minutes. That too was refused. As I knew that Federal Chancellor Kohl would make a speech at the ceremony, I telephoned him and asked him to make at least some mention in his address of the tragedy of the gypsies. Helmut Kohl did this readily, and in a moving way.

I have thus been able, here and there, to help the Sinti and Romany at least on the sidelines. On one occasion one of their convoys was held up at the Dutch frontier, and I succeeded, by a telegram to Queen Beatrix, in having it permitted to move on. On another occasion I was able, as an expert witness in a trial, to make a West German court realize the tragedy of the gypsies. At the Simon Wiesenthal Center for Holocaust Studies in Los Angeles we have deliberately staged a number of events to commemorate the tragedy of the gypsies as well as that of the Armenians, in order thereby to demonstrate our close links with all victims of genocide.

Far more important for the Sinti and Romany, however, would have been political representation. In 1979, a 'US Holocaust Memorial Council' was established, whose task it is to ensure, by means of a variety of events, that the tragedy of the victims of the Nazi regime is not forgotten. On this Council sat voting representatives not only of the Jews but also of Poles, Russians and Ukrainians – but not gypsies. Efforts in that connection by the International Association of the Romany were in vain. To help them I wrote a lengthy letter to Elie Wiesel, the president of the Council. A few months later I received an answer, from his secretary, that the appointment of members depended on President Reagan. The International Association of Romany and the Society for Threatened Peoples thereupon wrote long letters to President Reagan – which ended up with Elie Wiesel. In the end I turned to Wiesel again, this time with the suggestion that one of the more than thirty Jewish members of the Memorial Council might be replaced by a gypsy. To this letter I received no answer at all. When I subsequently published this 'correspondence' in our annual report – because I felt the attitude of the Holocaust Memorial Council to be unjust – I received a number of copies of other letters in which all kinds of people had approached Wiesel with the request that he should support the claim of the gypsies. But the only thing the Holocaust Memorial Council ever did for the gypsies was a kind of memorial hour in September 1986. Only after Elie Wiesel had given up his presidency were we informed that the newly formed board had invited a gypsy representative, Professor Hancock (who also represents the Roma in the United Nations) on to the Council.

In 1986, when the Nobel Peace Prize was awarded to Elie Wiesel, the gypsy organizations decided to go to Oslo and protest. This got me into an exceedingly unpleasant situation. It was well known that I had been a friend for many years of the Sinti and Romany leaders. No doubt Elie Wiesel would hold me responsible for such a demonstration: he would accuse me of injured vanity because he and not I (who was likewise a candidate) had received the Nobel Prize. I therefore had a prolonged telephone conversation with Romany Rose, the president of the gypsy organization in Germany, in order to prevent the demonstration. I succeeded, though not without some gnashing of teeth.

I believe nevertheless that the disappointment of many Sinti and Romany about the behaviour of those who suffered alongside them in the concentration camps is understandable and justified – especially their disappointment with the Jews. And yet we share so many experiences: the Sinti and Romany are like us dispersed among other nations, they are like us surrounded by a thousand deep-rooted prejudices and, like us, are not yet at the end of their sufferings. Auschwitz is branded into their history as it is into ours.

Modern interpretations of the concept of 'nation' list 'common destiny' as one of the most essential criteria. In that regard I feel bound to every gypsy who has gone through the horrors of Auschwitz.

28

Jews and Palestinians

'Isn't it tragic,' I was asked by a young German who no doubt regarded himself as a great moralist, 'that the creation of Israel, that attempt to redress the injustice done to the Jews, has only given rise to fresh injustice. Israel has a national home – but the expelled Palestinians are the new Jews.'

No, it is not tragic. The creation of Israel was the only possible and the only correct reaction to Auschwitz. There had to be a country in the world where the Jews were the landlords instead of tolerated guests, a place of refuge in the truest meaning of the word, even for Jews who live in other countries. And that country could only be located in Palestine because only there could the Jews pick up the threads of their own past: they had carried Israel with them in their prayers for two thousand years.

Israel's mere existence has revalued every Jew in the world. The image of the state of Israel has refuted, once and for all, the image our enemies have drawn of us over the centuries. This state has shown that the Jewish people, if they are not persecuted or enslaved, if they are not barred from certain occupations or forced into others, if they are able to develop freely in line with the laws of nature, turn into a self-assured and proud nation, just like any other nation. It has proved that we Jews are not born only to be victims or, at best, to escape persecution through special abilities or talents. All this means that we can also act. Anyone expecting that Jews could never commit a war crime, never persecute someone unjustly, or perhaps even never kill, merely shows that he still does not regard us as the equals of other nations – equals in good and in evil. Anyone siding with us only as long as we play the part of victim has, in a different way, remained the same old anti-Semite.

Unfortunately this new form of anti-Semitism has been spreading in West Germany and Austria in recent years. It has developed a vocabulary, whose special infamy resides in the fact that it is borrowed from anti-Fascism. It began by making it acceptable, and later even fashionable, to call Israel 'Fascist', or at least 'near Fascist', where there should be astonishment at the fact that a country which has been in a state of war for decades is still capable of so much freedom and democracy. But for Germans to call Jews 'Fascist' is a double advantage: for one thing it helps to make Nazi Fascism seem more harmless (since evidently all nations, including the Jews, incline towards Fascism), and on the other it helps to execrate the Jews (after all, how evil a nation must be to apply Fascist practices when it has experienced them itself).

This was even more blatantly in evidence during the campaign in Lebanon. Feelings ran high, not so much because the Israelis had invaded Lebanon at all, but because they had shelled Palestinian positions amidst residential areas, so that numerous civilians were killed. Not only *Nationalzeitung* but also some entirely reputable newspapers raised the question of whether one could remain silent in the face of these 'Israeli war crimes'. Yet even the briefest inquiry from any expert on military law would have told them that the legal situation was exactly the reverse: a war crime is committed by whoever installs a military position in the middle of a civilian residential area, so that in the event of hostilities the civilian population must inevitably suffer. But once again the question of whether Israel had committed war crimes was, to Germans and Austrians, not a matter of rational reflection (like, for instance, the war crimes of British, Dutch or French troops) but a question of their own redemption. If the Jews, too, were committing war crimes then the German war crimes wouldn't have been quite so bad – and how villainous of the Jews to indulge in war crimes when they themselves had suffered them in the past. Naturally, the Israeli 'war crimes' were immediately associated with something which they resembled even less – the mass murder in the concentration camps. (That is why, in this context, I never use the term 'war crimes' but Nazi crimes: the murder of the Jews was no war crime but a crime which merely happened to be committed during the war.)

Only this can explain the delighted enthusiasm with which the German and Austrian press took up the massacres of Sabra and Shatila. Here, finally, the equation was complete: the Germans committed mass murder of helpless people – the Jews do exactly the same when they get a chance. I believe that a survey would show that no more than 10 per cent of the public knows that at Sabra and Shatila it was not Israelis who did the murdering, but Christian Lebanese. And even the few who do know it believe that the Israeli army deliberately opened the camp gates to the murderers.

The most monstrous manifestation of this attitude can be observed most recently: reporting the disturbances in the occupied territories, in the course of which something over 200 Palestinians have been shot, the popular press referred to an Israeli 'final solution' of the Palestinian problem. But even highly reputable papers did not shrink from speculating whether the Jewish state was not perhaps paying back the Palestinians for what the Nazis had done to the Jews. Rudolf Augstein most clearly articulated the secret hopes of the Germans in Der Spiegel: 'It won't do for Ariel Sharon, with his share of responsibility for the butchery in the Sabra and Shatila camps, to settle down like a king in the captured Arab Old City of Jerusalem, while we in West Germany are still hunting down the last SS henchman who, at the time, was just eighteen.' That is just what they would like. The issue, at long last, was to be no longer the crimes of the SS henchmen, but the more important crimes of the Jews.

Augstein, needless to say, vigorously rejected the charge that this argument was the foundation of his piece – the moment one operates on rational ground an intellectual of his calibre instantly reveals his superior knowledge of history. But the inner conflict with Nazi guilt operates in the emotional and subsconscious sphere: Germans and Austrians want the Palestinians to be the 'new Jews', so that they can, at long last, forget the dead Jews.

What is particularly conspicuous in Germany is occurring also in the press of other countries, albeit in a much milder, attenuated form – but it is happening. Typically it is most noticeable in the USA, where an increasingly critical attitude towards Israel is fed from two totally different sources: first, from an anti-Semitism that is quite widespread in certain parts of the country, and secondly, from the guilty conscience of many Jews who have still not come to terms with the fact that they neither suffered in the concentration camps nor helped to establish the state of Israel. This guilty conscience, which for a long time induced in them an excessively pro-Israeli stance, now threatens to flip over into exaggerated criticism. Added to this is the naivety and self-righteousness of many Americans, and their wish to be loved by everyone, including the Arabs. There is certainly a change of mood taking place in America, making it increasingly difficult for any government to adopt an unambiguously pro-Israeli attitude.

This is a matter the Israeli government should bear in mind; it should make some kind of public relations effort. The continually victorious state of Israel cannot forever rely on the sympathy shown to 'victims'. On my lecture tours in the USA I am, with increasing frequency, being questioned on the Palestine problem, and discussion is becoming ever more difficult because opposing views are becoming increasingly radical. It is not always possible, as it was in a discussion at the University of Texas at Austin, to defuse the explosive climate from the start.

'Mr Wiesenthal,' I was asked by a young man sitting in a row of Arabs, 'you have told us a lot about the crimes of the Germans. Can you tell us when Israel will return the land it has stolen from the Arabs?'

'You want a date from me?' I asked, to gain a little time for reflection.

'Yes, a precise date,' came the answer from about twenty voices in unison.

'Very well,' I said, 'I'll try.' In the front row of the auditorium sat several representatives of the Jewish organizations which had invited me, staring at me with a mixture of despair and horror. They clearly thought I had gone out of my mind. I tried to reassure them by a slight nod before giving my answer as calmly and slowly as possible: 'The precise date will be one day after the Americans have returned Texas to Mexico.'

Some day it will have to be realized that it is impossible to establish a state without some people, who have been living in the region, finding their rights curtailed. (Because where no people have lived before it is presumably impossible for people to live.) One has to be content if these infringements are kept within bounds and if relatively few people are affected by them. That was the case when Israel was founded, whatever criticism one may have of the British. After all, there had been a Jewish population settled there for a long time, and the Palestinian population was comparatively sparse and had relatively numerous options in giving way. There could have been living space for all.

It was not the Jews who expelled the Arabs; it was the Arab High Committee that called on the Arabs of Palestine to leave the country in order later to return with the victorious Arab armies. (In Haifa and many other localities the Jews begged their Arab neighbours to remain – but they had scant success.) Thus – not because the Jews did not wish to coexist with Arabs – was the refugee problem born. Only as a result of the war which followed, only due to the fact that the Arabs wanted to wipe out the newly created state of Israel, was a climate created in which many Palestinians believed they could not coexist with the Jews, as well as some Jews who did not feel they could coexist with the Palestinians.

However, the Middle East need not even then have become the powder keg that it is today, had not the surrounding Arab countries claimed for themselves that portion of Palestine which had always been earmarked for the Palestinians, or if they had received the Palestinians in a different manner. But by deliberately confining the refugees in camps along the frontier they ensured that the aggression of those affected would be preserved for generations.

Let us imagine that West Germany had acted similarly: instead of integrating the thirteen million ethnic German refugees who flooded across its frontiers after the war, from all conceivable countries, it would have stationed them along the frontier with East Germany or with Czechoslovakia – I believe there would have been no peace in Europe. Austria too integrated 100,000 ethnic Germans instead of keeping them in camps along the frontier. The deported Sudeten Germans, who also suffered an injustice, were given an opportunity to come to terms with their position, and by now none of them would wish to return to their former houses. Admittedly, a few high-sounding demands might be voiced at meetings of Sudeten German associations, but ultimately all concerned have accepted the fact that there has been a redisposition in Europe, and there would be an outcry in the international press if the Sudeten Germans attempted to question that new order with terrorism, let alone with an armed struggle. Or take the South Tyroleans: they too have suffered a wrong. Of course the region between the Adige and the Isarco used to belong to Austria, and its inhabitants wanted to live in Austria. But the First and then the Second World War drew a new frontier, and all those concerned have respected it. The Italians have granted the South Tyroleans a large measure of autonomy, and I doubt whether a plebiscite there would nowadays go in Austria's favour.

If Jordan, the minority of whose population is Palestinian, had granted the Palestinians a similar kind of autonomy instead of locking them up in camps, there would be no Palestinian problem today. As it is, it has become one of the insoluble problems of our day – and a Jew living in Vienna would do well to refrain from giving advice. I can only express my conviction that, for Jews and Arabs, there cannot, and must not, be any other way but coexistence. History has sentenced them to coexistence, and they should help history along: by putting the wish to share a future common destiny above all the dividing elements of the past. If it is possible for Jews once again to live with Germans, then it must be possible, at some time, for Palestinians and Jews to live together too.

For my grandson's bar-mitzvah my daughter invited her Arab friends as well. They brought their children along, and thus their children and our children played together. When one has watched that, one can still hope – despite newspaper reports of unrest and deaths.

29

Jews and Jews

In 1945 I made the acquaintance of an American officer of Jewish extraction, who belonged to one of the units which had liberated the concentration camps and had seen the horror with their own eyes. One evening we were sitting together at my flat, talking about the war, more especially about the part which the world had then – during the war – played in our fate. We were both of us, for somewhat different reasons, interested in that issue. I therefore asked my American friend to send me, after his return to the United States, cuttings from American Jewish papers published in the autumn of 1943. I addressed the same request to my friend Bar Yosef, who had, within the framework of the organization Bricha, helped Jews to enter Israel illegally. I asked him to send me Palestinian newspapers from that period.

My requests were met: within a few weeks a soldier brought me a package from America, full of cuttings from *Morgenjournal*, *Forwerts*, *Tog*, and others, published in the USA at the end of August and the beginning of September 1943. That was the time when the world had, from a number of credible reports, learned about the greatest mass murder in history.

And what were the Jewish papers in New York reporting? Weddings, bar-mitzvahs, various events of Jewish and society life. On one occasion, squeezed between these topics of absorbing interest, was a BBC report to the effect that a large number of Jews had been rounded up in the Białystok ghetto, deported and probably shot in a nearby forest.

The Hebrew papers, which I got a friend to translate for me, were no different: there was a report, some four or five pages long, about a refugee who had entered Palestine illegally via Romania and Turkey, and about life and death in a ghetto – but on the front page was an account of an Arab raid on a kibbutz, during which, thank God, no human lives were lost, though two cows had been killed. Reading these papers I asked myself if we were still the same people.

As long ago as just after Hitler's rise to power the Austrian press had carried extensive reports on how the Jews were faring in Germany. The first reports, indeed the first books, were published then about German concentration camps. The journalist Leopold Schwarzschild, who had escaped to Switzerland, published a monthly journal there, in which he described German excesses, and the Nuremberg race laws were there for anybody to read. By the time a German industrialist had informed Jewish organizations that the Nazis were about to embark on the 'final solution', it was obvious in Switzerland, in 1943, what was happening in Poland. A detainee by the name of Wrba had escaped from Auschwitz and had written an account; this reached Switzerland by a roundabout route and from there got to England.

The scale of the disaster could not, of course, be suspected and the public probably did not want these stories to be true – but it must have been clear that frightful things were being done to the Jews under the Nazis. In fact, there were better opportunities for being informed outside the Third Reich than within Germany or Austria. A German listening to the BBC was committing a punishable offence – not so a Briton or an American. The account of the escaped Auschwitz prisoner was accessible there to anybody – in Austria or in Germany some drunken soldier on home leave might at best recount what he had witnessed in the east, but he was in danger of being punished for breach of security. Quite recently many foreign newspapers, in connection with the Waldheim affair, blamed the Austrians for having tried to look the other way – but surely this charge applies at least as much to the reaction of the free world at that time, and indeed to the reaction of the Jews. Where was there then, even in the Jewish papers, an appropriate outcry or a daily reminder in the form of a demonstration?

I was suddenly reminded of stories I had heard from the concentration camps, of Jews fleeing from one country to another, from one ghetto to another, only to be caught by the Nazis anyway. When Eichmann's men then demanded, from the ghetto administration, the first so-called 'emigration' list, that list was invariably headed by the names of those who had found 'asylum' in the ghetto. The 'alien' Jews. Thus the Jewish Council in Holland put the German Jews first on its list. And much the same happened in France and in other countries. Common membership of the

Jewish people was not sufficient reason for finding some other, more humane, way out, or for refusing to collaborate in any way with the Germans: why not let them do the 'selecting' rather than make Jews sully themselves? Yet Jewish councils which preferred suicide to collaboration were the exception.

I know that it would have been no use: both would have been gassed just the same – but we would have kept our moral integrity. Years later, when, for my own satisfaction, I was searching for an explanation for that failure and, in my thirst for knowledge, followed the history of our people back through the centuries, I found that in the darkest Middle Ages there existed, in each Jewish community in Europe, an institution serving the diametrically opposite purpose: a fund of assistance for foreign Jews. In the Middle Ages ships were frequently captured by pirates who then kept the passengers – Jews, Christian merchants, priests – somewhere in the Libyan desert in order to demand a ransom. As there was no mail and no telegraph then, such a ransom could be raised only from the nearest community. And this was nearly always successful: it was invariably the Jews who first had their ransom paid by other Jews, who were strangers to them.

While the Jews were living in ghettos they felt like one family. When emancipation – thank God – brought down the ghetto walls, the Jews became part of the population of their host country. And this, inevitably, meant the loss of some of that sense of community. We sought the road to equal rights by way of assimilation and a loosening of our inner ties. And that is what we lacked at the time of Nazi persecution. Otherwise it would not have been possible for Alois Brunner to establish his 'Jewish police', who helped him drag Jews from their homes and pile them on to trains bound for Auschwitz.

For us, too, there remains from the period of the Third Reich a part of history we have yet to come to terms with. No one else has a right to blame us for it – but we ourselves must face up to it some time. We have done very little to condemn Jewish collaboration with the Nazis. When, after the war, I demanded that those who had abused their office in ghettos or concentration camps be removed from Jewish committees, I was told that 'this would diminish the guilt of the Nazis'. I have nevertheless managed to make my view prevail, at least at the conference of Jewish refugee camps, because I argued, successfully, that we must not expose ourselves to the danger of others pointing out that there were in our ranks men and women who did not behave unimpeachably. I am proud that this ruling was called the 'lex Wiesenthal'.

Jews are living in more than eighty nations of the world under governments which might exert pressure on them – that is why we have a vital interest in declaring that collaboration with the enemy is to us the worst of all possible crimes. Alois Brunner's 'Jewish police' should be a cause for shame not only to Germans and Austrians, but also to us Jews.

30

The Right Hand of the Devil

Among Third Reich criminals still alive, Alois Brunner is undoubtedly the worst. In my eyes he was the worst ever. While Adolf Eichmann drew up the general staff plan for the extermination of the Jews, Alois Brunner implemented it. Eichmann demanded that the Jews should be registered, assembled and deported – Brunner registered, assembled and deported them. His importance is best illustrated by the example of southern France. There, too, an order existed to have the region 'cleansed of Jews'. But the French population, in collusion with the Italian occupation forces, torpedoed its implementation: the deportations existed on paper only. Until Alois Brunner arrived and got the trains rolling.

One might say that Eichmann was the head and Brunner the hand, but that would belittle Brunner's part: he was a hand with a head. His principal achievement was the invention of Jewish collaboration. By persuading the Jewish communities, partly with threats and partly with promises, to help him in the registration, assembly and deportation of its members, he accelerated the deportation transports on a scale which earned him Eichmann's admiration.

It is impossible to say which of the two, Eichmann or Brunner, was worse than the other. They were an equal pair of angels of death. Adolf Eichmann, however, was tracked down, chased half-way around the globe, and hanged. Alois Brunner lives unmolested in a villa in Damascus. Everyone knows his address, it is known by what means he transmits money to his family, and now and again one of the big magazines carries an interview with him, in which he regrets having been unable to complete cleansing the world of Jews.

For me, Alois Brunner first took on concrete outlines at the beginning of the 1960s – albeit in a strange and involved, roundabout way. The Eichmann case had then dramatically brought my name and work into the limelight, and all kinds of people were suddenly offering to help me. The most important of these was 'Alex', whose story I have outlined in my book *The Murderers Among Us*. Alex had found an entrée to an organization whose task was to support former Nazi bigwigs. Presumably the members of that organization were themselves Nazi criminals who were now on the run under false names and with false papers. I would, therefore, rather not use those names here but refer to them in the manner Alex did: he called them 'the fat one', 'the short one' and 'the scraggy one'. Even though he was not enjoying their full confidence and was not privy to all their plans, he did succeed, from time to time, in catching hold of a snippet of what they happened to be planning.

As for instance in March 1961, when Alex called on me at my flat in Linz, all excited. 'I've learned something', he came out in a rush, 'which on the one hand seems quite logical, but on the other is totally beyond belief. I think it's only the tip of the iceberg. It's a case of kidnapping. But in fact it's about Eichmann.'

'But he's in jail,' I ventured to object, 'in the most secure prison on earth; guarded and watched like no other man. He isn't left alone for a minute, he can't take a step without supervision.'

'All that may be true,' replied Alex, enjoying his superior knowledge. 'But it isn't Eichmann they want to kidnap. That would indeed be hopeless. If I understood correctly, they want to kidnap somebody else, somebody they can exchange for Eichmann.'

Thrilling as this piece of information may have been, there was nothing I could do about it at that moment. Neither did I know how seriously one was to take such stories – in the circles in which Alex moved there was often a good deal of bragging about fairy tales – nor was it possible, supposing his story was correct, to warn all potential victims. 'Stay close,' was all I could say to Alex, 'but don't show your interest too obviously in case you betray yourself. Because that might easily cost you your neck.'

Shortly afterwards I left for Jerusalem to attend the Eichmann trial. When I returned six weeks later I was anxious to see Alex as soon as possible. I was then expecting to move into a flat in Vienna's tenth district, and we decided to meet at the nearby restaurant in the Südbahn railway terminal. But no sooner had Alex walked up to my table than a sixth sense made me certain that we were being watched. 'Someone's watching us,' I whispered, and Alex reacted with lightning speed. He apologized loudly for having sat down at my table, got up and left. In the evening he phoned me at home and confirmed my suspicion. 'One of my mates saw me with you. He immediately questioned me about it outside; what, he wanted to know, did I have to talk about to that man Wiesenthal? I told him that I had no idea that the man was Wiesenthal. I had gone to a table, I told him, and sat down, and suddenly the man had angrily asked me to leave: Listen, this table is reserved, I'm waiting for a friend. So I apologized, got up and left.'

Alex was lucky: his friends accepted his story and evidently continued to trust him. Otherwise he would hardly have got hold of the information I received from him at my Vienna home in October that year. 'I am now pretty well in the picture about the essence of the planned operation,' he told me. 'But it's over now.'

'Alex, why do you take such pleasure in talking in riddles and making me guess?'

'I am not talking in riddles. But it's not so simple. Well then: the most important man is Alois Brunner, a former member of Adolf Eichmann's staff, who says that he was Eichmann's right-hand man. This Brunner now lives in Damascus and does deals through various firms and sham firms. One of these firms is called Thameco and imports medical equipment from Germany, on which he allegedly makes considerable profits. This Brunner, then, had planned to help Eichmann, that is to free him. This is what he planned to do: an important Jewish personage was to be kidnapped and offered as an exchange for Eichmann. Probably the Syrian secret service was involved in the affair. But I don't know that for certain. The fat one, you know who I mean, spoke of an Arab by the name of R—— from Aley in Lebanon, who had travelled to Vienna to bring greetings and maybe also money to the Brunner family. This R——, so it seems, was to take charge of the whole operation. The man they wanted to abduct is Nahum Goldmann, the president of the World Jewish Congress and of the World Zionist Organization. He was known to visit Bonn frequently for negotiations with Adenauer, and to stay there, as a rule, for some time. That would have been the chance to kidnap him.'

'And who is to carry out this operation?' I inquired.

'Who was to carry it out?' Alex corrected me. 'Because the business is over now. It's possible I only heard about the whole thing because it did not come about. The affair, you understand, had begun to spread: Brunner has a friend in Hamburg, whose name I couldn't discover and I didn't wish to ask too obviously about it. He got in touch with this man and asked him to look out for a good commando squad, best of all former members of the Brandenburg division. In point of fact, one of them agreed, provided a sum of 30,000 Deutschmarks was made available to him for the operation.

He was promised that amount, but he evidently didn't quite trust this promise and wanted assurances. But the clients didn't want to discuss this until later. Then the man told one of his former comrades, presumably his former superior officer in the Brandenburg division, and asked his advice. This man thought the whole operation was much too risky and after a short period of reflection he advised him to refuse outright.'

'And so the business petered out?' I asked.

'No,' said Alex, 'presumably not yet. They seem to have found someone else. But I couldn't quite make sense of what I heard. If I got it right, it was like this: the officer from the Brandenburgers who rejected the idea had apparently worked for the West German security service or may still be working for them. It seems that the organization discovered this, and so they assumed that he would report the matter to the authorities. At any rate, when a few Arabs, who had nothing to do with the business, were questioned by the German police, our Arab, that man Rayes, called the whole operation off for good. It had been blown, he said, and it would be too dangerous to pursue it further.'

According to Alex they had already set up a hiding place where Goldmann was to have been kept prisoner. As Brunner realized that at that moment not even an Arab state would be prepared to hold the kidnapped president of the World Jewish Congress on its territory in order to exchange him for Adolf Eichmann, he decided to make use of Rayes's connections with the FLN, the Algerian Liberation Front. Rayes was the Lebanese representative to the FLN in Geneva, and although the FLN did not yet possess a state of its own, there was a part of Algeria where they were in control. There the kidnappers could have found a hiding place, along with their victim Goldmann, and stated their terms. The entire plan seems to have collapsed when Rayes correctly concluded that the Israelis wouldn't surrender Eichmann even in exchange for Nahum Goldmann. Anyway, the trial ran its course undisturbed, and as Eichmann was sentenced to death and executed, the operation had become pointless by 31 May 1967: no one would exchange a corpse.

Thus went the tale, as Alex told it to me in 1961 and as, shortly afterwards, it was rather vaguely published in the socialist *Arbeiter-Zeitung*, to which it had obviously been leaked. In 1985 Brunner, talking to a German journalist, confirmed all of it in principle, except that according to him the principal figure was a Syrian captain by the name of Lehan. For me, however, this was merely a detour that was to lead me close to Alois Brunner before very long. There was a realistic chance in the sixties of arresting Brunner in Europe.

Worldwide interest in Brunner was a logical consequence of the Eichmann trial. Only then did this man's role emerge before the public eye.

Alois Brunner, born in 1912, was not exactly a picture-book SS man – any more than Adolf Eichmann had been. Certainly he didn't look like a man whom the Nazis would have sent to one of their 'Lebensborn' brothels in order to breed a fine, pure, blond, blue-eyed race. He was of medium height, with dark hair, with a slightly hooked nose, and altogether looked as if Jews and gypsies might have been mixed up in his ancestry. From one of his former comrades, Dieter Wisliceny, we know that his appearance got Brunner a nickname: SS men who didn't like him called him 'Jew Süss'. Brunner would proudly tell his friends that he had attended a police college in Graz. What he did not mention was that he spent only three months there (from October 1932 to January 1933). But at the age of nineteen he joined the Nazi party in Fürstenfeld in Styria, and by September 1933 he already belonged to its innermost circle: along with Kaltenbrunner, Eichmann, Reder and Haider (the father of the extreme right-wing politician Jürg Haider) he went to Munich illegally in order to join the 'Austrian Legion' – a paramilitary organization composed exclusively of Austrians, which planned to conquer Austria, if need be by force of arms.

But that, of course, was not necessary. When on 11 March 1938 the Nazis crossed the German–Austrian frontier no one opposed them. On the contrary, the only obstacles they had to overcome were cheering inhabitants who again and again broke through the cordons to present flowers to the marching troops. Nor did the Austrians have to be forced into anti-Jewish excesses: there were plenty of volunteers among the crowd which in the first week of April smashed the fronts of Jewish shops and the windows of Jewish homes. Adolf Eichmann, not finding himself in any way impeded in his work, was able to devote himself fully to his future task – the deportation of the Jews. In the then Rothschild palace on Theresianumgasse he set up a Central Office for Jewish Emigration which was to become the central office for the extermination of the Jews. One of his very first collaborators was a good friend from his Munich days: Alois Brunner.

Together the two were so successful that immediately after the German entry into Czechoslovakia a similar office was established in Prague: Brunner could handle the extermination of the Viennese Jews on his own. Having meanwhile been promoted to officer in the SS security service, he became the head of the Vienna Central Office. His range of activities covered both the granting of emigration permits to Europe and overseas, and the assembling of one-way transports – to the east, in other words Poland. Brunner proved his mettle. Eichmann called him his right-hand man, and with good reason.

Under the original plans a city with about 180,000 Jews would have required deployment of a huge number of SS men for identification, registration and deportation. Brunner conceived the idea of leaving these jobs to the Jews themselves; this would save German manpower. The Jews would have to be so intimidated and (by means of promises) so corrupted that they became useful dummies serving the SS. Eichmann agreed, and so Brunner organized the so-called 'Jupo' (Judenpolizei, or Jewish police) from men made available to him by the leaders of the Jewish community. They did not wear uniforms but carried appropriate identification, and Brunner promised to protect them and their families against harassment, arrest and deportation. The Jewish community administration itself was enlisted for the registration of the Jews. Later, at Brunner's behest, it addressed an appeal to the members of the Jewish community to report for work or resettlement in the east. And there really were people who, under the stress of daily harassment by some sections of the population, actually volunteered for such 'resettlement'. Alois Brunner announced through his 'pickers-up' – as the Jews called the Jupos – that those who volunteered first would get the better jobs in Poland. He invented a Jewish reservation in Lublin, which of course did not exist, and dispatched his transports of 'volunteers', one after another, to the east. Their final destination was virtually always the gas chamber.

Naturally, Brunner wanted a proper reward for his idealism. He moved into a villa in Hietzing and filled it with furniture, carpets and paintings stolen from Jewish homes. Other Nazi bosses in Vienna who also coveted Jewish treasures had only to knock at Brunner's door. His people knew where valuables were to be found. If the Jewish owners of fine homes did not emigrate on their own accord – which was then still possible – they were placed on a deportation list. Concierges had to see to it, on Brunner's orders, that no valuables were removed from their homes: that was the privilege of Brunner's men. In part they stole for themselves, and in part they gave generous presents to other top Nazis. There were, of course, some Nazi bigwigs who did not wish to be given presents – they 'purchased' their items: Baldur von Schirach, the governor of the 'Ostmark' (the Nazi term for Austria), for instance, bought a painting by Lukas Cranach for 500 Reichsmark. But this price seemed too high to the 'vendors', who threw in a couple of antique Flemish tiles as well.

At the end of November 1941 Brunner closed down the 'emigration office'. By then there were only deportation transports to Poland, to Riga and to Minsk. He travelled in person on one of these transports (to Riga) and en route shot the Jewish ex-banker Siegmund Bosel. This was a kind of foretaste – all the others on the transport were taken straight to the Rumbula woods near Riga for execution; pits had already been dug for them.

By February 1943 Brunner had deported 47,000 Viennese Jews. His career advanced with corresponding speed. Having joined the SS in 1939, he was promoted to Untersturmführer on the Führer's birthday in 1940, Obersturmführer on 9 November the same year, and Hauptsturmführer on 30 January 1942, the anniversary of the Nazis' seizure of power. The Reich Security Directorate valued him highly. In October 1942, when Eichmann was not entirely satisfied with the operation of the Berlin 'Central Office', he summoned Alois Brunner with a number of his Jewish assistants to the German capital, so he could personally instruct the local Gestapo on his Viennese experiences.

Whenever Eichmann wanted to speed up the deportations he called on Alois Brunner. As, for instance, in February 1943, when he ordered him to Salonika. There was a long-established Jewish community there: Jews from Alexandria had found a home there as long ago as 140 BC. Most of the Jews encountered by Alois Brunner, however, were descendants of the Sephardic Jews expelled from Spain in the fifteenth century, who had found asylum in Salonika under the rule of the Turkish sultan. It was a proud, culturally outstanding community, with Jews working in all occupations, from load-carriers up to university professors.

These 50,000 Jews, as well as some 8000 from Macedonia, were to be freighted by Brunner to the extermination camps of Auschwitz and Treblinka within a few weeks. For this he made use of the experience he had gained in Vienna. At the very outset he had twenty-five prominent Jews taken hostage and threatened to have them shot unless his instructions were obeyed. After that he got the Jews to organize their own ghetto. It was set up in a part of town which the Jewish philanthropist Baron Maurice de Hirsch had created fifty years earlier for Jews fleeing Tsarist Russia. Survivors recall Brunner running through the streets like a madman, ensuring law and order with pistols in both hands.

With the exception of a few thousand Jews who succeeded in escaping from Salonika to Athens, he deported all the inhabitants of the ghetto. This was known to the entire German occupation force in Greece, with the exception of Kurt Waldheim. Eichmann himself visited Salonika only once: a man like Brunner did not need hustling, he always performed superbly.

Theft, of course, was not forgotten, any more than elsewhere. Brunner had marble slabs, intended for gravestones, confiscated from Jewish stonemasons in order to line the bathrooms of SS leaders with them. And in 1943, having just organized nineteen transports from Salonika to Auschwitz and Treblinka, he – rightly – considered the Jewish cemetery unnecessary: a surviving photograph from those days shows a large swimming pool for German officers faced with gravestones from that cemetery.

When Eichmann assigned a new field of activity to his man Brunner in June 1943 – he sent him to Paris – the total of Jews deported from Salonika stood at 44,000.

Prior to Brunner's arrival in Paris, 50,000 Jews from France had already been deported to the east, mainly to Auschwitz. The main transit camp, from where the transports were dispatched, was Drancy near Paris – but this did not seem to Brunner to be secure enough. He dismissed the French guards and set up his own police, composed of Jews. At the same time he established a kind of Jewish council in the shape of the Union Générale des Israélites de France (UGIF). Then he began to rehearse the Viennese model: with the assistance of the UGIF, his 'Jupos' and only a handful of SS men, he had the country 'cleansed of Jews' within a mere fourteen months.

Brunner worked with cunning. When word began to get about that the deportations were to the extermination camps, he had fictitious postcards from allegedly deported Jews disseminated, from which it emerged that they had arrived in good order and had already found work. And he also worked with terror. It was said that the walls of his office showed splashes of blood and bullet marks. One day, when he was not satisfied with the performance of the Jewish supervisory staff, he dispatched its members to Auschwitz by the next transport.

Brunner interrupted his stay at Drancy only twice: once for a lightning visit to Auschwitz along with Eichmann in order to show the camp to the Mufti of Jerusalem, Amin el Husseini.* The second break in his stay was of a strictly official nature: following the fall of Mussolini, Brunner went to the German-occupied Italian zone around Nice in order to speed up the sluggish deportations from there. As the task of gathering the Jews in this region was different from the situation in Paris, he took with him seven SS leaders who had particularly distinguished themselves in Vienna.† On

---

* Amin el Husseini was a bitter enemy of the Jews. During the twenties he had repeatedly organized attacks on Jews in Jerusalem, Hebron and other towns. The British, who then administered Palestine as a mandated territory, placed him under house arrest but he managed to escape. He went to Iraq, where he helped to organize the rising against the British. He was again arrested but once more managed to escape and went to Berlin. There he helped raise a Muslim SS division. He met Hitler several times and always vigorously opposed any endeavours (which began towards the end of the war) to halt the deportations. He saw the end of the war in Bad Gastein, from where he moved to Paris. The Yugoslavs had him on their list of war criminals, but the Mufti succeeded in finally making his way to Cairo. It is likely that he and Brunner met there again at some time and that the Mufti supported his unlucky soul-mate as best he could. Brunner certainly told journalists about such a meeting.

† Hauptscharführer Brückler from Vienna, Oberscharführer Josef Wiesel from Vienna (a former bank official), Hauptscharführer Josef Ullmann from Klosterneuburg (the camp chief of Drancy), Oberscharführer Zitha from Vienna, Oberscharführer Herbert Gabing from Vienna, Rottenführer Oskar Reich from Vienna (in his day a well-known footballer) and Rottenführer Josef Koppel.

15 September 1943 Brunner and his men arrived in Nice and stayed at the Hotel Excelsior.

Until then the Jews in the Italian-occupied region of France had been able to lead a more or less tolerable life. The local population stood by them, and the Italian occupation authorities, as far as possible, obstructed Hitler's wish to deport them. Before withdrawing they quickly destroyed the only comprehensive list which revealed who, as a Jew, was receiving food ration cards. It took a man like Alois Brunner to get southern France 'cleansed of Jews'. His principal assistant in this task was a Hauptscharführer by the name of Rolf Bilharz, who, under the cover name Gautier, organized a group of French informers to whom he paid a hundred francs for every Jew they discovered. The money came from the proceeds of the valuables stolen from Jews.

Deportation was arranged by means of a cattle truck which was attached every third day to the Nice–Paris express, with a hundred Jews crowded into it. Over a period of three weeks 1700 Jews were thus removed from the French Riviera to Paris. Thence their road led straight to Auschwitz. By the time Brunner left France he had deported 23,000 Jews from the south.

He was next to prove his talents in Slovakia. Slovakia was not an occupied country but a satellite state which had modelled its laws on those of Germany. Hence the Jews were outcasts. When Brunner arrived, two-thirds of Slovakia's Jews had already been deported, but then there was a hitch. There were another 25,000 Jews who were to be deported but who meanwhile were held in different labour camps. An aid committee, tolerated by the Slovaks and headed by Rabbi Weissmandl and Gisi Fleischmann, endeavoured by means of gifts, bribes and interventions to make the life of the Jews in these camps as bearable as possible. Deportations did not proceed at the usual rate. That was why the German ambassador, Ludin, had asked for an expert – Brunner.

It was a time when the defeat of the Nazis was already taking shape and the Red Cross was trying to visit the concentration camps. Himmler himself was shaken in his belief in final victory and was considering what there was still to be saved. He therefore sent Standartenführer Kurt Becher to Hungary and devised a plan for an exchange: living Jews against foreign currency and lorries. Becher opened negotiations with representatives of the Hungarian Jews – their secretary was the lawyer Dr Rezsö Kastner. The aim was to make contact with the American Jewish Joint Distribution Committee by way of the representatives of the Swiss Jews. Himmler gave the number of Jews he was prepared to offer in exchange for lorries, raw materials and money, as one million.

Brunner nevertheless continued to pursue deportation with all possible vigour. It was almost as if he feared that the premature success of Becher's negotiations might rob him of the purpose of his life. But his fears were unnecessary. Although Kurt Becher had a meeting on the Swiss frontier with the president of the Swiss Jewish communities, Sally Mayer, no specific agreement was reached. Meanwhile another committee member, Joel Brand, was sent, with Nazi consent, first to Turkey and then to Palestine, in order to inform the Jews of Palestine of this opportunity to save their co-religionists. But Joel Brand was taken prisoner by the British and was unable to complete his mission. Eichmann thereupon declared himself ready to put a number of Jews 'on ice' while awaiting the end of negotiations; he would thus hold a forfeit for any exchange deal.

Brunner's superior in Slovakia, Dieter Wisliceny, was informed of these negotiations and tried to allow for them by ordering a 'hold'. But Brunner was so obsessed with his hatred of Jews that nothing could stop him. He simply ignored Himmler's plans and ran the deportations on his own account. Gisi Fleischmann thereupon asked for an appointment with him. Brunner, however, tried to bring her to heel with the method he had used on Jewish representatives in Vienna, Salonika and Paris: a mixture of promises and intimidation. Eventually he had her put in chains at the Sered camp, but Gisi Fleischmann remained firm. Brunner failed to discover how she had managed to make contact with foreign Jewish organizations. Thereupon Brunner, furious, deported her to Auschwitz, even though Standartenführer Becher and Dieter Wisliceny intervened on her behalf. He gave her a letter to hand over to an SS officer on arrival. The sheet contained only two words: 'Return undesirable'. She arrived in Auschwitz on 18 October 1944. This day is also thought to be the date of her death.

During his short stay in Slovakia Brunner managed to deport an additional 14,000 Jews.

He next went briefly to Hungary to assist with the deportation of some 12,000 people, then he made a tour of inspection at the Terezín camp in Bohemia, and in March 1945 he returned to Vienna to visit his wife. He realized that the war was over and that any survivors from the camps would be seeking him out. The documents he had signed would likewise be eloquent testimony against him in any trial. He therefore returned once more to Czechoslovak territory, removed his SS uniform, and by the time the Third Reich collapsed he was an inconspicuous German civilian. Along with other Germans Brunner came to West Germany and there, under the name of Alois Schmaldienst, made a living as a truck driver − for the American army. Schmaldienst was a distant relation of his, a man he was certain would not be searched out. From Munich Schmaldienst-Brunner moved further north. Some believed he went to the Gütersloh area, others to the Hamburg region.

Brunner was careful: there might, after all, be someone who knew that he was hiding behind the name of Schmaldienst. That was why he wished to leave Germany. But the only papers he had were documents regarding his expulsion from Czechoslovakia in 1945 or 1946, as well as an American work permit. He therefore needed a passport and allegedly received one from a man called Georg Fischer. This man later told a journalist that he looked so much like Brunner that there had been no need for a new photograph. He had simply given him his passport and a few weeks later reported his own to the police as 'lost'. Brunner received an Egyptian visa in 1954, in the name of Georg Fischer, and went to Cairo. With his new passport Brunner looked for a job in Egypt. About that time, in the early fifties, Germans were much in demand as experts in the Middle East. Many years later he told a journalist that he had met a Nazi propaganda man there, by the name of Johannes van Leers; on another occasion he stated that he had called on the Mufti of Jerusalem, Amin el Husseini. The Mufti had advised him to go to Beirut or Damascus.

Brunner's later story runs like any secret agent's story from that turbulent period in the Middle East. Now and again he would meet old acquaintances, who recommended him to others. But the Syrians initially did not really trust him: he was arrested and confessed his true identity as well as the nature of his occupation during the Nazi period. After that, Syria admitted him with sympathy. Friends of Brunner's in Austria subsequently reported that in the 1950s and 1960s Brunner had carried out a number of tasks for Syria against her enemies in Lebanon and had thus definitively earned his host country's full support. The German embassy in Damascus renewed Brunner's passport in the name of Georg Fischer – whether it is still valid or whether he has meanwhile acquired Syrian citizenship I do not know.

Changes in the Syrian regime do not worry Brunner: to the Syrians he is a man who, even though it was many years ago, has earned great merit in exterminating Jews. That implies a position of respect and favour. The Syrians do not see the slightest reason for extraditing him to any other country, even though not only France but Austria and Germany, too, have been endeavouring to get him extradited. Instead the Syrian police guard his house and protect him from unwelcome visitors.

The Eichmann trial meant a certain upset in this idyllic existence. The indictment inevitably also outlined Brunner's part in considerable detail, numerous witnesses referred to him, and Eichmann himself put some of the responsibility on to him. In our own archives, too, we already had a number of witnesses' depositions against Brunner. The most shattering of these was from my friend Albert Welt, who published the paper *Der neue*

Weg in Vienna. Welt, who during the war was still a Romanian citizen, had learned that his mother had been put on Brunner's deportation list. As in 1940 Romanian citizens were still safe from deportation, Welt obtained from the Romanian consulate general a petition concerning his mother; with this he went to see Brunner. Brunner scanned the letter, tore it up and laughed: 'Your mother's already on the train, but it hasn't left yet. Go back to that Romanian and tell him to write me a letter saying that he has no objection to your accompanying your mother.'

Other statements which gradually accumulated at my office differed from this only in insignificant details. But it was six years before I was able to add an update to that steadily growing file. This one might have been crucial.

In September 1967 Alex, after a longish absence abroad, visited me again in Vienna. 'Simon, what news of Brunner?' was his first question.

'Unfortunately none,' I had to admit.

He had only been waiting for this. With a secretive smile he indicated that he knew something.

'Why are you looking at me like that?' I asked him. 'Or have you brought Brunner along with you? Where is he? Have you left him in the hall?'

'No, but he's coming.'

Although this was the last thing I would have expected to hear from him, I was prepared for something of the sort after his preamble. 'Coming where? To Vienna?' I asked in a matter-of-fact way.

'I don't think to Vienna, but not too far away. He's got problems with his other eye – you remember he lost one from a letter bomb, and apparently it often happens that the other is then affected. From friends of his family I've heard that he has made contact with a specialist in Switzerland. It's very likely he will go to Switzerland for treatment and perhaps even for an operation.'

I stopped acting blasé. This was news; this was an almost unique chance of getting hold of Brunner. We simply couldn't afford to make a mistake.

Alex claimed that he would even be able to discover the exact date of Brunner's arrival in Switzerland. It therefore would be simplest to have him arrested at the frontier: after all, there were warrants of arrest out against him in three separate countries. Nevertheless I had serious misgivings. In the Mengele case I had had the worst possible experience of Switzerland and its authorities when, in response to my information, they merely expelled Frau Mengele. I therefore decided that the Swiss authorities should be the last to hear about Brunner's arrival. Instead I got in touch with Senior Public Prosecutor Dr Adalbert Rückerl, the director of the Central office for the investigation of Nazi crimes in Ludwigsburg. I had known this splendid man for many years and I knew that I could talk to him openly. We made the following arrangement: in order to avoid being accused of inhumanity, (strange as it sounds, one has to think of that even when arresting mass murderers), all action was to be postponed until after Brunner's eye treatment operation. In the meantime the German authorities were to take all necessary steps and make preparations to have him arrested as he was leaving the country.

However, Dr Rückerl informed me of an additional problem: it would not be at all easy to get Brunner to face trial in France – that was ruled out by the so-called 'transfer agreement'. This paradox needs a rather lengthy explanation. As early as the final phase of the war, proceedings began in the liberated parts of France against Germans who had committed crimes on French territory. Proceedings and sentences against such criminals were handled by French military tribunals, which based themselves on extensive incriminating documentation – witnesses' statements, captured German documents, material collected by the Resistance. In many cases, however, the accused themselves were absent: the worst criminals had long gone to ground in Germany or Austria, where they were hiding out or living under assumed names. Following the establishment of West Germany a so-called 'transfer agreement' was concluded with the three western Allies. One of the stipulations of that agreement was that persons already sentenced by Allied courts – whether by the International Military Tribunal in Nuremberg or by other Allied military tribunals, such as the French – could not be tried again by a German court of law.

This gave rise to considerable injustice. Many of those criminals who were initially given tough sentences by Allied courts subsequently had these reduced or altogether remitted by way of amnesty. Which meant that frequently they had behind them a shorter term of imprisonment than those subsequently tried by German courts and given equally tough punishments for lesser offences, who actually had to serve their sentences. In no other case was the injustice as great as with criminals who had committed their crimes in France – because, as I mentioned above, few of the top criminals had been tried by French military tribunals in person. A lot of them were tried *in absentia* – including, in particular, many SS leaders who had worked with the Gestapo, with the commander-in-chief of the security police, with the security service or with the Jewish department. As an example I should like to list four men tried in France *in absentia*, for the most serious offences, and sentenced to life imprisonment or death, who live entirely free in Germany today, without ever having had to spend a single day in prison: SS Obersturmbannführer Kurt Lischka, who between 1941 and 1943 was the permanent representative of the chief of the security police, Dr Knochen, and for a time was commanding officer of the security police and the security service under the commander-in-chief of the security police in Paris; SS Obersturmbannführer Heinz Röthke, who from 1942 to 1944 was the officer for Jewish questions under the commander-in-chief of the security police; SS Sturmbannführer Herbert Hagen, who was a departmental head under the commander-in-chief of the security police and personal assistant to the Senior SS and police chief for France, Brigadeführer Oberg; and SS Oberscharführer Ernst Heinrichsen, who was on the staff of the Jewish department of the commander-in-chief of the security police.

On 18 September 1950 Lischka was sentenced *in absentia* to lifelong forced labour by the military tribunal in Paris for participation in numerous crimes. Röthke was acquitted on 22 March 1949 by the Paris military tribunal, but subsequent investigations, newly discovered documents and witnesses' statements now incriminate him gravely. Hagen was sentenced to forced labour for life by the Paris military tribunal on 7 March 1956, *in absentia*. Heinrichsen was sentenced to death by the military tribunal in Paris on 18 September 1950, also *in absentia*, for numerous murders committed by him in person. All these sentences were for participation in the deportation of Jews. After all, some 70,000 French citizens had been involved, and only a few of them survived that merciless time. But Lischka, Röthke, Hagen and Heinrichsen were moving about freely. The French judiciary did not demand extradition because the relevant trials had already taken place, and the German judiciary had to observe the 'transfer agreement' which made it impossible for these men to be tried again. An application by the public prosecutor's office, challenging this state of affairs, was rejected by the German federal court. Germany subsequently tried to come to a special agreement with France on these four cases, but it was not ratified until 1974.

At the time of my conversation with Rückerl the problem still existed in all its complexity. Brunner, sentenced in France *in absentia*, could not be tried for the same crimes by a German court. But this was a problem which we were hoping to solve once we had got hold of him. For the moment there was little more we could do but wait for Alex to notify us. He was still fairly confident that Brunner would shortly come to Switzerland. News did arrive from Alex – but it was different from what I'd been hoping for.

'Just imagine!' he told me over the telephone. 'A Linz bulletin of the old comrades' association, *Linzer Turm*, has published the names of ten people who are being warned against travelling to France. Brunner is among them. The list of names is published under the heading "Warning by the Austrian Red Cross". The ten names include personal data and place of birth, to make quite sure there is no misunderstanding. And I can tell you something else, something that's not in the rag: Brunner's family was also warned personally. It was obvious the warning concerns not only France but the whole of Europe.'

Alex rang off and I felt stunned. The very next day I called on the director of the Austrian Red Cross, Hans Sefcik: 'Since when has it been the Austrian Red Cross's business to warn people who are wanted by the public prosecutor for crimes they committed under the Nazis? Is that one of the tasks of the Red Cross? Would you also warn cheque forgers, white-slave traders and other common criminals? Is it your service's practice to warn people not only in writing but also through trusted individuals?'

Hans Sefcik gave me the following reply, which I here quote in full: 'During a congress of the Red Cross Society in Holland the director of the German Red Cross approached me during a break, slipped an envelope into my jacket pocket and said that it had to be dealt with at all costs. It was a list of the names of thirty persons who should not travel to France because they ought to expect difficulties there. He did not explain to me why these people must not travel to France, and the names meant nothing to me. We therefore notified all the families we could trace.'

'There were thirty names on that list. In *Linzer Turm*, however, only ten of them are listed – how is that?' I inquired.

'Those ten we couldn't find, so we asked the association to publish their names.'

'And you thought nothing of it?'

'No. Our search service often carries out similar actions.'

The warning list handed to the Austrian Red Cross had the names and dates of birth followed by their SS ranks or membership, as well as the dates of sentences passed on them by courts. Moreover it was marked 'strictly confidential'.

I realized that this must be part of a much more extensive operation. Not only those sentenced in France were to be warned, but presumably all those whose Nazi past had not yet been fully explored. Soon I realized the reason: the German judiciary was just then trying to forestall the impending expiry of the statute of limitations by intensifying their inves-tigations. This represented a threat to men like Brunner – and that was what they were to be warned against.

I immediately got in touch with Dr Rückerl of the Central Office in Ludwigsburg, because I realized that these warnings concerned not only Austria. Rückerl told me, as expected, that the Red Cross had of course not received any such list from Ludwigsburg. All he knew was that the German Foreign Ministry, at the request of the Ministry of Justice, had approached many countries in order to identify the people who had committed crimes in the German-occupied countries. One of those coun-tries had been France. That was all he knew at the moment, but he would look into the matter at once, and if the director of the German Red Cross had given such a list to the director of the Austrian Red Cross, then this proved that there must also have been a list of wanted German war criminals in existence, as Austria herself had not requested any list from France. Soon afterwards Rückerl phoned to tell me how it had all happened: the legal protection department of the Foreign Ministry in Bonn had passed the list on to the German Red Cross, and they had leaked parts of it to the Austrian Red Cross.

I therefore embarked on a multi-track operation. I wrote to the then German Federal Chancellor, Kiesinger, with a request for clarification, as well as to the prosecutor general in Bonn, whom I asked to examine whether the files of the legal protection department of the Foreign Ministry amounted to 'succouring' of criminals, or possibly to a breach of security. And I laid a criminal action with the prosecutor general in Hamburg: the question was to what extent the German Red Cross had committed the offence of 'succouring'. In Austria I handed the Minister of Justice, Dr Klecatsky, a lengthy letter complete with documentary evidence. Klecatsky ordered an investigation of the Austrian Red Cross by the Ministry of the Interior and demanded a report.

On 27 March 1968 I informed the Austrian and foreign press. Reactions were appropriate: in the Dutch parliament a question was asked whether it was desirable henceforward for the Dutch Red Cross to maintain relations with the German Red Cross. Major American papers published letters from readers urging the public not to make any donations to the American Red Cross if it continued to maintain relations with the German Red Cross. The American Red Cross thereupon most urgently requested the German Red Cross for an explanation, and subsequently published the following statement in their letters columns: 'The French authorities realized that the Germans concerned were unaware that they had been sentenced, and therefore supplied the government of West Germany with a list of names of persons convicted. The German government was then under an obligation to notify the persons concerned that they had already been sentenced. The list contained no addresses except, at the most, addresses which were known before the war. On this point the German government, as was customary, enlisted the search service of the German Red Cross. The list of convicted Germans comprised 733 names. The search service of the German Red Cross established that 105 of them had died, 311 were untraceable, and 294 had already been traced. This operation was performed at the request of the German government.'

Similarly absurd was the reply sent me by the German federal chancellory: it claimed that the list given to the Red Cross had not been the official list from the French government, but one compiled by French lawyers. For one thing, this should not have made any difference: for another, it was a lie. But truth had no chance then. Thus the prosecutors general in Cologne and Hamburg, as well as the managing chief public prosecutor in Bonn, informed me in brief notes that there was no case of 'succouring' because no proceedings had been started by Germany against those who had been warned; the charge of 'succouring' only applied to such proceedings.

I flew to Hamburg to call on the prosecutor general and to suggest that he have the premises of the Red Cross searched, in order to establish whether there was any other material kept there which would represent succouring of Nazi criminals. As the prosecutor general was not present, I was received by his deputy. He listened to me politely, noted down what I knew about the warned men, and once more explained the legal position to me. When I mentioned a search at the Red Cross, he merely reacted with a rhetorical question: 'Why not also at the archbishop's?'

I therefore began, on my own, to interest myself in the legal protection department. And as chance would have it, the head of that department, Legation Counsellor First Class Dr Johannes Gawlik, turned out to be the same Dr Gawlik who, in 1945 and 1946, had been defence attorney for the SS at the Nuremberg Military Tribunal. When I then arranged for the German government, and in particular Foreign Minister Willy Brandt, to be flooded with letters of protest, the spokesman of the Foreign Ministry, Dr Jürgen Rufuhs, emphasized that it was not only the right but the duty of the federal government to disseminate such warnings. It was obliged, regardless of the persons concerned, to notify German citizens that they might encounter difficulties abroad.

A journalist thereupon put the good question why, in that case, the Foreign Office did not also hand over to the German Red Cross the Interpol list of wanted persons. Surely smugglers and swindlers were entitled to the same facilities as Nazi mass murderers? Dr Rufuhs did not react to that question. Nor to the one about whether the German government's duty to protect its citizens also extended to Austrian mass murderers such as Alois Brunner.

When, at a press conference, I called the whole business a 'crime against the concept of the Red Cross', the head of the search service of the German Red Cross, Dr Kurt Wagner, answered that he had 'a clear Red Cross conscience' in the matter. But then the idea of the Red Cross has had to suffer a few blows in the past. After 1933 the German Red Cross was Nazified and taken over by the SS. Henceforward Jews and other persons regarded as opponents of the regime were excluded from Red Cross care. The managing president of the German Red Cross, Reich Physician Dr Ernst Robert Grawitz, was promoted to SS Gruppenführer and his record was such that a week before the end of the war he committed suicide in Potsdam. As one of those who had been involved in experiments on humans he would otherwise have presumably found himself in the dock at Nuremberg. Grawitz was not the only one to choose death by his own hand: the Reich Physicians' Leader Dr Leonard Conti, a prominent member of the German Red Cross management, also committed suicide, either from fear of being indicted or from a not entirely clear Red Cross conscience.

The wartime role of the International Committee of the Red Cross in Geneva was likewise anything but glorious. The Committee considered concentration camps on German or German-occupied territory to be an internal German matter and did not intervene even once with the Reich government in the interest of the Jews, or later against the extermination of the Jews (for which, incidentally, lorries painted with a Red Cross were used in Auschwitz). Not until the summer of 1944, when the Wallenberg operation started in Hungary, did the International Committee deign to undertake some steps there. The first contacts made by the International Red Cross with the German leadership in the matter of concentration camps date from April 1945 – even though the existence of gas chambers had been known since, at least, the summer of 1943.

No doubt because this history gave them a particularly clear conscience, Red Cross officials after the war helped vast numbers of Nazi criminals to flee overseas, by arranging forged papers for them in cosy cooperation with Bishop Hudal. Seen in this light the warning given to Alois Brunner was no more than the continuation of a well-tried tradition.

The legal protection department of the Foreign Ministry, however, claimed that it had passed on the ominous list simultaneously to the Red Cross and to the prosecution authority in Ludwigsburg. Quite apart from the absurdity of such a procedure, if it had actually taken place, this statement was also untrue: the lists received by the Central Office in Ludwigsburg rather belatedly already had annotations by the Foreign Ministry – including, against some names, the shorthand gloss of the Foreign Ministry, 'Has been notified.' In view of this evidence the Foreign Ministry eventually had to admit that the list had, after all, first gone to the search service and only later to Ludwigsburg.

My attempts, in view of all these obvious inconsistencies, to get some proceedings going eventually ended, after prolonged correspondence, with the illuminating explanation from the public prosecutor's office that the Red Cross had regarded its action not as a 'warning' but as 'a necessary measure within the framework of its search service'. On 1 January 1969 came the official notification that the case had been dropped. I tried to appeal, pointing out that the Foreign Ministry had at least acted in breach of its internal rules of procedure by notifying the Red Cross and only later the prosecution authority. Surely that was a strong indication that someone knew very well what they were doing. But I realized that I was flogging a dead horse: a little prostitute who warns her pimp that the police have questioned her is locked up. But Alois Brunner may be warned with impunity. There has never again been such a favourable opportunity to seize him.

Brunner is living in his villa in Syria, and that country's leaders would not even dream of extraditing this murderer of Jews. Brunner, the Syrian authorities stated, could not be found at the address given. Reporters from a German magazine found him without difficulty and published a lengthy series of photographs and interviews. Nor did the postman have any problem finding him. In July 1980 Brunner, alias Fischer, had a package delivered to him which had been posted in Austria and allegedly contained medicinal herbs. In a covering letter the 'Association of Friends of Medicinal Herbs' in Karlstein apologized that they could not send the ring-bound books ordered by Brunner from 'God's Pharmacy for Your Health' but instead had found some other books with a similar content. When Brunner opened the package it exploded. Of the fingers of his left hand, only his thumb remained. Despite this successful postal delivery Syria continued to maintain that Brunner could not be located.*

When a book was published in Yugoslavia about the tragedy of the Jews of Macedonia, showing that Brunner, acting on Eichmann's orders, was also responsible for the deportation of 8000 Macedonian Jews, I asked the president of the Jewish community, Dr Kadelburg, to request the Yugoslav government to intervene with the Syrian government, with whom it had friendly relations. I personally addressed myself to the Yugoslav government in this matter twice, through its embassy in Vienna – but without success.

When I was invited to make a speech in Skopje on 11 March 1986, the forty-third anniversary of the start of the deportations, I accepted on condition that Yugoslavia took the necessary steps for Brunner's extradition. I never went to Skopje.

*In 1988 the West German government again applied for Brunner's extradition. The Syrian answer was the same.

31

The Infestation of the Police

The Brunner case is by no means the only one in which institutions which could be assumed to help justice prevail, have impeded rather than promoted the search for war criminals. The reason is simple: large numbers of old Nazis continue to sit in key positions. After the war it was virtually impossible to eliminate them all. Judiciary, police and most other authorities would probably have collapsed if all the ex-Nazis had been removed from them. This was a particular problem in the case of the police, which, after all, was to play a decisive role in hunting down Nazi criminals. Instead the wanted men were not infrequently warned by their old comrades, whose job it was to look for them. A police officer not too high up in the hierarchy was often more useful than a top man – because as a rule he was the first to see the material and the last to take a decision on it.

The transfer of jobs from the Hitlerite police and security services into the police departments of a reborn Austria and West Germany was uniformly smooth. A typical case was that of Heinz Riedel, a former unit commander in the secret field police: he had killed a number of people in the Soviet Union who were described as 'suspected of being partisans'. After the war he joined the criminal investigation police in Schleswig-Holstein, where he rose to departmental head in the Criminal Department of Schleswig-Holstein. When it became known in 1964 that he was being investigated for participation in mass murder, this did not lead either to his dismissal or even to his suspension. He continued in police service until March 1974 – a few days prior to the main hearing in his trial –

when he reached pensionable age and went into retirement.

That trial, incidentally, also unrolled in quite a typical way: Riedel did not deny the murders at all, but merely stated that, instead of having his victims liquidated by an execution squad, he had handed them over to a 'gas truck'. He had considered this more humane than shooting. The background of the argument was as follows: for Riedel's offence not to be subject to the statute of limitations it would have to be qualified as 'especially cruel or vicious'. Whether this qualification applied to death in a gas truck was judged by an expert appointed by the court, Professor Dr Emmanuel Steigleder; in his expert opinion, Steigleder explained, the victims would have lost consciousness within sixty to ninety seconds of the exhaust gases being directed into the truck. Until then they would merely have suffered from vertigo, slight discomfort and slight cramps – these, by themselves, were not sufficient for the presumption of 'cruelty'. The jury accepted this expert opinion: the murders of Kriminalkommissar (retired) Heinz Riedel had been committed 'neither cruelly nor viciously'. He left the court a free man.

I do not know Dr Emmanuel Steigleder's background. In Austria such an expert opinion would not have surprised me at all, as a number of forensic psychiatrists had a lurid Nazi past behind them. The most lurid no doubt was that of Primarius (or Chief Surgeon) Heinrich Gross: he had been responsible, at the Steinhof psychiatric hospital, for having several hundred children, who were suffering from a brain disorder, killed by injection. The nurses who had given the injections were convicted. Gross, who had ordered them, remained a free man. With this career record Heinrich Gross became the most important and most prominent forensic psychiatrist in post-war Austria.

However, it was not just a case of many individual police officers or forensic experts being directly transferred – there was also the instance of an organization which was taken over in bulk just as one of the worst criminals of the Third Reich left it: Ernst Kaltenbrunner's Interpol. This international police organization, founded in 1923 on the proposal of the Viennese police chief, had its head office in Paris and coordinated the international fight against crime. In 1938 it was decided to move its headquarters to Vienna. Shortly afterwards came the Anschluss, and Reinhard Heydrich became president of Interpol. He ordered the office to be moved from Vienna to Berlin. There are probably only a handful of people who know that the Wannsee conference, at which the extermination of the Jews was decided on 20 January 1942, was held at the Berlin office of Interpol.

Following Heydrich's assassination Kaltenbrunner became president of Interpol. He immediately used it in various ways for his own purposes. I have already mentioned that Interpol's card indexes made it possible to identify those professional forgers who were subsequently to manufacture forged pound notes which were to have thrown the British currency into chaos. Simultaneously, however, these card indexes also made it possible to trace those forgers who were manufacturing false baptismal certificates or false passports for Jews. The Gestapo for its part utilized the Interpol records to discover a number of people who, because of some youthful sins, might be blackmailed and then enlisted as Gestapo spies.

As the Nazis were occupying practically the whole of Europe they were able to let Interpol branches in most countries carry on as before, at most complementing them with a few of their own people – except that orders now came from Heydrich or Kaltenbrunner. Thus the USA, for instance, was a member of Interpol, and interestingly enough only since May 1938, that is, after the occupation of Austria. Not until 3 December 1941, four days prior to Pearl Harbor, did J. Edgar Hoover, the FBI chief, instruct his subordinates to sever contacts with Interpol. US membership in Heydrich's Interpol repeatedly worried the US Congress. In 1977, under the new Freedom of Information Act, the correspondence between the Nazis and the FBI was published. American newspapers reported that the FBI had informed Interpol which Americans on the 'wanted' lists were Jews. Although normally the religion of a refugee was never recorded, the FBI supplied Kaltenbrunner with 'wanted' lists containing indications on 'Jewish types', 'Jews' and members of the 'Jewish race'.

Interpol, however, acted not only against the 'Jewish types' among the criminals; any Jew in hiding or living under a false name was, to them, *ipso facto* a criminal. To track down such people was part of their duties. There was a special file (Interpol experts described it to me as File S) which contained all information concerning Jews in hiding. According to information which I was unable to verify File S was allegedly taken to Paris when the Interpol head office was moved back there. I therefore wrote a letter to the French Minister of Justice Robert Badinter in 1983, and he promised to investigate the matter. Unfortunately it did not produce anything.

A large portion of the extensive Interpol archives is said to have been destroyed in Berlin at the end of the war. At any rate, the search for it remains unsuccessful. However, as Berlin was captured by the Russians, it is possible that some of the files fell into their hands. A smaller portion was carried off by the Interpol secretary, Karl Zindel, on his flight in April 1945. He only got as far as Stuttgart, so this portion has survived.

The first post-war president of Interpol was Florent Louvage, head of the Belgian criminal investigation police before the war, and during the war – apparently without problems in cooperating with Heydrich and

Kaltenbrunner – head of Interpol in Brussels. I knew of quite a number of Interpol officials after the war to whom much the same applied. During the years of 1968 to 1972 the president of the federal criminal office in Wiesbaden, Paul Dickopf, became Interpol president. In my SS service list of 1945 he is still listed as an SS Untersturmführer and member of the security service. On the other hand, it was known that during the war (in 1943) Dickopf had escaped via Belgium and France to Switzerland in order to make contact there with the Americans. As a rule, SS officers who escaped were immediately placed on the 'wanted' list. During the 1970s a number of writers, notably S. Baram and Y. Vaughan, turned their attention to Interpol and stated that they were unable to discover any German search for Paul Dickopf – which gave rise to some debate about the Dickopf 'escape'. At any rate, the Central Offices for the investigation of Nazi crimes in Ludwigsburg, Dortmund and Cologne have told me informally that while Dickopf was president of the federal criminal office one could hardly expect help from him in tracking down Nazi criminals. I am inclined to say that the same applied very largely to Interpol as a whole.

32

The Infestation of the Judiciary

At least as problematical as the infestation of the police with former Nazis was, and still is, the infestation of the judiciary with hanging judges and hanging prosecutors. Unfortunately even people dedicated to 'the law' found surprisingly little difficulty in subordinating themselves to the Nazi state of lawlessness. As in the case of the physicians, it seems to me that the reason for this stems from the basically apolitical attitude of university-educated Austrians and Germans. Admittedly, Austrian jurists had never in the past had an opportunity to serve a democratic constitutional state, and German jurists enjoyed that opportunity for a short period only. In spite of the enshrined independence of the judiciary, it was accepted that the law had to serve the rulers, and in the case of the state prosecutor even his title proclaims him as the attorney of the state, and hence also, if it so happens, of a state of lawlessness. The French Revolution and the Enlightenment fell far short of adequately permeating the Austrian or the German judiciary with their ideas. They never saw themselves as the guardians of 'civil rights', but rather as an extended arm of the ruler for controlling the citizenry. In Austria, moreover, 'judicial positivism' had done much to shake the popular sense of justice. The Christian idea of a God-given 'natural law' was replaced by the positivist theory that the law was simply that which was moulded into legislation by the state. Whereas in the Anglo-Saxon world a judge passes, as it were, individual judgements, drawing for support on specific cases in the past, the jurist in Austria and Germany (as in most countries which have adopted Roman law) feels a duty solely to an abstract legal system. So long as he moves within that system he believes that, in the truest meaning of the phrase, he is 'within the law'. He believes that it is of no concern to him what that 'law' consists of or how it has come about. The circle of a basically apolitical attitude is closed on itself.

I realize that this apolitical attitude, usually commended as 'being above politics', also has its advantages, for instance compared to the American system, where some judges are actually elected. I am also aware of the advantages of a self-contained legal system over Anglo-Saxon 'case law'. All I am trying to do is to explain that rooted within the Austrian and German legal system there were, and are, plausible reasons for the caving in of so many of its exponents.

Regrettably they were permitted after the war to extricate themselves from their responsibility for countless criminal judgements by means of a device typical of the system: in test cases they were assured of impunity provided their actions and verdicts at the time had been in line with the law as then valid. No one asked whether a regime exercising power by illegal means is capable of creating valid law. If it is so, then Austrian and German judges would also have to practise according to the Mafia's code of honour should that organization succeed, with the aid of a few machine-gun-toting killers, in occupying parliament.

I do of course admit that the purging of an infested judiciary machine within a state that has to continue functioning is a well-nigh impossible task. Such a purge, needless to say, would have to proceed in line with the law – and who was to supervise this if not the very judiciary that was to be purged? Probably there were simply too many Nazi judges in Austria and Germany for all of them to have been dismissed. Nevertheless, it would have been an act of the most elementary hygiene to compel at least some of the incriminated people, by pressure of public opinion, to seek retirement, and to get rid of those whose sentences overstepped even the laws valid at the time.

Certainly the savage sentences of Dr Filbinger caused a sensation in West Germany. Yet the attempt made by the deputy chief prosecutor in the Nuremberg trial, Professor Robert Kempner, to open up the problem of Nazi judges on the basis of the sentences pronounced by them was successful only in two instances: a judge who had sentenced to death a Jew named Katzenberger on the patently false charge of 'racial defilement' – sexual relations with an Aryan – was sentenced to a term of imprisonment, and another judge, who had passed ninety-seven death sentences in Berlin, was charged thirty-five years later and hanged himself before his trial opened.

In Austria even such exceptional cases did not exist. When the journalist

Oscar Bronner (the future founder of the news magazine *profil* and at present engaged in establishing a new daily paper in Austria), in a special issue of the journal *Forum* in 1965, pointed to a number of senior judges who had pronounced the most inhuman death sentences, Minister of Justice Broda fully supported the men he attacked, even though the victims of those hanging judges included Social Democratic resistance fighters. To this day public delegations attend the 'Floridsdorf Spitz', a spot in Vienna's twenty-first district, to commemorate three men executed there on 8 April 1945: Lieutenant Alfred Huth, Senior Lieutenant Rudolf Raschke and Major Karl Biedermann. Four days later Vienna was liberated by the Allies. Yet the prosecutor of that special court martial, the then Lieutenant Dr Otto Rothe, saw the proceedings through to the end. Rothe went into retirement in the 1970s as President of the Senate of the Supreme Court in Vienna.

By way of illustrating conditions in the German judiciary I should like to quote the case of Judge Dr Franz Schuhmacher. Schuhmacher was senior field judge of the German occupation forces in Holland and there, in August 1943, he dealt with the case of a student, Gerard Frank Smits. Smits had been found in possession of leaflets and a pistol – without ammunition – and for this offence had been sentenced to twelve years of penal service on 10 December 1943. This was possible under the law then prevailing. That sentence, however, did not seem enough to Dr Franz Schuhmacher: he objected to General Friedrich Christiansen at what he thought an excessively lenient sentence and demanded the death penalty. General Christiansen quashed the verdict and ordered a retrial before a court martial. But this tribunal also sentenced Smits to 'only' twelve years. Dr Schuhmacher objected again and another trial was ordered – this time under Dr Schuhmacher's presidency. The accused man's counsel, Dr de Pont, tried in vain to object to Dr Schuhmacher on grounds of bias: the court, including its legally qualified senior field judge, declared itself free from any bias.

On 7 March 1944 Smits was sentenced to death. Immediately after the sentence Dr de Pont appealed to General Christiansen not to confirm the death sentence but to convert it to a prison sentence. In his application he pointed out that the presiding judge, Dr Schuhmacher, had himself framed the indictment and ensured the quashing of the two earlier sentences. This was a reason for barring him from the court, even under valid German military criminal law. Christiansen did not reply.

I had come across this general in an application by a Jewish ex-serviceman in Holland, who had lost both his legs in the First World War, and who was hoping that this might save him from deportation. Instead of an answer to the applicant General Christiansen made the following gloss, in his own hand, on the application: 'A Jew's a Jew, with or without legs.'

The Dutch judiciary assessed Dr Schuhmacher's procedure, as described above, as murder and on 7 March 1946 put his name on the international list of Nazi criminals. Dr Schuhmacher became a senior public prosecutor of the Limburg provincial court in West Germany.

After having been informed about the case by relations of the executed Smits I wrote a letter in October 1969 to the Minister of Justice of Hessen, Dr Johannes Strelitz, asking him to examine the charges against Dr Schuhmacher. Thereupon Dr Schuhmacher, at least, applied for retirement. His present attitude to his past emerges from an 'explanation' he gave of his action then: he had realized, he said, that only one-third of all death sentences passed were actually implemented at the time, and therefore he could afford to pronounce sentence of death even in less serious cases. I suggested that his pension claims might be examined. Without success.

Yet Dr Schuhmacher's action was not even in accordance with the 'non-law' valid at the time. First of all, he infringed the law by brushing aside the rules on bias, in order to sentence Smits at all. In conjunction with his two previous objections to more lenient sentences this was sufficient grounds for the presumption that Dr Schuhmacher's exclusive and entirely personal intention had been to deprive Smits of his life. Added to this was what, earlier on, I called the fundamental problem of Nazi justice: an organization practising state power illegally cannot, to my mind, create a law. Holland had been attacked and occupied by the Nazis: hence the presence of the Germans in Holland was illegal. Following the flight of the Dutch government and the surrender of the army the Germans were, at the most, 'entitled' to maintain order in Holland by means of valid Dutch laws. But no one could be sentenced to death in Holland for the possession of leaflets or a pistol.

The judiciary, however, is surprisingly inventive when it does not wish to assess a judge's sentence of death as murder. Even in cases where it was proved that judges had come into court with death sentences all prepared and ready, this was qualified not as murder but as manslaughter. The statute of limitation for manslaughter was fifteen years, and, as the cases were not uncovered earlier, these judges remained untroubled.

33

Who Has the Right to Murder?

The following story is also an illustration of the Nazi judiciary, in this case an SS police court. It is important for two reasons: first, because it shows that lawyers regarded the murder of Jews as a perfectly normal and permissible activity, and secondly, because it demonstrates that an SS man was not allowed to murder just as the spirit moved him. Adolf Eichmann demanded a well-organized mass murder, performed obediently and in accordance with his instructions. Individual intoxication with killing was forbidden.

Although I had been greatly concerned with the matter, this astonishing verdict by an SS police court only came into my hands in 1971. It concerns a man by the name of Max Täubner, an Untersturmführer in the 1st SS Infantry Brigade and on the headquarters staff of the Reichsführer SS, Heinrich Himmler. I was well acquainted with that brigade. I have on my shelves its war diary, which recorded painstakingly how many 'members of gangs' they had been able to annihilate day after day without any losses of their own: under the pretext of 'fighting against partisans' helpless civilians, especially Jews, gypsies and Communists, were rounded up behind the front and shot. The victims in the main were old people, women and children.

When I first interested myself in Täubner I didn't know that four years later I would come across an Austrian who had likewise been a member of one of these murder brigades, the then president of the Liberal Party of Austria, Friedrich Peter, whom Bruno Kreisky had chosen (assuming appropriate election results) to become Vice Chancellor of the Republic of Austria. But I shall write about this in a later chapter. Max Täubner's story may help to present a vivid picture of the activity of Peter's brigade as well.

In 1941 Untersturmführer Max Täubner was sent with a workshop platoon to the 1st SS Infantry Brigade in the Ukraine. On 12 September he arrived in the little town of Zwiahel and learned from its Ukrainian mayor that some three hundred Jews were being held at the local prison. That was a drain on personnel and food; the Ukrainian mayor therefore asked that these Jews be shot. Täubner obliged him: his squad left 319 dead.

On 17 October 1941 Täubner with his platoon reached Sholokhovo, where, in passing as it were, he killed 191 Jews. A few weeks later he was in the small town of Aleksandriya. There he found 459 Jews who had so far escaped 'resettlement'. Täubner had them rounded up and shot, hanged or beaten to death. While Täubner was playing his accordion, in between executions, one of his subordinates, Sturmmann Rudolf Nikolaus Wüstholz, staged a kind of gladiatorial contest: he encouraged two Jews to have a go at each other with spades and promised the survivor not to shoot him.

Needless to say, he did not keep his promise: the promise of a German to a Jew had no validity.

What I am describing here is no atrocity propaganda, nor the 'typical exaggeration' of a survivor, but the almost verbatim record of the SS police court's case against Max Täubner. However, anyone thinking that Täubner had to answer for the murder of 969 Jews would be mistaken. The court merely accused him of acting on his own initiative and committing unnecessary excesses. 'The Jews', the relevant passage of the verdict reads, 'must be exterminated and there need be no regret about a single one of them killed.' Extermination, however, was not to be conducted on anyone's personal initiative. Admittedly, Taäubner had to be given credit for 'considering himself entitled to take a personal share in the annihilation of Jewry' and for his motive, which had been 'genuine hatred of Jews'. But this did not change the fact that he had acted without proper authority. Especially as in Aleksandriya he had allowed himself to get swept away 'into atrocities unworthy of a German and an SS leader'. Germans murdered cleanly.

More serious, however, were two other counts in the indictment. Täubner had in a letter advised his wife to get an abortion, and he had sent her several photographs of executions to impress her. In this he evidently succeeded, because his wife had proudly shown them to a number of friends. By so doing he had committed an offence against the official secrets regulations of the SS, and the court left no doubt about the weight it attached to this offence. 'As a result of being developed in Southern Germany,' it recorded, 'the photographs could easily have fallen into enemy hands and could have been used for enemy propaganda.' On 9 July 1943 the court therefore sentenced Max Täubner to ten years' imprisonment.

Täubner lodged an appeal with Heinrich Himmler: he was, he said, a fanatical Jew hater and had therefore determined, at the very beginning of the Russian campaign, to finish off 20,000 Jews. He had been convinced, in the case of the unauthorized executions he was charged with, of acting fully and entirely in the spirit of the Führer, and his deeds had been an unreserved commitment to Hitler's aims. I don't know whether Täubner's petition was successful. At any rate he served only two years of his sentence, then the war was over and he was released.

When I began to interest myself in his further fate I learned that in 1949 there had been proceedings against him before the criminal court in Memmingen in West Germany. The subject of the trial was the murder of Jews recorded in the SS verdict. It took the court exactly a year to drop the case: under the principle of *ne bis idem* it was not permissible for a man to be punished twice for the same offence. Yet the verdict of the court martial had clearly explained that Täubner was being punished not for the murder of Jews but only for acting without proper authority and for excesses in the execution of the murders. The most weighty count of the indictment, anyway, had been his breach of secrecy.

I therefore addressed a lengthy account of facts to the Central Office for the investigation of Nazi crimes in Ludwigsburg, to Senior Public Prosecutor Dr Ludolf at the provincial court Munich I, and to the court in Memmingen. I demanded that all three authorities should reopen the case because the principle of *ne bis idem* had been wrongly applied. After all, this was a matter of something like a thousand Jews. It could not be right that the only punishment for such a crime was two years in prison, which in any case had been imposed largely for forbidden photographs and encouragement to abortion. Evidently my arguments were regarded as running counter to logic, as none of the three authorities could see its way to reopening the case.

We next tried a roundabout route: I laid a criminal charge at the Stuttgart public prosecutor's office against Täubner's accomplice, Rudolf Nikolaus Wüstholz, who, according to the verdict of the court martial, had incited Jews to kill one another. First Public Prosecutor Rolf Sichting, who had detailed knowledge of the case, prepared the indictment most meticulously and passed it on to the provincial court in Heilbronn. There, in April 1973, proceedings actually began. Wüstholz, as usual, was produced as a free person and, as usual, he couldn't understand at all why he was being charged with that business 'after thirty-three years'. He only had the vaguest recollection of events at that time, and he only once roused himself from his lethargy when his former superior officer, Max Täubner, entered the courtroom to give evidence as a witness.

'Wüstholz is sitting there as if he'd come to the wrong wedding,' the journalist Gudrun Weiss, who sat next to me on the public bench, whispered. And it really was an absurd spectacle: the man who obeyed an order to commit murder was in the dock, while the man who had given the order was now giving evidence as a free citizen. (And, needless to say, because of wartime injuries he now had gaps in his memory which he was unable to fill.)

The result of this legal farce was that Wüstholz was sentenced on 24 May 1973 to two years' imprisonment. His counsel, Dr Albert Vogel, appealed, but the appeal was rejected by the federal court in 1975. Dr Vogel then tried a petition for clemency, and to that end also turned to me with the request that I support Wüstholz. Punishment, he argued, was surely pointless several decades after the deed; prior to the war Wüstholz had never done anything wrong, and since the war he had 'led an honest and unimpeachable life'. Only because he was drafted to Täubner's unit at the time had he been involved in actions which were not in his character at all. I did not answer the letter. It is not in my power to forgive Wüstholz on behalf of the people who met their death through him. But I well understood the unease which the judge, and also Dr Vogel, felt during that trial. It is depressing to see the small fry in jail while the big fish get away.

34

Himmler's Chief Legal Adviser

The trial of Rudolf Wüstholz continued to interest me for another reason too. There was another witness, whom I would like to talk about here separately: Heinrich Himmler's former chief legal adviser and today an attorney in West Germany, SS Oberführer Horst Bender. He was called as a witness because, on Himmler's behalf, he had made available to the SS court martial in Munich on 26 October 1942 a document which covered the legal assessment of the shooting of Jews without orders or authority. I quote verbatim: '(1) In the case of purely political motives [for the murder of Jews] there shall be no punishment, unless the maintenance of order calls for one. In that event there can be either conviction by a court under Section 92 or Section 149 of the Military Criminal Code, or disciplinary punishment. (2) In the case of self-seeking or sadistic, or sexual, motives [for the murder of Jews] there shall be punishment by a court, in certain instances also for murder or manslaughter.'

It was this order by Heinrich Himmler that the court martial made the basis for its decision against Maz Täubner, and in the trial of Rudolf Wüstholz Dr Bender was asked to explain how Himmler had come to issue it. The court had before it, among other evidence, the notes which Bender had made for his report to Himmler. They revealed clearly that Himmler, not a lawyer himself, would sign only what Bender proposed to him. Personally, I would have imagined that Dr Bender, confronted after the war with his activity, would distance himself from it or argue that he tried to avoid something worse by stipulating in his draft that, under certain conditions at least, the murder of Jews was punishable. Common sense, if nothing else, should have suggested that kind of argument to Dr Bender. Yet in no way did he dissociate himself from what he had stated thirty-three years earlier. Anyone listening to him during the Heilbronn trial was bound to gain the impression that he still inclined to the legal opinion that the murder of Jews from 'political motives' was permissible.

To my mind this represented not only the objective but also the subjective facts of accessory to murder (in the legal sense), and on these lines I laid criminal charges against Horst Bender with the Central Office of the provincial judiciary in Ludwigsburg and with the prosecutor general of Baden-Württemberg. After all, Bender was thirty-seven in 1942, he was a lawyer, he was not acting under duress, and his offence was not subject to any statute of limitation. With the same justification I addressed myself to the Chamber of Lawyers in Stuttgart, requesting them to consider whether Himmler's legal adviser was a suitable member of the legal profession in a democratic state. The President of the SS Court in Munich, Dr Günther Reinecke, had had his licence as an attorney withdrawn after the war, and it was difficult to see therefore why the man on whose legal opinion Reinecke had based himself should go scot-free.

The Chamber of Lawyers, normally an institution which goes into action even when a lawyer behaves with unseemly rowdiness at a nightclub, declared itself not competent and referred me to the Ministry of Justice of Baden-Württemberg. The prosecutor general replied that he had passed on my criminal charge to the public prosecutor's office in Stuttgart for examination. (This is exactly what the Central office of the provincial judiciary had done with all the documents at its disposal.) The Stuttgart public prosecutor's office worked with unusual speed: it stopped proceedings against Bender without further investigation, on the grounds that there had already, in 1961, been proceedings against him with the same evidence and notes for his report, and that these proceedings had likewise been stopped.

I appealed against this to the prosecutor general, within the prescribed period: to my mind, I argued, Bender's recommendations represented a legalization of the murder of Jews, and I was unable to share the opinion of the prosecutor's office that he had practised his work as Himmler's adviser 'not to the disadvantage of the Jewish population in Germany or in the German-occupied territories'. After all, in October 1942 about half the Jewish population had still been alive, and the murder machine might well have undergone a certain slowing-down if there had been no order explicitly declaring the murder of Jews for 'political motives' exempt from punishment. SS men who, until then, might have believed that by killing a Jew they laid themselves open to punishment, and for that reason might practise a certain restraint, were told that this was not so. Finally I pointed out that neither in 1961 nor now had any attempt been made to examine Bender's general legal activity within the SS or to consider what other offences he may have been guilty of. The case excited a good deal of attention among the public, because of Bender's position in Himmler's immediate proximity: a number of lawyers and notaries did not wish to be members of the same Chamber of Lawyers as Bender and supported my complaint in writing and by word of mouth. We even made a last legal attempt: Frau Erna Birnbach accused Bender of the murder of her cousin Blauner through Obersturmführer Philipp Grimm at the Plaszów concentration camp. The shooting, Frau Birnbach pointed out, had taken place without orders, out of 'politically motivated' hatred of Jews. Whatever inhibitions Grimm may have had could not have come into effect because the Bender decree made him feel authorized to commit murder.

As expected, however, the public prosecutor's office dismissed the charge. Only Professor Robert Kempner, whom I had also consulted on this matter, succeeded with his arguments: the decision to stop proceedings should be rescinded because the Stuttgart prosecutor's office had not instituted sufficient investigations. So the Stuttgart prosecutor's office began new investigations – and again stopped proceedings. I once more appealed to Prosecutor General Weinmann, using the same arguments as in the earlier appeal. It was finally rejected by the Minister of Justice. Dr Horst Bender, chief legal adviser to Heinrich Himmler, continues to be an attorney in West Germany.

35

An Avenue in Berlin

One would have thought that people who were politically so utterly wrong in the past would display a certain reluctance to seek public office again, and that they would show even greater reserve when finding themselves, by some chance, confronted with the past.

But this is not so. An astonishing number of former party comrades have an irresistible need to hold public office again and to adorn themselves with new honours. They are met on the most unexpected occasions, but one may rest assured that their attitude will be the expected one – they will attempt to make Nazism seem harmless.

The following incident is of slight practical significance – it only involves a street name – but it reveals the world of ideas in which some people continue to move.

One of the many friends I have made through my work is Professor Hector Gouverneur, English interpreter to the president of Venezuela. For years we had only corresponded with one another, but in 1979 he visited me in Vienna and we were able to talk face to face.

On that occasion Gouverneur told me that in 1973 he had written to the mayor of Berlin, proposing that a street be named after Jesse Owens, the winner of four gold medals in the 1936 Olympic Games. My friend wanted to do something for coloured people against Nazi racism. After all, the black man Owens had managed to steal the show from Hitler's master race by winning the 100 metres, the 200 metres and the long jump, as well as a fourth gold medal in the 4×100-metre relay race.

Hitler, who had hoped for a demonstration of physical superiority by the Nordic race, was so irate that he refused to shake hands with the triumphant Olympic victor.

That was why, Hector Gouverneur's proposal explained, a street at the place where these games were held should be named after him. This would be a refutation of racism at an historic spot.

The proposal, however, was not taken up, even though Gouverneur had addressed himself also to the former mayor of Berlin, Willy Brandt, who was known to be receptive to such ideas. The authorities had passed the application from one desk to another, and nothing had come of it in the end.

I thought Gouverneur's idea good and meaningful. It is important to raise symbols. People often understand them better than a prolonged explanation. I also thought it important to show that Hitler's racism concerned not only the Jews, but that anti-Semitism was merely the extreme escalation of a general racism. This is why not only Jews but everybody should feel threatened by it.

I decided to consult with the German ambassador to Israel, Dr Klaus Schütz, who had himself been mayor of Berlin. Schütz suggested I write directly to the present mayor, Dr Dietrich Stobbe; he for his part would support my request by a letter.

But Stobbe's reply was a refusal: the regulations on naming streets stipulated that they could be named only after people who had been dead for no less than five years. Living persons were ruled out on principle. Only once had an exception been made to this rule – when, after the Berlin blockade, a Lucius-Clay-Platz was named after the joint initiator and organizer of the air bridge. For Owens, one could read between the lines, such an exception was not possible. He was not even dead yet but was living happily as a highly honoured citizen in Chicago. I couldn't really wish him dead merely to meet the Berlin rules for naming streets. Instead I notified the press and, as a result, a number of articles were published whose authors, like me, felt that Berlin might show itself a little less bureaucratic when an issue of fundamental symbolism was at stake.

Anyway, Owens went some way to satisfy the authorities: while I was still corresponding with Stobbe he died of lung cancer at the age of sixty-six. I seized this occasion for a renewed appeal to the Berlin municipality: they might pass a resolution to set aside the five-year rule and name a street – ideally the avenue leading up to the stadium – Jesse-Owens-Allee (Jesse Owens Avenue).

In 1983, ten years after my friend Gouverneur wrote his first letter, the matter was handed over to the district authority of Charlottenburg, which was in charge of street names. A few months later I received a letter from the new mayor of Berlin, the present Federal President Richard von Weizsäcker: it had been decided to make the exception and the renaming would be performed as soon as possible, on 11 March 1984, with an appropriate ceremony.

At the beginning of 1984 I was in Los Angeles and there talked to Mayor Tom Bradley, who had been a personal friend of the black sprinter, about Berlin's impending Jesse Owens Avenue. Bradley, in whose city the next Olympic Games were due to be held, thereupon requested the mayor of Berlin, which is twinned with Los Angeles, to invite him to the ceremony.

In vain. Neither Tom Bradley nor Hector Gouverneur nor myself was invited for 11 March. When, somewhat put out, I requested the new mayor of Berlin, Diepgen, for an explanation (von Weizsäcker had meanwhile become Federal President), he told me that the German Olympic Committee and not the Berlin city government had organized the festivities. The president of that committee was Willy Daume, who also delivered the commemorative oration. He used the occasion to turn the meaning of the renaming upside down: it was not correct, he informed an astonished audience, that Hitler did not wish to shake hands with Owens. What happened was that the previous day Hitler had shaken hands with a German woman athlete, and that had led to a complaint by the Belgian president of the International Olympic Committee: a handshake was against Olympic custom. The next day, therefore, Hitler had observed the rules and avoided shaking hands with the black American. No racism, just respect for Olympic practices.

I thereupon looked up the account of the scene as recorded by Hitler's neighbour on the dais, the erstwhile Reich Youth Leader and former Nazi party boss of Vienna, Baldur von Schirach, in his memoirs *Ich Glaubte an Hitler* ('I believed in Hitler'): 'The star of the 1936 Olympic Games was the sprinter Jesse Owens, a coloured American. When Hitler was in the stadium he would congratulate the victors in his box. When Jesse Owens had won the 100-metre event, Hitler said: 'The Americans should be ashamed of themselves to have Negroes win their medals for them. I won't shake hands with this Negro.' In vain did Jammer-Osten [the Reich Sports Leader] implore him to receive the hero of the Olympic Games in the interests of sport.'

I don't know what induced Willy Daume to come out with a version so totally at variance with the above account. Perhaps it was his Nazi party number 6098980.

36

Heil Hitler, Teacher

One thing that is perhaps even worse than a Nazi policeman or a Nazi lawyer let loose again on mankind, is a Nazi teacher once more let loose on young people. The problem was that there had been no profession with a higher percentage of Nazis: the majority of all teachers in the Third Reich were members of the Nazi party. Admittedly, a young teacher looking for a job simply had no other choice: without party membership he need not even apply. The Nazis were determined to bring up young people exclusively in their own ideas.

This high degree of infestation faced the education authorities in Germany and Austria with a virtually insoluble problem after the war. I recall a conversation with the provincial governor of Upper Austria, Dr Heinrich Glaser, who had himself spent a year in a concentration camp and who admitted to me: 'We must reopen the schools with Nazi teachers – or else we can't have any teaching at all. To have a supply of young teachers who are free from Nazi ideas will take a whole generation.' What happened therefore was typical of Austria: because they realized that the problem of Nazi teachers could not be satisfactorily solved, it was decided to make no differentiation at all – not even such differentiation as could easily have been made, for instance between party members and murderers. Thus, among the members of the 1st SS Infantry Brigade, which behind the front in the Soviet Union had massacred civilians – old men, women and children – there was a surprisingly large number of teachers. Most of these, when proceedings against them had been halted by the judiciary, went back to their occupation. Friedrich Peter, whom I have mentioned before and will again, became a provincial school inspector despite his past in the SS.

The Austrian school authorities even deliberately let a man continue in his job after he had been convicted of murder in Italy. I came across his story on the occasion of a lecture in Turin, when one of my audience, Vittorio Ovazza, told me with tears in his eyes about the fate of his family. His nephew Ettore, twenty at the time, had tried to find asylum in Switzerland, but had been expelled by train back to Italy, where he was seized by the SS. Presumably someone had forced him to betray the hiding place of his family: his parents, Riccardo and Nella Ovazza, and his fifteen-year-old sister Elena had found refuge in a place on Lake Maggiore, hoping that by means of their considerable wealth – they had converted all their belongings into money and jewelry – they would survive there. Instead they were shot by the SS in October 1943, along with a British prisoner-of-war, and then cremated in the central heating plant of a school at Intra near Verbania on Lake Maggiore.

In July 1955, SS Hauptsturmführer Gottfried Meir, born in 1911 in Weyr Feldkirchen in Carinthia, was charged with their murder and sentenced, *in absentia*, to life imprisonment. Meir, who was again living in Carinthia, appealed against the verdict through an Italian attorney, but the appeal was dismissed by the Supreme Court in Rome. The Italian authorities thereupon demanded Meir's extradition from Austria. As was to be expected, Austria did not comply with the extradition request because Meir was an Austrian citizen. True, proceedings against him were hurriedly instituted in Austria – and this is where this story really begins. The trial, which opened in Klagenfurt in 1957, ended, as did so many Nazi trials in Austria, with his acquittal. It may well be that the trial would have taken a different course if the prosecution witnesses had turned up in person from Italy. But they maintained that they had never been notified. The acquitted Meir, member of the SS Leibstandarte Adolf Hitler (the unit of which Walter Reder, too, had been a member), left the courtroom a free man and has since been headmaster of the village school of Tonfeld near Wölfnitz.

As Vittorio Ovazza had given me power of attorney to take every step on his behalf that might serve the interest of his murdered family, I first of all got in touch with the Ministry of Justice in order to have the limitation on the case suspended. (At that time Austria still had a twenty-year statute of limitation for murder.) Next I approached the then Minister of Education, Dr Piffl-Percevic, and inquired how he could justify a situation where a man validly convicted of murder in Italy was educating schoolchildren in Austria. The minister replied that he was 'not happy about the case' – even

I never suspected that he would be – but that authority in this matter lay solely with the provincial education board in Carinthia. The national executive of Socialist Freedom Fighters, whom I contacted, thereupon appealed to this board. I don't know if anyone is now happy about the Meir case, but the SS officer continued as headmaster.

I therefore set out to collect 'new evidence'. A clue was provided by the Italian verdict which named a witness called 'Peter', who appears to have worked as an interpreter and in that capacity had been present at the execution of the Ovazza family. We discovered that this Peter's surname was Zorzi and that he had not, as assumed, been killed in action in Russia but was living in Vienna. He was thereupon questioned by the police and made a statement to the effect that he had helped to incinerate the bodies in the central heating plant of the school in Intra. This restrained statement begins to make sense in the light of the statement of another witness, the SS leader Fetzer from Hanover, made before the Osnabrück court. Fetzer, a company comrade of Meir's, there stated that Gottfried Meir had given the order for the Ovazza family to be shot and that Peter Zorzi had participated in the shooting.

With this incriminating evidence in my hands I requested an urgent audience with Minister of Justice Broda, submitted to him my power of attorney from Vittorio Ovazza and the incriminating testimonies, and asked him to inform me of any further steps taken by him. I never received any such information.

37

'This is the Punishment for the Children of Warsaw'

Austrians accounted for only 8 per cent of the population of the Third Reich, yet Nazis from Austria were responsible for half of the murders of Jews committed under Hitler. There were two major reasons for this. For one thing, anti-Semitism in Austria was substantially stronger than in Germany, and more people, in consequence, had the psychological make-up required for cooperation in the extermination of the Jews. For another, Adolf Eichmann came from Linz. Although he was born in Solingen in Germany, he had come to Austria with his family at the age of four. There he acquired his anti-Semitism, and there he had friends and acquaintances. Thus, when he was chosen by Hitler to organize the murder of the Jews it was natural for him to invite Austrians into leading positions in his organization, and these in turn surrounded themselves with Austrian helpers.

One of these leading functionaries in the murder of the Jews was the Carinthian Odilo Globocnik. Initially Nazi party chief of Vienna, he subsequently, as SS police chief of Lublin, was in command of Operation Reinhard, the programme for the extermination of the Jews which, after Reinhard Heydrich's death, was given this name in his honour. His assistants once more were Austrians: Hermann Höffle from Salzburg, in charge of Operation Reinhard as its chief of staff, and Globocnik's personal ADC Ernst Lerch from Klagenfurt, who figured at one time as acting chief of staff and at another as Globocnik's closest confidant and number two. In addition, there were another sixty-three

Austrians (whose names are known) who were active in Operation Reinhard.

Globocnik himself committed suicide in jail in Villach in 1945, but his assistants Höffle and Lerch remained virtually untouched until the Eichmann trial. It was only in the course of this trial that their role emerged more clearly and the judiciary, which had been soft on Nazis throughout twelve years of the Cold War, had to take some action against these men, who time and again had been mentioned in Eichmann's evidence. Even Austria's judiciary could not avoid going into action after the Austrian observers at the Eichmann trial, Dr Wiesinger, a senior police officer, and Leo Meier, had made a preliminary report to the Ministry of the Interior on the basis of interrogations by the Israeli police. In January 1961 Hermann Höffle was arrested in Salzburg.

A mechanic by trade, Höffle had joined the (then still illegal) Nazi party at the age of twenty-two. On 1 February 1937 he was appointed leader of SS Sturmbann I/76. His first action was the Kristallnacht (the Night of Shattered Glass). This so impressed Eichmann that he recommended him to Globocnik. Trained at the officers' school in Dachau, he first commanded a few smaller forced-labour camps and in the late summer of 1942 was dispatched to Warsaw. But the list of his crimes starts even before Operation Reinhard. From the office of the SS police chief of Lublin he conducted the 'expatriation' of Jews from Mielec and Rzeszów prior to being responsible, from Lublin, for the deportation of 310,000 Jews from Warsaw to Treblinka, Sobibor, Belzec and Majdanek. When he was chief of staff of Operation Reinhard the number of dead he was responsible for exceeded the two million mark. In the hierarchy of the Nazi crime syndicate he ranks equal with Globocnik, immediately below Adolf Eichmann.

All this I imparted to the Austrian Ministry of Justice and to the Vienna public prosecutor's office, in prolonged conversations, in order to make them see that the Höffle trial would be the second biggest of all – after that of Eichmann. Newspapers throughout the world would report on it, and Austria's judiciary should therefore make a special effort in order not to look foolish. In view of Höffle's vast range of activities there was a relatively large number of witnesses. From Israel we received the names of fourteen Viennese Jews who had survived deportation to Majdanek and could give evidence on Höffle's activities. In all, according to my calculations, 8400 Viennese Jews had been taken, in seven deportation transports, via Izbica and Diepol, to Majdanek, and there killed.

We also got in touch with the archives of the Polish underground movement in London, under the control of General Pelczyński, and received copies of reports made, at the time of the crimes, by Polish resistance fighters and sent to London by couriers. Everywhere Hermann

Höffle emerged as a key figure in the deportation of the Jews from Warsaw. A survivor from Warsaw, Alfred Zimmermann, now living in St Louis, Missouri, described Höffle's 'work' as follows: 'On 18 July 1942 Höffle marched into the Warsaw ghetto at the head of a squad who started to pick up children. Children who ran away were fired at with machine guns. This went on for three days. Some time later streets were blocked off on Höffle's orders and the Jews were given five minutes to get ready. Anyone taking longer was shot; the rest were taken to Treblinka.' There they were not shot but gassed.

Höffle knew what he was doing. But there were at least moments when his suppressed conscience broke through. One of his subordinates, Michalsen, giving evidence in West Germany, stated that Höffle, shattered by the death of his two children (twins who died from a disease) burst out at their graveside: 'This is the punishment for the children of Warsaw!' But the following day he resumed his merciless business as firmly as ever.

I don't know to what extent absolutely unscrupulous murderers existed, the kind who are never haunted, even for a fraction of a second, by such thoughts. I am inclined to believe that in most of them some residual conscience continued to exist under a heavy armour of ruthlessness, that they quite simply could not afford to give way to a sudden urge of conscience – for how was one to continue living when one suddenly realized that one had murdered hundreds of thousands of innocent human beings? Men like Höffle, therefore, in a manner of speaking, anaesthetized their conscience: they pretended to be doing nothing other than obeying the Führer's orders to cleanse the world of a plague. With each murder they committed the armour round their consciences grew thicker, until they became inwardly extinct and consisted of nothing but that armour. To me, at any rate, this is the only explanation of the fact that so few of these mass murderers were overtaken by their consciences even after the war, when they had time for reflection.

Nor, for that matter, was Höffle. When he was arrested by the Americans and taken to the Glasenbach camp near Salzburg, he acted like any other criminal trying to escape justice. He claimed that he was being mistaken for an SS Gruppenführer called Hermann Höfle, who actually existed, but who was his senior by fourteen years and had been executed in Czechoslovakia. He tried the same trick again when he was arrested in 1961 and immediately gained the support of *Salzburger Volksblatt* with a front-page story headed 'He Has to Suffer for his Namesake'.

On 21 November the examining judge of the Salzburg provincial court sent a comprehensive account of the case to the competent court: Höffle was under suspicion, as chief of staff for the SS and police chief Odilo Globocnik, of having collaborated in the forcible deportation of hundreds of thousands of Jews to the extermination camps of Treblinka, Sobibor, Belzec and Majdanek. In addition, he had personally and with full responsibility directed the deportation of the Warsaw ghetto to the Treblinka extermination camp.

To this end Höffle had on 22 July 1942 summoned the Jewish Council and issued orders for all Jews resident in Warsaw to present themselves at assembly points. Only the members of the Jewish Council, their Jewish staff, as well as Jews needed at the hospital or in German enterprises were exempted. Cyncially, as always, the Jews were invited to take with them food for three days, as well as baggage up to fifteen kilograms and, in particular, their valuables. These were immediately taken from them at the extermination camps and dispatched by the truckload to Berlin, unless of course they were stolen by the camp guards.

Every day, the Jewish Council was instructed, 6000 Jews had to present themselves at the shipment point. Anyone resisting or refusing was to be shot out of hand. The operation ran until 6 October 1942. By that date the population of the Warsaw ghetto had been reduced by 310,000. There is no precise breakdown on how many were shot and how many gassed. Höffle personally took part in the shootings. He himself on 5 November 1943 recorded his participation in the operation 'Harvest Festival', a mass shooting in the district of Lublin with the following note: 'Result of Harvest Festival 15,000'. Against this figure the 4674 Poles killed in the same area as part of a resettlement operation represent almost a negligible quantity.

Höffle's comment on the charges against him runs as follows: 'The clear-out operation, at least so long as I was in command ... proceeded entirely smoothly, unbloodily and humanely. I saw no atrocities of any kind against the Jewish persons to be evacuated, let alone murders ... Not only did I not commit any atrocities myself ... but I did not witness atrocities or murders by other members of the SS. Nor did I hear of any such actions, not even as a rumour. If nevertheless ... atrocities or even murders were committed against Jewish persons, then this was done without my knowledge and against my orders, and so secretly that it remained hidden from me.' Nor did he realize 'that the Jewish persons to be evacuated' were earmarked 'for death in the extermination camps'. That such extermination camps existed had 'neither been disclosed [to him] by superiors nor reported by subordinates'. These camps had not even 'existed in the rumours which came to [his] ears'. As for gassings and shootings, he, Höffle, chief of staff of Operation Reinhard, had only learned of them from the press after the war. Perhaps in connection with the Eichmann trial: on 31 May 1960 Eichmann told his interrogator, the Israeli police captain Avner Less, that in the summer of 1942, when he was visiting Lublin, he had been conducted by Höffle through the extermination camps to form a picture for himself of their operation.

In all the Höffle file eventually covered eighteen volumes, each of them of about 500 pages. The number of victims of Operation Reinhard and of the Treblinka, Belzec, Sobibor and Majdanek extermination camps assigned to it was then estimated at one and a half million; present estimates tend to put it at over two million. I had certain doubts – I believe, justified doubts – that the Salzburg prosecutor's office would be up to a trial of such magnitude. Even more I feared the Salzburg climate: Austria's reputation would suffer irremediable damage if a Salzburg jury were to react to this murder of millions of people with an acquittal.

At the beginning of December 1961 I therefore called Dr Warbinek in the Ministry of Justice in Vienna, requesting him to have the Höffle case delegated from Salzburg to Vienna, considering that there were in Vienna two public prosecutors with a training in contemporary history and an intimate acquaintance with the field of Nazi crimes, Dr Coca and Dr Breycha. The Salzburg public prosecutor and the Salzburg investigating judge thought on much the same lines; they stated that they would collapse under the weight of the documents. But Minister of Justice Christian Broda was against any such delegation. His attitude only changed when it transpired that Höffle was enjoying countless privileges while in detention in Salzburg. He was allowed repeated visits from his old comrades, who conferred on how they might help their former chief. Apart from Jürgen Lassmann and Reinhard von Mohrenschild we were also given the name of a visitor called 'Aunt Berta', who in reality was Höffle's personal secretary in Lublin and Warsaw, Berta Gottschalk. When she was questioned by the authorities she said exactly what Höffle wanted to hear: she knew nothing about the deportation of Jews, any more than she did about their further fate. So the file went to Vienna after all. The Ministry of Justice nominated Public Prosecutor Dr Coca to handle the case.

One day I was talking to the president of the Salzburg Jewish community, Hermann Einzinger, when the conversation turned to the Höffle case. 'A good thing,' I remarked, 'that Höffle will now be facing trial in Vienna.'

'What do you mean?' Einzinger asked in surprise. 'Surely he continues to be held in Salzburg.'

At first I couldn't believe it, but it really was true: the file had been transferred to Vienna, but the 'enclosure', Höffle, had been overlooked. I approached the chief of the Vienna prosecutor's office, Court Counsellor Mayer-Maly, and he questioned Public Prosecutor Dr Coca as to how this oversight could have occurred. Coca's answer is typical of the conditions in which the trials of Nazis were prepared in Austria: he had been so swamped with work that he hadn't got round to questioning Höffle in person. He therefore hadn't missed him. Only then was Höffle moved to Vienna.

On 20 August 1962, ten weeks after his transfer, he hanged himself in his solitary cell. Maybe a spark of conscience had, for the second time in his life, broken through the armour of coldness which two million dead had built around his awareness. However, this confession of guilt on Höffle's part failed to break through the armour of indifference which, here and there, the Austrian judiciary was showing towards the great slaughter in Poland. Instead of being convicted for Operation Reinhard, this operation unequalled even against the background of the extermination of the Jews, Höffle's 'twin' in the operation, Ernst Lerch, formerly personal ADC to Odilo Globocnik, is presumably to this day living the life, in Klagenfurt on the Wörthersee, of a respected elderly gentleman.

38

A Café in Klagenfurt

SS Sturmbannführer Ernst Lerch, Globocnik's ADC and for a time also his chief of staff, is a colourful personality. In 1932 he was a waiter in Paris and there, in a German club, came into contact with Nazis. In 1934 he returned to his native Klagenfurt and joined the illegal SS. As he had made a little money he was in a position to open a café, which became a meeting place for Carinthian illegal Nazis. This is how he made the acquaintance of Franz Kutschera, Ernst Kaltenbrunner and, more particularly, Odilo Globocnik. As early as 1936, while still an 'illegal', he was made an Obergruppenführer for his merits and put in charge of the Carinthian illegal security service. In 1938, after the Anschluss, came the decisive leap forward: Lerch became SS Haupsturmführer in the Reich Security Directorate in Berlin. At his marriage to a Gestapo employee, Helmut Pohl and Odilo Globocnik acted as witnesses.

Globocnik had originally been Nazi party chief of Vienna; after the invasion of Poland, when he was made an SS Gruppenführer and appointed SS police chief for the Lublin district, he sent for his friend Lerch and made him his personal ADC and chief of staff of the Lublin SS. Following the Wannsee conference in 1942 this office had but a single task: the implementation of the 'final solution'.

That January construction was begun on the Treblinka, Belzec, Sobibor and Majdanek concentration camps. After that Globocnik, in close cooperation with the Reich Security Directorate, made sure he was supplied with suitable command personnel, preferably men with experience of euthanasia institutions. Thus Franz Stangl, following his 'training' at the euthanasia institution Schloss Hartheim, became commandant of Treblinka, his Hartheim colleague Franz Wagner became deputy commandant of Sobibor. Experience gained at Hartheim, Hadamar, Grafenegg or Sonnenberg was directly applied to the extermination camps: in connection with the euthanasia killings of the mentally disturbed or the disabled it had been found that gas was the most suitable method for killing the maximum number of persons in the minimum time. Experiments were still going on with regard to the type of gas. Thus the gas chambers of Belzec were initially fed with the exhaust gases of marine diesel engines, but these repeatedly broke down in Poland's low temperatures, so that 'production hold-ups' arose. Only the employment of Cyclon-B solved all problems, and the murder machine then operated at full revs.

Always assuming that enough material was fed in. The deportation of Jews to the extermination camps was a major logistical problem. After all, there was a war on, and rail tracks and roads, rolling stock and lorries were needed for the Russian campaign. It was necessary to deprive the fighting forces of some of their capacity in order to utilize it for the murder of the Jews. The staff planning of these extermination transports was the task of the Austrian Franz Novak, who, as 'stationmaster of death' was eventually sentenced in Vienna to nine years' imprisonment, of which he served all of six. In the Lublin district the control of these trains was in the hands of Ernst Lerch, who had been entrusted, by Globocnik's letter of 15 May 1941, with the department of Jewish affairs for the region.

But, needless to say, Ernst Lerch knew nothing about the murder of the Jews, any more than Hermann Höffle did. When his name kept cropping up in German trials in connection with Operation Reinhard and when members of a German special commission questioned him in Klagenfurt, he could not remember anything – except that no wrong was done under his command. The prosecutors from West Germany were mystified to find Lerch a free man. 'When will his trial be taking place?' they asked me; 'in Germany people with half his crimes to answer for were convicted long ago.' I could only shrug.

In 1964 there was a personnel reshuffle in the Ministry of the Interior. The new chief of the state police was Herr Straka, who had spent the war in exile and later became security director of Carinthia. Straka therefore knew of the crimes Lerch was charged with and drew the attention of his party colleague Hans Sima, the socialist provincial governor, to Lerch's case. At least, Straka suggested, prominent Socialist Party members should avoid the Café Lerch. But Sima remained just as unimpressed as his party colleagues: The Café Lerch – where an unsuspecting young man, Udo Beckelmann, played the piano before he became, as Udo Jürgens, one of the most popular entertainers in the German-speaking countries – continued to be the meeting place of the red VIPs just as, prior to 1938, it had been that of the brown VIPs.

It can well be imagined that in this climate the proceedings against Lerch only made very slow progress. I therefore intervened once more with the Ministry of Justice, and in 1971 the file was in fact delegated to Vienna. Legally Lerch's vital contribution to mass murder was assessed as 'remote accessory to murder', because in the view of the authorities Lerch had 'only' been a so-called desk murderer. This figment, however, collapsed when one of Lerch's subordinates, the SS leader Hermann Worthoff, senior police officer and chief of the Gestapo in Lublin, stated in evidence during a trial in Germany that Lerch, as ranking officer, had overseen the liquidation of thousands of Jews from the Majdan-Tatarski ghetto in a wood near Krepiec. After this testimony the Klagenfurt café owner was finally arrested. However, his counsel filed an objection with the Supreme Court to the transfer of the case to Vienna, and this was upheld: the 'Klagenfurt climate' was not envisaged in the criminal code as a reason to transfer proceedings. The case, therefore, was returned to Klagenfurt, and the first action of the Klagenfurt judiciary was to release Lerch.

The trial opened on 15 May 1972. Like Höffle – and indeed like nearly all Nazis in virtually all their trials – Lerch denied everything: he had done nothing and he had known nothing; besides it must be a case of mistaken identity. Helmut Pohl, seventy and hard of hearing, did not bother even to understand most of the prosecutor's questions, let alone to answer them. All important evidence incriminating Lerch was only read out: the witness Runhof stated that Lerch was, after Globocnik, the second highest SS officer and as such was of course directly involved in all the actions of his superior. SS Oberscharführer Mantke recalled a 'Jew operation' near Lublin and was certain that the order for it had come from Lerch. A string of witnesses accused Lerch of mass executions in connection with the clearing out of the Polish ghetto in Lublin and with the so-called 'Harvest Festival'.

Lerch did not deny that these actions had taken place – but he personally had had no part in them whatever. The principal prosecution witness, a certain Richard Türk, who was to have appeared in the box on 18 May, was prevented from appearing by illness. The few witnesses from the ranks of the SS who gave evidence in person in Klagenfurt had only known Lerch slightly and knew nothing about him.

The public prosecutor realized that these proceedings in Klagenfurt would end in acquittal unless personal testimonies were finally brought in instead of read affidavits. On 18 May 1972 the trial was suspended and adjourned *sine die*. The president of the court, Dr Kugler, wished to use the legal assistance procedure for once more specifically questioning the witnesses Türk and Worthoff, who were then facing trial in Wiesbaden for participation in the mass liquidation of Jews. Thereafter the case against Lerch was to be resumed. To this day that has yet to happen.

After I had received repeated queries from abroad I inquired about this from Prosecutor General Dr Marschall, who promised me to make inquiries in Klagenfurt. Without success. So I requested Major-General Albert Guérisse, the president of the Internationale de la Résistance, to intervene with the Ministry of Justice – among the victims of Operation Reinhard were citizens of several European countries, so that retribution for their deaths must be seen as a European matter. The Ministry of Justice left unanswered the letter from the Internationale de la Résistance. I finally asked my friend Hermann Langbein, the secretary of the International Camp Community, to call on Minister of Justice Dr Broda. He was informed that the Lerch case had long been closed. Christian Broda, a former Communist and fierce opponent of the Nazis, was now implementing a silent amnesty for Austrian Nazi criminals.

39

A Shrug by the Minister of Justice

As I write this book Austria is being swept by a veritable wave of scandals. There is a public prosecutor who made common cause with a cheat, a judge who released people under detention in return for money, the director of an insurance company who defrauded his firm, a Minister of Construction who dipped his fingers into the trade union chest, a Minister of Finance who gave false evidence; there was the scandal of the Vienna General Hospital, where thieving went on right and left, of the freighter *Lucona*, which allegedly had been blown up, and of the state-owned armaments firm Noricum which broke all laws by supplying heavy guns to Iran.

Stricken with the Waldheim affair and branded as inhabitants of a 'scandal republic', Austrians are beginning to reflect on how this has come about. Although they arrive at the most varied conclusions, they all agree on one thing: a crucial contribution was made by the long-term Minister of Justice in the Kreisky government, Christian Broda. The periodical *profil* carried lengthy accounts of criminal proceedings in the border area between economics and politics, which had been brazenly dropped during the Broda era. The more dramatic and politically explosive the cases were, the less anxious was the prosecuting authority to discharge its task of uncovering crimes and convicting the criminals.

Many Austrians, especially socialists, who esteemed Broda for his humanitarian efforts in reforming criminal law, for years closed their eyes to his attitude – and I cannot understand it myself. As a Communist, Broda belonged to a resistance group during the war. The group was arrested and all its members were accused of high treason. Broda alone got away with his life, and after a few weeks regained his freedom. After the war he displayed astonishing leniency towards Nazi criminals. 'These people should have been executed immediately, in the first few years after the war, in one great purge,' he used to say when among friends, 'but now there's got to be peace.' When the journal *Forum* revealed that a considerable number of hanging judges and hanging prosecutors continued to serve in the Austrian judiciary, Broda publicly took sides with those under attack – who, incidentally, included the public prosecutor who had at one time acted against him.

This was Broda's spirit in all criminal proceedings against presumed Nazi criminals: from hundreds of cases which, at the beginning of the 1970s, were dropped on his instructions, I should like to pick out only one – not an especially significant case but one which illustrates how much better the West German judiciary was operating than the Austrian. In February 1980 a young man by the name of Vadim Meniker turned up at my office: he had been sent to Vienna by the Jewish Agency to look after Jewish émigrés from the Soviet Union who wished to go to Israel via Vienna. Meniker, himself a Soviet émigré, had known my name while still in the Soviet Union, because I was repeatedly and viciously being attacked there by various papers and for a variety of reasons. That earned me his sympathies, and he wished to meet me. As one does not often meet people who during the war lived in the German-occupied part of the Soviet Union, I seized this opportunity to put my usual question to Meniker on how he had managed to survive.

This is the story he told me. He was still a child at the time and suffering from tuberculosis. To cure him they had taken him to a sanatorium by the name of Yeshil-Adda in Yalta in the Crimea. In August 1941, two months after the German surprise attack against the Soviet Union, he had been moved from there to another sanatorium in the Teberda river valley in the Caucasus. Teberda was an idyllic spot which served as a water reservoir during the summer. From the windows of the sanatorium one could see the eternal snows on the Elbrus range. By then the hospital was becoming a refuge for no fewer than 1500 children evacuated from the sanatoria of Yalta and Evpatoriya, attended by 200 doctors and male and female nurses. The head physician was a Jewish woman doctor whose name was Dr Elizaveta Sheyman and who, judging by Meniker's account, was a woman as splendid as Adelheid Hautval, about whom Dr Lingens from Auschwitz had told me.

To begin with, the remote hospital with its young patients was safe. Even when the region was conquered by Romanian troops in the summer of 1942 there where no excesses – either against the children or against the local population. But then the Romanian troops were replaced by German troops.

It is, unfortunately, a fairy tale that the Wehrmacht managed to distance itself from the general murdering. A directive from the High Command of the German Armed Forces, dated October 1941, for instance, contained this passage: 'The soldier in the eastern territories is not only a warrior according to the rules of war, but also the exponent of a ruthless national ideology ... That is why the soldier must realize the necessity of hard but just vengeance against those subhumans, the Jews.'

The sixth Army under Field Marshal Erich von Manstein did realize this. Within a few days of the Germans' arrival in Teberda doctors and nurses who were Jews had to wear the Jewish star. Dr Sheyman, suspecting what was in store for her, tried to save at least the children entrusted to her care. She knew that among the patients there were fifty-four Jewish children and so she began, together with a nursing sister, to forge their medical records. Name and nationality were changed: dark-haired children became Romanians, fair Jewish children were turned by Dr Sheyman and her helper into Ukrainians and Russians. 'Myself, I was blond,' Vadim Meniker told me, 'so they made me a Ukrainian.' But then a Russian nurse, who was having an affair with a German soldier, noticed the changes in the records and told him about it. Thus everything had been in vain. It must be feared that Dr Sheyman, when she was shot along with all the other Jewish nursing staff, knew that her efforts had been to no avail.

A few days after the execution – time and again the children had been alarmed by the rifle salvoes – a big closed lorry arrived in the hospital yard. The three SS men who came with it went from ward to ward, collecting the Jewish children from their beds. Only Vadim Meniker and a young Jewish girl were overlooked. The remaining fifty-two Jewish children were driven out of the building and forced by kicks into the solidly built freight box of the gas truck, where they had to be piled on top of one another. Thus, as a package of small spasmodically jerking bodies, they died

In consequence of the Soviet offensive at Stalingrad the Germans had to withdraw from the Teberda valley again in February 1943. But it took another three weeks for the Soviets to march in to repossess the region against the furious resistance of the native Cherkess people. During the five months of the German occupation the sick children were cut off from all food supplies, because Field Marshal von Manstein adopted the attitude that 'the provisions given us by the fatherland must not, even if there are shortages, be distributed, through some misplaced sense of humanity, to prisoners or the population.' Five hundred children did not survive.

Meniker was among those who were saved. His father, who was employed at the Ministry of Food in Moscow, again held him in his arms at the beginning of March, after a long odyssey, having first had to discover where the children had been evacuated from the Crimea. It was David Meniker who had closely investigated the fate of the other children and told his son about it. 'He is seventy-five now and lives in Moscow,' Meniker told me. 'If he is needed as a witness he can be reached any time.'

On the strength of the data given me by Vadim I began to put two and two together. Caucasus 1942, after the invasion of German troops: at that time there were two Einsatzkommandos (special squads) in the region – special squad 12 and special squad 13. I got in touch with the Central Office for the investigation of Nazi crimes in Ludwigsburg and soon learned that my calculations had been correct: at the time in question special squad 12 had been in the Teberda valley. It was also known that part of the squad had been under the command of an SS Obersturmführer by the name of Weber, who, along with two other SS men, was held responsible for the killing of the children. Weber could not be found but his case was pending at the public prosecutor's office Munich I.

I made contact with Munich and was asked to send them Vadim Meniker's statement. At the same time I learned that the murder of the children had also been the subject of proceedings in the Soviet Union. Five statements by Russian witnesses were available to the Munich prosecutor's office. Moreover, two SS men, Alfred Maywald and Wilhelm Eder, had been on record, along with Weber, as fellow suspects ever since 1969. As Maywald, too, had not been found anywhere, investigations were now focusing on Eder – and he was an Austrian. In 1970 the German judiciary authorities handed over the entire material, complete with witnesses' statements on complicity, to the Austrian judiciary authorities.

In Austria preliminary investigations into Eder – whose membership in the notorious special squad was known about – had been running since 1963 under reference 15St25474/63. Such membership in itself made the person concerned guilty of multiple murder, as the sole task of these special squads had been the killing of Jews, Communists and gypsies behind the front. In this particular case, however, there were also testimonies from several Russian women referring expressly to these three men, who had worked as the gas truck crew in the Teberda valley. These testimonies had been recorded immediately after the war and submitted by the Russian prosecutor to the Nuremberg tribunal on the subject of 'special squads'. There was a high degree of probability that the witnesses – their names are Tolupanova, Zubenka, Musina, Makaeva, Strilyaeva, Khorolskaya and Kalinich – were still alive in 1970. Whether the Vienna prosecutor's office made any attempt to question them again in connection with Eder, I personally, knowing that office, would venture to doubt. The one thing that is certain is that proceedings against Eder were dropped. And this was not the only case. In all there were eighty-six Austrians, known by name, who had worked with various special squads, their work consisting everywhere solely of murder. Proceedings were started against sixty-five of them. The only one indicted, in 1963, was a Dr Schönpflug, who had served with special squad C; he was even found guilty and sentenced to twelve years' imprisonment. The case against Wilhelm Eder, who had likewise belonged to special squad C, appears to have been shelved as early as the 1960s. The new incriminating evidence from West Germany seems to have resulted in its being dropped for good.

As the statute of limitation for murder had not yet expired, and as I was now in possession of an important new piece of testimony and, moreover, could at any time obtain a second one – from David Meniker – I called on Department 11 of the Ministry of Justice and requested Prosecutor General Karl Marschall to resume the suspended proceedings against Eder. About the middle of 1980 the Vienna prosecutor's office notified me that Mr Meniker's testimony did not represent new evidence and that, in consequence, there were no grounds for resuming the proceedings.

For Wilhelm Eder, being under suspicion of murdering fifty-two innocent children had no damaging consequences. Throughout the investigations conducted against him he served, untroubled, as a police official in Wels, and on completion of twenty-five years of service received a commendation from the Austrian federal president for his loyal service to the republic. Included in those twenty-five years were also the seven years from 1938 to 1945, hence also the time when Eder was a member of a special squad in the Soviet Union, and therefore in the Teberda valley.

I don't know what went on inside Vadim Meniker's mind when I told him that the public prosecutor's office had seen no reason to resume proceedings against Wilhelm Eder. I don't think it was hatred that rose up in him – rather that boundless astonishment that grips us victims whenever we are confronted as a matter of course with the continued existence of our tormentors. He would like to see that man again, Meniker said. See what a person looked like who could live with the memory of having broken into a sanatorium in order to kill fifty-two children. See what he would do when confronted with one of the two victims who slipped through his fingers. I understand that wish, and for just that reason I didn't want to let Meniker go and see Eder in Wels on his own. It seemed to me best to have him accompanied by a journalist who could, on the one hand, record Eder's reactions and, on the other, restrain Meniker from any rash action.

But the conversation was entirely undramatic. When the journalist – Christian Ortner of *profil* broached the subject of the Caucasus, and more particularly the operation against the children's hospital, the old man had the frequently-heard standard reply pat: 'I only did my duty, I was behind the front, and that included fighting the partisans.' He had never had anything to do with sick children or Jews. And in view of the fact that equally horrible things were now happening in Kampuchea and Vietnam, and equally innocent people were being killed, he couldn't see why these ancient matters should be warmed up again.

Who could blame him? A year later I was a guest at the Alpbach European Forum, where the role of the judiciary in dealing with the past was to be discussed. Among those present was the former Austrian Minister of Justice, Dr Broda, who had meanwhile relinquished his office in favour of the liberal jurist Dr Ofner. I used the opportunity for explaining to him, quoting the Eder case, how incomprehensible the behaviour of the Austrian judiciary seemed to me. His reply was a shrug.

But in fairness to Christian Broda his attitude should be viewed in connection with the trend of his party: over the years the Socialist Party of Austria had become the principal apologist of former Nazis.

40

Kreisky's Brown Harvest

In 1945 the Socialist Party of Austria, under the impact of the newly ended war, resolved that no ex-Nazi should hold office in its organization. By 1970 four out of eleven ministers of the (single-party) Socialist government were former activists in the Nazi party, one of them an SS man. Between these two dates lay a development whose workings can be explained in one sentence: both major parties, the Socialists as much as the Christian Socials rallied in the (Conservative) Austrian People's Party, realized that support from ex-Nazis would be vital for any future majority. The party which attracted more Nazis to itself faster would have the majority in parliament.

Until 1966 the country was governed – as it is today – by a Grand Coalition. In it the Socialists – among other reasons because of the electoral law – were invariably the weakest partner. The party's ambition to make use of the ex-Nazis was therefore that much greater: only with their help could it hope to rise to the top. That was why, as early as 1947, it rescinded its ban on ex-Nazis in party office, so it should carry no unnecessary handicap in the race for the votes of the 660,000 registered Nazi party members plus their families. There were a number of things which ensured a very slight lead for the Socialists: first their (by and large) anti-Fascist past gave it somewhat greater freedom of action, while the Austrian People's Party would immediately be accused of representing a 'bourgeois bloc' the moment it moved closer to the Nazis. Secondly, the Socialists as a rule provided the Minister of the Interior, who, as supreme police chief, exercised considerable influence on how ex-Nazis were handled. Oskar

Helmer, in particular, used this position for making it clear to the guilty that they had least to fear from the Socialists. Moreover, there was a considerable shortage, among the Socialists, of people with a university education – owing to the Holocaust and to post-war emigration. But as the party had to fill a large number of posts simultaneously – in Austria all heavy industry and banking are nationalized and thus, in a manner of speaking, party property – they had a lack of suitable candidates. This led them, more often than the Austrian People's Party, to resort to ex-Nazis, who willingly changed their party allegiance in order once again to be driven about in an official Mercedes. The United Austrian Iron and Steel Works thus acquired a package of industrial managers who now served the relevant Socialist minister just as willingly as they once had the Führer. Well into the 1960s the Association of Socialist University Graduates, with its acronym BSA, was referred to by those in the know as the BSS.

While the two major parties were eagerly absorbing ex-Nazis willing to assimilate, the Old Faithfuls assembled in a party of their own, the 'Association of the Independent' from which subsequently the Liberal Party of Austria developed. The Association of the Independent was a virtually sterling Nazi Party – to speak of ex-Nazis would be a falsification of history. Practically all its top officials had been Nazi party members and quite a few of them had served prison sentences after the war, which the old comrades regarded as marks of honour. This group subsequently also provided the hard core of the Liberals. However, the generation of incriminated fathers has since been joined by the generation of non-incriminated sons and daughters. In later years some genuine liberals also strayed into this party, and from the camp of apolitical protest voters it gained further entrants, and this trend still persists. Nonetheless, a person's attitude towards the past continues to be the greatest common denominator. Admittedly, not every Liberal follower nowadays claims that, strictly speaking, the Allies are to blame for the Second World War, but they still object to 'the whole responsibility being put on German shoulders'. Admittedly, only the hard core still talks of the 'Auschwitz lie', but the view is generally held that 'the concentration camp victims simply raked in the restitution millions after the war'. Admittedly, it is now rarely disputed that war crimes were committed by the Germans, 'but one should not forget the Allied war crimes'. Whereas the Association of the Independent was in fact a continuation of the Nazi party under a new flag, the Liberals are a party which trims its sails to the wind, never forgetting that the mast is anchored in a brown base.

For the major parties, therefore, political collaboration with the Liberals was taboo. Although they did not officially attack that party as the catchment bowl of former Nazis (because they did not wish to offend their own former

Nazis), and although they occasionally made use of it in forcing their coalition partner to make concessions, a sharing of power in government was unthinkable. The Liberals were not fit to mix with polite society. It was one of Bruno Kreisky's historic achievements to have freed them from that ghetto and made them fit to govern. In the late 1970 elections, as is well known, the Socialist Party of Austria first achieved a relative majority. But instead of forming a coalition government with the Austrian People's Party, as had been expected, Kreisky caused negotiations to break down and formed a minority government which, to everybody's surprise, proved viable. In the crucial vote on the budget it was supported by the Liberals.

The price for this obliging vote was an electoral reform which made it easier for small parties, such as the Liberals, to get into parliament, while it became even more difficult for the large parties to achieve an absolute majority. True, Bruno Kreisky was to pull off this trick twice more, but under normal circumstances Austrian heads of government, unless they resort to the (in democratic terms questionable) option of a Grand Coalition, will always depend on the Liberal Party to swing the balance. A party whose most 'liberal' minister, Friedhelm Frischenschlager, brought back the war criminal Walter Reder with a handshake, thus gained a lasting influence on Austrian politics.

In 1970 a so-called small coalition of the Socialists with the Liberals would not have been possible – it would have foundered on the resistance of the (still powerful) anti-Fascist wing of the Socialist Party. Yet eight years later, when the Socialists had lost their absolute majority, a small coalition was no longer a problem for the Social Democrats: Bruno Kreisky had systematically demolished the opposition to former Nazis. A vital part of that policy had been his demonstration to Austrians that having been a member of the Nazi party was in no way a blot on one's escutcheon. Not even in the sense that having once been so disastrously wrong might stop a person from seeking positions of political power now – for didn't this suggest a lack of one of the most important prerequisites: political foresight?

At any rate, Bruno Kreisky straight away invited four Nazis into his first cabinet: Minister of the Interior Otto Rösch (Nazi party membership number 8595796), Minister of Construction Josef Moser (number 6269837), Minister of Transport Erwin Frühbauer (number 10033793) and Minister of Agriculture Hans Öllinger, who had actually risen to Untersturmführer in the SS. When even Austrian newspapers questioned Öllinger's appointment, Kreisky reacted as he always did in such situations. He did not reflect for a moment whether he might not in fact have made a political mistake, but instantly went on the offensive: instead of declaring – which would have been entirely possible – that he had been kept in the dark about Öllinger's past and that he would not have appointed him had he known about it, he stood squarely by his attacked Minister of Agriculture. Until it was proved that he had committed a crime, he should be permitted to hold any political office in Austria. Admittedly, Öllinger subsequently resigned 'on grounds of health', but Kreisky's remarks had already crucially changed the emotional climate. 'If even the Jew Kreisky takes the view that thirty years after the war one should no longer talk about SS membership,' more and more Austrians argued, 'then surely we too can adopt that view.' Öllinger's successor, appointed by Kreisky, was Oskar Weihs (Nazi party number 1089867).

In Austria only a few journalists were outraged by these events, but when *Der Spiegel*, using my researches, proved that no less than one-third of the Austrian federal government consisted of ex-Nazis, a storm of outrage swept through the world. In any other country it would have been inconceivable for even a Nazi sympathizer to hold even the meanest political post. In Holland a former NSB member could not even become the mayor of a village; a Quisling was proscribed in Norway as much as a Pétain follower was in France. Even in Italy, where Fascism used to have a considerable base and where quickly changing governments used up hundreds of politicians, no ex-Fascist ever rose to ministerial honours. Yet Austria expects the world to let her rank equal with these countries by declaring herself 'Hitler's first victim'. Four ex-Nazis out of eleven ministers cast the first shadow on this self-presentation – a long time before Waldheim. The irritation threshold had been exceeded as even Kreisky's friend Paul Lendvai put it in the *Financial Times*.

Kreisky's irritation threshold had also been exceeded. Not, however, with regard to the treatment of ex-Nazis, but with regard to me. The fact that he had made incriminated men ministers was not to blame for Austria's international reputation being in jeopardy – it was I who was to blame for informing *Der Spiegel*. Not his hobnobbing with Nazis, but my activity deserved to be condemned. To do this Kreisky chose the party congress of 11 June 1970, which was to have been proclaimed as the victory congress but was now in danger of being overshadowed by the affair of the Nazi ministers. Originally the Chancellor had hoped that Minister of Transport Otto Probst would launch the attack on me. Probst had himself been a prisoner in the Dachau and Buchenwald camps, and it would therefore have suited Kreisky's books if he, of all people, had let fly at me. But Probst declined. His task was taken over by another man who discharged it from an overfull heart: the then Socialist Party Central Secretary and future Minister, first of Education and later of Foreign Affairs, Leopold Gratz.

Gratz had attended the Napola Nazi elite school, and although I have always been careful to differentiate between youngsters sent to the Napola by their parents and adults who had voluntarily joined Nazi organizations, Gratz evidently felt personally attacked. Otherwise I cannot explain the emotions of this politician, normally fonder of the foil than the sword. 'How much longer will we tolerate this private organization for vengeance?' Gratz shouted into the hall, calling my documentation centre a private secret police whose spies were hunting innocent people. Bruno Kreisky entirely supported his central secretary and added a trend-setting statement: 'Even a Nazi party member or an SS man should be permitted to hold political office in Austria, so long as he has not had any crimes proved against him.' It never occurred to him that his and Gratz's statements were incompatible. 'Let us assume that Kreisky is right,' I tried in a conversation to provoke the reactions of journalists. 'In that case we should re-integrate the Nazis provided they have committed no crimes. But how do you discover whether they have or have not committed any crimes? Surely only by investigation – but this Herr Gratz objects to: in his eyes that is "the work of informers, spies and secret avengers".'

Although Gratz and Kreisky earned a lot of applause in Austria, mainly from the tabloid *Kronen-Zeitung*, they had clearly somewhat underrated foreign reaction. The international press, which had otherwise shown great respect for Kreisky, commented on his and Gratz's behaviour with outrage. Delegations of former victims of persecution protested in front of Austria's foreign missions, and I received quite a number of symbolic invitations, including one to luncheon in the US Senate and another to dinner at the House of Commons, with Winston Churchill's grandson acting as master of ceremonies for eighty invited guests. Countless letters encouraged me in my work and urged me not to be deterred by any kind of pressure. And yet the pressure exerted on me then was scarcely perceptible compared to what was to come my way in connection with the so-called 'Peter affair'.

41

The Peter Affair

It was the beginning of September 1975 and Austria was about to go to the ballot box for the Nationalrat, the Austrian parliament. I had just returned from a holiday and felt refreshed enough to tackle a job I had been putting off for weeks: tidying my desk. Only someone who has seen my desk can have an idea of what that means. As a rule there are two stacks of files on it, and tidying up means looking at each individual sheet and deciding whether to file it away or continue work on it. Some of the papers I would have looked at cursorily before and would now examine carefully, others would be new and I would try to sort them into their proper places. Others again might be ancient but could acquire new meaning in new contexts. One of my most important gifts, the one which enables me to conduct investigations as a one-man band where normally a whole team of experts would be needed, is an almost photographic memory and a skill, like a computer's, for rapidly making all kinds of cross-links. Sorting my papers is therefore one of my most laborious but, at the same time, one of my most creative activities. There is always an element of a treasure hunt about it, and I have hardly ever failed to come across something unexpected. Thus it was again this time.

Among the many papers I scanned was a list of SS Unterführer (junior leaders) due to go on an officers' training course. Those concerned were members of the notorious 1st SS Infantry Brigade, which earned itself a sorry reputation for its crimes in the Soviet Union. I ran my eye over the list of names and stopped about half-way down. 'Friedrich Peter,' it said there. That was the name of the then chairman of the Liberal Party of Austria.

I got my secretary to look up Peter's date of birth, and when it tallied with the list I knew that I was holding a bombshell in my hands. Like most insiders in Austrian politics I knew that Peter had been in the SS – except that the talk had always been of the Waffen-SS, which was essentially a fighting unit. Not until the end of the war was the Waffen-SS amalgamated with other SS units and involved in crimes, so that the International Military Tribunal in Nuremberg included it among the criminal organizations. During the earlier years of the war, on the other hand, a man belonging to the Waffen-SS as a rule had no more and no less to answer for than any other German soldier. Peter's membership of the Waffen-SS had never therefore induced me to make any particular investigations. Yet now his name was on a sheet of paper dating from 1942, describing him not as a member of the Waffen-SS but, even then, of the general SS. And the SS man Friedrich Peter had served not just in any SS unit, but in one of the most notorious murder brigades of the war.

A war diary of the 1st SS Infantry Brigade had been published, through some irony of fate, by the socialist Europa-Verlag publishing house in Vienna. It represented a collection of testimonies to continual mass murder: the brigade was operating behind the front, with orders to control the territory and to 'cleanse' it. This meant that any Jews or Communists the unit came across were dragged from their beds house by house, village by village, driven to the surrounding woods and shot. My friend Peter Michael Lingens was subsequently involved in a case in which it was laid down that it was permissible to refer to the brigade as a unit which, week after week, was engaged in the mass execution of civilians, including old men, women and children.

Among other things, the 5th company, to which Friedrich Peter belonged, was principally responsible for the massacre of Lelchitsy, described in a report by the headquarters staff as follows: 'On 4.9.41 Lelchitsy was reached by strong reconnaissance forces and captured. No losses were reported. Booty: 60 rifles, 11 machine guns, 15 hand grenades, 22,115 rounds of rifle ammunition; moreover 38 prisoners were taken and 1089 Jews shot.' The shootings took place a short distance from the village. The Jews had to dig deep pits and position themselves in front of them. In this manner they could be conveniently shot so they fell into their graves. In a criminal trial held in West Germany in connection with this massacre the witness Lawrenc described the conclusion of the operation as follows: 'As the men of my platoon rallied we passed a sandy hill in open ground, with a few SS leaders standing by it. I saw that behind it was a pit, which was partially covered with sand, and that the SS leaders were firing their pistols into the covered pit. I marched past with my group at a distance of a few metres and could see clearly that the piled-up sand was moving, moreover as if there was some life left underneath. I therefore had to assume that an execution had taken place at that spot. And that some victims had apparently been buried alive.'

That, roughly, was what the routine work of the 1st SS Infantry Brigade was like. As soon as it was involved in real fighting it failed lamentably, so much so that the commanding officers of the participating Wehrmacht units complained to the Commander-in-Chief East – only to receive in reply the following explanation: 'The Reichsführer of the SS [Himmler] desires that this SS unit, which was never intended as a fighting force or for frontline deployment, be treated by the General Command, in the event of faulty performance, with appropriate indulgence and understanding care . . .'

So much for characterization of the 1st SS Infantry Brigade. The characterization of Friedrich Peter includes the fact that he was decorated by that brigade. And, nevertheless, he had no compunctions about sitting in the Austrian parliament as a deputy of the Liberal Party or about being a candidate for the position of Vice-Chancellor of the republic. This was because it was generally expected that in the 1975 elections the Socialists would no longer win an absolute majority. In that event it was obvious that Kreisky would go into coalition with the Liberals, which would automatically make Friedrich Peter the second most important man in the state. I don't believe that one has to be a Jew or a Nazi victim to find this thought intolerable.

My first idea was to call a press conference to publicize the case at once. But then I remembered that I was living in Austria: I would be instantly accused of wishing to influence the elections to the disadvantage of the Socialists and Liberals and in favour of the Austrian People's Party. I therefore dismissed the idea of an immediate press conference and cast about for an alternative: I decided to inform the Austrian federal president. To this end I compiled a dossier which would characterize the brigade: a few daily entries from the war diary conveyed an adequate picture. This dossier I presented on 29 September 1975 to President Dr Rudolf Kirchschläger.

Kirchschläger read it was profound shock and thanked me for having passed it on to him first, and not having publicized it: this would ensure that people would vote on issues and not on the past of a politician. He had the dossier photocopied and sent both to Peter and to Kreisky. Ambassador Wilfried Gredler described their reaction in a chapter of his book *Österreich zuliebe* ('For Austria's Sake'): Peter had been rather shaken but Kreisky had even then declared that whatever Wiesenthal might have written was of no consequence to him. If he needed the Liberals to form a government he would call on them. In that case Friedrich Peter would become Vice-Chancellor and Wilfried Gredler Foreign Minister.

I have never followed an election with a greater feeling of suspense either before or since. I felt certain that Kirchschläger would not accept Peter as Vice-Chancellor, but I also suspected the outbreak of fury on Kreisky's part that this would entail. But the outcome was different. Kreisky just managed a hair's-breadth majority for his party and did not need the help of the Liberals. Peter's hopes of the Vice-Chancellorship had, for this time at least, been dashed. Henceforward he would 'only' be a member of parliament.

On 9 October I held a press conference at the Hotel de France and handed the journalists the material I had prepared. I also told them that I had handed the same dossier to the federal president before the elections, in order to prevent Peter's appointment in the event of the election results designating him for the Vice-Chancellorship. The radio's *Midday Journal* broadcast the explosive story, and during the next few hours my office scarcely coped with the copying of the documents – so many journalists were asking for the dossier.

Peter himself said little. He had, he explained, been just a soldier, he had neither seen shootings nor heard of them. If any had in fact taken place this must have been while he was on leave. Nor had any of his comrades ever told him anything about atrocities.

It ought to be pointed out that during the period that Peter served with the 1st SS Infantry Brigade no home leave was, as a matter of principle, granted from the eastern front, and that Friedrich Peter's company had been involved in shootings not just once but week after week.

Austrian television reported on the press conference on the evening of 9 October. Both Peter and I were invited to comment, but Peter would only give his comment over the telephone. It ran as before: 'I did not participate in operations of this nature, but did my duty as a soldier.'

It was not Peter, however, but Bruno Kreisky, who the following day, having returned to Vienna from a trip abroad, reacted publicly: in front of millions of television viewers he began to revile me viciously. My action was 'outrageous' and in truth directed only against himself. Friedrich Peter had merely served me as a pretext. Besides, he had known Friedrich Peter for many years and believed what that upright democrat had told him about his wartime past. Peter assured him that he was not guilty of any crimes whatever, and that assurance was enough for him. That Friedrich Peter had kept silent throughout about his membership of the 1st SS Infantry Brigade did not bother the Chancellor.

Peter Michael Lingens described the effect of Kreisky's intervention on the public in the periodical *profil*: 'On the morning after Simon Wiesenthal's revelations about Friedrich Peter's past I gave a lift to a craftsman I know. About fifty, an ex-serviceman, a Social Democrat, but not particularly interested in politics. I was the more surprised by his spontaneous reaction: "He can't tell me that those were military operations. A thousand dead on the enemy side and only two among our own men! After all, we were all in the army ... But he'll probably go now. He doesn't have to sit in parliament. He really doesn't need to."'

The following evening Bruno Kreisky took up the Peter case on television. When Lingens spoke to the same man the next morning, his opinion had veered round: 'One would really like to know why that Wiesenthal is raking all this up now; he'll really have to prove it.'

Lingens described this incident in such detail to demonstrate how the public attitude to the Peter case was balanced on a knife-edge. How unsure, malleable and changeable it was. Bruno Kreisky threw the whole weight of his personality on to the scales in order to turn public opinion in the direction which, in a sense, was the predictable one: 'There's got to be an end some time – and why is that man Wiesenthal still allowed to live here ... ?'

More that anyone else, this Jewish Chancellor, who had to flee from the Nazis and whose relations were murdered by the Nazis, set the definitive yardsticks by which the Austrian public measures its own past. He has set them for years ahead. And consistently: by breaking the taboo which had excluded the Liberal Party, as the catchment of ex-Nazis, from negotiations in forming a government; by consolidating his minority government after his 1970 electoral victory by a *de facto* pact with that party, and by inviting into that government more former Nazis than any Chancellor including Seyss-Inquart had before him; by fully supporting his short-term Minister of Agriculture Öllinger when it was discovered that he had belonged to an SS formation; by pointing out how Nazis and socialists had jointly suffered under the Dollfuss regime; by likening the detention camp of Wöllersdorf, set up by the pre-war Austrian corporate state, a camp where the political detainees played football, went for walks and received visitors, to the extermination camps of the Third Reich; and now by regarding Friedrich Peter's twenty months' service in a brigade engaged week after week in murder, as compatible with holding top political office.

What induced Kreisky to act like that would deserve a lengthy study of its own. What is certain is that he was successful: the mere fact that he publicly attributed to 'that Herr Wiesenthal' a 'Mafia' organization won him at least 100,000 votes. For what can be pleasanter than having a 'victim' confirm that which one had always thought: that to have been a Nazi was no greater a mistake than to have served the corporate state. That having been an SS man was merely a tragic turn of fate, on which one had no influence. That the extermination camps had in reality been neither so bad nor so unique: Auschwitz was just a bigger Wöllersdorf. And murder brigades were fighting units. The real culprit was someone else: Simon Wiesenthal, 'allegedly a graduate engineer'.

In point of fact the next six weeks were the worst time I have experienced since the war. I was a leper in my new home, and only the thought that I had survived even Hitler prevented me from emigrating. It should be realized that Bruno Kreisky exercised an absolutely magic attraction for the public. People looked up to him as to their father, emperor and god all rolled into one. Even critical intellectuals hung on the lips of the 'Sun King', as he was universally called, as though he were offering them a revelation. Austrian journalists, with very few exceptions, were eating out of his hand. Anyone else attacking me would certainly have reaped widespread applause: among the public I had the image of an implacable avenger who had some poor innocent little Nazi for breakfast every day. The guilty conscience, which inevitably gripped many Austrians as soon as they were reminded of the war, now turned, in accordance with a well-known psychological mechanism, into aggression against me, because I would not cease keeping that memory alive. But now I was being attacked not just by anybody but by Bruno Kreisky, who could say all the things which were normally said against me only by the extreme right-wing press – because he was immune by virtue of his Jewish birth.

Worse than Kreisky's frontal attacks, made almost daily in interviews, were the underhand attacks I mentioned earlier. Thus he would refer to me on principle as 'Herr Wiesenthal, allegedly a graduate engineer', suggesting that I was not quite entitled to my degree. His continuous references to the 'Mafia' and the 'Feme' (a secret association committing revenge murders) were garnished with the hint that it was surely time to establish by what right I was running my so-called office in Vienna. Even more sinister suspicions were disseminated by the Chancellor, initially between the lines of his interviews. Until, on 10 November 1975, he really ran amok at a press conference for foreign journalists: 'There is nothing I have in common with Herr Wiesenthal, nor must he arrogate any such thing to himself. You understand me? Herr Wiesenthal, I maintain, had a different relationship with the Gestapo from mine. Yes, there's proof. Can I say more? Everything else I shall say in court. My relationship with the Gestapo is unambiguous. I was its prisoner, its detainee. And I was interrogated. His relationship was different – I believe I know this. And it will be possible to determine it. Surely what I am saying here is bad enough; he won't be able to dust himself down with a libel action, as he intended. It won't be as simple as that; this is going to be a big case.'

Kreisky's remarks caused enormous outrage throughout the civilized world. The federal German public prosecutor Rolf Sichting, who had been in charge at Stuttgart of the trial against the guards of the concentration camps and the Lvov ghetto, and therefore knew the story of my life in detail, permitted the journal *profil* to quote him verbatim: 'The accusations against Simon Wiesenthal, that he was a collaborator of the Gestapo, are an infamy. I stand by this word, I will answer for it. No other word would be appropriate.'

The 'big case' with the Chancellor unfortunately never materialized. Although I took out an action against Kreisky, he enjoyed immunity as a member of parliament. And although he declared with a grand gesture that he would waive his immunity, he knew perfectly well that parliament would never approve such a waiver in connection with a defamation suit. That, in that case, he would 'set aside his parliamentary status' remained an empty promise.

Incidentally, the 'big case' likewise failed to materialize in the dispute between Friedrich Peter and me. Peter had been compelled by his party colleagues to sue me because I had stated that no proof was 'yet' available that he had committed murder in person. It followed therefore, Peter argued, that I thought him capable of such murders. The court thereupon accumulated endless evidence – all statements made during trials in Germany of members of the 1st SS Infantry Brigade were made available – and as the number of dead kept rising, the number of months which Peter spent serving with the 5th company steadily decreased: suddenly he claimed to have served with that unit not twenty but only fourteen months. In 1968, in a first interrogation of which we only then learned, it had still been twenty months, and in 1943, in his CV he had likewise referred to twenty months. Commenting on this discrepancy Peter's attorney Dr Brösigke, simultaneously also the attorney of the extreme right-wing paper *National- und Soldatenzeitung* and subsequently promoted to president of the Audit Office, observed: 'In that case Herr Peter simply made a mistake twice.'

When the number of persons murdered by Peter's brigade had, according to testimony before the court, reached 360,000, the case was adjourned. From time to time we submitted further documents to the court and otherwise waited for the next hearing. For seven years in all – until one day Friedrich Peter's attorney wrote to my attorney that Herr Peter wished to withdraw his suit against me: he was not interested in continuing the case.

This then was the Friedrich Peter whom Bruno Kreisky championed with the whole weight of his personality, whom he would have made Vice-Chancellor in his government, and in whom he saw not the slightest reason to remove him from parliament. Instead he wanted to see me removed from Austria, and for that won the applause not only of the tabloid *Kronen-Zeitung* but also of the German *National- und Soldatenzeitung*, which opined that his attacks against Wiesenthal would never be forgotten.

But that was evidently not enough for Kreisky. He also won over the last anti-Semites to his side. When a Dutch journalist ventured to point out to him that his remarks were apt to irritate his Jewish fellow citizens, Kreisky snapped at him: 'I have no Jewish fellow citizens, I know only Austrian compatriots.' When the Israeli journalist Zeev Barth pointed out that he was manoeuvring himself into a tricky situation by pretending that he did not belong to the Jewish people at all, the Chancellor lost his composure: 'The Jews aren't a people, and if they were a people then they are a repulsive one.' When *Der Spiegel* quoted this remark Kreisky reacted in a letter to the editor: as he did not regard the Jews as a people they could not therefore be a repulsive one.

That the Jews are not a people is one of Kreisky's favourite themes. He is fond of endlessly lecturing journalists, in particular, about it, and they are mostly too polite to interrupt him. Everything he was saying, he would claim, had long been scientifically proved, but the Jews would not have it so. Some time he might write a book about it . . . When the Israeli journalist Oberbaum, actually the last Israeli accepted by Kreisky, asked him how, as Federal Chancellor, as a Foreign Minister for many years, as a diplomat and a statesman, he could insult Israel, the Jewish people, Begin or me in this manner, Kreisky replied with endearing frankness: 'When I hear the names Begin or Wiesenthal I just can't restrain myself.' To Kreisky we are the same 'eastern Jews' that we are to many Viennese; he does not wish to have anything in common with us. It is bad enough for him to be connected with the Jewish people at all – but to be connected with us is intolerable.

I have often asked myself where Kreisky's rejection of all things Jewish came from: he must be the only Austrian Jew not to see himself as a Jew. I think the most accurate explanation is probably the one attempted by Peter Michael Lingens in *profil*: anti-Semitism in Austria is so strong that a sensitive child of Jewish origin has only two choices: either he resists that pressure by demonstratively avowing his Jewishness, even though by doing so he enters a kind of ghetto, or else he tries to evade that pressure by continually trying to prove to those around him that he is not really different from them. There have therefore always been prominent Jews, especially in Vienna, who tried to be more Austrian than the Austrians. And being an Austrian simply includes a pinch of anti-Semitism, which *vis-à-vis* 'eastern Jews' increases to almost physical aversion. A Jew striving for total assimilation must adopt that anti-Jewish attitude. When men like me remind Kreisky of his Jewish descent he feels accepted by them and, as it were, exposed. For this reason – and not, as he pretends, because of our political conflicts – he hates me.

That hatred went rather far: the leader of the parliamentary Socialist Party, Heinz Fischer, threatened quite openly to set up a parliamentary commission of inqury against me, to lay my evil activities before the public at long last. It should be understood that such commissions are provided for by the Constitution in order to examine controversial actions by state authorities, for instance a ministry. In Austria, needless to say, this instrument is hardly ever used because the political parties very rarely want anything examined. When, for instance, the former Minister of Finance Hannes Androsch ran an investigation against himself for tax evasion and instantly acquitted himself of this charge, the Socialists naturally refused to initiate a parliamentary investigation of that strange procedure. And even an extensive arms deal done by the state-owned industry with Iran, the kind which, as 'Irangate', kept a commission of inquiry in the USA busy for months, has not been examined by the Austrian parliament to this day. What they now wanted to examine – even though such an examination ran counter to the law – was my 'Mafioso' activity as a 'Nazi hunter'.

The situation became exacerbated to a colossal degree. Austria's largest-circulation paper, *Kronen-Zeitung*, carried an attack on me almost every day. I was quoted in remarks which I had made in totally different contexts months and years before, in order to prove what harm I was causing the country. Letters to the editor demanded not only the immediate closure of my office but also my expulsion. Our documentation centre on the Rudolfsplatz was swamped by letters of vilification, and when more and more threats were scribbled on the walls of the driveway, the management of the building asked me to move out. There were many elderly people living in the building, especially Jews, who could not cope with having their windows smashed all over again. I took his point and moved to the office on Salztorgasse, where the documentation centre is to this day.

The situation had become an intolerable strain on the whole Jewish community in Vienna. The aggression against me was, in a sense, directed against all Jews. It was not yet possible then, as it was later, during the Waldheim affair, to berate 'the Jews' generally. But it was safe, since Bruno Kreisky was doing so himself, to go for the Jew Simon Wiesenthal and to throw at him all that one would have liked to throw at the Jewish community as a whole. Instinctively the Viennese Jews felt that the hatred directed at me might eventually hit them all – and they were gripped by understandable panic. There was anxiety even in Israel: the country depended on Vienna as a transit station for Jews emigrating from the Soviet Union to Israel and it was thought possible that Kreisky, in his fury with me, might close this door to the refugees. Thus it came about that both my Viennese friends and my friends in Israel implored me to make a compromise and to come to some form of truce with Bruno Kreisky. Last but not least, my wife Cyla also implored me: she believed she was entitled to spend her golden years at least a little like other women, going to the theatre together, sitting in cafés, or walking through the marvellous parks of our local district of Döbling, where other walkers were now calling out insults at us. That probably was the main reason why I agreed to a compromise, one negotiated by my friend Dr Ivan Hacker, president of the Vienna B'nai B'rith and later also president of the Jewish community. Kreisky stated in parliament that he had never accused me of collaborating with the Nazis, and I withdrew my suit against him.

There was nevertheless to be a court action in this matter. Peter Michael Lingens, the publisher of *profil*, mentioned by me on several occasions, had called Kreisky's behaviour 'immoral', 'monstrous' and 'undignified' in several articles. Kreisky authorized the public prosecutor's office to act against Lingens: as these words had described the Federal Chancellor this was no longer a mere private action. The proceedings took a rather strange course. Kreisky did not deny having said all the things Lingens had claimed he had said. Although he had in the meantime declared that he had never suspected me of collaborating, he now accused me anew in the court proceedings: he would prove that I had collaborated with the Nazis, there was sufficient evidence, and he would submit it if desired.

The court did not concern itself further with these grotesque charges. But they were subsequently repeated in a neo-Nazi periodical. And when I sued that periodical Bruno Kreiksy offered to testify to the correctness of its account. The hearing ended, as expected, with a finding against the brown rag, the court having established that my persecution under the Third Reich was documented down to the last detail and that there was not even a shadow of a suspicion of my having collaborated with the Nazis.

I don't know to this day what, apart from his hatred, induced Bruno Kreisky to make that reckless suggestion. He himself on one occasion mentioned a letter he had received from South America. This was from a former SS man who had, moreover, been wanted by the police after the war for extensive fraud, and who, in that letter, claimed to be acquainted with me and that I had been a Gestapo informer in Bucharest – a city I have never been to in my life, either during the war or since.

Although Kreisky had reiterated his immoral and monstrous theories, Lingens was found guilty of libel, and the Supreme Court confirmed the verdict. Lingens thereupon turned to the International Court in Strasbourg, which came to the unanimous conclusion that by sentencing Lingens Austria had infringed the right to freedom of expression. Ten years after

Lingens's sentence the Austrian Republic had to repay his fine and his legal costs, and ever since it has been lawful to state that Kreisky's behaviour in the Peter affair was 'immoral, monstrous and undignified'.

The affair did not seriously damage either Kreisky or Peter. Kreisky continued to be the much-admired Sun King. Peter continued as chairman of the Liberal Party and member of parliament. Although in 1983 he was replaced as party chairman by his younger colleague Norbert Steger, he remained leader of the parliamentary Liberals. In 1983 Kreisky lost his absolute majority and announced his resignation. But before his departure, while still Socialist Party leader, he installed that coalition government, along with the Liberals, which was to suffer such dramatic shipwreck because of its inability to come to grips with Austria's economic problems. The Vice-Chancellor of that coalition government was the new Liberal Party leader, Dr Norbert Steger, but Bruno Kreisky was anxious to show his gratitude also to his old friend Friedrich Peter. He proposed him for the second highest office in the state, the 'third president of the national assembly'. But this time the ex-Chancellor suffered a defeat. Whereas in the past, when Kreisky still wielded absolute power, only a few people protested publicly against his stand in the Peter affair, there were now thousands of artists, journalists and intellectuals who, in paid advertisements, manifested their opposition: it was intolerable that a member of a murder brigade should be promoted to president of the Austrian parliament. When the foreign media also took up the issue, Peter withdrew his candidacy.

In 1983 he resigned from parliament on grounds of old age. All three parliamentary parties gave him a standing ovation.

42

The Animal Lover

Some time during my dispute with Bruno Kreisky and Friedrich Peter I was interviewed about my work by *Der Spiegel*. I said then that only a Don Quixote would try to get a criminal case started against Nazis in Austria – they never came to trial anyway. Between 1971 and 1972 hundreds of proceedings against presumed Nazi criminals were suspended in Austria. During the next four years five of the eight cases still pending ended with an acquittal by the jury. Evidently in order to prove my statement to *Der Spiegel* wrong the Austrian judiciary after all – in November 1975 – hauled one Nazi criminal before a court: Vinzenz Gogl.

Gogl was an old customer of mine. My attention had first been drawn to him in March 1964 by a fellow inmate of Mauthausen named Walter Kehraus. He had discovered that the SS Unterscharführer was living as a respected citizen in the small town of Ottnang-on-Hausruck, and he came to see me in the hope that I might upset Gogl's idyllic existence. Kehraus had witnessed Gogl driving two prisoners up against the electric fence. That used to be a favourite game of the guards: they would throw a cap down near the wire and order an inmate to bring it back. If he refused he was shot for his refusal. If he tried to recover the cap he was shot for approaching the electric fence, which was forbidden. Kehraus, however, had also observed Gogl on another occasion: as a member of an execution squad which liquidated two Italian carabinieri who had escorted prisoners to the camp. There was a risk that the carabinieri might talk about what they had seen there, and it seemed more sensible to silence them.

I had not experienced Gogl in person, because I did not get to Mauthausen until February 1945. But I was familiar with his name from later
conversations with inmates, and I had a vague memory of having already
recorded some testimonies against him. But these were no longer in my
possession because in 1954, at the height of the Cold War, I had shut down
my office and sent all my files, except my Eichmann dossier, to Yad Vashem
in Israel. But of course Kehraus's deposition was enough to take out a
criminal action, and as Gogl was living in the Hausruck area the notification
went to the provincial court in Linz. Gogl vigorously denied all four
murders.

Meanwhile, however, I had written to Yad Vashem and asked for my
material on Gogl. This actually includes a letter from a former inmate,
Simon Lifschitz from the Bavarian township of Marktredwitz, where a
refugee camp had existed. 'I am personally acquainted with Gogl,' he had
said in the letter, 'for I spent a whole year at the Ebensee camp. He has to
answer for at least a hundred Jewish deaths: I saw him shoot them or beat
them until they were dead. I am prepared to give evidence as a witness at
the trial, and I know a few other people who were with me at Ebensee.'

I photocopied this letter and passed it on to the Ministry of the Interior
in Vienna. Unfortunately my attempts to find Lifschitz were unsuccessful:
he had emigrated from Bavaria to America, but had not shown up in any
Jewish community there.

On the other hand I discovered the testimony of a Yugoslav journalist,
Hrvoje Macanović, who had given evidence against Gogl in Zagreb, and
within a short time an appeal by the organization of Mauthausen ex-
prisoners was overwhelmingly successful. A whole series of witnesses made
their depositions at the Linz court. The Linz public prosecutor distilled
from them a 103-page indictment: Gogl had driven prisoners towards the
electric wire fence, whereupon they were shot dead from the watchtowers.
He had shot numerous prisoners himself, as well as participating in the
shooting of Dutch and British airmen who, instead of being taken to a
POW camp, had been brought to Mauthausen. And on 6 September 1944,
according to the indictment, Gogl led British and Dutch paratroopers to
the so-called 'Vienna dyke', where they were told to drag stones up the
186 steps. When the prisoners of war refused, they were driven by blows
up the steps to an opening in the electric fence, from where they were
pushed out. They plunged to their death 100 feet below.

The reading of the indictment took up three days. The public prosecutor
announced that he would call twenty witnesses, the first of whom was
Walter Kehraus. All the witnesses made precise statements which incriminated the accused most gravely. But among the public in court there was
an atmosphere which anticipated the verdict. A number of former SS men

shouted encouragement to their old comrade and mocked the Jewish witnesses by interjections. 'You might have thought the year was but 1942, not 1972,' I was told by a friend who had attended the hearing. (I myself had made it a practice, whenever possible, not to attend a trial, because witnesses would invariably come up to talk to me and this would then be interpreted by defence counsel as attempts on my part to influence their evidence.)

The hearing was concluded on 5 May and the jury retired. Six hours later the foreman of the jury announced the unanimous verdict: not guilty on all twenty-three counts. Not guilty of the liquidation of Allied paratroopers on 6 September 1944; not guilty of the murder of a Wels resistance group on 18 and 19 September 1944; not guilty of the killing of two French detainees during the night of 15 November 1944; not guilty of the murder of a young Russian whom Gogl, according to the testimony of the witness Erich Gussmann, had beaten on the head with a bottle until he collapsed dead; and not guilty of the countless routine murders in Mauthausen and its ancillary camp Ebensee. There was uproar in court when the verdict was announced. Louder than the outrage of ex-prisoners were the cheers of th ex-SS men. The acquittal occurred on the anniversary of the liberation of the Mauthausen concentration camp.

When the press asked for my reaction I found it difficult to control myself: the Gogl case had been well prepared. There were unquestionable and convincing testimonies by witnesses. But the atmosphere surrounding the trial had been weird from the start: although Gogl was charged with numerous murders he defended the case as a free man. SS men were permitted to make derogatory remarks about the witnesses. Several witnesses stated that attempts had been made to suborn them. Normally such an acquittal would have been set aside by a judge for 'patent error of the jury', but nothing of the sort happened. This acquittal was almost as bad as the crimes it condoned: it was a Nazi demonstration.

This, in fact, was one of the greatest problems about Nazi trials in Austria. These trials have to be by jury, and the jury alone decides on the issue of guilt. In the case of trials in Graz or Linz one had to expect acquittal as a matter of principle, in trials in Vienna one had to expect it as a rule. That was why as early as the 1960s I proposed that former political persecutees and former Nazis should equally be debarred from juries in Nazi trials. Indeed I wonder whether trial by jury is really a sensible institution for political or politically tinged offences − for which it was never invented. A professional judge with his legal training usually has more scruples before sweeping aside all evidence and rules of logic. He moreover runs the risk of his judgement being quashed by the next highest court, and he knows that a multiplicity of such revisions might damage his career. Jurors, on the other hand, need not care about their verdict being overruled.

The Gogl verdict, too, was overruled. The Supreme Court declared an error by the jury and ordered a retrial, this time before a Vienna jury. It was not until 1975 that proceedings were actually opened. Once more frightful events were described. But most of the witnesses' statements now had to be read out, as the bulk of foreign witnesses refused, after the Linz trial, to set foot in Austria again. Gogl's stereotyped answer to all charges was: The witnesses are lying or else they are confusing me with someone else.

The SS men did not sit in the courtroom in Vienna; instead they appeared as witnesses for the defence. Max Krämer had been sentenced to twenty years for murder by an American court; when questioned about this by the judge he said: 'I drowned two Jews while washing, I killed three with a coal shovel because they didn't want to work. Two I pushed into the sewage plant, and one I kicked in the throat until he was dead. One Jew I flung into the furnace, then he disappeared.' About Gogl, of course, Krämer had nothing but good things to say: he did not remember him ever striking or maltreating a prisoner. He didn't believe Gogl could have done anything like that.

A second testimony likewise was out of the ordinary: it was by a witness called Magnus Keller who had been appointed camp elder by the SS. This honour usually went to convicts with previous sentences. During his interrogation by the Allied military tribunal in Dachau in 1946 Keller had still stood squarely by the prisoners and had called Gogl one of the most dangerous murderers in the Mauthausen and Ebensee concentration camps. Keller testified on oath that the Unterscharführer, along with the second camp elder, a man called Dehler, had shot dead two resistance fighters from Wels. But in the Linz trial Keller's testimony had suddenly changed: he could not recall his evidence to the American military tribunal; all he knew about Gogl was that he had been a protector of the prisoners. Keller did not even come to Vienna: his testimony was read out. There had in fact been rumours at the time of the Linz trial to the effect that Frau Gogl had travelled to Munich with a jewelry box in order to soothe Keller's memory. When the Vienna court questioned Gogl on this point, he confirmed that, along with his wife, he had seen Keller. But of course without a jewelry box .

In the newspapers the reporting of the Gogl trial coincided with my conflict with Bruno Kreisky. Everybody knew that Gogl was a case from my files and was facing court on my initiative. The tabloid *Kronen-Zeitung* printed scarcely an issue without accusing me of operations of secret vengeance, vindictiveness, and damaging Austria's reputation. A number of foreign reporters attended the trial, and the verdict was seen as having some symbolic significance: the jurors answered the question on Gogl's responsibility for the death of the British and Dutch victims with three 'guilty' and five 'not guilty' votes. On all other points of the indictment Gogl was found not guilty by an even bigger majority. Together with his wife he left the courtroom a free man.

If I wished to be sarcastic I might say that this verdict also saved me some unpleasantness. The leader of the parliamentary Socialist Party, Heinz Fischer, reacting to my clash with his boss Bruno Kreisky, had been considering a parliamentary commission of inquiry that would make me see reason, in other words induce me to withdraw my suit against Kreisky. But now the central secretary of the Socialist Party, Karl Blecha (presently Austria's Minister of the Interior) let it be known that 'following Gogl's acquittal we cannot set up a commission of inquiry against Simon Wiesenthal'. That would not have looked good to the international press.

The trial of Johann Vinzenz Gogl was the last Nazi trial in Austria. A newspaper quoted the then senior public prosecutor at the Vienna provincial court, Dr Werner Olscher, echoing the argument of his mentor Christian Broda: 'Who is it that benefits from the Nazi trials? If for some decades such a man has been socially and politically integrated, I consider it pointless and unnecessary to tear him out of the social fabric.'

Johann Vinzenz Gogl is to this day one of the socially most valuable members of the municipality of Ottnang-on-Hausruck: he has two children, is a superb watchmaker, and is entirely devoted to his pets. Visitors to his home were able to admire fourteen budgerigars, several cats and a dog from the dogs' home.

43

The Waldheim Case

At the beginning of 1986, when it was known that the conservative Austrian People's Party would put forward Dr Kurt Waldheim, the former Secretary General of the United Nations, as its candidate in the presidential elections, two members of the Austrian resistance movement called on me. They wanted to know if I had anything on Waldheim. Both were members of the Social Democratic Party and I could not help asking them where they had stood in the Peter case. 'I had a fat dossier against Peter, but you weren't interested.' My visitors were at a loss for an answer, and as I was anyway unable to tell them anything about Waldheim they left my office empty-handed.

Shortly afterwards I received a letter from a former Auschwitz inmate, whom I had known for dozens of years and who was also a long-standing member of the Socialist Party. He asked me to support a historian, Dr Georg Tidl, in an Austrian television documentary programme about the Wehrmacht general Panwitz and his Cossack division. I was astonished at the interest shown by Austrian television in this issue, but when the author of the letter also telephoned to ask for my help, I agreed.

A few days later Tidl himself was on the other end of the line. He too told me about the planned TV documentary, and when I again expressed surprise at the fact that, all of a sudden, television was interested in the Cossack division – which was moreover a pure fighting division – he came clean: 'Waldheim is reputed to have been in that division. In February 1945 the smashed Cossack division had been amalgamated with an SS division – which meant that Waldheim had been a member of the SS.

'Have you actually researched into whether the people from the Cossack division had a chance of resisting incorporation in the SS?' I enquired.

But to him the matter was more simple: whether or not he had wanted to be one, Waldheim had been an SS man.

When I asked whether that was all he could produce against Waldheim, Tidl observed that he was still at the beginning of his work. I suggested he ring me when he was a little closer to the end.

Seven years earlier I had received an inquiry on Waldheim. That time friends from Israel had shown an interest in him. It had struck them that, as Secretary General of the United Nations, Waldheim had so emphatically sided with the Arabs and against Israel, that it was possible it might have been the result of a Nazi past. The question interested me too, and I phoned my friend Axel Springer in Berlin and asked him to make inquiries for me at the Documentation Center there as soon as possible (I myself would have had to accept an endless waiting period). Springer's answer came by return of post. Its contents, according to the observer's point of view, were either satisfactory or disappointing: Waldheim had not belonged to any Nazi organization. Attached to this negative report was the infor- mation from the 'Wehrmacht information office' that Waldheim had repeat- edly been in hospital and that he had served as a lieutenant with Army Group E in the Balkans.

After my telephone conversation with Dr Tidl I fished out that Wehr- macht information again, to discover whether General Panwitz's Cossack division was mentioned in it. But there was no mention of it anywhere, let alone any incorporation in the SS. If Dr Tidl had again phoned me I would have told him. But Tidl evidently was busy.

By mere chance I learned that the legal adviser of the World Jewish Congress, Eli Rosenbaum, had been visiting Vienna – allegedly even twice – without visiting me or even telephoning me. This surprised me because I knew the WJC people from the days when Nahum Goldmann was president and when the brothers Jacob and Nechemiah Robinson were actively helping to bring Nazi criminals to justice. When the two died, Dr Karbach took over their department, and with him, too, I had been in continuous contact. Following Dr Goldmann's departure I did not hear from the WJC for a long time, until it staged a congress in Vienna in 1985. I attended only on the first day, and for some time it was even doubtful if there would be a second day. The reason was that many delegates demanded that the meeting be cut short in protest against the Reder–Frischenschlager affair. The Austrian Minister of Defence, Dr Friedhelm Frischenschlager, had welcomed SS Obersturmbannführer Walter Reder, sentenced for mass murder in Italy and just released from detention at the fortress of

Gaeta, by shaking his hand on his arrival in Austria and thereby causing a worldwide storm of indignation. Even in Austria criticism was loudly voiced and the Opposition demanded Frischenschlager's resignation. But the Liberal Party, to which he belonged, stood squarely behind him, and the Socialists, who together with the Liberals formed the government, did not wish to affront their coalition partner. With the party discipline typical of them, all Socialist deputies voted against the Austrian People's Party's motion of censure. Only with difficulty, and because members of the board of the Jewish community were begging the WJC, was the congress seen through.

I think it probable that some of the people who later played a part in the Waldheim affair may have been active then as intermediaries between the Socialists and the WJC. In February 1986 the news magazine *profil* published Kurt Waldheim's service book, from which it emerged that he had been in the Mounted Corps of the SA and in the Nazi Students' Association. This event had for some weeks been preceded by rumours about the alleged Nazi past of Kurt Waldheim. I knew from the publisher of *profil* that they had been receiving anonymous hints and photographs. *Profil*, however, did not regard the photos as providing any strong evidence. Finally journalists from that magazine learned that some old Socialists had wept on the shoulders of their Austrian People's Party friends about something quite awful being about to surface in the matter of Waldheim. There was a plan, they said, to make a big splash with Waldheim's Nazi past. These reports would be published not in an Austrian paper but abroad. The whole spectacle, the alarmed comrades are reported to have said, would run 'like a production at the Burgtheater'. This they didn't think right, even if it harmed their political opponents, the Austrian People's Party.

The editors of *profil* pursued this and similar rumours and eventually discovered that the *New York Times* was in possession of a voluminous Waldheim dossier which it would shortly start publishing. Furnished with this information, *profil* approached Dr Waldheim and advised him to reveal his wartime past on his own accord. He would have to expect, however, that the editorial office would check his information most painstakingly. Waldheim agreed, even though – typically – he gave away nothing about his SA Mounted Corps membership nor about his service in the Balkans. With his approval a *profil* editor, Johannes Czernin, inspected Waldheim's army record, which until then had been under lock and key in the Austrian War Archives. To everyone's surprise the record contained the information on Waldheim's membership in the SA and in the Nazi Students' Association.

My friend Peter Michael Lingens published an exceedingly well-balanced commentary in *profil*. Membership of the student's association was harm-less, he said; this was necessary even to obtain a room in a students' hostel. The SA, admittedly, while still illegal had been an unsavoury organization of rowdy brawlers, but anyone joining it after the *Anschluss* did not thereby manifest any deep ties with Nazism but probably just a certain opportunism. The charge against Waldheim was not so much that he had committed those youthful sins as that, rather irritatingly, he had in his memoirs portrayed himself almost as a victim of Nazism.

Waldheim objected: he had merely belonged to a riding club and didn't know it had been incorporated into the SA. He himself had never signed a membership form of the SA and therefore had not regarded himself as a member. (In point of fact no SA document with Waldheim's signature has been found.) He had likewise found himself in the students' association without his knowledge when all the members of his youth group were automatically enrolled.

The article in *profil* could well have triggered off a meaningful discussion of Waldheim's credibility – if the World Jewish Congress had not started up the machinery of its long-prepared campaign a few days later. While the *New York Times*, as predicted, carried its first report on Waldheim, the WJC proclaimed Waldheim a hard-line Nazi and a well-nigh convicted war criminal. The case developed a colossal media dynamism: the world's newspapers vied with each other in producing new incriminating Waldheim material, and the WJC added its comments.

For a long time what Waldheim offered in his defence scarcely made any impact internationally. People who hardly knew the difference between the SA and the SS found the question of whether a riding club could, without the knowledge of its members, be incorporated in the SA way above their heads. Even less did they realize that the Mounted Corps in the Third Reich had become a catchment bowl for opponents of the Nazis, who, for a variety of reasons, had to be 'members' somewhere and did not wish to be in the Nazi party. In fact, Kurt Waldheim was a fairly good illustration of those constraints: his father was a committed Christian Social Party man, who immediately lost his post under the Nazis. In the regional records of the Nazi party the family was listed as emphatically anti-Nazi, and Kurt Waldheim himself had, immediately before the Anschluss, distributed leaflets calling for a 'No' vote. Because of that he had been beaten up by the Nazi hitmen. For anyone wishing to complete his studies at the Konsularakademie against such pressures, it was more than sensible to join the Nazi students or the SA horsemen voluntarily, to avoid difficulties.

One may think it more heroic to accept such difficulties knowingly – but in view of conditions prevailing at the time one should be careful not to condemn too severely the opportunism that was inevitably spreading. University graduates, for instance, who were unable to prove membership of at least a small Nazi club had virtually no hope of finding a post in the civil service. That may have been a matter of irrelevance for the sons of rich families – but it was by no means irrelevant for Kurt Waldheim, who came from a modest background.

Nevertheless I believed from the very outset that the credibility of the former UN Secretary General left something to be desired: a person of his standing might be expected to speak on his own initiative and fully about all he did at the time, instead of having every detail painfully extracted from him. But this is still some way from being a 'hard-line Nazi', and even further from being a 'war criminal' (these terms were used by the WJC long before those Yugoslav documents turned up which proved that Waldheim at least knew about war crimes). It was along these lines that I answered all the telephone calls which came into my office – and they numbered a dozen per hour. I said that we had made inquiries earlier at the Documentation Center in Berlin and had been unable to learn anything to Waldheim's discredit. He had not been a member of a Nazi organization, because the National Socialist Students' Association and the SA Mounted Corps were not, for the reasons I've outlined above, subject to registration in Austria.

But it was of course possible that the WJC possessed evidence which we did not know about. The Simon Wiesenthal Center in Los Angeles therefore got in touch with the Secretary General of the World Jewish Congress, Israel Singer, to find out what they had on Waldheim. Singer stated explicitly that he had been promised weighty material from people close to the Austrian government. Now I understood why Eli Rosenbaum had come to Vienna: evidently to gather preliminary information. That I was not involved may have been for two reasons: for one thing, the subject matter of my telephone conversation with Dr Tidl might have got about and there might have been some anxiety that the laboriously constructed charges could collapse in the light of my precise acquaintance with the facts. (I have occasionally encountered this journalistic phenomenon: journalists being reluctant to see a good story spoilt by excessively detailed research.) But I also think it possible that I may have been thought biased: in connection with my dispute with Bruno Kreisky in the Friedrich Peter Affair a number of Austrian People's Party politicians – especially the then future President of the Austrian National Bank, recently deceased, Stefan Koren – had taken my side, which had given rise to the rumour that I was an Austrian People's Party member. At any rate, I have frequently been accused of failing to attack Waldheim for that reason.

The truth was simpler. I was not prepared to attack Kurt Waldheim as a Nazi or a war criminal because, from all I knew about him and from all that emerged from the documents, he had been neither a Nazi nor a war criminal.

As for his credibility, I have always questioned that – except that no one in Austria or in New York cared about it during the first few months. The WJC – in spite of its grandiose name no more than a small Jewish organization of inferior importance – used the Waldheim case to get itself into the headlines of the major American papers, headlines at first readily made available to it. (It was only gradually that newspaper editors discovered the real complexity of the issue, and from that point onward began to differentiate between the accusations of the WJC and their own findings.)

But it was in Austria that the activities of the World Jewish Congress turned into disaster: on 9 March 1986 *profil* carried an interview with the Director of the WJC, Elan Steinberg, and its Secretary General, Israel Singer. In this interview the two WJC officers indulged in grotesque threats, not only against Waldheim but against all Austrians. If Waldheim were elected President, they said, every holder of an Austrian passport would feel the effects of it when he went abroad: he would find himself surrounded by a 'cloud of mistrust'. The result of the interview could have been predicted: even those Austrians who until then had regarded Waldheim as an incompetent opportunist began to defend him. And the numerous anti-Semites at last had grist for their mill: evidence at last of the 'world-wide Jewish conspiracy'. A lot of young people, especially for whom anti-Semitism no longer was an issue, were confused. Thus a young man phoned me to enquire why he should feel ashamed when travelling abroad, seeing that he wasn't going to vote for Waldheim and that there had not been a single Nazi in his family. 'What, Herr Wiesenthal, do the Jews have against me?'

For the first time reference was again being made to 'the Jews', instead of people saying: 'Elan Steinberg of the World Jewish Congress' or 'Israel Singer of the World Jewish Congress'. In a population with a deep-rooted traditional anti-Semitism, a population which had undergone seven years of *Stürmer* indoctrination, the ideas of Nazism could not have died from one day to the next. The men of yesterday were only too ready to say: 'Now you see how right we were – now you see what they are really like, the Jews.' But even the fellow travellers were glad of a belated excuse: 'There are some bad sides to the Jews, that's a fact all right.' And the young people, who scarcely had any personal experience of Jews, were confused: 'Could the Jews really be what some people say they are?'

It is true that all these reactions are ultimately anti-Semitic to various degrees (or at any rate reactions rooted in the anti-Semitic tradition), but this does not mean that officials of a Jewish organization have the right to trigger off such a reaction needlessly, to provoke it. Least of all is it the right of two young Jewish officials who live in the USA, while we Austrian Jews are the ones to suffer the consequences. But we were not asked – even though, according to its statute, the WJC would have been obliged to consult with the local Jewish community or, at the least, inform it of its intentions. The desperate efforts of Dr Hacker, the recently deceased president of the Vienna Jewish community, to persuade Singer and Steinberg to retract their interview were unfortunately to no avail. Instead there was an internal split: some young people who – thank God – had only known Nazism by hearsay, now felt obliged to be more merciless than the men and women who had spent years in the concentration camps of the Third Reich, and supported Singer and Steinberg. Especially as this was an opportunity for getting rid of some of the older board members. But these young people, too, were functionaries: their views did not coincide with those of the members of the Jewish community who had to live day in and day out with a more or less pronounced Austrian anti-Semitism. A member of that community phoned Mr Singer and complained to him.

'How many Jews are there living in Austria?' the WJC Secretary General enquired.

'Seven thousand.'

'Well then,' Mr Singer suggested, 'why don't you just emigrate?'

In a Canadian Jewish paper he grandly declared that 'the cause' had made it necessary to accept the hardships the Austrian Jews would face.

Inappropriate as the reaction of the WJC was, so of course was the reaction of a number of Austrian institutions. The Austrian People's Party, which had made Kurt Waldheim its candidate, daily during its campaign aroused anti-Semitic sentiments which it then claimed it had 'not wished to arouse'. Its chairman Alois Mock missed no opportunity to pillory 'certain circles' on the east coast for having fanned a campaign against Austria, and with this phrase once more helped the WJC to become 'the Jews'. The same line was taken, even more noisily, by the Secretary General of the Austrian People's Party, Dr Michael Graff (who later had to resign because of a serious anti-Semitic impropriety); needless to say, Kurt Waldheim had no objection to this kind of election campaign.

The biggest gutter press daily in the country, *Kronen-Zeitung*, which had distinguished itself earlier with a highly controversial series about Jewry, was daily adding fuel to the flames, and the broadsheet press hardly lagged behind. Both kinds of papers were able to gauge the success of their reports by a series of anti-Semitic letters to the editor – not to mention the turns of phrase which once again became acceptable in tavern talk. I know of several cases of taxi drivers refusing to take Jewish passengers. In this respect the Waldheim affair, though not essentially designed to do so, in fact stirred up and made apparent what had long been regarded as dead: anti-Semitism has in no way been overcome in Austria.

This in turn gave rise to justified concern among the Jewish community in the USA. It was suddenly recalled that Austria had made no kind of restitution to the victims of Nazism, on the grounds that Austria did not exist during the war. It was conveniently forgotten that, under the Kreuznach agreement, Austria after the war was only permitted to keep extensive German assets because she undertook to compensate victims of Nazism appropriately. People also remembered the curious role which Kreisky had played in all discussions on Israel. Waldheim, who had become UN Secretary General upon Kreisky's proposal, had in that post simply followed the policy which is propagated by the 'Sun King' to this day: the prime objective of Austria's Middle East policy is not security or recognition for the state of Israel, but must instead be the establishment of a Palestinian state. His friendship with Gaddafi and Arafat did not make him especially popular in the USA.

None of this did Austria's image in the USA any good. Behind the traditional sympathy for the land of the Vienna Boys' Choir and the Lipizzaner horses a good deal of criticism had been building up even before the Waldheim case. While Austria was no longer quite as popular as before, Waldheim was altogether one of the most unpopular figures in the USA. The majority of Americans anyway regard the United Nations as an unnecessary and incompetent organization, and Waldheim as its most unnecessary and most incompetent Secretary General. Even people who realized that the majority in the UN consisted of Communist and Third World countries could not understand why Kurt Waldheim was quite so eager to join their side.

Least of all, of course, could the Jews understand it. They were aware that the resolution 'Zionism is racism' was adopted in his era, and they also remembered his refusal, when visiting Yad Vashem, to cover his head, or his statement that the Israeli rescue operation in Entebbe was 'a breach of international law'. Kurt Waldheim was seen by the Jews – for understandable reasons – as an enemy, and now the World Jewish Congress saw a unique chance of painting this enemy brown and dressing him up in the uniform of a war criminal. The American public in general and the Jewish population in particular were only too happy to believe that image.

Waldheim himself reacted with the diplomatic finesse which had characterized him as UN Secretary General. When it was pointed out that he had served in the Balkans with a unit involved in extensive war crimes, he stated that he had 'only done his duty'. This assured him of the approval of the so-called war generation within Austria, which had been using this phrase for decades to run away from all responsibilities. That it might also be possible to say that it would have been difficult to avoid military service does not seem to have occurred to many members of that generation, any more than it did to Waldheim. One of my pleasanter experiences, however, within that unpleasant affair was the fact that many young Austrians found Waldheim's formula particularly repellent and contrasted it with a different categorical imperative: if there was such a thing as duty, then it was their duty to resist.

No one, however, demanded such heroism from Waldheim. It would have been entirely sufficient for him to find clear words to describe his wartime past. As a man who knew so much – owing to his position on the staff Waldheim was one of the best-informed officers – he should have stood up as a witness to that period and informed the younger generation about the bestialities of the Nazi regime. Instead, Waldheim missed no opportunity to sweep the Nazis' predatory war in the Balkans on to the same pile as partisan resistance, and the shooting of hostages by the German Wehrmacht with the excesses of the partisan struggle. Instead of making a statement, belated though it would be, he had to be confronted with a document each time before his memory would stir. Thus he told an interviewer from *profil* that he had known nothing about illegal reprisals in the fight against the partisans, only to declare three days later, faced with a flood of documents bearing his signature, that surely the fact that hostages were shot was generally known.

Shortly afterwards he claimed that he had only learned from the newspapers about the deportations of Jews from Salonika. When thereupon I declared that by this remark Kurt Waldheim had forfeited all credibility, he telephoned me and the following dialogue developed:

'Herr Dr Waldheim, the Jewish community in Salonika was one of the largest and most ancient in the world and your headquarters was less than five miles from Salonika. It is impossible that you didn't notice anything about the deportation of the Jews.'

'Believe me, I knew nothing about it.'

'The deportations went on for six weeks. Some two thousand Jews were deported every other day; the military trains which brought down equipment for the Wehrmacht, that is for your people, took away the Jews on their return run.'

'I had nothing to do with it.'

'Surely you were often at the officers' club: did no transport officer ever mention these things?'

'No, never.'

'The SS at the time had no provisions for the Jews, so the Wehrmacht made available for each Jew one loaf of bread and twelve olives. Every supply officer knew about this. Did none of them ever talk to you either?'

'No.'

'You would go into Salonika time and again. The Jews made up almost one-third of the population there. Did you never notice anything? Jewish shops being locked up, groups of people being escorted through the streets, an air of depair?'

'No. I didn't notice anything.'

I could only reply what the commission of historians likewise made clear in its report: 'I cannot believe you.'

By his public attitude towards the deportation of the Salonika Jews, if for no other reason, Kurt Waldheim made himself unacceptable to me as a Federal President. But the WJC was still trying to brand him a war criminal. Their basis was the well-known list of Yugoslav War Crimes Commission, according to which Kurt Waldheim was wanted for murder. When I first learned of that list I sent a telegram to the Yugoslav Premier Milka Planinc, requesting her to publish all the documents on Waldheim which existed in Yugoslavia.

She replied the same day – she happened to be in Vienna – only to say that Yugoslavia did not interfere in the internal affairs of Austria. I didn't let matters rest there but flew to the USA to persuade UN Secretary General Pérez de Cuéllar, to ask the Yugoslavs officially to publish their evidence. To this day this has not occurred.

Nevertheless, a fairly clear picture emerges from the available documents. The charges against Waldheim go back to a German officer who was himself guilty of the massacre of which he accused Waldheim (and who was also executed for it). A second incriminating testimony came from a soldier whose widow was interviewed by *profil*: she stated that her husband had confessed to her that the accusation was false. It had been a general principle during interrogations to attribute responsibility to someone who was already safely abroad. In point of fact, Waldheim never hid after the war but became the secretary to the Minister of Foreign Affairs, Karl Gruber, a meritorious resistance fighter. The Yugoslavs themselves never requested Waldheim's extradition, evidently because they realized that their file was insecurely documented. Presumably it was in existence only because it was thought possible to use it for blackmail. Meanwhile a carefully researched book has appeared on the subject: *The Missing Years* by Professor Robert Herzstein. Certainly the proposition that Waldheim was a war criminal can in no way be maintained on the basis of the material at present available to us. The accusations of the World Jewish Congress were rash. As I once put it to a WJC official: 'I am in the habit of researching first and making accusations later. You made an accusation first and only then started researching.'

The undifferentiated manner in which Kurt Waldheim was attacked has undone years of educational work in Austria: in a vast number of lectures, interviews and personal conversations I, and other people, had tried to show that a distinction had to be made between the indifferent, the fellow travellers and fanatical Nazis; that just any Wehrmacht officer could not be equated with a member of a murder brigade; that although Hitler's war was a criminal war, it must nevertheless be distinguished from war crimes, and that war crimes have to be distinguished from crimes merely committed during the war. The 'Waldheim case' once more blurred all these distinctions.

What I find frightening is that only in the Eichmann case did I witness a similar measure of media interest in Nazi crimes. Yet one man had been one of the worst criminals in world history, and the other had not even been a Nazi. One had been responsible for the murder of millions of Jews, while the other had only been clumsy enough to deny his knowledge of the deportation of the Salonika Jews. Rarely have I witnessed such a confusion of values and words. Thus the WJC held a conference in Geneva in April 1986 under the chairmanship of Israel Singer, at which a certain Kalman Sultanik, vice-president of that organization, made a speech. In it he said literally: 'Waldheim, who sent the Jews to the gas chambers, is being supported and defended by the prominent Jew Simon Wiesenthal.' When, at that, the representative from Austria, Paul Gross (now president of the Jewish community), asked to speak, Israel Singer decided to close the discussion.

Even in my own office I had experience of how the Waldheim case could induce a seemingly sensible, seemingly decent, person to commit an incomprehensible action. One of my staff, Mrs Silvana Konieczny-Origlia, took a copy of a private letter to me, believing that she could thereby prove Waldheim to be a war criminal who was being protected by me. The letter was from Professor Fleming, later to become a member of the commission of historians, and it contained a number of documents concerning British prisoners of war, with the note that I was the only person who did not possess them. Careful researches, however, disclosed that these documents had been discussed in Der Spiegel two weeks earlier and that Greville Janner, MP, an old friend of mine, had already addressed a question about them to the British Foreign Office. But my employee knew nothing about this at the time, and passed the letter on (naturally without my knowledge) to the Italian journal Epoca, which thereupon made it into a big story against me. The Italian journalist Fiamma Nierenstein accused me of having suppressed the evidence in order to help Waldheim; other papers took up the accusation, and on French television Serge Klarsfeld had a real go at me. A week later Epoca carried an article which Elan Steinberg had written against me. My friend Paul Gross telephoned the WJC to speak to Steinberg, but he was not available. From talking to his secretary it emerged that the WJC director had written that article considerably earlier. If it had not taken so long to translate it into Italian it would presumably have appeared alongside Mrs Konieczny-Origlia's 'revelations'.

There is a cynical explanation for all these phenomena: the World Jewish Council and a few other people had got their teeth into the business and were not prepared, under any circumstances, to admit their mistakes and reduce the charges against Waldheim to a reasonable level. They were, in a sense, urged on by their own success to make their announcements true: somewhere a document had to turn up that would unmask Waldheim as a war criminal – otherwise his accusers would be exposed as slanderers. It was undoubtedly that kind of thinking that played a part in the continuation of the Waldheim case.

But there is also another, more charitable, explanation: young Jews who could not comprehend that their parents did not resist more (and whose knowledge of the period is too slight for them to know how difficult such resistance would have been) were now, half a century too late, performing something they saw as resistance. In the absence of a more suitable figure they magnified Kurt Waldheim into the symbol of the persecutor and were now going all out for him, by proxy, as it were, for their parents. Added to this is the fact that many American Jews have something akin to a sense of guilt in their subconscious anyway, for not having done enough for the persecuted Jews of Europe during the war. The Waldheim case offered them an opportunity to take a demonstrative stance. Disinformation from some American television services and newspapers was a further factor. And the rest was provided by anti-Semitic incidents in Austria. The Americans therefore concluded that the WJC had been correct with its charges against Waldheim and Austria. The Austrian anti-Semites saw themselves justified in their anti-Semitic actions by the attitude of the WJC and the reaction of the Americans. Thus the vicious circle continued.

I had hoped to cut that Gordian knot by proposing, on the very day of Waldheim's election, 8 June 1986, that a commission of historians be set up to determine, to the best of their knowledge and conscience, the truth and nothing but the truth. On 8 February 1988 the commission of historians arrived at the result I had expected: Waldheim had known about what he denied knowing. He had been in 'consultative proximity' to war crimes, but he had not been personally involved in any way.

I thought that Waldheim would use this opportunity to resign without loss of face, for the sake of Austria: one cannot remain Federal President when one has been publicly proved to lack credibility – and it is the duty of every Federal President to serve his country. Waldheim's resignation would have done a service to Austria's international reputation. Yet Kurt Waldheim decided differently: he is willing to live in conflict with the truth. That induced me, on 9 February 1988 on Austrian television, to call on him to resign. Simultaneously I appealed to the intellectual elite of the country to draw their conclusions with regard to Waldheim. Not because he was a Nazi or a war criminal, but because he had shown himself unworthy of his office and of his responsibility.

A committee was formed which took up my appeal, and thousands of people, including the leading cultural figures and intellectuals in Austria, rallied every week in the Stephansplatz, the square around St Stephen's cathedral, to demand Waldheim's resignation. Opinion polls revealed that the percentage of those in favour of Waldheim's continuation in office had declined to less than forty. At this point the President of the WJC, Edgar Bronfman, went to Brussels to protest against Austria's admission to the EEC. Since then the Waldheim supporters have again topped 50 per cent and are increasing in number with every further statement made by the World Jewish Council on Austria.

44

In dubio contra
ebreo

The fuss around the Waldheim affair once more reminded the public of a fact which I regard as incomparably more serious: Austria has compensated the survivors of the Nazi terror as slowly and as niggardly as possible. Not only Jewish victims but all Nazi victims. Although Austria took over this obligation from the Germans in exchange for being allowed to retain so-called 'German assets' (predominantly enterprises set up in Austria by the Germans), the Austrian republic never dreamed of paying the Nazi victims anything like what the Federal Republic was paying them. Initially Austria's compensation payment was all of five Schillings per day in Auschwitz; only after vigorous protests did the country draw level with the Germans who had been paying five Deustschmarks from the start. For loss of pension or damage to health the Austrians paid only a fraction of the German compensation figures.

Nevertheless, the Austrian public is still under the impression that Nazi victims were simply raking in the money and had greatly enriched themselves. This climate was typical of all restitution proceedings, from which I am deliberately picking out one which was economically of marginal importance, so that Austria cannot make the excuse of inadequate financial strength. This was compensation for *objets d'art* stolen from private homes. To deal with such matters speedily and correctly would only have been a question of taking the necessary trouble. I came across this (to me unusual) subject through a letter from an old lady in New Zealand, who described how she had left Vienna in 1939: 'They gave me exactly five minutes to pick up my coat and handbag – everything else I had to leave behind.' Now the author of this letter wished to know if I could possibly help her to recover an oil painting which she regarded as relatively valuable, because 'I am getting on and there are bills to be paid.' It had taken her about two years even to discover where such 'ownerless' paintings were being kept: in the storerooms of the Federal Monuments Office in the Hofburg. But she gave up the attempt to find out whether her painting was among the lot. She suspected, she wrote, that this was not my usual field of activity, but maybe I would be successful in this matter too.

The Nazis, as is well known, had committed the greatest thefts of art objects in history: anything of value was removed from Jewish homes, and in the occupied countries the museums were looted. The Führer was regarded as a collector of taste, and he planned to present to his home town of Linz the greatest art collection in the world – bigger and more beautiful than the Louvre, the Uffizi and the Prado all rolled into one. As he was in the process of incorporating the whole of Europe it was easy enough for him to act the Maecenas: the 'Rosenberg staff' was given instructions to loot the conquered museums. The stolen treasures were packed in crates marked AH (for Adolf Hitler), but these did not reach their addressee intact: Herman Göring stole some of them by having the lettering changed to HG. When I thought about compiling a collection of documents on this subject, Albert Speer sent me a few pencil sketches made by Hitler of the proposed exhibition building. I was speechless when I turned the sheet over and looked at the date of the sketch: the first, more modest, design dated from October 1938, while the other, a more showy one, was made at the Führer's headquarters on 4 January 1943 – the time when the German armies were bleeding to death at Stalingrad.

After the war the Allies discovered the stolen works of art in a salt mine near Altaussee, and Austria established a commission to examine the stocks. Paintings stolen from museums or galleries were relatively quickly returned. But when it came to private collections whose owners were missing the authorities preferred to wait for them to come forward, rather than searching for them. The fact that lying in the storerooms of the Federal Monuments Office were countless less valuable paintings, which had simply been taken from private homes, was not known to anyone at all. It was a remarkable achievement by the old lady in New Zealand to have discovered it. How remarkable, I was to find out when I started a search myself. The first place I called on was the Monuments Office, where a lady State Custodian told me that private individuals were not entitled to receive any information from her whatever. When I remarked that in that case I would seek the help of the press she suggested the Ministry of Finance. There I had the following, entirely friendly, conversation with the official concerned:

'How many paintings whose owners are unknown do you have under your care?'

'Well, that's difficult to say. One would have to make a new inventory.'

'How many belong to victims of racial or political persecution? Two hundred? Three hundred?'

'I'd say considerably more.'

'Ten thousand?'

'That's probably too high an estimate.'

'Why hasn't a list of these painting ever been published? That would give their owners, now scattered throughout the world, a chance of reclaiming their property.'

'My dear Herr Wiesenthal, there's no need to publish any such list. The art trade and collectors know everything about the more important paintings. Word gets around.'

'Let's assume word doesn't get around to a small town in New Zealand, where an elderly Jewish lady is living on charity. She could sell her painting and enjoy the final years of her life.'

'Hm.'

My suggestion that a catalogue of all paintings and other *objects d'art* in store be compiled and sent out to every Austrian consulate throughout the world was met with a wringing of hands in despair: 'Do you realize what this would mean? We'd drown in a flood of letters.'

I encountered a similar shocked reaction at the Federal Office for the Protection of Assets. There they feared an 'incredible paper chase' and a 'series of law suits': 'You've no idea what things were like when the Allies pulled out in 1945. We returned sequestrated property to its alleged owners. But then others claimed the same items. Heavens above, you wouldn't believe the things that happened. And, strangely enough, everybody fought over the valuable items. No one wanted the rest of the stuff.'

'Are you saying that you want to wait until all has become state property?' I asked.

'Applications for restitution had to be submitted by the end of 1965. Later applications can no longer be considered.'

If the owners did not know of this time limit it was just too bad for them.

By October 1965 I'd had enough and handed the whole story over to the press, whereupon the then Foreign Minister Dr Bruno Kreisky wrote to me to say he supported my idea of a catalogue. (I made a mental note of this: it was the only time that Kreisky ever supported anything I proposed.) On 16 April 1966 the then Minister of Finance Dr Wolfgang Schmitz informed me that he and the Minister of Education had 'thoroughly examined' the matter. The 'problem raised' by me 'could best be solved by a federal law, to be probably known for short as the "Art Property Settlement Law". I have already directed that the draft of such a law be prepared ... The envisaged federal law will make it possible for claims to such art property to be asserted within a certain period of its enactment. I hope that you too will welcome this proposition.'

I welcomed it, and the old lady in New Zealand waited. It took another three years for the Austrian parliament to pass the Art Property Settlement Law. Though not without simultaneously doing something for the former Nazis. In the same sweep parliament approved the so-called Intermediate Periods Law, under which Nazis suspended from office after the war would have that time included in the calculation of their pensions. At any rate, the official *Wiener Zeitung* now published a copious list of art treasures which presumably would still be lying in the storerooms of the Federal Monuments Office if the old lady had not written to me. I quote a few items from it: 657 oil paintings, 84 watercolours, 250 pastels, 53 woodcuts, 43 sculptures, 365 silver items, 3343 coins. The paintings included a Van Dyck, a Frans Hals, a Ruysdael, a school of Titian, a Brueghel the Elder, a Boucher, as well as pictures by Böcklin, Alt, Caravaggio, Correggio, Feuerbach, Gauermann, Waldmüller, Spitzweg and many others.

The periods for lodging claims were also extended. Except that by then only half of the former owners of the stolen items, at most, were still alive, and their heirs were now expected to supply the most detailed information on works of art they often only knew of from hearsay. Needless to say, the authorities – because of the 'series of lawsuits' – demanded an exact description, with special emphasis on precise dimensions, as if most Jews, just before being arrested, had walked through their homes with a tape measure to measure their pictures. This enabled the Austrian republic to engage in further chicanery: a valuable painting of Klimt, for instance – now hanging in the Albertina – was not returned because the measurements supplied by the family claiming it were one inch out from its actual dimensions. I took the liberty therefore to write a letter to the Minister for Science and the Arts, Frau Herta Firnberg, summing up my experience as *in dubio contra ebreo*.

I did not realize how accurate I was. Only while writing these memoirs did I come across the book, published by Amalthea-Verlag, of a young English historian, Robert Knight, which reproduces the until-then secret minutes of the ministerial council meetings of the Austrian government between 1945 and 1952 on the issue of compensation for Jewish victims of Nazi terror. The title of the book (so far published only in German) is a verbatim quotation from the Socialist Minister of the Interior Oskar Helmer, a suggesstion followed by virtually all his colleagues: 'Ich bin dafür, die Sache in die Länge zu ziehen' (I am in favour of procrastinating in this matter'). There probably exists no better document to illustrate the real problem of Austria: there is not so much a danger of a new Nazism gaining ground in the country as of the ancient anti-Semitism smouldering on undiminished. In spite of Auschwitz. And even though there are scarcely any Jews left in Austria.

The government members whose statement Knight reproduces were none of them Nazis; one of them, Karl Gruber, had resisted Hitler and another, Leopold Figl, had been in a concentration camp. Yet the minutes bristle with anti-Semitic remarks. Gruber could not see why the Jews who had 'gone abroad' should receive any compensation at all, and Foreign Minister Leopold Figl observed that 'the Jews simply want to get rich quick.'

A memorandum from the State Chancellery for Foreign Affairs on the 'foreign policy and international law aspect of compensation claims by Jewish Nazi victims' reads like an anti-Semitic pamphlet from the 1930s, or like the commentary of a leading Austrian daily on the Waldheim case in the 1980s: 'The Jews play a big role in world foreign policy, firstly because they control a large part of the press through which they exert their influence on world public opinion, and secondly because they have managed to induce the governments of other countries to champion their claims. In this the Jews have succeeded the more easily as international finance capital is largely in Jewish hands. Among pro-Jewish governments are, above all, the British and American governments (the USSR, as far as is known, has not so far commented on the Jewish problem in Germany and Austria). It is not for nothing that Jewry has been described as the fifth world power, against whose opposition Hitlerite Germany was destroyed.' So it was not the Jews who were destroyed in Auschwitz, but Hitlerite Germany that was broken by Jewish hostility!

Because of this towering influence exerted by the Jews on politics the Austrian government decided on a compromise: Austria would pay as little and as slowly as possible. Thus in the case of 'ownerless' art objects only a portion of the paintings were claimed because only a portion of those concerned were informed. The finest paintings from that stock found their way into Austrian embassies and museums. The less valuable objects were stored in a Carthusian abbey at Mauerbach near Vienna, and would have remained there if the 'Jewish press' had not once again 'exerted its influence on world public opinion'. In December 1984 the American journalist Andrew Decker of *Art News* published an article which also appeared, in abridged form, in the *New York Times*, and which asked the question of whether the Austrian federal government was intending to enrich itself with stolen property. Minister for Science Dr Heinz Fischer thereupon issued an 'explanation': what was in museums and in embassies would remain in Austria, and what was in Mauerbach could be claimed by the victims of persecution. This, however, did not satisfy the 'pro-Jewish governments' or the Jewish-manipulated 'world public opinion', and after much toing and froing the then Federal Chancellor Fred Sinowatz was induced to find a proper solution: the term for lodging claims was once more extended, and anything that remained unclaimed at its expiry was to be valued and sold at auction. The proceeds of the auction were to be passed on to the victims of persecution through Jewish and non-Jewish organizations. The old lady in New Zealand had meanwhile died.

It is the continuing Austrian anti-Semitism which lends real weight to the Waldheim case. The statements made during his election campaign by all kinds of senior politicians are a good deal worse than his now famous 'I did my duty.' Waldheim had merely been too maladroit to avoid this standard sentence, which is used in Austria also by people of complete integrity to explain that they had no other choice. Worse than Waldheim's continual appeals to the 'wartime generation' (which were bad enough) were the appeals of various Austrian People's Party top politicians to the anti-Semitic instincts of the Austrians. Whenever they referred to 'certain circles' they encountered a wave of unspoken agreement: one did not have to put up with any more from that 'unscrupulous lobby from the east coast'.

Opinion polls, the accuracy of which is continually being argued about, present a picture which, even at best, is bad enough. Depending on interpretation, 30 to 70 per cent of all Austrians nurture more or less serious anti-Semitic prejudices. The most frightening is a poll by the IMAS Institute from the 1970s, when Austria was still having to be careful lest the published result should damage her international reputation: according to its figures 35 per cent of all Austrians would be unable to marry a Jew, 45 per cent believed that if a Jew was 'doing something good' it was only 'from calculation', and 21 per cent thought it better that there should be no Jews in Austria at all.

This last wish has been very largely fulfilled: at the turn of the century there were 1,225,000 Jews in Austria, though 900,000 of them were in my native Galicia and in Bukowina. In 1910 Vienna recorded 175,000 and in 1923 as much as 201,000 Jews. In 1945 there were 240. At present there are approximately 10,000 Jews in Austria, of whom 9000 live in Vienna – which is just over five per 1000 inhabitants of the city. The role played by Jews in the Austrian economy, in Austrian banking, in the Austrian press and even in Austrian culture is accordingly marginal. Austrian anti-Semitism can manage without Jews. It seems to be hereditary.

It is generally accepted that anti-Semitism is proportional to the Jewish percentage of the population. That percentage was biggest in Poland and in Austria. Moreover, anti-Semitism certainly has a Catholic root, which again was operative in Poland and in Austria. Finally, both these countries were having identity problems: Poland was forever being partitioned, while Austria, initially a diffuse multinational state, shrank from a great power to a small country. To strengthen the cohesion of its own group during such identity crises it was useful to blame a wicked outsider – the Jew.

This anti-Semitism, however, with its multiple roots in the past, now evidently no longer needs a logical justification to survive into the future. The hope that Auschwitz may have put an end to it is fundamentally mistaken: Auschwitz on the contrary created, especially among Austrians, enormous subconscious feelings of guilt, which are best assuaged by arriving at the conclusion that the Jews were themselves, perhaps not entirely but surely 'a little', responsible for their own fate: by being the way the Waldheim case had revealed them as being. Of course, one should not therefore have sent them to the gas chambers immediately, but for Austria to have no Jews at all would still seem the best solution for one Austrian out of five.

The Waldheim affair stirred up all that mud. This has a lot of drawbacks but also some advantages: one knows where one stands. And for the first time it became obvious that there exists also a 'new Austria' which, as a political force, has actually adopted just this name: a whole number of, in the main, young artists, journalists, scientists and intellectuals, determined to oppose vigorously anti-Semitism wherever it raises its head. Even the present Federal Chancellor Franz Vranitzky and the Vienna chairman of the Austrian People's Party, Erhard Busek, though they do not belong to that group, may be counted among it by their outlook.

Judging by my own position, I might say that for the first time alongside the people who curse my work, there are also some who approve of it quite officially (which would have been unthinkable a few years ago); for the first time I am receiving honours – from newspapers, from the public, and even from the state – while ten years ago they wanted to expel me. I am not saying that things are good – but they are getting better.

45

The Auschwitz Lie

In January 1988 Austrian television began broadcasting a series entitled *Zur Person* ('Personal Encounter'). I was invited as the first guest and was interviewed by the well-known Austrian journalist Franz Ferdinand Wolf. The interview was broadcast live from the Vienna Josefstadt Theatre.

Within minutes of the beginning of the transmission shouts were suddenly heard. 'Murderer!' someone called out. And 'You're a liar!' Three men leaned over the balustrade of the first tier and threw stacks of leaflets into the audience. The state police had observed them entering the theatre, but 'under the law' had not been allowed to intervene until the three had become 'active'. Their leader was an old acquaintance: Gerd Honsik, head of the Austrian 'Foreigners Halt' movement and editor of the periodical *Halt*.

As I write these lines the latest issue of that periodical is being distributed outside Vienna's schools. Austrian juveniles thus receive information such as, roughly, the following: 'Why was the Anschluss annulled? Stupidity? Spinelessness? Crime? The regime owes us an answer!' *Halt* even offers some poetry by printing the ballad 'War of Flowers', by an unknown poetess whose heart overbrimmed with these stanzas:

> War das ein Jauchzen, als der Führer kam,
> das Volk seinem Wege wuchs zum Strome,
> wie eine Flut, die schier kein Ende nahm.
> Und alle harrten, daß er komme, komme.

Und jeder wußte, was sein Kommen hieß:
(hat nie geschmeichelt und hat nichts verborgen)
das nicht zum Dulden – das zum Kämpfen wies,
sein Weg auf seiner Suche nach dem Morgen.

Im Beilfallstosen hören sie ihn nahen,
und sehen ihn im offenen Wagen kommen.
Es wächst der Urschrei brüllend zum Orkan,
und alle sind vor Seligkeit benommen.

So wie ein hunderttausenköpfig Tier
erhebt die Menge sich zu wildem Leben
und angestrampelt wie ein schneller Stier
stampft die Begeisterung auf Hitlers Wegen.*

The ballad ends with the exclamation: 'Give generously! So we can hold out!'

Halt, of course, as it expressly points out in every issue (print run 30,000 copies), is 'more than a newspaper! *Halt* is struggle against the lie.' The lie it sets out to struggle against is essentially the lie of the gas chambers which, allegedly, never existed in the Third Reich. To support the lie, *Halt* quotes an alleged document dating from 1948, implying that there were no killings by poison gas in Mauthausen or certain other camps. That document is signed by one 'Müller, Major', and one 'Lachoud' testified 'to its correctness'. Both are said to have been members of the military police service with the Allied military command. According to information from the Austrian Ministry of the Interior, no such office ever existed. Nearly all other *Halt* articles dispense similar nonsense.

But should one fight against such journals? Should one sue them? Should one ban them? I believe one should. The youngsters who have these rags thrust into their hands are often very ignorant about the Third Reich. If they are served up such a concoction of lies and alleged evidence some of them, at least, may be impressed. What must impress them even more is that nobody is taking any action against these articles, from which they are

---

* The jubilation when the Führer came, / the people along his road grew into a river, / like a flood which truly had no end. / And all were waiting for him to come. // And everyone knew what his coming meant: / (he never flattered and never concealed anything) / something pointing not to suffering but to struggle, / his road of search for a morrow. // Amidst the roar of cheers they hear him approach, / and see him coming in the open car. / The primal shout grows roaring into a hurricane, / and all are stunned by bliss. // Like to a hundred-thousand-headed beast / the crowd rises up to savage life / and stampeding like a swift bull / enthusiasm tramples along Hitler's paths.

bound to conclude that if these statements are not stopped then they must probably be true. We should not allow this kind of conclusion.

I believe, moreover, that the state must observe its own laws, and these laws stipulate that neo-Nazi activity is punishable. The journal *Halt* constitutes the continuous offence of neo-Nazi activity. This is obvious to anyone reading it, even though the authors are forever using certain protective formulations designed to present their outpourings as a scholarly historical discussion.

I would, however, urge that the dissemination of such matter be made an offence in itself. My reason is that National Socialist activity in Austria carries a minimum punishment of five years' imprisonment, and because no jury would wish to put anyone behind bars for some idiotic scribbling, this kind of trial invariably ends in acquittal. If, on the other hand, the punishment were a matter of months then the offenders would be sentenced. Unlike many of my friends I do believe that there is a good case for making the allegations that 'Auschwitz is a lie' a punishable offence. It has never yet been made for scholarly reasons but has always served the exclusive aim of making Nazism seem harmless and/or agitating against 'the Jews' who are allegedly spreading that lie.

This is opposed by the view that the denial of the existence of gas chambers actually testifies to a relatively decent attitude: those concerned thereby admit that it would be a crime to gas Jews – and they don't wish to see Hitler accused of such a crime. This may be true of a few lunatics who actually regard the gas chambers as Allied constructions. In fact, however, one is dealing with people who may be insane but who are also cynical: they deny the gas chambers just as Hitler had denied his intention ever to wage war. I believe, moreover, that the survivors of the Holocaust, just like the members of any religious community, are entitled not to have their martyrdom mocked. The claim of the 'Auschwitz lie' is a slap in the face of all those who have gone through the martyrdom of Auschwitz, and indeed a slap in the face of their children. On the soil of Germany, which bears the responsibility for Auschwitz, it seems to me entirely legitimate to protect the survivors and their children against such slaps by penal legislation.

There is a difference between an American leaflet and a paper published in Austria or West Germany spreading the lie of the 'Auschwitz lie', and a difference between a mentally unbalanced American being responsible for it and a practising West German lawyer. For my part, I am certainly determined to make use of the facilities provided by the law against incorrigible people like that, even though this will sometimes assume the character of a grotesque mini-war which I would normally regard as beneath me. The fact is, I not only believe that the brochures of those people are less harmless than they are sometimes depicted, but that the people themselves, ridiculous as they are, could be dangerous. (I can think of no one more ridiculous than Adolf Hitler.)

A good illustration of my thesis is the attorney Manfred Roeder from Bensheim in Hesse. He came to my attention as the author of the preface to the brochure *The Auschwitz Lie* by Thies Christophersen. Thies Christophersen had spent the war at Rajsko, an ancillary camp of Auschwitz, where Auschwitz inmates were used as forced labour: attempts were made then to grow plants at Rajsko from which rubber might be obtained for German industry. I don't know what induced Christophersen to dispute that there had been gas chambers in Auschwitz or that Jews had been murdered there: the Rajsko inmates were indeed not gassed, because they were needed. It is conceivable that Christophersen became so involved in his theses that subsequently he did not want to retract them. In view of the overwhelming evidence for mass murder at Auschwitz this would suggest mental derangement, but there will always be a few lunatics. The problem only arises from the fact that such balderdash has actually been published and that the preface by an attorney has stamped it as a serious contribution to the discussion.

I therefore wrote to the Chamber of Lawyers in Frankfurt and demanded that disciplinary proceedings be instituted against Roeder. Roeder's reaction was the publication, in his periodical *Bürgerinitiative* (*Citizens' Initiative*), of a letter of vilification by a former Austrian Nazi called Munk, who was wanted by the provincial court in Innsbruck for fraud and had therefore fled to Argentina. In that letter, posted in Argentina, Munk asserted that I had not been in a concentration camp for a single day, that in reality I had no engineer's degree, and that during the war I had been an informer of the Security Service in Bucharest.

I sued, and the hearing was held in the court of Roeder's home town of Bensheim in Hesse. The walls of the courthouse were decorated with small swastika flags, and four policemen with dogs escorted me through a cordon of some two hundred 'citizens' whose 'initiative' in Roeder's sense of the word consisted of catcalls: 'There's a stench of garlic here ... Down with international Jewry ... Judah perish ... Hitler hasn't gassed all the Jews ...,' their scanned comments belying the 'Auschwitz lie'. The courtroom, too, was filled with Roeder's supporters and the judge explained how he saw the proceedings: 'We are not at the Nuremberg Tribunal here, which passed its sentence on the grounds of falsified documents.' Indeed we were not at the Nuremberg Tribunal: the judge, in no way up to the publicity of the case, adjourned the proceedings as soon as they had opened.

The newspapers were indignant at this open demonstration of neo-Nazism and the Minister President of Hesse apologized to me for the incidents. Whereupon Manfred Roeder instantly went on to the offensive again: he called West Germany a 'Zionist republic' and, regarding this as the peak of mockery, framed its sovereign eagle in a Star of David. However, he committed the mistake this time of personally insulting a number of German politicans also, who took out actions against him. These actions were combined into one, and in February 1976 new proceedings took place in Darmstadt. There Roeder was finally sentenced – bound over for seven months of good behaviour.

The good behaviour looked like this: in the spring of 1980 bombings took place in several German towns, for which a 'Deutsche Aktionsgruppe' ('German Action Group') claimed responsibility. In August there followed an act of arson against a refugee hostel, when two Vietnamese lost their lives. In their investigations of this the German police eventually succeeded in arresting six members of the German Action Group – their leader was Manfred Roeder. On 28 June 1982 he was sentenced to thirteen years' imprisonment for 'heading a terrorist association'.

Anyone thinking that only lunatics would have taken Roeder's verbal attacks on me seriously would be mistaken. In Austria not only the paper of former SS men, *Der Kamerad* ('The Comrade'), published the Hermann Munk letter, but even Federal Chancellor Bruno Kreisky referred to it when, as reported in an earlier chapter, he accused me in an interview with a foreign correspondent of having worked for the Gestapo.

When I sued *Kamerad* for the Munk letter, the SS old comrades' association submitted to the court two essential witnesses in support of the truth of Munk's allegation. One was the former SS leader Jan Verbelen, who had been sentenced to death in Belgium *in absentia* and in 1963 had been arrested in Austria at my instigation, though of course acquitted there. The other was Bruno Kreisky. A pity no one took a photograph: the Chancellor of the Republic and the ex-SS man and right-wing extremist on the same page.

Needless to say, neither witness knew anything to support Munk's allegations. Munk himself had already been questioned in Buenos Aires, by way of the legal assistance arrangement, at the time of my suit against Roeder, and had declared that what he had written was not based on personal knowledge but had been told him by a German, who unfortunately was no longer alive. *Kamerad* was convicted of slander because, as the judge stated, the journal had been unable to produce 'even a shadow of proof' of its accusations.

But being unable to produce even a shadow of proof of their allegations has never bothered the neo-Nazis – nor has it ever stopped them from denying the most crushing evidence against them.

46

The Test Case

A person denying the existence of the Auschwitz gas chambers is invariably
either an old Nazi or a neo-Nazi. Moreover, he is probably a fool, for he
is venturing out on ground where, except with children or mental defectives,
he has no chance of success. The circle of those willing to go along with
his arguments will remain extremely small, at least for the next few decades.
The professional neo-Nazi therefore will rather tend to present Auschwitz
in a relativist light. He will deny not the gas chambers but the figure of six
million dead, and he will try to offset them by the dead of Dresden or My
Lai. As for the murder of Jews in the Third Reich, he will either tacitly
approve of it or he will try to present it as a wrong decision by a few
disagreeable types such as Eichmann or Himmler. Certainly he will not
even try to disseminate the lie of the Auschwitz lie, because he would find
himself offside.

Yet there is another argument by which persons leaning towards Nazism
can be instantly identified: the quarrel about the *Diary of Anne Frank*.
'Isn't the genuineness of that book rather controversial?' is one of the stock
questions by which people try to probe where their interlocutor stands. Or
sometimes more directly: 'But this is allegedly [probably, obviously] a
forgery.'

The neo-Nazis know why they are attacking that book with such
vehemence: to my mind it has moved more people than the Nuremberg
trials or even the Eichmann trial. Because here average people were suddenly able to identify with an average victim and experience another

person's fate as their own. The state of mind of a young girl forced to hide in an attic does not surpass our powers of imagination as, for instance, the account of an inmate who has survived the hell of Auschwitz may. The *Diary of Anne Frank* is the fortunate instance of a personal report which, on the one hand, radiates unadorned authenticity and on the other displays such a measure of literary quality that it is capable of captivating any human being.

Added to this is the story of the discovery of the diary, which could not have been bettered by a publicist: on 1 August 1944 Anne Frank, in hiding from the Gestapo along with her family and a few friends in an attic in Amsterdam, confided to her diary: 'If I'm watched like this I start by getting snappy, then unhappy, and finally I twist my heart round again, so that the bad is on the outside and the good is on the inside and keep on trying to find a way of becoming what I would so like to be, and what I could be, if ... there weren't any other people living in the world.' These are the final words Anne Frank wrote in her diary. Three days later there was that knock at the attic door which the occupants had been fearfully awaiting for two years. The door was broken down, five uniformed men stepped in and arrested those in hiding – Anne Frank, her father, her mother, her brother, a further couple and their son, and a dentist. A Dutchman had denounced them, and they were now taken to Auschwitz, to be moved from there to Bergen-Belsen. Otto Frank, Anne's father, was the only one to survive, so that he was later able to report what occurred that morning: 'The SS man found a small writing case and asked if it contained jewelry. I told him there was only paper in it. He flung the papers, including Anne's diary, on the floor and stuffed our bits of silver and Hanukkah candelabrum into his briefcase. Had he taken the diary with him, no one would ever have known anything about my daughter.'

Anne Frank lost her life at Bergen-Belsen in March 1945. A year later her father returned to Amsterdam and went to that attic. The diary was still lying where the SS man had flung it down. It became the most important book written about the Third Reich, the *Diary of Anne Frank* has been translated into more than thirty languages and provided the model for a stage play and later a film. The Anne Frank House in Amsterdam has become a place of pilgrimage and countless young people travel to Bergen-Belsen every year to stand there in remembrance of the dead and to pray. Anne Frank's diary has gone straight to the heart of young people and drawn a response from them. That is why the neo-Nazis had to do anything they could to question its authenticity.

One evening in October 1958 a friend phoned me at my flat in Linz and asked me to come to the Landestheater at once. A performance of the *Diary of Anne Frank* was being disturbed by anti-Semitic demonstrators.

I did in fact see a gang of juveniles between fifteen and seventeen, mostly secondary-school pupils, who were shouting their slogans into the auditorium: 'Traitors! Arse-lickers! Swindlers!' From the gallery they threw leaflets into the stalls, in which they were more specific: 'This play is a swindle. Anne Frank never lived. The Jews have invented the whole business to squeeze out more compensation. Don't believe a word of it. It's all pure invention.'

The incident was symptomatic. Everywhere in Austria and in Germany the old Nazis, new Nazis and fellow travellers who did not want to be reminded of the past, were making countless attempts to unmask the book as a fraud. One of these, at a secondary school in Lübeck, even led to a lawsuit: a senior master by the name of Lothar Stielau had publicly declared the book to be a forgery and had thereupon been sued by Anne Frank's father. Three experts in court had confirmed the authenticity of the book and the court had found against the 'teacher'. But even such a verdict was questioned by the Nazis: experts could be bought, and the German judiciary dared not antagonize the Jews.

Two days after the incident in the Landestheater I was sitting with a friend in a Linz café discussing the leaflets. A few secondary schoolboys sat down at the next table, and my friend addressed one of them whose parents he knew well: 'Were you there during the demonstration, Fritz?'

'Unfortunately no, but some of my classmates were.'

'And what do you think of it?'

'Well – it's simple enough. There's no proof Anne Frank ever lived.' Anyone could claim that she was in a mass grave at Bergen-Belsen, anyone could get hold of an old exercise book and write something or other in it, anyone could 'find' that exercise book in an attic.

'But surely Anne Frank's father is still alive.' I objected.

'That doesn't prove anything.'

'Hang on, her father testified that they were arrested by the Gestapo.'

'Yes, yes, we know all that.'

'Suppose the Gestapo official was found who arrested Anne Frank. Would you accept that as proof?'

With a grin the young man accepted this bet: 'Okay, if he admits it himself.'

This gave me the idea of finding the man who, fourteen years earlier, had arrested Anne Frank in a house in Amsterdam. And absurd though it seemed, I felt convinced I'd succeed.

An appendix to the diary provided my first clue: a man called Paul Kraler, a Dutch employee of the firm Kohlen and Co., which had been owned by Anne's father, remembered how, after the Franks' arrest, he had tried to intercede for them at Gestapo headquarters in Amsterdam. On that occasion he had spoken to the official who had arrested the family, an SS man from Vienna, whose name began with something like 'Silver'. Kraler's account drew sneering comment from Austrian Nazis: everybody knew that the name 'Silver' did not even exist in Austria – further proof that the Anne Frank story was phoney. To me, however, it was obvious that 'Silver' was presumably 'Silber'. He was certainly an Austrian (he didn't really have to be a Viennese, as many Austrians abroad referred to themselves as coming from Vienna), and he need not have held senior rank in the SS. He had probably been a Rottenführer or perhaps just a private.

I found eight men called Silbernagel, who had been members of the Nazi party or the SS and were the right age. One of them, a former Obersturmführer, could be eliminated from the start because of his high rank – in recognition of which he had become a prominent official in Burgenland. The other seven would have to be looked into. I requested a friend to get in touch with private detective agencies and inquiry bureaux and tell all of them the same story: he had been approached for a loan by a man called Silbernagel and would like to know something about him. In this way we received a mass of information on Silbernagels with all possible first names – but the man we were searching for was not among them.

In 1963 I was invited to Holland by Dutch television and visited the Anne Frank memorial – I laid my hand on the wall the young girl had touched, as if I could draw strength from it for my researches. For the moment, however, I was moving in a totally wrong direction: the Dutch suggested that the SS man I was looking for might not have been called Silbernagel but Silbertaler. Prior to the war a few people of this name had lived in Vienna, but they had been Jews. Eventually I found three Aryan Silbertalers, but they were beyond suspicion for different reasons.

On my next visit to Amsterdam I happened to talk to two friends of mine who were familiar with the Anne Frank case. Ben A. Sijes was employed in the Netherlands Institute for Second World War Documentation and Mr Taconis was a senior Dutch police officer. Together we scrutinzed the list of people who had worked for Eichmann. As I was about to leave, Mr Taconis observed that he had some reading matter for me for my trip: the photocopy of a telephone directory of the Gestapo in Holland, containing over 300 names.

My flight to Vienna took two hours. I settled down in my seat and scanned the Gestapo list. I had almost dropped off when I came to the page 'IV Special Squad'. Under 'IV B4, Joden (Jews)' I read:

> Kempin
> Buschmann
> Scherf
> Silberbauer

I was sure: this was my man.

No sooner had I got back to Vienna than I pounced on the telephone directory. But there were quite a number of Silberbauers in Vienna and there would be a lot more in telephone and address books for the rest of Austria. I was in too much of a hurry to enlist a detective agency once more to follow up every one of them. This time I could proceed more systematically. I knew that most of the officials of Department IV B4 had come from the German and Austrian police forces, mostly from criminal investigation branches. My Silberbauer therefore had presumably been with the Vienna police – and perhaps he still was.

I telephoned Dr Josef Wiesinger, the head of Section II C in the Ministry of the Interior, with whom I was on good terms, and burst out with my conviction: 'I've found the Gestapo man who arrested Anne Frank. He's a Vienna policeman by the name of Silberbauer.'

'What's his first name?' asked Wiesinger, not entirely convinced.

'That I don't know.'

'There are at least six men in the Vienna police with the name of Silberbauer – so which of them do you mean?

To me this seemed a perfectly easy investigation. One need only look at the men's personal files and discover which one had been with Department IV B4 in Amsterdam in August 1944.

'Submit an inquiry in writing to my office,' Wiesinger suggested and wished me good luck.

On 15 October Sijes and Taconis came to Vienna and jointly we called on Dr Wiesinger. 'What emerged from the search for Silberbauer?' I asked.

But Dr Wiesinger waved my question aside. 'I am sorry, we haven't got that far yet in the matter.'

This was not so: on the morning of 11 November *Volksstimme*, the paper of the Communist Party of Austria, published a sensational story: Inspector Karl Silberbauer had been suspended from duty because he might have to face criminal proceedings for the part he had played in the Anne Frank case. Radio Moscow was also instantly sure about who was to be commended for this coup against neo-Nazism: 'the vigilance of Austrian resistance fighters and other progressive elements'.

I phoned Dr Wiesinger, who squirmed with embarrassment: 'How were we to know that Silberbauer would blab it out? We expected him to keep his mouth shut.'

I was to learn later that Dr Wiesinger had been instructed from above to keep the whole business secret. Silberbauer had been suspended from duty on 4 October with orders not to say a word about the matter. But the irate police inspector (this is the second lowest rank in the Austrian police) did not follow instructions. He complained to at least one colleague that he was 'having some bother because of that Anne Frank'. The colleague, it so happened, was a member of the Communist Party and so the story got into *Volksstimme*.

Meanwhile journalists the world over were getting hold of the case. A Dutchman, Jules Huf, was the first to succeed in interviewing Silberbauer (I had given him his address).

'Aren't you sorry for what you did?' Huf asked.

'Of course I am sorry. Sometimes I feel positively like an outcast. Each time I want to take a tram I have to buy a ticket now, just like anybody else. I can no longer show my police card.'

'And what about Anne Frank?' Have you read her diary?'

'I bought the little book last week to see if I was mentioned in it. But I'm not.'

'Millions of people read the diary before you did. But you could have been the first to do so.'

'That's quite true. I never thought of that. Maybe I should have picked it up after all.'

Had he done so, the diary of Anne Frank would not have shaken the world's conscience.

I never again saw the secondary schoolboy I talked to in Linz and I don't know what he is doing now. Sometimes I should have liked one of those youngsters to come to me and say: 'Yes, Herr Wiesenthal, you have convinced me.' But to admit that one has been the victim of an error requires courage. And that, unfortunately, is what neo-Nazis almost invariably lack.

47

So-Called Security

My life in Austria has not always been entirely free from danger. At the beginning, when I still had my office in Linz, I was known only in specialist circles: on the one hand, to the Austrian security authorities and to the American departments concerned with Nazi crimes, and on the other to the Nazis. Among the public I was then scarcely known; word spread only gradually that there was a person searching for hidden SS men – and that was then no disgrace. My contact with the Americans, moreover, automatically assured me of a kind of respectful distance: one didn't attack a man who was occasionally seen in the company of an American officer.

I was never really in danger from those I actively pursued: for one thing, those people were too shrewd and too careful to stage anything against me – much as professional criminals are generally careful not to attack a police officer. For another, they were possibly too burnt out, or too much concerned with their own escape, to mount any major operation. I could also believe that the idea of killing a Jew had suddenly become taboo for them: that was something one simply couldn't afford to do immediately after the war.

The only person who then dared to attack me physically was – a Jew. In the summer of 1946 survivors from the Polish town of Tarnów had made statements to me incriminating a member of the Jewish police by the name of David Zimmet. One day Zimmet suddenly appeared in my room and was about to go for me with a knife. Luckily there were no ball-point pens then: we used pen and ink. I hurled my inkwell into my attacker's face and started yelling. That was the only attempt ever made against my life.

Maybe I only imagined that I was safe: when one has twice in one's life been in a hopeless situation, a hair's breadth from death, yet escaped an execution squad, one believes, albeit irrationally, that one cannot be shot by anyone. I never therefore took any particular safety precautions. Admittedly, after a few physical attacks by youngsters, apparently neo-Nazis, I was permitted to carry a pistol for my own defence, but I realized that this was ultimately pointless: against a professional killer I wouldn't stand a chance anyway, and against amateurs I didn't need it – amateurs are better looked in the eye and talked to. For a long time, therefore, one only had to ring the doorbell at my office to be admitted. Of course I looked through the peephole which most front doors in Austria have to see the face of my caller – but I never left even former SS or Gestapo men waiting outside.

I probably believe that one dies when one is destined to die and that one lives as long as one is destined to live; bullet-proof vests and alarm systems make little difference. Red Army Factions have killed people who lived inside fortresses and were driven around in armoured cars, but each increased security measure had merely produced increased efforts to get round it – and ultimately the individual is always powerless against terrorism. One can smash only the terrorist scene. Everything I had lived through merely confirmed me in my fatalism, most of all an incident whose meaning was revealed to me only later. I was probably never since the war in greater danger of my life, and yet I escaped it by pure chance – though I didn't wish to call it that.

The Mauthausen concentration camp is in the immediate vicinity of Linz, and on 5 May commemorative ceremonies are held there to mark its liberation by the Americans. I was invariably invited to attend these ceremonies. In the early 1970s, therefore, I was once more participating and got into conversation with the members of a Soviet delegation. These former inmates from Russia had probably seen me at some previous meeting or else knew me from newspaper photographs: anyway, they came up to me in a friendly manner, and as I have been able to speak Russian since childhood, or at any rate understand it, I was able to converse with them quite easily. It struck me that one of them, a young man, was speaking Russian with such a heavy accent that he could not possibly come from the Soviet Union, not even from one of its provinces. In point of fact, he told me that he was from South America and was studying in Moscow. His companions explained to him who I was: I was tracking down Nazi criminals and bringing them to justice. I had played a vital part in tracking down Eichmann.

Thereupon the young South American took my hand in both his hands and softly muttered: 'I thank you.'

In 1978 Hans Joachim Klein — who had been involved in the attack on the OPEC conference in Vienna — broke with the extreme left-wing scene. He has since lived in secrecy, having to hide both from the judiciary and from his former comrades in the 'Revolutionary Cells'. In 1979 Rowohlt published a book, *Rückkehr in die Menschlichkeit — Appell eines ausgestiegenen Terroristen* ('Return to Humanity — An Appeal by a Former Terrorist'). Among other things it reproduced an interview given by Klein to the French paper *Libération*, in which he mentioned attempts on the lives of certain persons, planned by the 'Revolutionary Cells': 'Wilfried Boese had suggested to Haddat [the leader of the terrorist operation at Entebbe] to make an attempt on the life of the Eichmann hunter Simon Wiesenthal. The reason was that Wiesenthal cooperated closely with the Mossad, the Israeli secret service. But when the project was discussed, Carlos said 'that it would be lunacy to want to shoot that type, for he is an anti-Nazi'.

I had seen several photographs of Carlos, who was a South American studying in the Soviet Union before embarking on his terrorist career. I felt convinced that I had met the man in the photograph before — that 5 May in Mauthausen. (My friend Dr Prem Dobias, who was also present at the time and had subsequently seen pictures of Carlos, confirmed my belief: 'There's no doubt, that's the same man.')

I always find it shocking that people can drift into extreme left-wing terrorism from what are often exceedingly honest anti-Fascist convictions. People like young Gudrun Ensslin, who went from identification with the victims of the Vietnam War, via protests against the Vietnam War, to terrorist strikes against American institutions and eventually into an aimless terrorist existence. Ulrike Meinhoff is probably the best-known example of a young woman who initially devoted herself warmly to the weak, to the victims of society, and ultimately made innocent people the victims of her terrorist actions.

The explanation probably calls for psychology, or even psychopathology. When a person who has not himself suffered any pain identifies so much with the pain of others, even though he scarcely knows that either and at most has heard or read about it, then our joy over that person's commitment should always be tempered by a dose of suspicion: is there not such a thing as pathological yearning for pain as such? Does the person concerned not, self-pityingly, see himself in every sufferer? Is he not trying, in a kind of megalomania, to redeem the sufferers only to exalt himself? Is sharing another's sufferings not important to him in the same way as it is to the sadist — who is always a masochist at the same time?

This process, it seems to me, must have taken place in the minds of the members of the 'Revolutionary Cells' (the Bader-Meinhoff gang, the Red Army Faction): in the end they cause suffering only to delight in it. Suicide in Stammheim prison is a logical consequence: murder of oneself produces the enjoyment of supreme suffering.

There are young neo-Nazis with a similar psychological make-up. In numerous trials I have come across youngsters who, at one time or another, have gone through a phase of great personal engagement for a 'good cause'. But it was never a 'cause' they knew from personal experience, or that they knew anything about. The sufferings of those they felt committed to were invariably beyond their national frontiers. In Austria it was then nearly always South Tyrol, the sufferings of the betrayed South Tyrolean population allegedly enslaved by the Italians, that the young Nazis were committed to. To listen to them, one might have believed that they had spent their entire youth on a South Tyrolean farm, watching the carabinieri beat up the farmer, rape his wife, and prevent his children from singing German songs. During the trials it usually emerged that they, who had thrown bombs and blown up pylons to fight for South Tyrol's freedom, had often never set foot in the region. All that mattered to them was to have a demonstrable object for their own enthusiasm, in reality for their own aggression.

Even the young Nazis who went for me did not do so because I had denounced one of them to the courts, or got their father, their uncle or their brother who had been an SS man, into prison (these would have been understandable and almost rational motives), but they fought against me as the representative of an idea. I stood for something, either Zionism, or the eternal revenge of Jewry, or the besmirching of the Nazi idea. It was no accident that a German and not an Austrian Nazi undertook the most serious attempt against me: in 1982 Ekkehard Weil escaped from prison in West Germany and came to Austria where he met up with men who thought like him. The group organized a series of outrages against Jewish figures – the biggest one on my home on 11 July 1982.

The explosive charge, which had been placed at the entrance to the building, caused considerable material damage, and even the house next door had all its windows broken. Admittedly I would only have been in danger of my life if the explosion had ripped open the nearby gas main, but this, undoubtedly, had not been part of the neo-Nazis' plan. (They were not therefore charged with attempted murder.)

Weil was sentenced to five years' imprisonment, but his aggression was still so unbridled in the courtroom that he tried to hurl himself at me and had to be restrained by a police officer.

This trial, incidentally, ended with convictions all round, against all nine accused, and for once represents good marks for an Austrian jury: when they start throwing explosives about in their own country, the young Nazis cannot expect any sympathy.

48

How to Deal with Opponents

More than twenty years ago I was invited by the 'Teutonia' students' fraternity to visit Baden-Baden to talk about coming to terms with the past. My opposing speaking was a certain Franzel, of whom I only knew that he was a Sudeten German living in Munich. Although all my friends tried strongly to dissuade me from speaking in such a setting, I went to Baden-Baden. Our job is to convince not those who share our views anyway but those who apparently still find it difficult to assess correctly what happened in the Third Reich. I thought it was a good sign that the 'Teutonia' men wanted to talk to me at all.

Of course there were some among them who had ulterior motives for inviting me. Like that young man who was the first to speak in the discussion and thought he'd put me in my place. His face flushed because all eyes were on him, he fired a sentence into the hall, which no doubt he thought tremendously effective: 'Herr Wiesenthal, we know you well. You have a Nazi for breakfast, another for lunch and yet another for dinner.'

Before he could carry on I interrupted him: 'You are mistaken. I don't eat pork.'

The ice was broken. There was an outburst of laughter, turning to non-stop applause. The questions which followed were entirely normal, reasonable and unpolemical, and I answered them calmly and factually. After the official discussion we continued our conversation in a smaller circle, and eventually I was asked to stay on an extra day to tell them more.

Many of the young men facing me simply did not know enough about that dark period. Many had been deliberately misinformed, but it was possible to discuss that misinformation with them. I began to realize how difficult it was for many of them to cope with a past in which their fathers, and often even their brothers, were personally involved. One of the participants in the discussion, for instance, had a much older brother who had been with the SS. He had shown his elder brother a photograph from an illustrated magazine, showing mountains of dead bodies in a concentration camp. Whereupon the respected 'big brother' had declared: 'This is a monstrous lie: those bodies are *papier mâché*. The Americans manufactured them after the war so they could turn their military victory over the Germans into a moral victory as well.'

From the way he was talking to me I realized that the young man had already developed some misgivings about his brother's explanation. Our conversation now gave me a chance to face him, eye to eye, and tell him: 'I have myself stood at the edge of such mountains of bodies. I have watched my friends drop into the pits next to me. Do you think I am lying to you?'

It is not always the worst types who are most provocative in such discussions. Behind their bold exterior often lurk the doubts which have long been aroused in them. Once they realize that one does not by any means 'have them for breakfast' they are then more easily and more quickly won over than those tepid ones who avoid all confrontation. I have remained in touch with many members of the 'Teutonia' fraternity, and some of them write to me to this day.

Humour, in my opinion, is one of the best bridges that can be built to an opponent. Every good joke contains a greater or lesser amount of aggression, and by getting rid of it in this way one can then speak more calmly. Nothing defuses as much as laughter. Behaviourists, as we know, maintain that laughter is a relic of showing our teeth in a way which tells the other individual that we will certainly not bite. People who have laughed together do not want to kill one another any more. Humour, however, should not only help us build bridges to our opponents, but it should sometimes be deliberately employed as a weapon: the neo-Nazis are best fought by making them look ridiculous. It should even be possible, in retrospect, to make figures like Hitler and Himmler objects not only of revulsion but also of ridicule. I cannot think of anything more ridiculous than that moustachioed Germanic dwarf with his tinted hair, who barked his speeches like a seal and then, like a string puppet, flung up his arm awkwardly and crookedly in the Hitler salute. One cannot nowadays watch film clips of his big speeches without laughing. Or stand amazed at the fact that this half-crazed, half-educated *petit bourgeois* actually managed to fascinate millions. This was probably due to the fact that, during his earlier speeches, people had far too rarely stood up to make him look ridiculous by a skilful counter-question. At least in dealing with the neo-Nazis we should, in my opinion, apply this recipe of ridicule every time. (Which is not to say that in serious cases we should not also resort to legal means.)

Unfortunately such laughter (quite understandably) is at times difficult for the survivors of the Holocaust. I remember, for instance, that on 20 April 1978 American neo-Nazis in Chicago wanted to stage a parade in honour of Hitler's birthday: they wanted to march in full uniform through the suburb of Skokie, where a large number of Jews live. Protests by the Jewish inhabitants were unsuccessful because the American Civil Liberties Union (ACLU) decreed that the First Amendment of the American Constitution guaranteed, even to neo-Nazis, the right to demonstrate and openly state their views. The ACLU happened to be represented by, of all things, a Jewish lawyer, who unhesitatingly put the words of the First Amendment above its sense: much as he personally abominated that parade, he yet had to defend the neo-Nazis' right to stage it, because the First Amendment was the law, and no one must set the law aside.

I was just then in Chicago for a lecture, and so I was drawn into the dispute. My friends asked me to phone the ACLU and talk to the lawyer. So I tried to explain to him that the issue here was not primarily freedom of opinion but a provocation. He should try to picture what would go on inside people who had lost their families through the Nazis or who were possibly still suffering from disabilities due to their persecution, and who would now have to watch men with swastika armbands parading outside their windows. 'These people need protection, not the twenty neo-Nazis.'

But the only reply I received to my objections was the same formula: 'The First Amendment permits it.'

After some twenty minutes of telephone conversation I had spent my arguments and reacted – with hindsight – not quite fairly: 'I have been told you are a Jewish lawyer; I don't know whether you are young or old, but I can tell you one thing, and you can write it down and hang it up over your bed: A Jew may be stupid, but it's not obligatory.'

This had swept away my anger, and I was once more relaxed enough to reflect on the situation. Unfortunately I was the only relaxed one, because all my friends in the Jewish Federation were firmly resolved to oppose the Nazi provocation by a huge counter-demonstration. Five thousand Jews were to march through Chicago to show that they would not stand for Nazi provocations. This seemed to me a mistake: it would only bolster the self-confidence of those twenty youths to know they could bring so many Jews out into the streets. They should be treated in exactly the opposite way: they should be ignored or, at most, made to look ridiculous.

So I made my counter-proposal: twenty young Jews should march through Chicago with a herd of pigs. The pigs should wear swastikas round their bellies, and one of them should have a moustache painted on, or else one of the young Jews should dress up as 'the greatest leader of all time' and trot ahead of the pigs. All the papers and major television stations would be invited. Why should the neo-Nazis always annoy the Jews? Why not, for a change, let the Jews annoy the neo-Nazis?

My proposal did not find favour. Another survivor, Sol Goldstein, with just as much right as me to speak on behalf of the victims, convinced the Jewish Federation that the mass parade was the better reaction. I still think it was the wrong reaction: it was disproportionate to the real neo-Nazi danger in the USA. The American police had to protect the neo-Nazis against the Jews. The media gave those sixteen misguided pubertal milksop faces (they had not even mustered the planned twenty) a degree of publicity they would never have enjoyed without the 5000 demonstrating Jews. People who, more than anything else, were ridiculous were able to feel like martyrs.

Of course, there is no patent recipe for how to handle neo-Nazis. While in one instance it may be correct to take as little notice of them as possible and at most to make them look ridiculous, in another case it may be necessary to react with firmness and resolution. The same big protest march which in Chicago, in view of the ridiculous nature of the swastika parade there, seemed inadequate to me would have been exceedingly useful in Austria or in Germany now and again, because in these countries neo-Nazism has to be seen against the background of a still not totally overcome Nazism. The American neo-Nazis are crazy outsiders. The Austrian and German neo-Nazis, admittedly, are also outsiders, but their ideas continue to meet with approval from at least a part of the population. Anti-Semitic actions, in particular, are certain in Austria of (at least discreet) applause.

A Dr Norbert Burger, whose political programme would presumably be described as neo-Nazi in any other country, managed to secure 140,000 votes in the 1980 presidential elections, and his ideological colleague, the hereditary health specialist Dr Otto Scrinzi, collected 50,000 votes in the 1986 presidential elections. Political tendencies hiding behind such political manifestations have to be taken seriously.

I believe that we must manage to find the right combination of determination with a relaxed attitude. We should not take neo-Nazis so seriously that we magnify their importance, but we must not underrate them to an extent that will encourage them to tweak our noses. If I had to draft a programme for dealing with neo-Nazis, it would be like this: instead of imposing a fine on them they should be gathered into a group and driven to Auschwitz or some other extermination camp. They should there be shown the mountains of shoes, the mountains of spectacles, the mountains of suitcases, each representing one dead. They should be made to remove with their fingers some of the grass growing around the crematoria until they come to the layer of splintered bones which have accumulated there. They should be made to look into one of the ponds at the bottom of which the skeletons lie to this day, and they should be conducted by someone who had gone through all this himself. This should be a quiet, friendly old man or a quiet, friendly old woman, someone who likes children, even confused children. And he or she should tell them about it, day and night, until they say: 'Yes, you have convinced us.' I have often conducted such conversations. And what seemed to me most important about them I propose to sum up in the following chapter. It is my bequest to young people.

49

To My Young Readers

Survival is a privilege which entails obligations. I am forever asking myself what I can do for those who have not survived. The answer I have found for myself (and which need not necessarily be the answer for every survivor) is: I want to be their mouthpiece, I want to keep their memory alive, to make sure the dead live on in that memory.

But we, the survivors have an obligation not only to the dead but also to future generations: we must pass on to them our experiences, so they can learn from them. Information is defence.

It is not enough that everything has already been recorded in books. A book, unlike a person, cannot be asked questions. A witness must be a 'live' witness. That is why at meetings of survivors I have invariably urged: 'You have children, you have grandchildren, your neighbours have children – you must talk to them. You must tell them everything you experienced, and provoke their questions so they can pass on your story. Only in oral accounts does memory stay alive.

*

In the spring of 1968 I gave a series of lectures at universities in the United States and in Canada. I talked to well-dressed, well-nourished, cheerful young people, and suddenly I asked myself: How can I make a person who has never in his life experienced hunger or cold understand what a piece of bread, a slice of turnip or a jacket meant then? How can I communicate to someone who knows death only from reading the papers, what a person feels like when he sees the smoke rising from the crematoria, knowing that the greasy, sickly smell comes from people who were yesterday marching down the camp streets in a long column? With what words can I describe to these young people the pain of a mother whose child is snatched from her hand and thrust among those earmarked for the gas chamber? Can one communicate the stench – communicate it so it produces sickness and nausea – which emanates from a cattletruck in which dead persons have stood among the living for a week, unable to fall down only because there was not enough space? Can anyone understand that mingled with the shock at a further death there was also always among the living a touch of subconscious gratification: a little more room in the hut, no more disturbance of one's sleep by the rattle in his throat? Can I communicate to anyone what I was feeling as I stood at the edge of a pit in which there were already hundreds of dead and in which I would have lain a few minutes later if a ludicrous accident had not interrupted the execution?

I am afraid that it is impossible to communicate all these experiences. We can speak and shape our memories into words. But these words, even if our listeners absorb them avidly, do not become reality in their minds again. What happened in the Third Reich is beyond one's power of imagination.

Sometimes I am seized by the fear that a few hundred years from now teachers and children in history lessons will be saying: in the twentieth century Hitler tried to set up a great empire in Europe under National Socialist leadership. Contemporary witnesses maintained that he had attempted to exterminate the Jews of Europe. There is talk of the poisoning of the Jews in specially established camps. It seems that excesses were in fact committed, though these accounts are probably greatly exaggerated.

This seems to me a fundamental dilemma: we are under an obligation to make young people realize how unique, how unbelievable, how exceptional the period of the Holocaust was. But by this very attempt we make it difficult for them to accept our accounts as the truth and as facts. The incomprehensible remains incomprehensible.

*

Men can do nothing other than decide that life goes on. It is probably impossible to live with the continuous awareness of fifty million dead, six million of them murdered Jews – otherwise one would go out of one's mind. And yet it sometimes seems to me just as crazy that only a few decades afterwards, one can act as though that mountain of corpses never existed.

*

I have sometimes wondered whether for my lectures I should seek words which would move my listeners to tears. But I think that would make it too easy for me: tears flow readily – a sloppy tearjerker at the cinema on the next corner will produce them. What I wish to produce is a knowledge of the horror and an awareness of the danger. I don't so much want my listeners to be shocked here and now, as that the shock may continue to be aroused in them throughout their lives. So I tell them not only that many cities of Europe had been levelled to the ground at the end of the war and covered with dead bodies, but I also tell them that they have been rebuilt and that life there continues. But how are they to know, when visiting Coventry or Dresden, Nuremberg or Frankfurt, that these new buildings stand on the rubble of yesterday? They should, when waiting for a train at a station, looking forward to a journey to the east, recall now and again that through that same station rolled trains with hundreds of thousands of people destined for death in the east. It would in fact be appropriate to place plaques in all those railway stations, reading: 'Between 1942 and 1945 trains passed through here every day with the sole purpose of taking human beings to their annihilation.' It is not possible to set up such tablets everywhere – but one can carry them in one's mind.

*

Associations of resistance fighters should never content themselves with commemorating resistance then, but should also fight for resistance now. There exist still inhuman dictatorships, whose violations of human rights should be condemned. There are also the beginnings of Fascism, which should not be passed over in silence. There is still anti-Semitism which should be branded. Anyone who kept silent about Polish anti-Semitism in the 1960s has betrayed his dead brethren.

*

Survivors should be like seismographs. They should sense danger before others do, identify its outlines and reveal them. They are not entitled to be wrong a second time or to regard as harmless something that might lead to catastrophe. Coming to terms with the past means also that we, the victims, must recognize the misjudgements we made. We must learn from our mistakes.

These mistakes include the belief that we can confront anti-Jewish hate solely by gaining respect for our achievements. These mistakes include our failure to comprehend, even after two thousand years, that we are invariably the first victims of discord – wherever a majority is whipped up against a minority it is the Jews who are eventually crucified. These mistakes include watching and waiting while there may still be time to act.

I remember the first few years after Hitler's seizure of power. I was then a student in Poland, and we all knew that he broke treaties, that he was rearming, that he wanted something from the Poles. But even the ones who were worried thought it was just the Danzig Corridor.

The Nazis were not such bad psychologists as is frequently claimed. Long before they attacked a country they endeavoured to sow discord in it. The simplest way was to stir up the majority against the minorities, and the minorities against each other. At a time when Hitler already had his plan of attack against Poland in his desk drawer and when German industry was already producing the weapons needed, the Polish parliament spent months debating whether Jews should be permitted or forbidden to perform ritual slaughter. Our mistake was our failure to realize that the combination of traditional anti-Semitism in nearly all the countries we were living in, with the radical character of Nazi anti-Semitism, was bound to lead not to a mere doubling but to an exponential increase in anti-Semitic outrages.

Strange though it may sound, we, a people persecuted for two thousand years, underestimated the danger of persecution by Hitler. Just because we had experienced so much persecution, and survived it, we nurtured a deceptive conviction that we could not perish. This totally unfounded assurance probably lent the Jews in Israel the strengh to create their state – but it also deluded the Jews in Europe into watching passively as Nazism prepared their extermination. Instead of resisting, or at least fleeing, the Jews believed that they could come to some arrangement with Hitler, Himmler or Heydrich. They were acquainted with *Mein Kampf* and yet did not fight against it.

*

Our mistake was the belief that the nation of Schiller and Goethe could not submit to a Hitler or Himmler. The Jews of eastern Europe were especially Germanophile because they were the exponents of German culture in that region. When they were expelled from Germany centuries before, they took with them into exile their language, Middle High German, and preserved it there. (The same, incidentally, was done by the Spanish Jews, who took with them their Old Castilian in the form of Ladino on their expulsion from Spain.) I clearly remember the wall of bookshelves in our flat in a township called Buchach: most of the books were in German. When my mother wanted to communicate something really important to me, she would take down a German classic and say: 'You know, he put it much better than me – this is what I want to say to you.'

This was how the bulk of the Jewish intelligentsia in Galicia was brought up: we saw ourselves as outposts and custodians of German culture in the east. Each glance at our shelves confirmed our conviction that Hitler could have no hope in Germany. We regarded him as a peripheral phenomenon which would soon disappear again. I was then drawing cartoons for Polish and Jewish newspapers, and in them Hitler was always ridiculous rather than dangerous. Our mistake was the belief that a person who had read Goethe would be unable to read *Stürmer*.

*

We failed in that we did not prevent social conditions from arising which facilitated Hitler's seizure of power. Whenever I speak to young people I also tell them about those millions of unemployed who were then out on the streets, about people with notices hanging from their necks reading 'Willing to do any job'. Anyone saying this about himself will also do the job of a Hitler.

We failed in that, as politicians, as entrepreneurs, as journalists, as members of the intellectual elite, we were unable to consolidate democracy, and indeed in that at times, with our criticism, we contributed to undermining the last remnants of its reputation. While we were questioning a great many things the Nazis had a clear answer ready for everything: it is all the fault of the treaty of Versailles, it is the fault of democracy, it is the fault of the Jews. We Jews, too, allowed Hitler to grow big.

*

It is occasionally maintained that Nazism, at least of the Hitlerite type, has no hope of revival. There might be other forms of Fascism, there might be other persecutions – but never again as in the Third Reich. I believe that myself, but I have learned that control is better than confidence. National Socialist cells continue to exist, and we have no guarantee that under different social circumstances they might not again grow into life-threatening tumours. There is a small but active neo-Nazi scene in Austria, there is a small but active neo-Nazi scene in West Germany, and there are major political groupings, and even parties, whose ideology is not too far removed from Nazism. Probably the strongest Nazi scene – not in percentages of population but in absolute figures – exists in the United States: in a city like Milwaukee there were, and still are, parades of youth organizations in Nazi uniforms and with swastika armbands. Similar provocations have occurred in other cities.

I once showed the Republican Senator Robert Dole and his wife Elizabeth, when they were visiting Vienna, a number of neo-Nazi periodicals published in the USA, which under cover of the First Amendment propagate racialism and hatred. They were both shocked, but assured me that American democracy and its inhabitants' love of freedom were strong enough to offer no chance to old or new Nazis. I hope so too, but German politicians in the 1920s used similar words when questioned about the prospects of a small bully-boy group around a certain Adolf Hitler.

Although I always hope that we may learn from history, I am also afraid that we might learn nothing new and will merely repeat the old mistakes under new conditions. One of these is that we believe that democracy should not immediately flex all its muscles to fight against Fascist groups. Another is that we are afraid to mobilize right against wrong. Most European countries, for instance, have laws prohibiting the stirring up of racial hatred – but we allow brochures preaching it to be distributed to children in front of our schools. All because of fear that we might curtail some freedom of expression. In the USA such laws do not even exist. When the judges and attorneys of Chicago chose me as their 'Man of the Year', I strongly criticized that state of affairs: only by means of legislation against the stirring up of hatred could the flood of neo-Nazi publications in the USA be contained.

The principal ingredient of such agitation continues to be hatred of foreigners: wherever neo-Fascists appear – whether in England, France, Austria or the USA – they call on the majority to resist 'swamping by foreigners'. Swamping by coloured people from the British colonies, swamping by coloured people from France's former colonies, swamping by Yugoslav or Turkish guest workers, swamping by Mexicans or Puerto Ricans. True, the Jews are not mentioned at the top of the list in these pamphlets – but two thousand years have proved that they are always the first to be done to death.

*

One day I was walking down a street in Chicago with my friend Gerry Bender, an attorney, and came across a man distributing handbills. Their text ran: 'The rabbis of Dallas murdered Kennedy.' The leaflet bore a regular imprint: the man distributing it was called Villis (judging by the name a Lithuanian immigrant), and there was his address and telephone number. I took the leaflet to the District Attorney to enquire if the First Amendment permitted it to be distributed. The following dialogue developed:

'True, I am a foreigner, but I am a great friend of the United States, whose army liberated me from the concentration camp. That's why I am shocked to see such a leaflet being distributed here.'

The DA cast his eyes down the leaflet, and replied: 'The man could equally well have said, "The barbers of Dallas murdered Kennedy." That of course would be the same kind of nonsense, but he can't be stopped.'

'But don't you see', I asked him, 'that there is a difference between the barbers and the rabbis of Dallas? Jews have been killed before because they were held responsible for a certain murder – the barbers not yet. Besides, the rabbi represents a religion recognized by the state as well as by several million US citizens.'

The district attorney instructed me: 'Now if this Billis or Willis or whatever had written "Rabbi Eliahu Cohen killed Kennedy," then one would have to look into the matter. As it is, he referred quite imprecisely to 'the rabbis', and there are therefore no grounds for intervention.'

This is one of the greatest difficulties in the struggle against anti-Semitism: that it is so difficult to make people see that a particular Jew so easily becomes 'the Jews'.

*

In the autumn of 1967 I gave a number of lectures to Jewish communities in the United States. I think it was in Cleveland that a middle-aged man came up to me and addressed me as follows: 'I am not a survivor of the Holocaust myself, nor do I have relations in Europe who have lost anyone – but I believe that your work is important.'

'Not so,' I said to him; 'you too are a survivor, only you don't realize it yet. Hitler declared war on every Jew in the world. In all the treaties he concluded with all sorts of semi-Fascist states in Europe the first clause always was "Give me the Jews". That's how it was in Slovakia, that's how it was in France, that's how it was in Hungary, that's how it was even in the Italian republic of Salo. Believe me, if Hitler had won the war and there had been a peace treaty with the United States, its first clause would have been, "Give me the Jews". Because he wanted all of the Jews. Only because Hitler did not win the war did you survive. Every Jew is a survivor, even one born after the war.'

In a television discussion I once said: 'Hitler not only murdered millions of Jews and millions of his adversaries, he also morally destroyed millions of Germans and millions of Austrians – what's more, for generations to come. To belong to the victims is terrible – but it is even more terrible to belong to the victim-makers.'

*

The children of those who under the Nazis were on the side of the victims and the children of those who belonged to the victim-makers are living alongside each other in Austria and Germany, and have to live with each other. How can we shape that coexistence in such a way that there shall never again arise a generation of victim-makers and of victims? I don't think there is any other solution than constantly coming to terms with the past, and learning from it. There is no point in minimizing guilt in order to make it easier for sons and daughters to bear the failure of their fathers and grandfathers, their mothers and grandmothers. The entire guilt must be patent – only thus can the entire guilt be understood.

*

It worries me that young people – particularly in the United States – may believe that the Third Reich could never repeat itself. Least of all in their own country. That is not so: hatred can be nurtured anywhere, idealism can be perverted into sadism anywhere. If hatred and sadism combine with modern technology the inferno could erupt anew anywhere. The poison-gas shells which fell on the Kurdish towns in Iraq and exterminated their civilian inhabitants within hours were manufactured here and now. Unless we are vigilant, the history of the twentieth century will read like this: the beast in human shape got hold of a machine gun and, for the first time, was able to exterminate anything that moved.

*

The combination of hatred and technology is the greatest danger threatening mankind. This applies not only to the high technology of the atom bomb, it applies equally to the lesser technology of everyday life: I know people who spend hours sitting in front of their television sets because they have forgotten how to communicate with one another. Soon there will be no need to learn foreign languages because there will be pocket computers into which one speaks one's own language and from which a foreign language will ring out. Human beings will increasingly communicate with each other through computers. Sometimes I have the terrifying vision of computers talking to each other without human beings.

*

Many young people put their hopes in the progress of our culture and our civilization. They consider it impossible for the beast in us to break out again, and fear a return to the Dark Ages only in Iraq or in Iran. They believe that the Ayatollah Khomeini is by now an almost ludicrous relic. I myself made jokes about Hitler when I was twenty, and mocked the rising Nazis in cartoons, because I too believed in the inevitable victory of culture and civilization over the Dark Ages.

In reality culture and civilization are only a wafer-thin layer, beneath which the beast continues to lurk within us. The fact that we have brains from which sprang the theory of the link between mass and energy protects us in no way against the theory being applied to annihilate us in a nuclear war. Our intellect does not only make us more rational, it also, unfortunately, makes us more dangerous.

Violence is like a weed – it does not die even in the greatest drought. Even in an age and in localities which provide more favourable conditions for happy coexistence among people than ever before, some people get together to commit acts of terrorism, to tyrannize aviation, the administration or politics. And violence survives any flood: the fact that countless millions were murdered during the Third Reich has in no way exhausted man's lust for murder. That is why even the smallest shoot of violence must be torn out by its roots the moment it is spotted. Because weeds luxuriate – within a few days they can strangle everything.

*

I have spoken to students on the problem of freedom and dictatorship at well over a hundred universities in the United States. Many young people today would wish to fight against the Gestapo, against the SS, against Hitler; they would like to save the Jews from being murdered and they would like to avoid a world war. These are heroic aims. But where they live is no Hitler, no Gestapo and no SS. They should understand that none of these existed in the 1930s either, that they grew, slowly and unnoticed at first, and then ever more quickly. Until it was too late.

That is why one must fight from the outset. 'You should', I tried to tell them, 'go into battle against the small injustices – often this takes just as much civil courage and bravery as the struggle against the great wrongs. If a person looks the other way when his colleague at work is unjustly slandered, if he likes the idea of perhaps stepping into his position, then he is acting no differently from the person who looked the other way when the Jews were made to scrub the pavements, and who was happy to move into their abandoned homes. I believe that the people who then went in for the great resistance would nowadays go in for resistance in small things.'

If a person today only wishes to offer the grand resistance to Hitler, then I suspect that he wants to dodge the lesser resistance against today's injustice.

*

One of the problems is that young people in western Europe and in the USA enjoy their freedom as something so self-evident that they no longer realize its worth. On my lecture tours I used to see time and again how little many of them value a social system which, for all its faults, grants them an unprecedented measure of freedom, prosperity and security. Sometimes I would try to make them realize the value of freedom and security by telling them about Israel: one day, walking through a cemetery and looking at the headstones of army graves, I noticed that none of those buried there had been older than twenty-four.

'Those Israelis', I told my listeners in Los Angeles or Chicago, 'were the same age as you. But they paid with their lives for their freedom. You, who are sitting in this hall, travel to Israel for a visit, you make criticisms that excesses are being committed there under a still not terminated state of war, you rely on the strength of the Israeli army as an outpost of the United States in the Middle East, and sometimes you feel proud that this land was wrested from the desert. But have you ever considered that your brethren there, who are just as young as you and who love life just as much as you do, have to defend their freedom anew every day? That they accept three years' military service? That they accept enormous economic difficulties in order to maintain their military strength? That, to repeat it once more, they risk their lives to defend that small patch of soil where, two thousand years ago, a relatively small group dug itself in to make a dream reality?'

'For an aim like that,' some young people in Cleveland or Boston would then say to me, 'we would also be ready to risk our lives.'

But this I am not ready to accept: one cannot be enthusiastic for the defence of freedom in Israel while disparaging the freedom one is enjoying oneself.

*

How does one explain to a young person what freedom means when he has been born to freedom? Can one appreciate the importance of air for breathing before one's air passages have been choked?

Young terrorists have declared under interrogation that the explosive charges flung by them were intended to shake the 'system'. This should be taken seriously: those bombs are their protest against a system that is incapable of communicating values and ideals.

*

It appears that only dictatorships have programmes for young people – democracies leave them to their own devices. Thus the young, especially in Germany and Austria, were left without ideals after the Second World War. We are witnessing the total exhaustion of the programmes of all political parties. There are no visions left, nothing that could inspire young people with enthusiasm. Everything that used to be fought for in the past has long been achieved – short working hours, long holidays, education, health, welfare for all. Even the new unemployed are being paid better by us than a skilled worker was in the past. The only thing that our age encourages in young people is consumption. But even that is becoming exhausted, and so we are confronted with the question: what are we to do to give meaning to our lives?

I am afraid that this state of affairs might create the conditions for a new dictatorship just as much as hardships, hunger and unemployment did in the past. Dictatorships have invariably first got hold of young people who have lost a sense of direction. Instead they instilled in them a madness. Then they put them in uniforms and kept them busy all day playing at war. Until they were ripe for real war. Until they yearned for a hero's death, without the least idea of how mean and dirty and ugly real death would be. Young people have a tendency to flee from meaninglessness into death. Dictatorships provide scope for that tendency. Democracies must learn to give young people a meaning to their lives.

Index